Multicultural Counselling

Multicultural Counselling

A Reader

edited by
Stephen Palmer

SAGE Publications
London • Thousand Oaks • New Delhi

First published 2002

 SAGE Publications Ltd
6 Bonhill Street
London EC2A 4PU

SAGE Publications Inc
2455 Teller Road
Thousand Oaks, California 91320

SAGE Publications India Pvt Ltd
32, M-Block Market
Greater Kailash - I
New Delhi 110 048

British Library Cataloguing in Publication data

A catalogue record for this book is available
from the British Library

ISBN 0 7619 6375 8
ISBN 0 7619 6376 6 (pbk)

Library of Congress Control Number available

Typest by SIVA Math Setters, Chennai, India
Printed in Great Britain by The Cromwell Press Ltd,
Trowbridge, Wiltshire

Dedication

I dedicate this book to Dr Pittu Laungani who has supported my work, been a loyal colleague and friend for over a decade. He has helped me to gain different perspectives on a range of issues. Although his views can cause some controversy, I have enjoyed listening to them.

Memories are odd, in particular the ones that stick in our minds regarding relationships and friendship. I first remember meeting Pittu when I was chairing a public health conference held at the Royal Society of Medicine. As one of the speakers could not attend, to avoid letting the delegates down I decided to take the opportunity to give a paper on how health professionals are largely responsible for creating their own levels of stress – a tough topic to speak on from a cognitive perspective. Pittu helped out by chairing the conference while I was speaking. We were no longer strangers. Later that day, his paper comparing the differences in stress between England and India etched a permenant impression on my mind. I became interested in his work. We continued to meet up at different conferences. Then in the mid-1990s, I enrolled on a PhD programme at South Bank University and Pittu was of great assistance as my advisor.

Thank you Pittu for your ongoing support, friendship and the great parties.

Contents

Editor

Professor Stephen Palmer PhD is a chartered psychologist (counselling and health), a UKCP registered psychotherapist, a certified REBT supervisor and a Fellow of the British Association for Counselling and Psychotherapy. He is Founder Director of the Centre for Stress Management and the Centre for Multimodal Therapy in London, an Honorary Professor of Psychology in the Centre for Health and Counselling Psychology, City University and Visiting Professor in the National Centre for Work Based Learning Partnerships at Middlesex University. He has written or edited over 20 books including *Counselling in a Multicultural Society* (1999, Sage) with Pittu Laungani. He is Honorary Vice President of the International Stress Management Association (UK) and of the Institute of Health Promotion and Education.

His special interests include stress management, brief therapy and multicultural counselling. His overseas work has included teaching counselling and psychotherapy in Beijing, China, Tokyo, Japan, and Wellington, New Zealand. He was given an award for his work on behalf of the Women's Hotline Counselling Service in Beijing. In 2000, he jointly received the Annual Counselling Psychology Award for his 'outstanding professional and scientific contribution to Counselling Psychology in Britain'.

Contributors

M.H. Abu-Rasain was a student attending the Masters in Counselling course at the University of Hull when co-writing the article (see Chapter 10).

Waseem J. Alladin is Chief Editor of *Counselling Psychology Quarterly: An International Journal of Theory, Research and Practice* and an Associate Member of the Institute of Directors. He is consultant clinical and counselling psychologist with Hull and East Riding Community Health NHS Trust, North Humberside, where he is the specialist in cognitive therapy.

Nick Banks, PhD is a Chartered Clinical Psychologist and a Senior Lecturer at the University of Nottingham Centre for the Study of Human Relations. He teaches counselling and has a private practice mainly as an expert witness for Courts of Law involving child care and family issues. He has research interests in cross-cultural counselling and to date has written the only evidence based book on cross-cultural counselling in Britain (*White Counsellors – Black Clients: Theory Research and Practice.* London: Avebury).

Joan L. Biever received her PhD in counselling psychology from the University of Notre Dame. She is the Dean of Graduate Studies at Our Lady of the Lake University of San Antonio since 1992. Her research and clinical interests include narrative and solution focused therapies with children and their families and the training needs of bilingual therapists.

Monte Bobele received his doctorate in counselling psychology from the University of Houston. He has completed post-doctoral fellowships in family therapy and health psychology. Dr Bobele teaches narrative and solution focused approaches and has presented and published extensively in this area. He is currently the training director of Our Lady of the Lake University PsyD programme.

Petrūska Clarkson is a consultant philosopher, chartered clinical, counselling, occupational and accredited research psychologist, registered individual and group psychotherapist, and accredited supervisor and management consultant with almost 30 years international experience. She has more than 150 publications (21 languages) in these fields. She is Honorary Professor of Counselling and Psychotherapy at University of Surrey, Roehampton, and teaches at PHYSIS, London.

Padmal de Silva is Senior Lecturer in Psychology at the Institute of Psychiatry, King's College, University of London, and Consultant Clinical Psychologist for the South London and Maudsley NHS Trust. His research interests include anxiety disorders, Buddhist psychology and eating disorders.

Shukla Dhingra is a counsellor and trainer at Loughborough University. She has worked extensively with black ethnic minorities, as a counsellor and as Head of an ESL Service. She has researched into the counselling needs of people of Asian origin and the access of black people to higher education. She has published in the field of bilingualism and cross-cultural counselling.

Aisha Dupont-Joshua is of mixed race originally from South Africa. She trained with the Nafsiyat Inter-Cultural Therapy Centre and London University, which gave her the tools for working with issues of race and culture in counselling. She teaches Inter-Cultural Counselling at Lambeth College, London and Southampton University.

Zack Eleftheriadou works in private practice in North London, and also at the Medical Foundation for the Care of Victims of Torture, where she works with refugee children and their families. She has been a supervisor, trainer and consultant in the field of cross-cultural therapy for many years. She has published widely, including the book *Transcultural Counselling* and is currently working on another transcultural text for mental health professionals.

Zoubida Guernina PhD in Psychology is a Chartered Health and Counselling Psychologist, trainer and supervisor who has taught psychology and psychotherapy in the UK and abroad. She has worked in Nafsiyat, in the NHS and other health centres. Her major research interests are in the psychology of mental health and psychotherapeutic effectiveness with vulnerable groups.

Garry Hornby is a chartered counselling psychologist who has taught courses on counselling in England, Hong Kong, New Zealand and Barbados and therefore has an interest in cross-cultural counselling. He also has an interest in the disability field and has published in this area.

Peter Jewel is Assistant Director of the Centre for English Language Teacher Education, Warwick University. He is also a practicing person-centred counsellor and counselling trainer, working as a lecturer, facilitator and consultant, with a special interest in multicultural awareness.

P.L.S. Khoo was a student attending the Masters in Counselling course at the University of Hull when co-writing the article (see Chapter 10).

Colin Lago is the Director of Counselling Services at Sheffield University. He has long been interested in and concerned about enhancing the effectiveness and provision of transcultural counselling and has authored several books including *Race, Culture and Counselling* (Oxford University Press, 1996). He is a fellow and accredited member of BACP.

Pittu Laungani is an Honorary Senior Research Fellow at the University of Manchester. His major research interests are in the psychology of mental illness, death and bereavement, stress, counselling and therapy, all from a cross-cultural perspective. He has published several books and over 60 research papers in national and international journals.

Roy Moodley is Assistant Professor in the counselling psychology programme at the Ontario Institute for Studies in Education of the University of Toronto. He has published papers on race, counselling and psychotherapy; masculinity and management; access to HE.

Zenobia Nadirshaw is an honorary Senior Research Fellow at the Ethnicity and Social Policy Research Unit at the University of Bradford. She was the first psychologist to chair the Transcultural Psychiatry Society (UK). She has recently completed a Department of Health funded study on clinical psychology and black and ethnic minority communities.

Yuko Nippoda is a UKCP registered psychotherapist with extensive experience in the field of counselling and psychotherapy in Japan and England. As a bilingual psychotherapist and counsellor, she has worked with clients on a wide range of issues from many different cultures. Her special interest is in cross-cultural issues, particularly issues between East and West, and she conducts research and has some publications on this subject.

Mary-Wales North is a bi-lingual psychologist who received her doctorate in counselling psychology from Our Lady of the Lake University in San Antonio. She specializes in services to Latino families and individuals. In addition to her clinical work, she consults on multicultural issues with schools, public service agencies and hospitals. She is on the Board of the Nebraska Association of Farmworkers and now works for the Tucson, Arizona Police Department.

Anita Pearce at the time of writing the article (see Chapter 18) was in the Department of Psychology, Manchester Metropolitan University.

Joyce Thompson is a counselling psychologist, consultant, trainer and supervisor currently practising in Jamaica. She was trained in the UK and facilitated training in Germany, the Netherlands and Monserratt. She is a fellow and life member of the British Association for Counselling and Psychotherapy.

Romeria Tidwell PhD, a UCLA full professor, licensed psychologist and educational psychologist, teaches courses in counselling theory, multi-cultural counselling, and assessment. Her research focuses on immigrants, minority and understudied groups and the practice of counselling, multicultural assessment and crisis intervention.

Pat Ward, M.A. trained as a teacher, social worker and later as a counsellor counselling in hospital and GP primary health care settings as well as higher education and specialist sexual abuse counselling services. She now teaches counselling in further education and has a private practice working with adults and children.

Amanda Webb Johnson at the time of co-writing the article (see Chapter 12) was at the Confederation of Indian Organizations (UK).

Acknowledgements

Chapter 1 by Colin Lago and Joyce Thompson was first published in the *Handbook of Counselling* (1997), pp. 285–302 and reproduced with permisson of Routledge, an imprint of Taylor Francis.

Chapter 2 by Aisha Dupont-Joshua was first published in *Counselling, Journal of the British Association for Counselling* (1997), 8 (4): 282–4, and is published with permission of the British Association for Counselling and Psychotherapy.

Chapter 3 by Zack Eleftheriadou was first published under the title of 'Multi-cultural counselling and psychotherapy: a philosophical framework', in *The Italian International Review of Psychology* (1992), 3: 21–9, and is reproduced with permission of the editor.

Chapter 4 by Colin Lago and Roy Moodley was first published in *Integrative and Eclectic Counselling and Psychotherapy* (2000), pp. 233–51, and is reproduced with permission of Sage Publications.

Chapter 5 by Stephen Palmer is a chapter adapted from two chapters first published in *Counselling in a Multicultural Society* (2000), pp. 153–202, and reproduced with permission of Sage Publications.

Chapter 6 by Zoubida Guernina was first published in *Counselling Psychology Quarterly* (1993), 6 (4): 365–70, reproduced with permission of Carfax Publishing.

Chapter 7 by Joan L. Biever, Monte Bobele and Mary-Wales North was first published in *Counselling Psychology Quarterly* (1998), 11 (2): 181–8, reproduced with permission of Carfax Publishing.

Chapter 8 by Nick Banks is an adapted article first published in *Counselling Psychology Review* (1995), 10 (3): 8–14, reproduced with permission of the editor.

Chapter 9 by Romeria Tidwell is an adapted article first published in *Counselling Psychology Quarterly* (1992), 5 (3): 245–9, reproduced with permission from Carfax Publishing.

Chapter 10 by P.L.S. Khoo, M.H. Abu-Rasain and G. Hornby was first published in *Counselling Psychology Quarterly* (1994), 7 (2): 117–31, reproduced with permission from Carfax Publishing.

Chapter 11 by Padmal de Silva was first published in the *British Journal of Guidance and Counselling* (1993), 21 (1): 30–4, and reproduced with permission of the Careers Research and Advisory Centre.

Chapter 12 by Amanda Webb Johnson and Zenobia Nadirshaw was first published in the *British Journal of Guidance and Counselling* (1993), 21 (1): 20–9, and reproduced with permission of the Careers Research and Advisory Centre.

Chapter 13 by Pittu Laungani was first published in the *International Journal of Health Promotion and Education* (1999), 37 (4): 142–55, and reproduced with permission of the editor.

Chapter 14 by Roy Moodley was first published in the *British Journal of Guidance and Counselling* (1998), 26 (4): 495–507, and reproduced with permission of the Careers Research and Advisory Centre.

Chapter 15 by Waseem J. Alladin was first published in *Questions and Answers on Counselling in Action* (1993), and reproduced with permission of Sage Publications.

Chapter 16 by P.A. Ward and Nick Banks is an adapted article first published in the *British Journal of Guidance and Counselling* (1996), 24 (3): 413–22, and reproduced with permission of the Careers Research and Advisory Centre.

Chapter 17 by Roy Moodley and Shukla Dhingra was first published in *Counselling, the Journal of the British Association for Counselling* (1998), 9 (4): 295–9, and reproduced with permission of the British Association for Counselling and Psychotherapy.

Chapter 18 by Anita Pearce was first published in the *British Journal of Guidance and Counselling* (1994), 22 (3): 417–28, and reproduced with permission of the Careers Research and Advisory Centre.

Chapter 19 by Petrūska Clarkson and Yuko Nippoda was first published in *Counselling Psychology Quarterly* (1997), 10 (4): 415–37, and reproduced with permission of Carfax Publishing.

Chapter 20 by Peter Jewel was first published in *Counselling Psychology Review* (1994), 9 (2): 17–34, and is reproduced with permission of the editor.

The editor and publisher would like to thank the various authors, editors and publishers for granting permission to reproduce the above material. Particular thanks go to Waseem Alladin and Tony Watts, who edited *Counselling Psychology Quarterly* and the *British Journal of Guidance and Counselling* respectively, for the periods from which a selection of the articles have been taken. Every effort has been made to trace all copyright holders and authors, but if any parties have been inadvertently overlooked, we shall be pleased to include an acknowledgement at the next opportunity.

Preface

By its very nature, editing a reader involves reading so many articles and chapters, and deciding which ones to include or leave out can be a burden. In the end, I decided to focus on the articles from 1990. Although this could imply that I only recently started this project, in fact, searching for articles was an ongoing process as new material was being constantly published. I decided to choose material that had made me think more about the challenging subject of multicultural counselling. During the period concerned, I had edited a number of counselling journals and had been on a number of editorial boards. This had given me an insight into what had been published. I had also collected various articles that I would use for teaching purposes. Thus, unwittingly, I had started editing this book a decade ago.

Why 'multicultural counselling'? In the UK, a number of terms have been used, including cross-cultural, Afro-centric, transcultural, black feminist, intercultural and anti-racist (see Moodley, 1999). They all have different meanings. Historically, for a number of reasons, in the UK the term multicultural counselling has been avoided. In this book, I have focused on material originally published in British journals and books, although some papers reflect practice outside the UK. Therefore, I have used the term multicultural counselling in the book's title although I have not altered the terms used by the authors of the individual chapters. I hope that this does not offend any readers who may align themselves to one of the approaches.

Why a book on multicultural counselling? When teaching, I did not find a suitable book that would cover a range of topics written from different perspectives. Single or co-authored books tend to reflect one perspective or approach. This book is inclusive and has chapters covering a range of views that the reader or I may or may not agree with. Can this lead to further reflection upon our practice? I truly hope so.

The book is aimed at students of counselling, counselling psychology and psychotherapy, experienced practitioners, as well as trainers and lecturers, who will discover a range of interesting chapters which may lead to reflection, discussion and debate. Authors were invited to update their material if they so wished. Each chapter includes four suggested discussion issues to help initiate further deliberation. Trainers and lecturers may find that the discussion issues could be useful essay topics.

The book is divided into four main sections: Counselling and Race; Theory and Practice; Ethnic Matching in Counselling and Psychotherapy; Research. The first section provides an overview to many of the issues raised in this book. As many chapters illustrated both the theory and practice of multicultural counselling, these two areas were included in the same section. There are 20 chapters in total providing an insight into counselling in a multicultural society.

Reference

Moodley, R. (1999) 'Challenges and transformations: counselling in a multicultural context', *International Journal for the Advancement of Counselling*, 21: 139–52.

PART ONE
COUNSELLING AND RACE

Part One provides a useful introduction to some of the key issues associated with multicultural counselling. It contains two chapters. In Chapter 1, Lago and Thompson contend that racism has to be addressed and worked with by counsellors in training who plan to practise in today's multicultural society. However, this process could be an intensely painful experience. White groups, after training, may experience vast realms of guilt and impotence, while black people may get in touch with powerful emotions such as depression. Lago and Thompson then consider cross-racial counselling partnerships and the issues that arise for practice. Interestingly, they suggest that the task of the black counsellor is beset with professional demands that would appear to exceed those of white practitioners. Seventeen guidelines are provided for counsellor practice.

In Chapter 2, Dupont-Joshua focuses on how to work with issues of race in counselling. She refers to relevant models to help counsellors assess the different developmental stages that the counsellor and client may have attained that aid understanding of the dynamics which may emerge during counselling. Dupont-Joshua provides an interesting case study, David, which illustrates how her attitudes influenced the tone of the relationship. These two chapters raise a number of important issues and help to set the scene for the rest of the book.

1

Counselling and Race

Colin Lago and Joyce Thompson

Issues

The subject of counselling and race is difficult to address in a clear manner, because as Jones (1985: 173) has put it: 'among other complexities, it is embedded in the fluctuating nature of race relations in our society and hence in a continually evolving sociocultural context'. At the heart of the subject there are several major debates that in part reflect contemporary views of 'race' in British society. The term 'race' used here is a broad one. We recognize that residing in Britain today are people from many races and racial origins. Many of these groups are likely to be disadvantaged, oppressed, or discriminated against by the dominant society (for example, the Irish, Jewish, Eastern Europeans, and so on). The specific focus, in this chapter, however, is concentrated upon the complex relationship between black and white people in Britain generally, and within counselling specifically. Nevertheless, in focusing on one specific set of relationships between black and white, it is hoped that more understandings might emerge implicitly for these other groups.

A major area of contention has centred around the extent to which counsellors require specialist knowledge of and sensitivity to race relations in Britain in order to counsel. One view holds that the knowledge and skills of counselling are all that is required with any client. The opposing view contains several major themes that may be summed up as follows:

(a) In order to understand relationships between black and white people today, a knowledge of the history between differing racial groups is required.
(b) Counsellors will also require an understanding of how contemporary society works in relation to race, the exercise of power, the effects of discrimination, stereotyping, how ideologies sabotage policies, and so on. In short, counsellors require a 'structural' awareness of society.
(c) Counsellors require a personal awareness of where they stand in relation to these issues.

From this debate a key question emerges that has sometimes keenly split different groups. Can or should white people counsel black people? In doing so, it is argued, they are substantiating, symbolically, the erroneous and pejorative view that black people are inferior, that black people require help, and worst of all that black people do not have, within their midst, their own capacity to resolve difficulties.

White people are already, self-evidently, rooted in white culture. Also, as counsellors they will have been trained in bodies of theory and practice that have either central European or US origins and emphases. Certainly, white American counsellors have often asserted that black people do not respond well to traditional methods of psychotherapy (Jones, 1985). Some black people within Britain assert that such methods are also culturally encapsulated within a white western view of the world and are consequently insensitive and totally inappropriate in their unthinking application to all counselling situations.

So far, we have concentrated on the white counsellor/black client counselling relationship. We do not wish this early focus to blind us to the black counsellor/white client relationship. Increasingly, black people are training in counselling and indeed some have already formed an Association of Black Counsellors (ABC).

The issues of race and racism exist, potentially, if not explicitly, within the above pairings as well as in the same-race counselling dyads (black–black or white–white). Whether covert or overt, very real dilemmas confront counsellors in terms of how subjects related to racism are managed in the process of counselling.

Further questions also exist for counsellor trainers. What is the knowledge base required in preparing trainees to work with clients of different racial origins? In doing so, are there specific individual skills that need to be disseminated? Many other questions arise out of the initial complexities already presented here. At the core of this maelstrom of debate, some of which has been painful and bitter, there exist a deep underlaying question that goes something like this. Given that relations between black and white groups over several centuries have been typified by oppression, exploitation, and discrimination, how might contemporary relationships within counselling be transformed into creative (rather than further damaging) experiences?

Racism – the major issue

It is our contention that the issue of racism has to be addressed and worked with by counsellors in training who plan to work in today's multiracial society. This view is not held by all counsellors and counsellor trainers in the field. Similar to earlier sentiments expressed by US psychiatrists (Thomas and Sillen, 1972), many white counsellors see themselves as caring, sensitive people who have chosen counselling precisely because they are concerned about other people. Therefore, they ask, how could they be racist in their practice? This genuinely held view does not take into account, however, a whole range of mechanisms, perceptions and experiences to which white people have been exposed throughout their lives. Such phenomena, if they remain unconscious, may affect the counsellor's behaviour and responses in ways that prove negative in cross-race counselling.

Notwithstanding the importance of this dimension, we are sensitive to the fact that any journey of exploration into the issues of racism will be, for many people, an intensely painful experience. White groups, after training, may experience vast realms of guilt and impotence. Black people, similarly exposed, may get in touch with powerful emotions such as depression and anger. Despite these apparently negative effects, our belief is that counsellors need to operate from a position of maximum awareness of self and of society.

Racism – the evidence

An abundance of research material clearly demonstrates that the black members of this society do not have equal access to the opportunities and provisions that exist within Britain (Coard, 1971; Dummett, 1980; Hartmann et al., 1974; Jowell et al., 1984; Jumaa, 1993; Skellington and Morris, 1992; Smith, 1977). As far back as 1971 the Census suggested that the unemployment rate among young people of Afro-Caribbean origin was twice as high as among white teenagers. In addition, Little et al. (1978) asserted that the incidence of young people going to an interview and not getting a job was four times as great for black teenagers compared with white teenagers. Smith (1997) also indicated that as total unemployment rose, the minority groups tended to make up a greater proportion of the total: in other words, unemployment rates for minority groups rose more steeply than rates of total unemployment (*Guardian*, 1994).

In the educational arena, Coard (1971) produced some frightening figures concerning the disproportionate incidence of black children in what were then termed 'educationally subnormal' schools. One race-relations selected bibliography confirmed that a considerable amount of research had emerged indicating that the average teacher had differential perceptions and expectations of poor and minority group children; that these differential perceptions were associated with differential treatment and teaching techniques; and that these in turn could lead to a depressed performance on the part of the children treated thus (Skellington and Morris, 1992).

The media also helps to perpetuate a view of black people that is pejorative. Research has revealed that a biased selection of issues concerning race is presented in the newspapers. Troyna (1981) reports that in a survey of major national and local newspapers, 47 per cent of all material on race issues were confined to the following themes: the National Front, crime, immigration, human interest, and 'normal'. Conversely, less than 10 per cent of items were devoted to housing, education, health, and employment. Some 25 per cent of all items in which West Indians were highlighted related to crime stories. Immigration was not dealt with as an issue of black people entering Britain but with seeking to keep them out. Perversely, white hostility existed outside the framework of 'race' news; such discussions focused on issues such as democracy, the erosion of freedom, and so on. Conversely, black hostility was firmly placed within the framework of race-related material within Britain. Unfortunately, space does not allow other examples to be quoted, though there do exist substantial negative findings in other socio-economic areas (for example, housing, health, street arrests, and so on).

This consistent pattern of disadvantage and discrimination is so widespread and uniform across institutions in our society that the underlying issues of racism and racist attitudes are self-revealing and self-evident. Running parallel to this assertion and, indeed, extending it is the statement in the United States Mental Health Commission Report in 1965, which cited racism as the number one health problem in the USA. Within Britain in recent years violence has erupted in several cities and racism has been cited as one of the major reasons for these occurrences.

Consequently, in any counselling relationship between counsellor and client where there is racial difference, aspects of racism must be assumed to exist and might also require focused attention. One immediate area for concern, then, within counselling is that of the relationship between client and counsellor. This is explored in more detail in the next section.

The cross-racial counselling partnership – issues in practice

The following considerations have been devised by the authors in order to demonstrate the range of issues potentially present in various cross-race pairings of counsellor and client. Some generalized views and attitudes have been included in order to aid the visibility of such issues. However, we acknowledge that they are somewhat simplified and are themselves in danger of serving to confirm stereotypes. We apologize if this occurs: it is not intended.

Let us imagine four scenarios featuring different racial pairings of counsellor and client, as illustrated in Figure 1.1.

Scenario I: Black counsellor/white client
The black counsellor It is most likely that the counselling training a black person would have received would have been, first, in a white, middle-class organization or institute, and, second, theoretically and culturally Eurocentric and American (i.e. US) in origin. Additionally, they are also likely to have been taught by white, middle-class trainers. Consequently, and quite contrary to a simplistic view of the situation, black counsellors, by virtue of their training and backgrounds, will have been predominantly geared to working with white people, not black people.

The aforementioned aspects of a black counsellor's training will hopefully constitute positive qualities towards working with white clients. However, in their lives as black people in white society, some will have

SCENARIO 1	SCENARIO 2
White client	White counsellor
Black counsellor	Black client
SCENARIO 3	SCENARIO 4
White client	Black counsellor
White counsellor	Black client

Figure1.1   *Possible scenarios of counsellor–client racial pairings*

experienced negative incidents and consequently feelings in relation to white people. For black counsellors, then, a serious element of their work with their white clients will be the nature of the countertransference that develops as the counselling unfolds (i.e. black counsellors' feelings and reactions to their white clients that occur during the counselling process). One might predict, therefore, that one element for discussion and exploration between black counsellors and their supervisors/consultants will be this very aspect, in order that the negative elements of the countertransference can be dealt with professionally, rather than being expressed inappropriately within the counselling encounter.

The white client Obviously, it is difficult to predict accurately the nature of a white client's response to working with a black counsellor. However, the range of responses is likely to be stimulated by the following questions:

- What is the white client's perception of a black counsellor?
- Does this change over time?
- Would the white client be reluctant to expose his or her difficulty to a black person because of his or her own (erroneous) sense of superiority?
- To what extent would the white client presume that the black counsellor will not understand his or her predicament?

In sum, what effects do the race, class, and culture of the counsellor have upon the client?

Questions in this section and the next have been deliberately employed to demonstrate the extent to which a multiplicity of responses might exist for each counsellor and each client. Unfortunately, space does not allow an expansion of these areas. Suffice it to say that it is hoped that the questions themselves may stimulate counsellors' reflections upon their own position.

Scenario 2: White counsellor/black client

The white counsellor Again, a series of questions can assist us in addressing, briefly, the issues for a white counsellor with a black client:

- How structurally aware of society is the counsellor?
- Do they have an understanding of the myriad disadvantaging mechanisms that exist in contemporary society in relation to black people?
- What class background are they from?
- What experiences of black people have they had?
- What effects, perceptions, and attitudes have these left upon the counsellor?

From experiences gained by the authors while involved in training groups, it seems reasonable to state that many white people are quite unable to cope with radical black perspectives and black people's pain and anger, specifically in relation to racism. Rogers (1978) has noted this phenomenon and suggests that white people who are effective in responding to oppressed groups seem to learn two attitudes. One is the realization and ownership of the fact that 'I think white'. The other is the ability to respond empathically, to be able to enter into the black person's world of hate, bitterness, and resentment, and to know that world as an understandable, acceptable part of reality. To achieve this ability Rogers (1978) suggests that the white persons themselves need to listen to their own feelings of anger at unjust situations. This is clearly something that could most usefully be done in training and therapy, in order that the fullest opportunities for personal learning may be gained.

From the perspective of power, this combination of white counsellor with black client has a potential danger, namely a perpetuation of the notion of white superiority. The white person, as the counsellor in this situation, has the power. The sensitive handling of that power is absolutely crucial. White counsellors have to work out ways of enhancing their own sensitivity and knowledge beyond the counselling framework. To pursue their curiosity, however justified they might feel within the counselling process, would be an unethical abuse of their power. Black clients so used would have every right to experience further anger and a sense of injustice.

The black client One aspect of colonial conditioning that many black people have experienced is that of viewing white people as positive, powerful, knowledgeable, intelligent, and so on. Consequently, such clients might have more confidence in a white counsellor. By contrast, black clients who are aware of the historical inequalities of the relationship between black and white people might be mistrustful of any meaningful interaction with a white counsellor. Indeed, it is unlikely that they would, knowingly, expose themselves to a white helper.

Some black clients might expect white counsellors not only to know their way around the British bureaucratic system but also to be able to influence that system on their behalf. The latter perspective raises further complexities as to the philosophical and theoretical nature of 'counselling' and how that equates with the reality of dealing with disadvantaged clients who are rendered less able, because of discrimination, to be effective in their world.

Suffice it to say, at least three different emphases have emerged in various counselling practices in relation to this quandary. One response has been for the counsellor to maintain the 'purist' perspective of engaging in therapeutic dialogue with the client, trusting that the client will learn sufficiently from this process to become able to deal with difficulties in their lives. An extension of this has been for some counsellors to offer educational teaching assistance to clients in areas such as assertion training. The third model has been the counsellor's adoption of an advocacy role on the client's behalf. Thus, based on the initial therapeutic work, the counsellor then moves towards negotiating with external agencies or persons on the client's behalf.

Scenario 3: White counsellor/white client

The white counsellor This is the commonly assumed combination of counsellor and client whenever counselling is discussed. Though race is not often an issue within such alliances, nevertheless it does from time to time figure within the dialogue. Indeed, when this occurs the counsellor may well be challenged in terms of his or her responses to the client. Thus, for example, what is the counsellor to do if the client uses racist language and conveys stereotyped views throughout the counselling? Should the counsellor confront these attitudes; accept them; ignore them; continue to work with the client in order (hopefully) to gain an understanding of the significance of such utterances and views; refer them to someone else?

Each of these questions contains significant quandaries for every white counsellor concerned with racial justice. Clearly, from the above questions dealing with a 'whites only' counselling situation, it seems self-evident to note the crucial importance of introducing issues of race into all counselling training courses. Race is still an issue even in apparently non-racial situations. This question, which can have real consequences for the counsellor–client relationship, needs considerable thought by counsellors.

The white client From the client's perspective, of course, they have a right to their views and to express them within counselling, even though they may be experienced as negative or objectionable to the counsellor. Indeed, these sentiments will also exist for many subjects that clients may bring to counselling. Self-evidently, the activity of counselling exists precisely to facilitate the expression and exploration of problems perceived by the client.

The white client might also assume that the counsellor will agree with his or her sentiments. Further, some clients might attempt to coerce their counsellors into colluding with their views on issues of racism, in the knowledge that they are both white.

Scenario 4: Black counsellor/black client

The black counsellor The actual content and direction of the therapeutic interview between black counsellor and black client might well depend upon the counsellor's perception of the client's problems. The counsellor might, for example, be tempted to deal with the issue of racism and to explore this at the expense of other issues or problems which the client is having to deal and cope with. Of course, the opposite tendency is also a possibility: that is, the counsellor may concentrate, perhaps inappropriately, on other issues at the expense of acknowledging the issue of racism as raised by the client. From the perspective of professional development it would be most important for black counsellors to check themselves for either tendency in order to further explore their own perspective on the subject. Also, black counsellors working with black clients are likely to find themselves caught up in ethical dilemmas stimulated by the client's own community. One such dilemma occurs when the counsellor supports the self-development of a client when that development is in conflict with the mores of the client's cultural group. Such dilemmas, if handled inappropriately or insensitively, could well create considerable difficulties, not only for the counsellor and client but also within the client's family, the local community, and the counsellor's agency.

In summary, the task of the black counsellor can be seen to have considerable consequences and is certainly beset with professional demands that would appear to exceed those of white practitioners. Blending British training with alternative traditional approaches and then having to cope with external consequences as well as with the client's internal world are formidable extra dimensions to the black counsellor's load.

The black client Some black people, because of their own upbringing, find it difficult to perceive other black people who themselves enjoy equal status to their white counterparts, as equally knowledgeable and skilful. Such people, as clients, might end up feeling that they have only received second best. Inevitably, this sense of disappointment could lead to a deterioration or withdrawal from the therapeutic process or a projection of inappropriate anger on to the counsellor. Conversely, there are black people who would welcome the opportunity of being counselled by a black counsellor by virtue of a perceived positive identification of the same values and belief systems as themselves, for example, 'I find it easier to talk to you, you remind me of my grandmother.' Such initial positive feelings of transference are likely to be a foundation for a good working relationship.

Further developments

Some of the responses outlined above, of both white and black participants, are more succinctly described within an emerging series of racial and ethnic identity development models developed in the USA (Atkinson et al., 1989; Helms, 1984).

These models have been hailed as the 'most important development in cross-cultural counselling research' (Lee, 1994) and are now being used on

American counsellor training courses as a guide towards counsellor understanding of both where they and their client are in relation to their differential stages of racial identity development. These models support our views, detailed above, that indicate that there will be some cross-race counselling pairings that achieve appropriate therapeutic development and there will be others that never manage to establish a minimum level working relationship. The identity development models admirably explain these difficult and complex dynamics and thus will be helpful to counsellors in their pursuit of appropriate therapeutic effectiveness. Pontoretto and Pedersen (1993) provide an excellent review of an increasing number of these models that have been researched and constructed in relation to different majority and ethnic communities in the USA. Equivalent research work and the construction of currently relevant models has still to be carried out in the UK. Nevertheless the above American models are a most useful general guide to any counsellors working in a cross-racial structure.

Principles

Tentative guidelines for counsellor practice

Although the previous section on cross-race counselling relationships concentrated on complex issues, it also introduced some ideas in relation to what we consider to be good practice. The following guidelines constitute a development of such principles of practice:

1   Attempt to gain an awareness and knowledge of your own culture and cultural style, race, and racial origins.

This apparently simple statement represents a considerably complex task for anyone to embark upon, certainly in relation to cultural 'style' (perceptions, behaviours, beliefs, and so on). As Hall (1976) has noted: 'Honest and sincere people in the field continue to fail to grasp the deep and pointing ways in which culture determines behaviour, many of which are outside awareness and beyond conscious control.'

It is our contention that it is crucial that counsellors know where they are coming from, culturally, historically and behaviourally. Only through having such knowledge and awareness will they be able to have a sense of their effect upon others as well as access to an understanding of the dynamic process that unfolds between them and their clients.

2   Specifically, attempt to gain more understanding of the historical and contemporary relationship that has existed and presently exists between your own race and that of your clients.

Such knowledge may be of enormous value in understanding your clients' present perspective. Historically, most relationships between black and white races have been based upon traditions of conquest, colonialism, exploitation, oppression, and so on. Further, the evidence cited earlier stresses the contemporary existence of racism in Britain.

Both perspectives might yield insights for the counsellor into how they may be perceived by the racially different client. Such knowledge will, one hopes, contribute to the sensitivity and awareness that the counsellor brings to the encounter.

3   Develop a 'structural awareness' of society.

This should include the effects of history, as well as an understanding of the myriad mechanisms of oppression and systems of discrimination that operate in society. Judy Katz's book *White Awareness* (1978) is an excellent reference work for training ideas and exercises. Indeed several trainees with whom we have worked have written essays and articles that have been stimulated by the impact of such exercises upon them. The importance of this guideline lies in its potential to demonstrate to each white counsellor how they, however unwittingly, can contribute to discriminatory procedures in society.

4   Attempt to gain knowledge of the client's culture, cultural style, race, and racial origins.

This is similar and complementary to our first guideline. One of the dangers of trying to learn about others is that of being tempted into simplistic beliefs and views of them based on inadequate, biased, or limited accounts. Such knowledge, therefore, has to be acknowledged as useful but limited. Indeed, willingness to change or modify one's views in the light of fresh experience is crucial.

In short, gain as much knowledge as possible, but also retain the ability to suspend that knowledge when working with a client. Extended awareness of how others live and view their lives will contribute to the extent to which counsellors may fully understand their clients.

5   Hold in mind that any breakdown in communication may be attributable to the dynamic process between you.

You are not 'neutral' in your communication form and the client is certainly not deficient, just different. Breakdowns in communication can be most disturbing to both participants in counselling. At worst, negative stereotypes may be reinforced on both sides. The following pointers might be helpful in this regard:

(a)   Attempt to be clear and concise.
(b)   Avoid use of jargon and colloquialisms.
(c)   Check out the accuracy of your understanding of what is being said.
(d)   Be clear about what help it is that you are offering.
(e)   Possibly allow more time for the interview.

6   Be aware (and beware) of your assumptions, stereotypes, and immediate judgements.

Some of these may be based on personal experience. Others may be gained from very old incidents, folk tales, parental influence, and so on. At worst, your assumptions and prejudices are likely to come between you and the client and operate as a barrier to real communication.

7   Remember that many concepts like truth, honesty, intent, politeness, self-disclosure, and so on are culturally bound.

This may affect what the clients feel they can or cannot say and to what degree they can expose their feelings in relation to the issues they are bringing. Also, by holding this guideline in mind, counsellors may be further assisted in suspending initial judgemental attitudes.

8   The dominant manner through which all counsellors operate is one that is underpinned by attention-giving and active listening to the client.

9   Be alert to your usage of language.

Words and phrases can be loaded with connotative and ideological meanings. Gaining an awareness of the effect of the language we use is a very difficult process as we are so used to the words we utilize. Specific efforts have to be made to 'decode' and understand the implication of our utterances. Thus, for example, there are many expressions that have racist undertones. To use them not only abuses the victim of them and, by association, your client, but also affects and reflects the speaker. At one level you become the abuser and, as such, consequently no longer the helper.

   Another aspect of language usage is contained in the following anecdote. This concerns a West Indian woman who arrived in Britain during the 1960s. She kept going to the labour exchange looking for a job. On her second or third visit, the woman behind the desk said, 'I'm afraid we still haven't found a job for you.' The West Indian woman replied strongly, 'I don't want you to be afraid of me, I want you to help me find a job.'

   It is virtually impossible to avoid such expressions as language is structured by them and is beset by them. However, what we can do, in addition to developing an awareness of them, is to broaden our range of vocabulary and expression in order that statements may be rephrased more appropriately or meaningfully. Sensitivity to clients' responses to your usage of language will also enable you to monitor the effect of what you are saying upon them.

10   Pay attention also to paralinguistic phenomena for they also can ensure that real communication does not occur.

Paralinguistic phenomena such as sighs, grunts, intonation, expression, silences, the structure of who says what and when, are determined by cultural and linguistic backgrounds. Research has revealed how powerful these phenomena can be upon the deterioration of the relationship between two people in communication.

This tenth guideline is intended specifically to complement the fifth, seventh, and ninth outlined above. Each, in their various ways, encourage counsellors to suspend initial negative judgements in response to their clients. Cultural and linguistic phenomena can have such profound negative effects on people who are culturally different. It is as if all the standard cues for understanding someone else have been removed. Yet the listener is not necessarily aware of this. They continue to hear the same language being used and fall into the trap of assessing the other person based upon their own regular criteria. Unfortunately, even these criteria are seldom conscious.

This general point is a most complex one and deserves considerable thought on the part of counsellors.

11 A more open and accepting approach to many models of counselling and helping is required within this sphere. (Remember also that this statement implicitly incorporates non-Eurocentric models of helping.)

At the moment in Britain there is available a whole variety of theoretically different courses of counselling training. Consequently, practitioners may become informed and skilled within a range of approaches to therapy. However, the vast majority of these have emerged from western societies.

What is more difficult to acquire are insights into non-western, traditional therapies that are based upon dialogue. Paradoxically, an insight into these therapeutic styles might greatly assist white western counsellors with black clients whose cultural origins are outside Europe. Thus, for example, one form of problem resolution in the Middle East is for the troubled person to consult various elders in the community. After gaining their views he or she then chooses a course of action based on the information gathered.

12 Monitor your own attitudes during the interview, especially in relation to feelings of superiority or power over the client.

This point has been addressed briefly, earlier in the chapter. It relates specifically to the areas of oppression and racism. As elements of countertransference it seems crucial that the counsellor reflects on the case with his or her supervisor or consultant.

13 There are circumstances in which it will be appropriate for white and black counsellors, in being sensitive to the issues of racism, to explicitly acknowledge and explore this topic within the counselling process.

The precise details of how, why, or when to do this can clearly not be predetermined by the guidelines here. It is however crucial that counsellors are knowledgeable and sufficiently comfortable with the subject that they can acknowledge its existence and facilitate the exploration.

14 We would encourage counsellors to proceed cautiously and be in favour of minimum contact rather than long-term work.

The former will hopefully be helpful, and the latter may become intensely complex and have a poor prospective outcome. In these circumstances, appropriate referral arrangements might prove more satisfactory.

15 Generate possible sources of referral to helpers or counsellors of the same race/culture as the client.

16 Similarly, try to locate a suitable consultant who has experience of or is of the same race as the client, if the client becomes a medium- to long-term one.

17 Explore the experience of consulting racially different people with your own personal difficulties or for therapy in order to gain an insight into what it is you are attempting with your racially different clients.

Space does not allow any further exploration of the ideas contained in the above section. We offer these tentative guidelines as a basis for good counselling practice in the present. Hopefully, as interest develops in this aspect of counselling, the research might guide the development of future practice in more defined ways. Many of the above issues are considerably expanded in recent books written on both sides of the Atlantic (Lago and Thompson, 1996; Lee and Richardson, 1991).

Future developments

Implications for counselling education and training

Counselling and race, as a topic, is still not dealt with on many existing counselling courses. Historically, also, such courses have not concentrated upon the society and the social milieux within which counselling takes place. Rather, there has been an emphasis on the development of self-awareness, the enhancement of existing skills and theoretical knowledge and a concentration upon micro-skills. We are fully in accord with such emphases in training. However, the perplexities we can now appreciate through counselling in a multicultural and multiracial community make it crucial that future training courses also make efforts to adopt a wider 'sociological' approach. Here, the term 'sociological' is used within the definition of 'structural awareness' as described earlier. It serves to imply the following:

(a) an increased understanding of today's multiracial society and the historical pre-conditions that contributed to its formation;
(b) the provision of experiential training in the areas of racism and cultural awareness and the development of anti-racist strategies;
(c) simulated exposure of skills practice with racially and culturally different clients;
(d) the opportunity for case discussion and analysis to highlight the complex range of data generated when counselling within this milieu.

Such a combination of approaches would help individual trainees to develop a connectedness between their knowledge base, their attitudes and preconceptions, and their ability to practise.

Sue (1981) links five characteristies of culturally effective counsellors: (1) having self-knowledge; (2) possessing an awareness of generic counselling characteristics and their relation to culture and class; (3) having an understanding of socio-political forces affecting clients, especially racism and oppression; (4) having the ability to share world views of clients, without being culturally encapsulated; (5) having mastery of an eclectic variety of skills and theories and an ability to choose which are appropriate for a particular client. To this list we would add having; (6) self-knowledge of our own cultural origins and one's present (culturally determined style; (7) an awareness of one's own perceptions of people who are racially different.

If a white person in counselling training pursues these general suggestions laid out above, then several implications are likely to emerge for their personal life as well as their professional one:

(a) a development of an attitude of concern for the creation of a racially just society and the elimination of racist practices;
(b) a development of personal apprehension or fear that they will become 'marginalized' within their own groups (friends, work, family) and become the subject of conflict or ridicule for holding such views;
(c) a need to acknowledge that combating racism is a long and painful process and consequently they will require stamina of purpose and motivation;
(d) the exploration of personal attitudes and the development of a knowledge base of how society operates discriminatory practices and implicitly invites individuals to make political, professional, and personal choices in the present and the future;
(e) firmly held beliefs about the theory and practice of counselling might have to give way to a more open appreciation of other models;
(f) the possibility of adding a 'preventive' educative function to their work in addition to the existing one of counselling individuals through disseminating such awareness (via workshops, community activities, and so on).

At the present time, unfortunately, there seems to be a shortage of informed and skilled trainers within this specific area. Further, it would seem important and necessary for counsellors involved in mixed race settings to avail themselves of supervisors who have the necessary width and breadth of knowledge required. Again, such consultants are rare.

The above elements reflect a somewhat 'chicken and egg' situation. Clearly this scenario constitutes a frustrating predicament. Viewed from a slightly less pessimistic perspective, there exists a variety of short courses available (one-day, weekends) dealing with these phenomena. Indeed, increased demands have been made on members of RACE (Race and Cultural Education in Counselling, a division of BACP) and the BACP to provide such facilities over recent years.

We can appreciate in the near future that, as a result of an increasing incidence of mixed race counselling partnerships occurring, appropriate training methods and consultative support mechanisms will develop. Beyond that, issues such as specialist accreditation of counsellors, supervisors and trainers for this specific element of counselling might have to be considered by organizations such as BACP and the British Psychological Society. However, the labelling of certain individuals in this way might carry the unfortunate implication that most of us do not need to address the issues and problems of race in counselling.

The path towards increased training opportunities for black counsellors will also not be an easy one. The authors are already aware of situations in some allied 'helping professions' where white trainers have been accused of racism for failing black students. The overriding concern of and challenge to training agencies is that of maintaining 'academic' standards while encouraging black students from a range of backgrounds, some of whom may lack prior qualifications. Unfortunately such predicaments may well cause many agencies to avoid offering training that is sensitive to the subject of this chapter.

We have begun to map out above a potential area of development for counselling courses and individual counsellors. Our own experience contributes to a view that these initiatives are long overdue and require immediate attention. However, in reality, we fear that some of the challenges presented by this arena might prove too formidable to engage with directly. A shortage of existing trainers and supervisors (Thompson, 1991) has already been acknowledged, and so too has the difficulty of encouraging black students, lacking traditional prior qualifications. A further barrier to comprehensive development is the lack of systematic research in two crucial areas, training and counselling practice. Such research might guide the formulation of sensitive and effective training programmes. It is our experience that some programmes in anti-racism education have had contradictory effects: that is, some participants have been further consolidated in their prejudicial attitudes. Trainers and researchers must therefore develop approaches to training that enable participants to explore these very difficult issues, without producing the contrary effects alluded to above.

Given the above apprehensions we predict that developments in train-ning in this field are likely to be slow and ad hoc. It seems reasonable to suspect that some counselling courses, whilst not fully incorporating major new modules on counselling and race, will offer short introductory seminars on the subject. A rather more modest expansion of general awareness might thus be created over time which might then act as a catalyst for the development of substantial initiatives at a later date. It is perhaps only in this way that enough experience might be generated for a coherent development of 'good' training to occur.

One example of a substantial initiative would be the development of a specific postgraduate counselling course focusing on this area. Certainly there is no shortage of theoretical or experiential training material to fill such a course. Trainees could be drawn from the various professions which already use counselling methods. The course would offer a specific body of knowledge and skill to equip participants, first, more ably to counsel those who are culturally or racially different, and, second, to counsel members of ethnic minority groups.

Other considerations for organizations offering counselling

Counselling is often seen as a middle-class activity, and thus as elitist, or certainly distant from the experience of working-class people, white and black. We believe that more effort needs investing in education, health and public relations programmes to counter this view and to increase general counselling provision. Counselling needs to be seen as a legitimate process for problem resolution.

Recent developments in training, in education, social services, and the National Health Service have seen an increase in the spread of counselling skills generally. However, this has not yet been accompanied by a visible expansion of counselling facilities, especially in areas having a higher incidence of ethnic minority peoples. With specific reference to coun-selling racially different clients there are very few specialist organizations offering help. Our view is that greater co-operation needs to take place between local authority and voluntary organizations and the different ethnic communities to stimulate the joint formation of projects that might be seen as directly relevant to the needs of those communities.

Much of this chapter has dealt with counselling as an activity that takes place between two people. There are other models of helping from around the world that are based on different assumptions, for example, working with families, working with community groups, using a series of counsel-lors in turn, and, so on. Co-operation and consultation between various elements of local communities might lead to the establishment of counselling agencies that are more sensitively appropriately equipped to help specific local communities. If counselling providers work only on a one-to-one model they might not only be guilty of cultural domination but will fail to provide the most relevant forms of help.

Given the present nature of Britain's multiracial society, it seems incumbent upon those whose concern is for the quality of people's lives generally to imaginatively expand that concern to all groups resident within Britain. It is not enough to assume that there already exists an adequate network of informed agencies and counsellors. Developments in training, provision research, and public information are all required so that any client, be they black or white, may have access to helpful counselling.

References

Atkinson, D., Morten, G. and Sue, D.W. (1989) *Counselling American Minorities: A Cross-Cultural Perspective.* Dubuque, IA: William C. Brown.

Coard, B. (1971) *How the West Indian Child is made Educationally Subnormal by the British School System.* London: New Beacon Books.

Dummett, A. (1980) 'Nationality and citizenship', in *Conference in Support of Further Education in Ethnic Minorities.* London: National Association for Teachers in Higher Education.

Guardian (1994) 'Labour figures show rise in reported race attacks in London', 18 March.

Hall, E.T. (1976) *Beyond Culture.* New York: Doubleday.

Hartman, P., Husband, C. and Clark, J. (1974) *Races as News.* Paris: UNESCO Press.

Helms, J.E. (1984) 'Toward a theoretical model of the effects of race on counselling: a black and white model', *The Counselling Psychologist,* 12: 153–65.

Jones, E.E. (1985) 'Psychotherapy and counseling with black clients', in P. Pedersen (ed.), *Handbook of Cross-Cultural Counseling and Therapy.* London: Praeger.

Jowell, R., Witherspoon, S. and Brook, L. (1984) *British Social Attitudes: the 1984 Report.* Aldershot: Gower/Social and Community Planning Research.

Jumaa, M. (1993) 'From the chair', *Race Newsletter,* 3. Rugby: BAC.

Katz, J.H. (1978) *White Awareness: Handbook for Anti-racism Training.* University of Oklahoma Press.

Lago, C.O., in collaboration with Thompson, J. (1996) *Race, Cultural and Counselling.* Buckingham: Open University Press.

Lee, C.C. (1994) An Introductory Lecture given at a conference entitled 'Race, Culture and Counselling'. Sheffield University, UK (July).

Lee, C.C. and Richardson, B.L. (1991) *Multicultural Issues in Counselling: New Approaches to Diversity.* Alexandria: American Association for Counselling and Development.

Little, A., Day, M. and Marshland, D. (1978) *Black Kids, White Kids. What Hope?* Leicester: National Youth Bureau.

Pontoretto, J.G. and Pedersen, P.B. (1993) *Preventing Prejudice: A Guide for Counselors and Educators.* London: Sage.

Rogers, C.R. (1978) *Carl Rogers on Personal Power.* London: Constable.

Skellington, R. and Morris, P. (1992) *Race in Britain Today.* London: Sage/OUP.

Smith, D.J. (1977) *Racial Disadvantage in Britain.* Harmondsworth: Penguin.

Sue, D.W. (1981) *Counseling the Culturally Different.* New York: John Wiley.

Thomas, A. and Sillen, S. (1972) *Racism and Psychiatry.* New York: Brunner/Mazel.

Thompson, J. (1991) 'Issues of race and culture in counselling supervision training courses'. Unpublished MSc thesis. London: Polytechnic of East London.

Troyna, B. (1981) *Public Awareness and the Media.* London: Commission for Racial Equality.

Discussion issues

1 Counselling and race is difficult to address in a clear manner.
2 In what ways, if any, has your journey of exploration into the issues of racism been 'an intensely painful experience'?
3 'In any counselling relationship between counsellor and client where there is racial difference, aspects of racism must be assumed to exist.'
4 In Britain is counselling a middle-class activity and thus elitist?

2

Working with Issues of Race in Counselling

Aisha Dupont-Joshua

I am a black woman of mixed race, and it has become very clear to me in the course of my practice that who I am, my attitudes and what I represent to clients are very important ingredients in the therapeutic relationship. Perhaps the most important part of my training took place in a mixed-race therapy group that I attended twice a week as part of my intercultural training. Here I thrashed out often very painful issues around my racial identify. I have constantly to work on this because I know that I cannot work with others on their racial identity unless I work on my own. The issue of race is such a clouded one that white counsellors usually go into what Patricia J. Williams (1997) calls 'the colour blind mode'. In her Reith lecture entitled 'The Emperor's new clothes', she says that race belongs to everybody except white people; they are not a race but are rather just 'normal'. Until white counsellors start owning their whiteness as part of their identity, and working on their racial identity development, they will be ill equipped to work across cultures, because their attitudes, who they are and what they represent to their black clients use vital ingredients in the counselling relationship.

Conscious and unconscious processes in the black/white dyad

As counsellors we are mirrors to our clients and to keep our mirrors clear we have continually to work on ourselves and our attitudes. Our attitudes on how we perceive 'the other' are very largely based on how we see ourselves and what we have been taught is socially normal. I wonder how many people reading this article have ever thought of themselves as white people. What does that represent – especially to black people – being normal, being in the majority, being historically dominant, having access to privilege, being part of what is considered aesthetically attractive, being in control. Of course on an individual level, this may not be true, but on a symbolic level, in relationship to black people, all these factors are present in the relationship.

I might add here that I use the term 'black' as a political term, not to describe the colour of one's skin, but rather to describe the collective experience of people of minority groups who have suffered racial discrimination in relationship to the majority white host culture.

Often when we talk about discrimination, racism and the historical abuse of black people, this brings about a huge cloud of guilt in white people – I am not talking about these factors to invoke guilt, no, only to make people aware that these factors are there, on a conscious or unconscious level for a meaningful relationship with black people in the counselling situation, and in life in general. Difference can be very threatening and in professional relationships, especially the counselling relationship, it is often managed by denial. Just focus on the presenting problem. However, transference issues will arise, regarding race and colour, and dreams may occur involving these issues – the unconscious will out. It is far healthier to bring these factors into the relationship and work with them. For what is happening in the counselling situation becomes a mirror for what is happening in other key areas of the client's life, and can be worked with very effectively, if acknowledged. Lennox Thomas (1992), in 'Racism in the consulting room', gives the example a therapeutic relationship between a white female client and a black male counsellor – where the effects of the blackness of the counsellor on the client were completely denied; she told him that she did not notice that he was black. However, a dream she brought to a session in the early months of counselling clearly showed that she was repressing her feelings. In the dream she was gradually becoming black – starting at her head the change of colour gradually worked its way down to her toes. Her fear in the dream was that her friends would not recognize her. She had started with ambivalence about being in counselling, but as often happens with people who have a poor sense of self, she became increasingly dependent on her counsellor and her dream related to her fear of merging with the counsellor and losing her individuality – her colour foremost. This dream revealed her feelings about dependency and individuation in the relationship and freed her to say that sometimes when she came to their sessions she had an image of her counsellor with a bone through his nose and a spear in his hand. She was upset about saying this but said that she feared that thinking about it would get in the way if she did not talk about it. Several months later, this led her to express her aggressive sexual feelings towards the counsellor. She was eventually able to recognize the aggressive warrior in herself, which she had previously projected onto the black counsellor.

Racial and ethnic identity development

Difference needs to be acknowledged right at the outset of the relationship, and, once acknowledged, can be used as a very useful tool to explore the social being of the client, as well as perhaps their racial identity. Of course, as a white counsellor, or a black one, you cannot help explore a black client's racial identity without exploring your own racial identity. Colin Lago and Joyce Thompson (1996), in their book *Race, Culture and Counselling*, have a very useful section on racial and ethnic identity development. Here, racial and ethnic identity development is described as being at the leading edge of thinking on multicultural counselling in the USA at the present time. These models attempt to describe a developmental process that people may go through in their quest to achieve a healthy sense of racial and ethnic identity. Clear and positive feelings about who we are enable us to respect and value others.

Helms (1984) suggests that there are five stages of white racial identity that affect attitudes, behaviour and emotions. To develop a healthy white identity requires developmental work, including abandoning individual racism, recognizing and actively opposing institutional and cultural racism, and becoming aware of their whiteness as an important part of their identity and internalizing a realistically positive view of what it means to be white. Helms' white racial conscious model (1984) suggests five stages of development – contact, disintegration, reintegration, pseudo-independence and autonomy.

1   In the *contact* stage there is an unawareness of the self as a racial being, with a tendency to ignore differences, together with an unawareness of minority groups, which is too problematic to take on and coped with by denial of the problem.
2   The *disintegration* stage involves becoming aware of racism – which tends to lead to feelings of guilt, depression and feeling bad. There is often a conflict between internal standards of human decency and external cultural expectations. The result is often an over-identification with black people, the development of paternalistic attitudes towards them to a retreat into white culture.
3   *Reintegration* is expressed as a hostility towards minority groups and a favouring of their own racial group.
4   The *pseudo-independent* stage is expressed by an increasing interest in racial groups' similarities and differences, together with a mental acceptance of other racial groups. There are limited cross-racial interactions or relationships with certain black people.
5   In the *autonomy* stage there is an acceptance, appreciation and respect of racial differences and similarities. Difference is viewed positively and there is an active seeking of opportunities for cross-racial interactions and relationships.

The process of the minority identity transformation involves moving from a white frame of reference, where the individual has a negative image of themselves for being black, to a positive black frame of reference. Atkinson et al.'s (1989) five-stage model is: conformity, dissonance, resistance and immersion, introspection, and the stage of synergetic articulation and awareness.

1   In the *conformity* stage, people of minority groups identify more strongly with the dominant culture's values, and tend to lack awareness about their personal ethnicity. There is often negativity shown towards themselves and other people of similar ethnic background.

The dominant group stereotypes about themselves and others are passively accepted.

2 During the *dissonance* stage, people tend to feel confusion and disillusionment about their previously held values, and an awareness of issues involving racism, sexism, oppression, etc. begins to develop. They begin to search for their own group's rolemodels and there are often feelings of loss and anger.

3 The third stage of *resistance and immersion* becomes more active and there is a rejection and distrust of the dominant culture and much greater identification with their own culture. The immersion into their own culture activates an interest in their own group's history, traditions, foods, language, etc. Activism often develops, with a challenging of oppression, frequently accompanied by a wish to separate from the dominant culture.

4 In the fourth stage of *introspection*, there is a questioning of the outright rejection of the dominant group's values, which can cause conflictual feelings about their loyalty to their own cultural group; this is part of the struggle for self-awareness.

5 *Synergetic articulation and awareness* express a stage of resolution of the previous conflicts and a sense of fulfilment in the search for a personal cultural identity. Other cultural groups' values, as well as the dominant group, are appreciated, together with a desire to get rid of all forms of oppression.

These are very useful sets of conceptualization for the counsellor's consideration, and enable a possibility of assessing the different levels of counsellor and client attainment on the development models, as a way of furthering understanding the possible dynamics that might emerge during counselling.

Case study

David was a young man of mixed race whom I worked with. He came to me in crisis, suffering from depression: he had become agoraphobic, he suffered from migraine and was dependent on cannabis as a pain-blocker. He wanted to find out where he fitted in society. His mother was a white English woman, who had been very protective of him. His father was a black man, originally from Barbados; he was of a violent nature, and mixed with white people as he did not like black people. His parents had separated when David was eight.

David was an attractive, masculine-looking, tall young man and had been in the RAF. However, he had a very ambiguous gender identity, and though he was rather popular with women and had a son, he felt that he was really a woman and considered having a sex change. His relationships with women had been clouded by these feelings and he was trying to negotiate a non-sexual 'girl' relationship with his current girlfriend. In his search for his racial identity David had become a DJ, and had become part of a black 'posse' – he joined a black community in Oxford, he had grown dreadlocks and a beard. However, after some violence, his friends were sent to prison and he now found himself lost and confused in his mother's house, unable to go out and smoking cannabis most of the time.

I am also of mixed race and found on my journey in search of my racial identity a long passage of rejection and acceptance of the whiteness and blackness in myself. The acceptance and peace with both those parts became the crux of our work together. I had difficulty with the details of David's gender identity and had to work on my feelings about this in supervision, but it became clear during the course of the relationship that this confusion was related to the confusion he felt in his racial identity and he was in a sense acting out his social marginalization. There seemed to be a splitting between the elements of whiteness and blackness, good and bad, and masculine and feminine in him. We established a dialogue between the different parts, sometimes through gestalt exercises and even gave the different parts names. This dialogue and acceptance of the different parts, each with a place, became a very healing element for David and became the building blocks to creating a positive sense of self. I encouraged him to develop his relationship with his son, and his positive fathering role, which he had never had with his father, helped him to develop his masculinity. He unconsciously related masculinity and blackness and, because he had had such a poor role model in his father, had difficulty with both these aspects of himself. He eventually went off to live in a mixed-race community in Liverpool, where he felt he could be himself.

Conclusion

I have used the above case study to illustrate how my attitudes towards the ambiguity in David to both race and gender were very important in setting the tone of the relationship. I could not have helped him find acceptance in the duality of his racial identity unless I had worked on my own racial identity. So to conclude, to give a clear reflection, the counsellor must continually work on their attitudes, on their own racial identity and also work with the aspects of race and culture reflected in the relationship.

References

Atkinson, D., Morten, G. and Sue, D.W. (1989) *Counselling American Minorities: A Cross Cultural Perspective*. Dubuque, IA: W.C. Brown.

Helms, J.E. (1984) 'Towards a theoretical model of the effects of race on counselling: a black and white model'. *The Counselling Psychologist*, 12: 153–65.

Lago, C. and Thompson, J. (1996) *Race, Culture and Counselling*. Buckingham: Open University Press.

Thomas, L. (1992) 'Racism in the consulting room'. *Inter-cultural Therapy*, Oxford: Blackwell Scientific Press.
Williams, P.J. (1997) 'The Emperor's new clothes' *The Reith Lectures*, London: Virago Press.

Discussion issues

1   In what ways could a counsellor explore her or his racial identity?
2   What are the advantages of the Atkinson et al. (1989) five-stage model?
3   Do you feel guilty about discrimination, racism and historical abuse of black people? If so, why?
4   Why is it difficult, if not, impossible for a white counsellor to help explore a black client's racial identity without first exploring her or his own?

PART TWO
THEORY AND PRACTICE OF
MULTICULTURAL COUNSELLING

Part two focuses on the theory and practice of multicultural counselling. The 12 chapters form the major part of this book and include a range of topics such as the philosophical framework for therapy, therapeutic approaches such as family therapy, counselling specific groups including those facing racism and discrimination, and frank talk(ing).

In Chapter 3, Eleftheriadou focuses on the underlying attitude and philosophy of counsellors and psychotherapists working in the transcultural field. The chapter proposes that an existential phenomenological philosophy provides an accessible framework for dealing with transcultural issues. A case study illustrates this with a female client who originated from the West Indies.

In Chapter 4, Lago and Moodley consider multicultural issues in eclectic and integrative therapy. They provide possible examples of racist theoretical underpinnings of therapy, citing some of Jung's work as well as other more contemporary works. A case study is used to highlight some of the implications of gender difference in transcultural therapy, discuss the therapeutic approach and explore the client's inner journey.

In Chapter 5, Palmer asserts that an idiographic approach aids multicultural counselling. By its very nature, it is transtheoretical and attempts to understand each client from his or her unique frame of reference. It is also compatible with the biopsychosocial model of mental health. Although it can be helpful to take a nomothetic perspective that focuses on the distinguishing characteristics of a group to which a person belongs, it may overlook important aspects too. Palmer suggests that multimodal therapy is a suitable idiographic approach and illustrates this with a case study.

Chapter 6 addresses the failure of western family therapy in dealing with cultural bias for 'ethnic minority families'. Guernina provides two case studies from cultural minority families to help clarify the assessment or intervention procedures used and gives a conceptual framework for cultural specific interventions. In Chapter 7, Biever and associates discuss ideas from postmodern narrative therapy including social constructionism and highlight its application to therapy with intercultural couples. It is suggested that postmodern therapies such as those based on social constructionism provide a framework for approaching the complexities of intercultural relationships, although accepting that the efficacy of the approach has yet to be examined.

In Chapter 8, Banks seeks to help counsellors identify difficulties related to discrimination and racism when offering stress counselling to black client groups. This is discussed within the context of black employees attending counselling and he stresses the need to acknowledge the personal, political and institutional structural factors that they experience. In fact, he asserts that the difficulty is not the stress but the racism. Chapter 9 by Tidwell focuses on crisis counselling. This is a short-term, directive psychotherapeutic intervention which is oriented towards the solution of practical problems and toward quickly re-establishing emotional equilibrium. In Chapter 10, the unique counselling needs of foreign students are covered. Khoo and associates review the literature, consider the issues concerned, and focus on how to develop competencies and relevant strategies for counselling this group. In addition, they select a number of guidelines recommended by the American Psychological Association which counsellors may find helpful.

In Chapter 11, de Silva discusses the principles and practices of Buddhism applied to the field of counselling. He believes that many of the Buddhist techniques could profitably be incorporated into therapy. He highlights that Buddhist literature contains references to a large number of cognitive and behavioural strategies such as graded exposure, modelling, stimulus control, distraction, and so on. In fact, this may be a surprise to many western counsellors.

Chapter 12 focuses on good practice in transcultural counselling from an Asian perspective. Webb Johnson and Nadirshaw discuss Eurocentrism in western psychiatry and its mind–body dichotomy. This contrasts with the more holistic eastern approach. It is suggested that psychiatric services are often discriminatory, culturally insensitive and inappropriate. This paper was published in 1993. The question we could ask ourselves is whether the situation in the new millennia has considerably improved. It would be great to think it has. Webb Johnson and Nadirshaw challenge stereotypes about the South Asian communities such as the assertion that Asians 'somatize' more than any other ethnic group. As many counsellors and psychotherapists would have noted, somatization is reported in white Europeans too. Useful guidelines for good practice for counsellors and therapists are provided in the final section.

Chapter 13 by Laungani argues that conceptions of mental illness and its treatment often stem from the normative, social and cultural constructions of mental illness. To understand mental illness, it is necessary to examine the salient normative beliefs, attitudes and values of a given culture, which guide behaviours at a personal, social and cultural level. He proposes a cross-cultural theoretical model that permits an examination and comparison of mental illness in India and Britain. He includes a section on the diverse therapeutic practices available in India.

Part Two finishes with a chapter by Moodley on 'I say what I like': frank talk(ing) in counselling and psychotherapy. He considers the black consciousness psychology or philosophy of Steve Biko. Aspects of the philosophy relating to empowerment, self-concept development, the internalization of racism and the racial identity of black people are discussed. The 'frank talk' method is explored. It is based on the idea of expressing freely what one feels and what one knows to gain and regain one's sense of humanity.

In reading Part Two of this book, it becomes apparent that many different perspectives on the theory and practice of multicultural counselling co-exist. There is a range of diverse approaches, each with their underpinning theory, providing their own suggestions on how to work with different groups. However, there is still a lack of research indicating what would be the most effective interventions or approaches to use when counselling in a multicultural society. What does exist is largely based on studies undertaken in North America, which may be less applicable to Britain. Jewel attempts to cover this topic in the last chapter of the book.

Transcultural Counselling and Psychotherapy: A Philosophical Framework

Zack Eleftheriadou

This chapter focuses on the underlying attitude and philosophy of counsellors and psychotherapists working in the transcultural field. Although the author has published subsequent papers to this chapter drawing from psychodynamic theories, for the purposes of this chapter 'therapeutic technique' is not addressed in depth. Instead the author raises fundamental questions on the actual underlying *philosophical framework* of transcultural therapy, such as: How do we uniquely and personally integrate the common social–cultural reality of our surroundings? How do we form a subjective outlook on the world? These questions need to explored by therapists themselves, before embarking on transcultural therapeutic work.

It is suggested in this chapter that a philosophical framework can be effective for the practice of transcultural therapy. The proposed framework is an integration of the existential ideas of Heidegger, Sartre, Yalom and Binswanger and the phenomenological ideas and methodology of Husserl. The existential/phenomenological framework is suggested because it accepts that the client is embedded in a socio-cultural reality, yet he or she has integrated this in a unique way. The assumption of this approach is that the individual creates a unique experience of the world; in other words has a subjective world view. The notion of a world view is not a static concept, but something that is always interactive with all of the person's experience and is always capable of change. It is recognized that both the client and the therapist hold differing world views or philosophies of life. Working in this way implies that before attempting to understand another person's world view it is essential for the therapist to have examined his or her own values, beliefs or unique philosophy of life. Consequently in therapy, the client's underlying values, beliefs and ideas are explored, in terms of the different modes of relating to the world: the physical, personal, social and spiritual/creative aspects. The therapist is at all times helping the client identify and clarify these, through the process of description, being non-judgemental and attempting to step back from his or her own values and assumptions. This process is illustrated through a case study.

Transcultural therapy is a product of the emerging pluralism in western countries. With the continual movement towards pluralistic societies there is a need for expansion of knowledge and for more openness to other cultural beliefs and practices. Most mental health workers are generally in agreement that issues of race or culture arise in the therapy room, and during supervision and between therapists. Nevertheless, what has tended to happen is that the concept of culture has been dismissed in therapy, and clients have been counselled according to western beliefs and value systems. Using a preformulated theory into which clients are slotted is of no benefit to any client, black or white. It is merely a system which tries to pin people down mechanistically into labels.

Alternatively, others have criticized this field insisting that there is no analysis so deep that it goes beyond culture. The purpose of this chapter is to provide a framework that could be applied to transcultural therapy.

The aim is not to argue about what is inborn and what is environmental or cultural, but instead to tackle the person-cultural context relationship as a whole rather than only the person or just the culture. It is suggested in this context, that culture can be transcended in the therapeutic process using existential/phenomenological analysis. The approach can be used more as a framework than as a systematic, prescribed way of working. This is a much broader model of therapy, a model that is transcultural rather than cross-cultural or intercultural. The difference is a crucial one because 'trans' denotes an 'active and reciprocal process'. Therapists in this setting are responsible for working across, through or beyond their cultural differences (d'Ardenne and Mahtani, 1989: 5).

Phenomenology and existentialism are both branches of humanistic psychology. Phenomenology was founded by the philosopher Edmund Husserl in the nineteenth century. 'Phenomenology' originates from the Greek words 'phenomenon' meaning appearance and 'logos' meaning study. It is primarily a way of viewing the world as it is created by the individual and there is an attempt to describe a person's experience rather than to seek causal explanations for it. It is believed that human beings are continually trying to make sense out of their world through the act of 'intentionality' (from the Latin word 'intendere' which means to stretch). Intentionality means that the mind stretches out into the real world and draws it to the self, so the experiential process is at all times interactive with the world.

Existentialism is a philosophy which has its roots in the seventeenth century. However, it is largely a product of the philosopher Friedrich Nietzsche in the nineteenth century, and Martin Heidegger, Jean-Paul Sartre and Martin Buber in the twentieth century. It is an interactive view of society concerned with the conflict an individual encounters as he or she confronts 'existence' (a term originating from the Latin word 'existere' meaning to emerge or to become).

Existential phenomenology is by no means an attempt to deculturalize therapy, but rather this framework is suggested because: first, the existential branch helps to examine fundamental ideas and assumptions of human existence, and second, it acknowledges that both therapist and client have differing worldviews. Phenomenology provides us with a methodology of attempting to 'strip away, as far as possible, the plethora of interpretational layers added to the unknown stimuli to our experience' (Spinelli, 1990: 15), in order to reach a more clear explanation of what is there. The therapist in this field must be explicit where his or her model(s) of working arise from, as it is important to recognize that counselling can never be value-free. It is always linked to social, political and historical issues (Katz, 1985). Not knowing what is culture-free in the therapeutic process puts us in a position of always needing to be open and flexible. Both participants, the therapist and the client, bring their socialization patterns, complex experiences, implicit theories of human nature and their unique philosophies of life into the therapeutic relationship. The relationship can be made more effective if we are aware of what each one brings, and specially, as therapists, how much we can influence the other.

Hence it is essential for the therapist to clarify his or her own ideas on life and on living generally. This includes familial and interpersonal relationships and values, religious or political ideas, and so forth (d'Ardenne and Mahtani, 1989). Therapy is not only a potential learning environment for the client, but also for the therapist. Indeed the therapist should be learning and using the experiences with the clients for self-growth.

Effective therapy requires many more important elements rather than just cultural knowledge. The therapist from the same ethnic background may be helpful to the client because there is a shared socio-cultural context. Nevertheless, there is often a danger when the therapist believes that the client will present certain issues because of his or her cultural background. And even if a client belongs to a certain culture, it does not imply that he or she holds that culture's views and values. If the client is perceived as representing a certain culture, the danger is that the complexity and uniqueness of the individual's own learning and experience is undervalued and stereotyping and prejudice may be the end product. It is important to remember that the client will eventually provide the therapist with all the cultural information that is necessary and relevant to the therapy. Existential phenomenological analysis is a process of engaging in a Socratic dialogue with the client in order to help the client discover himself or herself and his or her own uniqueness, in other words, to actually encounter and confront this self. Therapy is a process of attempting to make communication clear and explicit at all times. This means that meanings are not accepted as what they appear to be to the therapist, unless the client has confirmed this.

The therapeutic relationship should be as equal as possible and this may be achieved by focusing on the 'relationship'. This approach de-emphasizes therapeutic techniques since it is believed that too much of it can impede actual understanding of the client. Nonetheless, therapy can be effective if the basic skills of counselling are utilized (such as positive regard, non-possessive warmth, genuiness, concern, respect, a non-judgemental attitude (Rogers, 1961) and the toleration of ambiguity. These should be necessary attitudes in every therapist–client relationship (Pedersen et al., 1989).

The goals would be what the client has brought to the therapy, which belong to the appropriate cultural context, implying that the client's own concept of normality or health is used (Fernando, 1991). Therapy can provide clients with the opportunity to clarify and question and subsequently expand their world-view or:

> to enable clients to enter a new phase of development of their talent for life. Existential counselling is a training in the art of living. It involves learning to see the world and human existence anew, with interest and imagination rather than boredom and bigotry ... The sense that many more secrets are buried in the heart of existence brings more hope and undreamt joy in living. New meanings and possibilities are revealed and with them arises a source of motivation and courage. (van Deurzen-Smith, 1988: 26)

In existentialism, life is compared to art, which can improve only by practice, such as by facing problems and difficulties as well as pleasure. The person can try to uncover previous choices which restricted his or her being-in-the-world and to see himself or herself more clearly.

The actual problem is not seen as something that necessarily has to be changed, but as something that we can try to understand in a creative way. The ultimate goal is for the client to find his or her own truth and meaning and hence existential/phenomenological philosophy is something which must be experienced and deeply understood by the person (Suinn, 1985).

If a person takes the time to explore the direction that his or her life is going, then he or she can learn to accept himself or herself and situations, and change other aspects by choice. This follows the underlying assumption that we are changing beings, always in flux. This implies that we are not static and therefore always faced with freedom. As Sartre said, 'each man must invent his own values, and he exists authentically in so far as he strives to realise values that are really his own' (quoted in Macquarrie, 1972: 207). However, our freedom is embedded in the human limitations of illness, death, etc. These are general ideas, and what is important is to concentrate on the individual meaning of these facts. One must also take the responsibility for the consequences of his or her choices and for those with whom one interacts.

The first important element of therapy (arising from phenomenology) is to be able to be as bias-free as possible through a similar process to Husserl's epoché (Spinelli, 1989). Epoché is a process of stepping back as far as possible from any assumptions or prejudices. In therapy there is an immediate focus on experience as it happens, rather than basing the experience on theory, belief or reason. The counsellor must be open, continually checking and clarifying with the client. This is challenging because it may constantly require the skill of tuning into a totally new reality along with that culture's own meaningful and appropriate thoughts, emotions and behaviours.

Furthermore, it is demanding because the therapist has to deal with such a new world view that the therapist must be striving to push into the background his or her own philosophy of life. This is exhausting and tiring, and research has shown that it can evoke many feelings of incompetence and inadequacy (Pedersen et al., 1989). It may sometimes create a similar situation to the experience of culture shock. The situation may occur with any client since he or she may have a unique subjective reality and belong to a different subculture to the counsellor in age, socio-economic status, political party orientation, religion, etc. In a way, transcultural work highlights the issue of how, as therapists, we are not experts on the client's world view. The person is therefore allowed to be, that is, accepted for what he or she is. The client is seen as an autonomous person who can only change if he or she is motivated and has chosen to do so. The person can then choose how he or she should be in life.

The second element is called the rule of description. This is an attempt to describe immediate 'here and now' stimuli rather than formulating more abstract causal explanations of the client's experience. The immediate behaviour of the client is examined with a focus on what is actually being experienced, rather than how it was experienced or how the client would like to experience it in the future.

Another important notion of this process is the horizontalization rule or equalization rule. This is an attempt to avoid hierarchies in the description of the behaviour. All behaviour is perceived in equal rankings and all phenomena are accepted as being a normal part of the person's subjective reality. The therapist must show neutrality towards the client, by avoiding any criticism or judgements.

Within his or her cultural context (this includes subcultures he or she may be part of) the client has to develop a wider perspective, including an awareness of more choice. It is the therapist's role to work with that client within his or her world view or cultural net in order to understand what are cultural adaptions and patterns. Instead of dimissing the person as crazy or too different because his or her ideas are defined from a different reference point, the existential therapist works with that person not only with feelings and behaviours, but also by examining his or her basic value system. These are explored within the four modes of relating: the Eigenwelt, Mitwelt, Umwelt (Binswanger, 1968), and the Uberwelt (van Deurzen-Smith, 1988). The Umwelt is the natural world, or the environment. It is the meaning of this physical world to the person. The Eigenwelt is the private, intrapersonal world of the person. The Mitwelt is the public or interpersonal world of the person. However, there is still a different, although generalized view of the inner world of clients of different ethnicities. The Mitwelt includes all of the person's significant human relationships, interactions, and support systems which are largely culturally defined, such as people's relationship to their race, their ethnicity, organizational sphere, community group and broader societal issues (law, religion, economics, politics, etc. (Freedman, 1987). The Uberwelt is the spiritual aspect or that which is beyond. It is man's 'ideological outlook on life, the beliefs he holds about life, death, existence – those beliefs which underpin or are a basis for all subsequent beliefs and interpretations' (Spinelli, 1989: 129). It is the most creative part of us and the part which is still unknown.

The four dimensions make up the total existence of the person (Vontress, 1987). They emphasize that both therapists and clients from different cultures have adopted different social realities or world views. It is important for the counsellor to find out how these are translated into the client's subjective frame of reference. Using the above framework, we have a way of examining value systems, emotion, individual relationships, etc. Once the four modes of relating have been established, they can be then questioned. In the process, some aspects are owned and others are rejected or altered. It is not as important to find the roots of these social patterns (for example, whether they have stemmed from parental socialization or peers), but how the person feels about them, and what is meaningful for that person's life. The client and therapist can then work towards change and new meaning. This is a lifelong process for both client and therapist.

An example of how the philosophy of existential phenomenology was applied can best be illustrated with a female client who originated from the West Indies. This client sought therapy because she was experiencing anxiety every time she entered a car, particularly every time she took her a driving test. Her doctor had referred her for therapy after realizing that the prescribed relaxation pills were not alleviating her symptoms. Hence, she came to therapy with the goal of being able to drive in a relaxed manner, and consequently to pass her driving test. As time passed, it emerged that this anxiety was experienced in many other areas of her life: for example, in the presence of different individuals (including the therapist), and when she was among groups of people. As illustrated by this client, often a restriction in one mode of relating can be experienced in other areas.

Therapy was seen as a dialogue where she would slowly describe her experience of feeling anxious. This client's concept of anxiety may have similar aspects with other people, but for each individual there are unique components, such as this client's connection of anxiety to certain situations, certain times, settings. The clarification process is of value to the client and for the therapist, in order to understand the experience of what it is to feel anxious. In this way, the counsellor is not making assumptions based on experience of a similar situation as that reported by the client. As therapy progressed, this client began to explain how her experience of anxiety was that of feeling restricted and controlled.

Sometimes during the sessions this was expressed in the way she had her coat buttoned up to the top with her purse crossing over her chest.

In terms of her Eigenwelt she felt trapped and rather isolated from life, especially herself. She described living her life as an actress who does not really experience it actively. In her Mitwelt she began to describe how she was extremely dependent towards other people; such as her friends to drive her to places, her husband to control the finances at home and other aspects that would protect her from facing the world. The paradox was that she was dependent on others and yet she could not relate to them intimately. Her Umwelt also felt restricted in comparison to her life back in the West Indies. Back in the West Indies, she was more in touch with nature and loved the warm climate. She would always love to walk outdoors and feel the hot sun, look at the blue sky and pick fresh fruit. When she came to England she felt this as a restriction of her physical body, due to the climate and the distances of a big city like London. She could no longer walk to places and it felt like outside influences were now being imposed on her, like having to learn to drive in order to be able to go out and retain some independence. A person can often end up in this situation where he or she has lost responsibility for himself or herself and for his or her world. Many people who enter into the therapeutic enterprise have reached this point in their life where their choice and freedom seem extremely restricted. Draguns (1975) states that if there is one pancultural feature of therapy it is that of addressing the relationship of society with the individual. Frequently, this takes the form of social control. In this state of self-deception the person is not being authentic; that is not taking on values and beliefs which are truly meaningful.

During therapy we examined the four modes of relating and the client was encouraged to look at them in terms of three time dimensions: the past, present and future. The three dimensions enable the person to see what experience has been acquired and how he or she has interpreted the experience. In this case she was able to redefine some past aspects of her experience, explore her present life and to strive towards goals and aspirations of the future. This was evident in her Uberwelt, where creatively, she realized that she really enjoyed working with children and writing.

Additionally, ways for releasing physical frustration eventually emerged more and more in her passion for dancing, which she could pursue for hours.

In conclusion, existential phenomenology has been proposed as an accessible framework for dealing with transcultural issues because: first, it delves deep into fundamental questions of human existence. It is taken as a basic assumption that all the different manifestations presented in therapy are related to basic universal, existential concerns of life, such as death, anxiety, meaningless and isolation, regardless of race, ethnicity and culture.

Second, it acknowledges that both therapist and client have differing world views and it is a prerequisite as well as an ongoing process for the existential therapist to examine this. The therapist must acknowledge, understand and accept the client's cultural background. Existential phenomenology travels deep into the person's values, morals, assumptions and expectations. It explores a person's experience in terms of all the possible areas for connection to the world to discover what it is he or she enjoys, is capable of, as well as facing up to the limitations of oneself and life.

Most of the suggestions in this chapter, if displayed in a consistent and convincing manner during therapy, should be present in any psychotherapeutic communication and indeed many therapists do use them without conscious acknowledgement. Nevertheless, they are particularly applicable when working with clients from different cultural, ethnic backgrounds and those who present with cross-cultural conflicts.

Note

An earlier version of this paper was originally published under the title 'Multi-cultural counselling and psychotherapy: a philosophical framework (1992) in *Psychologos: The Italian International Review of Psychology*, 3: 21–9. The author would like to thank the journal editors for permission to republish the article.

References

Binswanger, L. (1968) *Being-In-The-World*. New York: Harper Torch Books.
d'Ardenne, P. and Mahtani, A. (1989) *Transcultural Counselling In Action*. London: Sage.
Deurzen-Smith, E. van (1988) *Existential Counselling in Practice*. London: Sage.
Draguns, J.G. (1975) 'Resocialization into culture: the complexities of taking a worldwide view of psychotherapy', in R.W. Brislin, S. Bochner and W.J. Lonner (eds), *Cross-Cultural Perspectives on Learning*, 273–90. London: Sage.
Eleftheriadou, Z. (1993) 'Application of a philosophical framework to transcultural counselling', *Journal of the Society for Existential Analysis*, 4: 116–23.
Eleftheriadou, Z. (1994) *Transcultural Counselling*. London: Central Publishing House.
Eleftheriadou, Z. (1997a) 'Integration of isolation: the cross-cultural experience', in S. du Plock, *Case Studies In Existential Psychotherapy and Counselling*. Chichester: Wiley.
Eleftheriadou, Z. (1997b) 'Cultural differences in the therapeutic process', in I. Horton and V. Varma, *The Needs of Counsellors and Psychotherapists*. London: Sage.
Fernando, S. (1991) *Mental Health Race and Culture*. London: Macmillan.
Freedman, J.A. (1987) 'Clinical sociology', in P. Pedersen (ed.), *Handbook of Cross-Cultural Counseling and Therapy*, 117–23. London: Praeger.
Ibrahim, F.A. (1985) 'Effective cross cultural counselling and psychotherapy: a framework', *The Counselling Psychologist*, 13 (4): 625–38.
Katz, S.H. (1985) 'The sociopolitical nature of counselling', *The Counselling Psychologist*, 13: 615–24.
Khan, M.A. (1991) 'Counselling psychology in a multicultural society', *Counselling Psychology Review*, 6 (3): 11–13.
Macquarrie, J. (1972) *Existentialism: An Introduction, Guide and Assessment*. Harmondsworth: Penguin.
Pedersen, P.B., Draguns, J.G., Lonner, W.J. and Trimble, J.E. (eds) (1989) 'Introduction', in *Counselling Across Cultures*, 3rd edn. Honolulu: University of Hawaii Press.
Pedersen, P., Fukuyama, M. and Heath, A. (1989) 'Client, counsellor, and contextual variables in multicultural counselling', in P.B. Pedersen, J.G. Draguns, W.J. Lonner, and

J.E. Trimble (eds), *Counselling Across Cultures*, 3rd edn, 23–52. Honolulu: University of Hawaii Press.

Rogers, C.R. (1961) *On Becoming A Person; A Therapist's View of Psychotherapy*. London: Constable.

Rogers, C.R. (1965) *Client-Centered Therapy*. London: Constable.

Spinelli, E. (1989) *The Interpreted World: An Introduction to Phenomenological Psychology*. London: Sage.

Spinelli, E. (1990) 'The phenomenological method and client-centred therapy', *Journal of the Society for Existential Analysis*, 1: 15–21.

Suinn, R.M. (1985) 'The sociopolitical nature of counseling: effective cross-cultural counselling and psychotheraphy', *The Counselling Psychologist*, 13: 684–91.

Vontress, C.E. (1987) 'Existentialism as a cross-cultural counselling modality', in P. Pedersen, (ed.) *Handbook of Cross-Cultural Counselling and Therapy*, 207–12. London: Praeger.

Yalom, I. (1980) *Existential Psychotherapy*. New York: Basic Books.

Discussion issues

1 Can a philosophical framework be most effective for the practice of multicultural therapy?

2 It is essential for the counsellor to have examined his or her own values, beliefs or unique philosophy of life before attempting to understand another person's world view.

3 What dimensions do you think make up the 'total existence' of the person?

4 When counselling transculturally, have you ever allowed your world view to clash with a client's world view? If yes, what have you learnt from the experience?

4

Multicultural Issues in Eclectic and Integrative Counselling and Psychotherapy

Colin Lago and Roy Moodley

During the last decade ideas about counselling and psychotherapy in a multicultural context have been developing gradually with a consequent increase in training possibilities, research and publications becoming available to practitioners. The actual practice of therapy with clients from different ethnic origins stimulates many questions. For example, why do ethnic minorities infrequently use counselling and psychotherapy services? If they do use them what are the reasons for early termination? Are there other cultural forums providing for the mental health needs of these groups? These questions have been addressed elsewhere (see Lago and Thompson, 1996; Moodley, 1998) and so we will not go into any details here, but suffice it to say that the research context for ensuring and developing good practice is still very limited.

The process of counselling and psychotherapy is constructed and constantly being reconstructed to attempt to meet the needs of those who engage with it. Issues of 'race', culture and ethnicity should play a central role in any formulation of therapy within the available theoretical models. It is becoming clear that there are theoretical limitations in the discourse of counselling and psychotherapy with relation to cultural diversity. Pedersen (1985: 45) asserts that 'there is no well defined consistency for cross-cultural counselling and psychotherapy either as a field or as a discipline'. He suggests that the developments thus far are the result of a few interested individuals trying to develop a process from much of the scattered material gained from related disciplines. Pedersen also indicates that the existing western European models of counselling and psychotherapy have been the only resources from which perspectives on cross-cultural counselling and psychotherapy have been gained.

Multicultural therapeutic competencies are extremely difficult to acquire, as inevitably we are primarily demanding of ourselves as practitioners to attempt imaginatively to 'indwell' and thus strive to understand the 'cultural' and psychological views of the world of clients who are culturally different to ourselves. This is clearly not the same as empathically indwelling in others' psychological views of the world who are culturally similar to ourselves, for here we have some semblance of possibility of understanding their cultural perspective as we (to a greater or less extent) share that heritage. But where both the psychology and culture are different then the task becomes much more formidable. (The term 'culture' used in this paragraph relates to all the aspects of society that one is influenced by and subjected to).

Complexities of terminology

In the following discussion of multicultural issues in eclectic and inte-grative counselling and psychotherapy, we consider how issues of 'race', culture and ethnicity engage with these therapies. The literature on this subject is also beset with its own complexity in relation to terminology and the resulting implications this has for therapeutic practice. For exam-ple, the practice is variously called: cross-cultural counselling (Pedersen, 1985), inter-cultural therapy (Kareem and Littlewood, 1992) and trans-cultural counselling (d'Ardenne and Mahtani, 1989; Eleftheriadou, 1994). Other hyphenated synonyms exist such as Afro-centric (Hall, 1995) and anti-racist (Moodley, 1992), as well as black feminist and politicized coun-selling (Pankhania, 1996). Sue and Sue (1990) discuss the same issues under a more general rubric of counselling the culturally different. There is also a tendency to discuss multicultural counselling and psychotherapy under a more sociopolitical nomenclature of 'race', ethnicity and culture. These ideas are developed in Carter (1995) and Lago and Thompson (1989, 1996).

Contemporary practice in the USA is to term the whole field as 'multi-cultural' which is presently being hailed as the 'fourth force' in coun-selling (Pedersen, 1991). Fassinger and Richie (1997: 83) suggest that in this paradigmatic change, in which the 'fourth force' is related to the 'dynamic, reciprocal relationship between intrapsychic forces and environ-mental influences related to one's cultural milieu', 'counsellors are trained to think complexly, rather than categorically' (p. 84). This is refreshing given that the history of labelling ethnic minorities in the UK is problematic and beset with complexity and controversy. However much these labels may have their own unique meanings, McLeod (1993) asserts that all approaches are essentially about the race, culture and eth-nic identity of the participants engaged in the counselling process. Our own intentions in writing this chapter are to encourage the reader both to critically examine their use of language and concepts within multi-cultural encounters and to recognize the complexity of the changes that occur in language use over time. Our overall concern is obviously to sup-port the optimum delivery of sensitive, competent counselling practice in multicultural settings.

Assumptions, theoretical approaches
and authors' limitations

Clearly it seems there are various ways in which counselling and psychotherapy with minorities is practised. In counselling the culturally different client, eclectic and integrative approaches are strongly recommended (Fassinger and Richie, 1997; Ponterotto, 1997) since potentially they offer the client a process that is broadly based and flexible. Any one 'purist' approach carries the danger of exposing the client to the hidden Eurocentric assumptions that are invariably present in conventional therapies. Another reason for advocating eclectic and integrative approaches with the culturally diverse is an understanding that members from these communities are already engaging in a form of socio-political eclecticism and so are skilled at understanding themselves in relation to different and sometimes opposing perceptions of themselves and their environment. In this chapter we have included:

- a brief review of the background and history of counselling and therapy in terms of 'race', culture and ethnicity;
- a discussion relating to issues of cultural sensitivity, world views and universal approaches.

In considering clinical issues we have focused on some specific aspects of clinical practice such as empathy, non-judgementalism, congruency and interpreting the transference. This is done through the discussion of a case study of a client in therapy with one of the authors.

A word of caution is included here for the reader in relation to the authors' views. Both authors are clinically experienced and have taught counselling. Their preferred theoretical models – person centred and psychoanalytic – do not comfortably fit into the integrative and eclectic schools. Their concerns, however, for sensitive informed practice in multicultural therapy are paramount and it is from this perspective and commitment that they have written this chapter.

Historical attachments

The history of counselling and psychotherapy in particular is rooted not only in its philosophical context but has also been shaped very much by its social and political contexts. Sashidharan (1990: 8) reminds us of psychiatry's position that is 'rooted in colonialism and in the theories of racial differentiation'. In this sense counselling and psychotherapy are no different. This understanding has increased the development of a critique of multicultural therapy supported by theoretical ideas from post-stnrcturalism, post-colonial and feminist theory. Some of the past ideas from 'race thinking' (Husband, 1982) still appear in the therapeutic processes today. Working with cultural diversity has always raised the objection that a single approach is problematic because its origin is located at a particular point within European culture. This can be further pinpointed as residing in particular individual people (usually men) who have developed the theoretical field, such as Freud, Jung, Adler, Klein, Lacan, Rogers, Ellis, Egan, etc. This realization begs questions of hegemonic patriarchy and negative masculinities.

During the 1980s and 1990s, the feminist movement, especially the French feminists, successfully interrogated the psychoanalytic movement for its gender bias in its theoretical formulations. The present critique through the discourses of 'race', culture and ethnicity still finds itself enveloped by themes that have repeated themselves viz. racism in the early literature of psychoanalysis (Dalal, 1988; Thomas and Sillen, 1972), cultural competence development (Pedersen, 1985; Sue and Sue, 1990) and socio-biological anthropology (Littlewood, 1990). The examples we offer below follow this pattern but offer a reminder that the background to any multicultural work in eclectic and integrative counselling and psychotherapy is made complex by this very history.

Racist theoretical underpinnings?

The initial tainting of the 'race' issue by Freud and Jung, for example, must be seen and understood in a wider historical context of the representation of 'otherness' socially, politically and medically when these authors were attempting to understand and articulate theories of human development and therapy. However, the racism that is inherent in their writing needs to be acknowledged and deconstructed. A reformulation of important and relevant concepts must be attempted and integrated in the development of the eclectic movement. For example, Jung postulated that the 'Negro has probably a whole historical layer less in the brain' (Thomas and Sillen, 1972: 239). This manifestly must be critiqued as racism but can also be seen in the light of other aspects of his awareness. At a further point in his writing he indicated that 'because the European does not know his own unconscious, he does not understand the East and projects into it everything he fears and despises in himself' (Jung, 1957: par. 8). The East here clearly being the 'other', as Jung understood it to be. Clearly Jung's position on 'race' was ambiguous and he obviously reflected more than the negative stereotyping of people from the 'Third World' than other writers of his time. According to Dalal (1988), Jung accepts stereotypes and only questions the deviation from them. Dalal offers a clear and detailed analysis of the deeply ingrained racist position that Jung took in exploring some of the major psychological processes he theorized. This useful analysis of the collected works of Jung reveals the state of thinking and the negative projections that found themselves in the analytical psychologies of this period. Although writers like Samuels (1988) and Rycroft (1988) accept the criticisms by Dalal, they nevertheless suggest that Jung's writing must be seen in the context of the thinking of his time and that value should be placed on the symbolic perception of his comments. However, valuing symbolic perceptions of those very comments is also problematic. What seems to us to be important is the possibility of using some of Jung's ideas in attempting to develop counselling and psycho-therapy with minority groups and not engaging in the contradictions that have been highlighted in Eweka (1990) and the subsequent critique by Phillips (1991).

Even Freud seems to have failed to 'self-analyse' this process in himself, as his 'self' was inevitably a product of his time. Freud's contention that the unconscious was a place below – different, timeless, primordial, libidi-nal, separated from consciousness, unmapped, dark and without light – was said to be 'discovered' at the same time that Africa was being actively explored and exploited (Moodley, 1991). Being critical of Freud's racism is necessary but problematic if the consequences lead to a complete dis-counting of the theories embedded in psychoanalysis. Eclectic and inte-grative therapy with culturally diverse groups can benefit greatly from both analytic and humanist ideas on childhood origins of emotional prob-lems. Psychoanalytic thought also embraces ideas on the importance of the unconscious, resistance and defences, and offers ideas on the thera-peutic relationship, objective identification and splitting.

Contemporary suspicions of racist practice

Notions, indeed accusations, of racism in some areas of therapy have continued to the present day. Kennedy (1952), after treating two black women, observed that the cause of their neurosis was the result of con-flicts arising from a hostile white ego ideal (cited by Carter, 1995). Sue and Sue (1990) indicated that minorities may be portrayed in professional journals as neurotic and psychotic. According to d'Ardenne and Mahtani (1989) the lack of sophistication in the host culture in understanding the impact of variables such as emigration, immigration and settlement has probably contributed to and significantly reinforced much of the racial stereotyping that already existed in the literature.

While much greater sensitivity now exists about counselling ethnic minority clients, the core processes still remain largely Eurocentric, ethno-centric and individualistic. As a way out of this dilemma and to avoid the stigmatization of this racist perception, the best option for the therapist might be seen to focus on the universal and world view models (Patterson, 1978; Pedersen, 1985; Sue and Sue, 1990).

The universal approach as problematic

A universal transculturalist model seems to place the multicultural coun-selling approach firmly in the realm of integrative and eclectic therapy where the clinical practice could be perceived as positively representing all things to all people. A therapeutic process that can be offered using sensitively and appropriately the ideas from different therapies to meet the needs of a heterogeneous, multi-ethnic, multiracial and multicultural group of people seems to fit the complexity of demands potentially made by clients. If this is possible at all, and indeed there are many questions raised about whether different philosophical, theoretical and practical strategies can be brought together, then we still have a situation that begs other questions. For example, McLeod (1993: 106) suggests that 'often, counsellors working in an eclectic mode may be relatively inexperienced and have limited training in the techniques they are employing'. Carter (1995) in citing Yee et al. (1993) suggests that despite the recent interest in diversity in counselling and psychotherapy the 'racial influence has not been well elaborated' (p. 23).

Clearly there are contradictions here. On the one hand, an eclectic or integrative approach appears to be best suited for multicultural work because of its flexibility and potential bringing together of the most appropriate aspects of all therapies to meet minority needs. However, such a process is likely to cause tension and suspicion among that community because it may be seen to lack direction and focus. In a situation where the counsellor appears to the client to be the 'cultural expert' (through life experience and knowledge) the counselling process could also be perceived to be problematic. Said (1978, 1993) offers a timely reminder in *Orientalism* and later in *Culture and Imperialism* by stating that 'the net effect of cultural exchange between partners conscious of inequality is that both people suffer' (p. 235). Perceived power differentials cannot be and must not be ignored within the multicultural therapeutic setting.

Pedersen (1985) suggests a process that was considered to be essentially client based rather than a counsellor generated one, called the 'cultural fit' or the conformity prescription. This asserts that the process is reformulated to fit the client. No doubt such a process as a tool in the hands of a culturally sensitive counsellor would prove to be an authentic empowering and therapeutic process. Our understanding of the 'cultural fit' model is that it would include theoretical ideas from a number of psychoanalytic, psychotherapeutic and counselling models, as well as taking account of the client's traditional practices of healing. A genuine eclectic and integrative approach where the process is altered, modified and reformulated to encompass cultural uniqueness and is conducted within the cultural norms and origins of the client's culture fits the 'cultural fit' conceptualization. If counsellors and therapists have also undergone self-exploration of their own 'race-thinking' and have a sophisticated awareness of their own cultural roots they will be in a better position to consider aspects of dissonance in their views of the client (countertransference, projections, stereotypical reactions, etc.).

Eclectic and integrative counselling and psychotherapy has an emphasis on individual autonomy and on the process of attaining optimum self-actualization. This process, however, if experienced outside the context of the social and cultural history of the client can impose additional aspects upon the client's false self (Lago and Thompson, 1997) with the danger of further exacerbating their condition, and thereby potentially increasing their anxiety and stress. Sometimes this could lead to more serious pathologies rather than ease the client's situation. Such an approach could also, through the focus on the individual rather than their collective group, separate him/her from the social and cultural archetypes which in normal times would have provided the boundaries for the ego.

A client who seeks counselling is in 'transition' (d'Ardenne and Mahtani, 1989), attempting to comprehend new realities and construct boundaries in relation to these states for a more integrated self. For some minority clients this can only be achieved through a group autonomy. Indeed this could be construed as a political enterprise. McLeod (1993), in discussing the relative merits of theoretically singular and pure approaches as against the eclectic method, suggests that there is a much larger question at stake. This relates to 'whether it is even in principle possible to create a universally acceptable framework for understanding human behaviour?' (p. 99). While it may be impossible or inappropriate for universal models to be developed, it nevertheless seems vital for counsellors to build a wide repertoire of theoretical frameworks, clinical skills and competencies to work with a culturally diverse group of people. The theory which underpins this thinking is based on the ideas that the meaning of illness for an individual is grounded in the network of meanings it has in a particular culture (see Good and Good, 1982; Littlewood, 1990). We would also wish to emphasize the suggestions made by researchers such as Doi (1963) who note that cultural ideas originating in one culture can be adapted and translated into the ideas, languages, and practices of another culture in the therapeutic process. The incorporation of cultural constructs that allow for the transferability of cultural paradigms into the therapeutic process will provide the therapist with the essential tool for effective intervention.

Cultural sensitivity

Several writers have indicated that the most important aspect of multicultural counselling and psychotherapy has to do with the levels of cultural sensitivity in the counselling process and in counsellors (Heppner and Dixon, 1981; Pomales et al., 1985; Wade and Bernstein, 1991). This has been emphasized, but not exclusively, as the acquisition of therapist skills and competence, knowledge of the cultural 'other' and an understanding of the world view of the culturally differed client (Lago and Thompson, 1996; Sue et al., 1992). However, when culturally sensitive counsellors work within this broader flexible way the many implications of their knowledge and sensitivities to the issues of culture and 'race' could be anxiety producing for them. The dynamics of locating the presenting problem becomes complicated because there is no clear base line for a potential hypothesis. A multicultural trans-theoretical integrationist view on what the client shares could easily confuse and upset the therapist striving for sensitivity.

Therapist influence and power

As one example of the above point, it is not uncommon for some therapists to interpret that an Asian woman who refuses to accept an arranged marriage is experiencing a deep inner conflict living in a western European style civilization. This is a conflict between understanding the culture as an outsider on the one hand and the theoretical ideas underpinning therapy and validating individuation on the other. The therapist is potentially torn (consciously) in two directions (understanding the client's culture and constructing appropriate therapeutic responses), and influenced unconsciously in a third direction (by the implicit values underpinning Western cultural values and psychotherapeutic theory). Sometimes the therapeutic process in such cases seems to have managed these crises through the therapist's exerting an influence on finding a resolution within the therapy. Some aspects of the resolution for these clients, on hindsight, may appear to be out of context with their own ethnic cultural origins. Inevitably, the unconscious cultural hegemony of the therapist may have influenced the client's perception of various cultural characteristics such as fundamentalism and sexism.

Counselling sets out to be an open, equalizing partnership, yet the reality of such a democratic process is constrained by a number of oppressive and unequal variables for black people. Sue and Sue (1990) are critical of processes that are imbued with contradictions between the ideals of counselling and the actual practice concerning the culturally different. They maintain that while 'counseling enshrines the ideas of freedom, rational thought, tolerance of new ideas, and quality and justice for all, it can be used as an oppressive instrument by those in power to maintain the status quo' (p. 6). Counsellors and therapists (like others in society who unconsciously perpetuate prejudice and discrimination), are subject to inheriting and repeating these negative aspects of human relating within the process of counselling. It is through the subtlety of the 'countertransference' process that the projection of such unconscious inheritance is manifested, causing untold damage to the client's self by reinforcing the stereotypes of racial and cultural inferiority while at the same time espousing ideas of equality.

Is the answer a culturally matched therapist? In a study of black client perceptions by Wade and Bernstein (1991), culturally sensitive counsellors were seen to effect the process more than the 'race' of the counsellor.

They point to culture and 'race' sensitivity training as the chief factor responsible for clients perceiving therapists as expert, trustworthy, attractive and empathetic. The study also found that counsellors who address cultural differences in counselling will positively affect clients' perceptions of counsellor credibility and attractiveness (also Sue, 1981), while those counsellors who lack cultural sensitivity, knowledge and awareness contribute much to the oppression of minorities (also Sue and Sue, 1990). They conclude that a humanistic process is possible if counsellors and therapists take responsibility to confront their own stereotypes and assumptions about human behaviour. Therapists also need to become aware of the client's world view and assumptions about human behaviour. In addition, therapists must take account of the historical, cultural and environmental experiences of the culturally different client. This appears to have been experienced by Phung (1995) who writes of her experience as a black client with a white male counsellor. The experience was one in which his 'openness', and his 'absence of defensiveness created a bridge of understanding'. Also his belief in 'justice', his 'interest in racism' and his acknowledgement of the 'difference in our worlds' had restored her 'faith that there were people who cared enough to want to heal the damage caused by racism' (p. 61). In addition, d'Ardenne and Mahtani (1989) recommend that counsellors examine their own cultural assumptions and develop a sensitivity to cultural variations and cultural bias of their approach when working with clients across cultures. These areas of core responsibility in multicultural therapy direct counsellors to the issues that need attention whatever their mode of practice.

Practical and clinical issues: Case study

Anna is a 26-year-old woman from North Africa who has been living in Britain for more than a decade now. As a result of experiencing bouts of depression she became withdrawn and uncommunicative at home and at work with colleagues. She decided to seek help. It was at this stage that she met with the therapist, one of the authors. The first issue confronting the therapist was whether or not to offer a handshake upon meeting. With many ethnic minority women, especially those from a Muslim background, it is taboo for men to make any physical contact, in or out of the counselling situation. The second issue that had to be faced was the building of an appropriate rapport with the client through the general opening conversation which accompanies the first contact. The development of a therapeutic relationship with some minority clients through the process of opening conversations can be anxiety producing. Clients from some ethnic minority communities, if not directly asked or invited to talk about their 'problems' and the kind of help or support they require, can tend to suspect a hidden agenda in the therapist. 'Small talk' (or light opening conversations) can be viewed as not being professional and competent. By contrast, a too direct interrogative beginning might be extremely offputting. Clients experience 'white institutional procedures' as often very formal, direct and non-humanistic procedures.

How to start and how to begin to create sufficient ambience for therapy to commence can already prove problematic with culturally different clients, especially for white therapists not trained in multicultural counselling and psychotherapy.

The first session

In the first session Anna presented herself as being 'depressed in the general sense but not clinically depressed'. She was asked to clarify this self-diagnosis and how she came about understanding this. She replied that she was aware of her thinking, her behaviour and her feelings and she felt the issue was not physiological so did not warrant any medication. It was clear from subsequent sessions that she shared many of the symptoms of depression as suggested by Rowe (1983) such as feeling valueless and unacceptable to herself, which clients deem as real, absolute and an immutable truth in their lives. She talked much about her arrival in England as a postgraduate student, the isolation she felt earlier in her life in this country and the separation from her family. She felt that much had to do with issues of 'culture shock' and her own lack of understanding the specificity of the host culture. She felt that although she did not fully assimilate into the host culture she now considered that she was a 'part of society'. Indeed, her children were born here and 'spoke like a native of the land'. However, the feelings of not belonging were prevalent. She still felt 'culture shocked'. The therapist encouraged further exploration.

Counselling and psychotherapy has generally embraced the term 'culture shock' as a useful tool for understanding such a person's situation. From a cognitive-behavioural perspective, a person who is understood to be experiencing 'culture shock' may be offered help through the process of (a) identifying situations that cause anxiety in that person; (b) the therapist would then enable the client to discover new skills to reinforce stress-reducing behaviours. This approach could be perceived as 'training' people in the 'appropriate social skills'. Clearly a serious (and erroneous) assumption could be made here by a therapist considering the client's behaviour as the cause of their conflict without any reference being made to the environment which they inhabit.

Apparently, at work Anna was constantly reminded that she was different because colleagues only connected with her when the context was: 'multicultural', 'Third World', black, or when she was referred minority women students for advice and guidance. She also shared the difficulty of being the only black woman in her department.

At this point the therapist was conscious of the dilemma of whether to offer self-discourse which reflected similar or almost similar experiences. Sue et al. (1995: 723) in their review of studies that investigated therapist characteristics influencing psychotherapy conclude that 'there is some evidence to suggest that the degree of intimate self-disclosure and interest in a client's culture or race have favourable effects'. Yet therapist self-disclosure as an open-ended strategy may lead to over-identification on the part of the client. For the therapist it may also produce 'blind spots' that inhibit or prevent their full understanding of the client's perspective (Shapiro and Pinsker, 1973). Also, indiscriminate use of the strategy might produce methodological confusion in eclectic and integrative approaches.

Some implications of gender difference
in transcultural therapy

Towards the end of the first interview session, the therapist and counsellor talked about the possibility of therapy in relation to the client's expectations, the therapist's method of working, times for meeting and the possible limitations on the therapy as a result of engaging in the process within the same organizational setting. She was reminded that the service offered male and female therapists and that she was free at any time to discuss a change of therapist if she wanted. The therapist explained to her that he would use a 'transtheoretical integrationist approach' as a result of his training and experience. It was agreed that the sessions would be weekly for six weeks, each lasting about 30 to 45 minutes followed by a session to review the situation. Although the client did not seem overly anxious about these arrangements, she nevertheless pointed out at the beginning that she understood the process to be male constructed, referring to Freud, Jung and the discourse of some of the French and Anglo-Saxon feminist critiques on psychoanalysis. It transpired that Anna's research was in African women writers. In a sensitive way she also confronted the position of the process being managed by a male therapist. Clearly it seemed that the issue of gender was important to her both academically and psychologically. Counsellors and therapists have been noted, through their knowledge and impressions of the various cultures of their clients, to have changed their style of counselling to accommodate the perceived cultural qualities and differences of their clients. However, for male therapists according to Smith (1985) the problems in counselling black women are related to the counsellor's 'lack of awareness, sensitivity, and knowledge of Black women's history, culture and life concerns' (p. 185).

At a personal and reflective level the therapist noted that he felt a deep sense of awareness of such issues as Islam, ethnicity and gender, particularly the relationship of masculinities to concepts such as power and authority. He could not help thinking that such pre-countertransference must be dealt with. Dupont-Joshua (1994) cites Kareem's (1988) thoughts on pre-transference and countertransference: 'the therapist who has definite ideas about groups of people who are different from themselves, and who lives in a society which projects negative images about particular groups of people has a precountertransference towards clients from such groups' (p. 204). For example, when a therapist is aware that a minority client is going to arrive there has already been a countertransference reaction even before the client steps into the room. Although both therapist and client in this circumstance were apparently relatively culturally matched (both originating from the African subcontinent), it was nevertheless important for the therapist that he understood the heterogeneity of this particular therapeutic dyad. This also meant for the therapist that he understood and internalized Kareem's words personally and did not reserve it as a criticism for his white colleagues, as sometimes the theoretical debate on racism apparently allows minority groups to do.

Therapeutic approach

Rogers's (1951) 'core conditions' for therapist behaviour were seen to be essential tools for the process with Anna. Empathic understanding (perceiving and understanding the life experience of Anna by the therapist imaginatively placing himself in her experiential, psychological world), unconditional positive regard (a non-judgemental acceptance of Anna as a person), and the congruence in which the therapist engaged with Anna in the therapeutic relationship were core components of the work. They also, however, needed to be understood in the context of ethnic minority clients. For example, the concept of empathy, understood linearly as a bond of similarity between individuals, proves problematic, as Lago and Thompson (1996) point out by citing Jones (1987) who asserts that empathy defined in terms of shared qualities cannot occur. There is a need for an empathy based on differences that focuses the imagination upon transposing itself into another, rather than upon one's own feelings. In this way, 'psychotherapists might achieve a complete understanding of culturally varied predispositions, personal constructs and experience' (p. 140).

Anna's existing knowledge of counselling and psychotherapy directed the way she wanted to explore her own issues of distress and concern. She typed out her dreams and brought these to counselling for a few weeks. In a ritualistic way she would read her dreams to the therapist and try to explain the background to some of the people and images. For example, events of the day or days before, especially work scenarios, would reshape themselves into scenes that she felt were explaining racist events. Frosh (1989) in 'Psychoanalysis and racism' states that 'while racism is a social phenomenon, it operates at more than just the macro-social level.... [It occurs] at the level of social organisations and in encounters between individuals' (p. 229). Sometimes counsellors can feel that the issues of racism are for the social scientist.

Facilitation by the therapist of a more dense and focused nature of a few of the images brought the client realization that the unconscious works in symbolic and metaphorical ways to unearth the buried material of the past. Dreams 'may contain ineluctable truths, philosophical pronouncements, illusions, wild fantasies, memories, plans, anticipations, irrational experiences, even telepathic visions' (Jung, 1934: par. 317), and are a 'spontaneous self-portrayal, in symbolic form, of the actual situation in the unconscious' (Jung, 1945: par. 505). However, the therapist refrained from any interpretations that he felt would lead to a reductive analysis at this stage in the process remembering the words of Klein (1990: 4): 'Some people are so dominated by their pain that they cannot concentrate on much else.... They need to complain to us until they are sure we mind about their pain before we can educate them into taking an interest in its unconscious meaning.' She also argues that those who are not accustomed to a psychological way (European psychological) of thinking 'need time' to appreciate reflection and interpretation.

There is also the argument that psychodynamic and psychotherapeutic strategies are more conductive to western Europeans. We have come a long way from what Patterson (1978) thought about this idea:

> Westerners are more used to introspection, more ready and able to engage in self disclosure and self exploration.... Persons from an Oriental or some other culture, on the other hand, are more reticent, more modest about talking about themselves or personal relationships ... psychotherapy as developed and practised in Western societies is not applicable in other societies. (Patterson, 1978: 234)

It is now becoming fairly apparent that using this argument, that the client's communication style problematizes counselling and psychotherapy with minority groups, is profoundly erroneous. We are also aware that some of the 'strait-jacket' theoretical positions held by practitioners negate any cross-cultural work. The eclectic and integrative approaches, it seems, have addressed this concern through clinical techniques which take account of what Patterson highlights, but at the same time they do not stereotype the client into universal categories.

The client's inner journey

Anna's exploration of her dreams went on for a few weeks. She seemed to like analysing her dreams through the symbols, reflecting on socio-political factors that contributed to her development, especially her childhood experiences. She was quick at deciphering the metaphors beyond the 'race' identity issue. It began to emerge that her childhood and upbringing were strictly Islamic and these values were in direct contradiction to the way she constructed her reality as an adult. Anna was aware that many of these learned childhood values infiltrated her relationship. For example, she would offer mixed messages about her role as an equal partner in the relationship and invite her partner to overindulge at her expense. At times she expected and demanded some of the 'inequalities' experienced by 'Third World' women or at other times projected a sense of dominance and matriarchy indicating that was more real for her. She explained these confusing positions as an expression of her upbringing in North Africa.

El Saadawi (1980: 13) offers an explanation of the kind of education a female child undergoes in Arab society. She states that: 'The child is trained to suppress her own desires, to empty herself of authentic, original wants and wishes linked to her own self and to fill a vacuum that results with the desires of others.' Furthermore, she states that Arab societies are 'passing through a transitional stage, and shifting over from cultural and social backwardness to a modernisim copied without any real understanding from the West. This modernization process does not prevent such societies from hanging on to many worn out traditions in the name of Islam and of Eastern moral values' (1980: 89). This seemed to be the process that Anna was undergoing within herself. Her search for the 'cultural primal scene', a return to the 'matriarchal womb' and a repositioning of her 'racial identity' were unconscious motivators in therapy. Women in Islamic societies who define an identity for themselves are struggling against the very fabric of that society. Such a process is imbued with the falsity of its construction and subsequently manifests itself in the development of the ego which is located in the imaginary. Removing the mutated layers and reaching into the depths of the real self through the images of Anna's dreams was a difficult and painful journey for her. But the 'illogicality; the indifference of the dreaming mind to convention and common sense, turned out to be of great value in forging new combinations out of seemingly incompatible contexts' (Koestler, 1964: 182). This provided Anna with the possibility of reframing her reality within the process of counselling.

The therapy sessions with Anna were generally held once a week. At the end of the contract of six weeks, a review took place and Anna continued for another eight months. Occasionally, however, the frequency was fortnightly or monthly. The sessions were also of different time durations (45, 30, 15 minutes). Here the therapist recognized and valued the fact that therapeutic moments can often occur outside westernized, professionalized notions of conventional sessional times, particularly in multicultural therapy.

Opposing cultural values

An issue we would like to discuss before we conclude is one that confronted the therapist with the complex aspects of morality, cultural sensitivity, religious differences and human rights. The value base of clients and their cultures can confront directly and forcefully the therapists' own beliefs and truths they hold about the world. For example, in one of the therapy sessions with Anna, the 'subject' centred on the issue of clitoridectomy. Anna had undergone the operation as a child. At this stage in her life the issue was now disturbing her to the extent that she felt the culture of her childhood and her parents had collaborated to mutilate her. She talked about circumcision on both males and females in her society and within Islam. The therapist reflected to her that this might be how she felt in this society, feeling castrated in the context she found herself. She retorted back in anger that she felt that the entire culture was oppressive and managed by men to subdue women. The therapist reflected that the anger might also have something to say about their therapeutic relationship. She responded with increased anger: her voice, her vocabulary, her facial intensity and her hand gestures were staccato and strong, different to the usually composed person who sat in the chair. It was to her mum she said that she wanted to express her anger. The therapist suggested she tried the Gestalt exercise with the two chairs. She engaged with this exercise till the session finished. The therapist also suggested she might want to do some drawings but that she might choose not to bring them to therapy. The question that she posed at the end was: 'Isn't this a human rights question, really?' Then she departed. The therapist was left thinking about many other issues such as cultural sensitivity, castration complex, female corporal mutilation, masculine aggression, power and oppression. What she had said was most profound. Indeed it was a human rights issue.

As counsellors and psychotherapists we must engage with ethical issues, wrestle with objective morality and cultural sensitivity in recognizing that there is a reality in which human beings are oppressed, pained, hurt and killed and that we need to make our own stand against these oppressions (see also Lago and Thompson, 1989; Samuels, 1993). Woolfe (1995: 38) asserts that 'It would be nice if counsellors were able to work in such a way that they were able to contribute towards resisting the growth of oppressive forces rather than just deal with their consequences.'

Conclusion

Lane (1995: 38) suggests that 'it is now recognised that an interactive view of counselling is needed which approaches in a wholistic way the social, cultural, economic and emotional issues facing us'. In sharing the experience of Anna we have tried to show that issues of 'race', culture and ethnicity can be explored in a culturally sensitive and psychosocial way. The use of varying clinical strategies from different and sometimes opposing approaches in an eclectic or integrative manner is compatible with the idea of 'cultural fit'. However, we also suggest that it can become complicated and oppressive if essential aspects of therapist competencies such as cultural knowledge, 'race' awareness and tolerance of differences are not appropriately developed in the practitioner or demonstrated in clinical applications. An eclectic and integrative approach offers the opportunity for a psychotherapeutic process to engage alongside the socio-political. Clearly in a process where the cultural metaphors are interpreted alongside the psychological and politically constructed images the client is more likely to be empowered. This in turn empowers the practice, the therapeutic discourse and indeed discourse itself.

References

Carter, R.T. (1995) *The Influence of RACE and Racial Identity in Psychotherapy.* Chichester: Wiley.

d'Ardenne, P. and Mahtani, A. (1989) *Transcultural Counselling in Action.* London: Sage.

Dalal, F. (1988) 'Jung: a racist', *British Journal of Psychotherapy,* 4 (3): 263–79.

Doi, L.T. (1963) 'Some thoughts on helplessness and the desire to be loved', *Psychiatry,* 26: 266–71.

Dupont-Joshua, A. (1994) 'Intercultural therapy', *Counselling: The Journal of the British Association for Counselling,* 5 (3): 203–5.

Eleftheriadou, Z. (1994) *Transcultural Counselling.* London: Central Books.

Eweka, I. (1990) 'Counselling the ethnic minority client: pitfalls and some likely remedies', *Counselling: The Journal of the British Association for Counselling,* 1 (4): 117–19.

Fassinger, R.E. and Richie, B.S. (1997) 'Sex matters. Gender and sexual orientation in training for multicultural counselling competency', in D.B. Pope-Davis and H.L.K. Coleman (eds), *Multicultural Counselling Competency.* London: Sage.

Frosh, S. (1989) 'Psychoanalysis and racism' in B. Richards (ed.), *Crisis of the Self: Further Essays on Psychoanalysis and Politics.* London: Free Association Books.

Good, B.J. and Good, M.-J.D. (1982) 'Towards a meaning-centred analysis of popular illness categories: "fright-illness" and "heat distress" in Iran', in A.J. Marsella and G.M. White (eds), *Cultural Conceptions of Mental Health Therapy.* Dordrecht: Reidel.

Hall, W.A. (1995) 'Afro-centric counselling'. Papers presented at the Second National Black Access Conference, June, Sheffield University.

Heppner, P.P. and Dixon, D.N. (1981) 'A review of the interpersonal influence process in counselling', *Personnel and Guidance Journal,* 59: 542–50.

Husband, C. (1982) 'Introduction: "race", the continuity of a concept', in C. Husband (ed.), *'Race' in Britain: Continuity and Change.* London: Hutchinson.

Jones, E.E. (1987) 'Psychotherapy and counselling with black clients', in P. Pedersen (ed.), *Handbook of Cross-Cultural Counselling and Therapy.* New York: Praeger.

Jung, C.G. (1934) 'The practical use of dream-analysis', *Collected Works 16,* trans. R.F.C. Hull. London: Routledge and Kegan.

Jung, C.G. (1945) 'On the nature of dreams', *Collected Works 8,* trans. R.F.C. Hull. London: Routledge and Kegan.

Jung, C.G. (1957) 'Symbols and the interpretation of dreams', *Collected Works 18,* trans. R.F.C. Hull. London: Routledge and Kegan.

Kareem, J. (1988) 'Outside in...inside out...some considerations in inter-cultural psychotherapy', *Social Work Practice*, 3 (3): 57–77.

Kareem, J. and Littlewood, R. (eds) (1992) *Intercultural Therapy Themes: Interpretations and Practice*. London: Blackwell.

Kennedy, J. (1952) 'Problems posed in the analysis of black patients', *Psychiatry*, 15: 313–27.

Klein, J. (1990) 'Patients who are not ready for interpretation', *British Journal of Psychotherapy*, 7 (1): 38–49.

Koestler, A. (1964) *The Act of Creation*. London: Hutchinson.

Lago, C. and Thompson, J. (1989) 'Counselling and race', in W. Dryden, D. Charles-Edwards and R. Woolfe (eds), *Handbook of Counselling in Britain*. London: Tavistock/Routledge.

Lago, C. and Thompson, J. (1996) *Race, Culture and Counselling*. Buckingham: Open University Press.

Lago, C. and Thompson, J. (1997) 'The triangle with curved sides: issues of race and culture in counselling supervision', in G. Shipton (ed.), *Supervision of Psychotherapy and Counselling: Making a Place to Think*. Buckingham: Open University Press.

Lane, D. (1995) 'New directions in counselling: a roundtable', *Counselling: The Journal of the British Association for Counselling*, 6 (1): 38.

Littlewood, R. (1990) 'From categories to contexts: a decade of the 'new cross-cultural psychiatry', *British Journal of Psychiatry*, 156: 305–27.

McLeod, J. (1993) *An Introduction to Counselling*. Buckingham: Open University Press.

Moodley, S.R. (1991) 'A theoretical model for transcultural counselling and therapy'. Unpublished MPhil thesis, University of Nottingham.

Moodley, R. (1992) 'Interpreting the "I" in counselling and guidance: an anti-racist approach'. Unpublished keynote speech at Derbyshire FE Counselling and Guidance Conference.

Moodley, R. (1998) '"I say what I like": frank talk(ing) in counselling and psychotherapy', *British Journal of Guidance and Counselling*, 26 (4): 495–508.

Pankhania, J. (1996) 'Black feminist counselling', in M. Jacobs (ed.), *Jitendra: Lost Connections, In Search of a Therapist*. Buckingham: Open University Press.

Patterson, C.H. (1978) 'Cross-cultural or intercultural counseling or psychotherapy', *International Journal for the Advancement of Counselling*, 3: 231–47.

Pedersen, P. (1985) *Handbook of Cross-Cultural Counseling and Therapy*. New York: Praeger.

Pedersen, P. (ed.) (1991) 'Multiculturalism as a fourth force in counseling' (special issue), *Journal of Counseling and Development*, 70: 4–250.

Phillips, M. (1991) 'Counselling the ethnic minority client ... a response', *Counselling: The Journal of the British Association for Counselling*, 2 (1): 10–11.

Phung, T.C. (1995) 'An experience of inter-cultural counselling: views from a black client', *Counselling: The Journal of the British Association for Counselling*, 6 (1): 61–6.

Pomales, J., Claiborn, C.D. and LaFromboise, T.D. (1985) 'Effects of black students' racial identity on perceptions of white counselors varying in cultural sensitivity', *Journal of Counseling Psychology*, 33: 58–62.

Ponterotto, J.G. (1997) 'Multicultural counselling training', in D.B. Pope-Davis and H.L.K. Coleman (eds), *Multicultural Counselling Competency*. London: Sage.

Rogers, C.R. (1951) *Client-centred Therapy*. Boston: Houghton Mifflin.

Rowe, D. (1983) *Depression*. London: Routledge and Kegan Paul.

Rycroft, C. (1988) 'Comments on Farhad Dalal's "Jung a racist"', *British Journal of Psychotherapy*, 4 (3): 281.

Saadawi, N. El (1980) *The Hidden Face of Eve*. London: Zed Books.

Said, E.W. (1978) *Orientalism*. London: Routledge and Kegan.

Said, E.W. (1993) *Culture and Imperialism*. London: Chatto and Windus.

Samuels, A. (1988) 'Comments on Farhad Dalal's "Jung: a racist"', *British Journal of Psychotherapy*, 4 (3): 280.

Samuels, A. (1993) *The Political Psyche*. London: Routledge.

Sashidharan, S.P. (1990) 'Race and psychiatry', *Medical World*, 3: 8–12.

Shapiro, E.T. and Pinsker, H. (1973) 'Shared ethnic scotoma', *American Journal of Psychiatry*, 130: 1338–41.

Smith, E.M.J. (1985) 'Counseling black women', in P. Pederson (ed.), *Handbook of Cross-Cultural Counseling and Therapy*. New York: Praeger.

Sue, D.W. (1981) 'Evaluating process variables in cross-cultural counseling psychotherapy', in A.J. Marsella and P.B. Pedersen (eds), *Cross Cultural Counselling and Psychotherapy*. Honolulu: East West Centre.

Sue, D.W. and Sue, D. (1990) *Counseling the Culturally Different: Theory and Practice*, 2nd edn. New York: Wiley.

Sue, D.W., Arrendondo, P. and McDavis, R.J. (1992) 'Multicultural counseling competencies and standards: a call to the profession', *Journal of Counseling and Development*, 70: 477–86.

Sue, S., Zane, N. and Young, K. (1995) 'Research on psychotherapy with culturally diverse populations', in A.E. Bergin and S.L. Garfield (eds), *Handbook of Psychotherapy and Behavior Change*, 4th edn. New York: Wiley.

Thomas, A. and Sillen, S. (1972) *Racism and Psychiatry*. New York: Brunner and Mazell.

Wade, P. and Bernstein, B.L. (1991) 'Culture sensitivity training and counselor's race: effects on black female clients' perceptions and attrition', *Journal of Counseling Psychology*, 38: 9–15.

Woolfe, R. (1995) 'New directions in counselling: a roundtable', *Counselling: The Journal of the British Association for Counselling*, 6 (1): 34.

Yee, A.H., Fairchild, H.H., Weizmann, F. and Wyatt, G.E. (1993) 'Addressing psychology's problem with race', *American Psychologist*, 48 (11): 1132–40.

Discussion issues

1 'Multicultural therapeutic competencies are extremely difficult to acquire'.

2 'Purist' approaches carry the danger of exposing the client to the hidden Eurocentric assumptions that are invariably present in conventional therapies.

3 Is an eclectic or integrative approach the best suited for multicultural work?

4 What are the advantages and disadvantages of eclectic and integrative approaches for multicultural work?

5

Counselling Idiographically

The Multimodal Approach

Stephen Palmer

It may be an idea to start with the generally accepted proposition that each client is a unique individual with a combination of different aspects and characteristics. Even identical twins brought up in the same family will have had different experiences, which may have affected them. Each twin may require a different style of counselling for maximum effectiveness. An idiographic approach to counselling attempts to cater for each client's uniqueness by counsellors examining their clients' personal experiences and problems which then guide the entire process of counselling (Ridley, 1995). Assumptions will not be made prematurely about either assessment or the subsequent therapy without first meeting the client and ascertaining their goals (if any). This may be in contrast to established forms of therapy such as cognitive therapy that focuses on cognitions and behaviour, and psychodynamic therapy that has an emphasis on earlier experiences and current transferences. Moodley (1999) has suggested that an approach is needed which can include traditional healing practices. But how can this be integrated into Eurocentric and ethnocentric approaches to counselling?

Ridley (1995: 82–5) has developed five principles, which he believes will help counsellors acquire a therapeutic mindset that enables them to counsel minority clients more effectively:

1 Every client should be understood from his or her unique frame of reference.
2 Nomothetic, normative information does not always fit a particular client.
3 People are a dynamic blend of multiple roles and identities.
4 The idiographic perspective is compatible with the biopsychosocial model of mental health.
5 The idiographic perspective is transtheoretical.

Understanding clients from their own unique frame of reference is based on the work of Rogers and his concept of empathy. Raskin and Rogers (1995: 142) describe it as: 'an active, immediate, continuous process. The counselor makes a maximum effort to get within and live the attitudes expressed instead of observing them, diagnosing them, or thinking of ways to make the process go faster. The accuracy of the therapist's empathic understanding has often been emphasized, but more important is the therapist's interest in appreciating the world of the client and offering such understanding with the willingness to be corrected'. Recently the term 'cultural empathy' has been used to describe the ability of counsellors to understand and communicate the concerns of clients from their cultural perspective (Ridley, 1995; Ridley et al., 1994; Ridley and Lingle, 1996). Cultural empathy has two dimensions: understanding and communication. To understand a client involves really grasping their idiographic meaning, which necessitates the counsellor not allowing any cultural bias to interfere with their perceptions. Communication involves the ability to demonstrate to the client that the counsellor has understood the client's idiographic experience. Also the counsellor ensures that he or she is using language that is meaningful to the client (Ridley, 1995).

A nomothetic perspective focuses on the distinguishing characteristics of a group to which a person belongs. Although this may be useful, the counsellor can overlook important aspects or characteristics about any individual within the group. In counselling the idiographic perspective avoids this particular problem. Ridley (1995) suggests that counsellors need to look at group norms, as long they do not necessarily expect to understand clients without first exploring their 'frame of reference'.

Each person is a member of overlapping groups with many roles and identities. To help the counsellor to understand the client, these will need to be explored. Idiographic role maps can be used to plot these many roles thereby helping the counsellor to imagine what it is like to be their client. Figure 5.1 is Paola's role map, which illustrates her various roles that help to contribute to the whole picture. Ridley (1995) suggests that to obtain an insightful look at the client, counsellors need to focus their attention on the centre of the diagram – in Paola's case her uniqueness as a person having nine cultural roles. Ridley suggests that viewed from this perspective, the client's idiographic experience – in our example, Paola – sets her apart from every other Italian, female, mother, wife, eldest sibling, daughter, Catholic, bank clerk and resident of London, England. Every role should not be ignored as each contributes to understanding Paola.

The biopsychosocial model of mental health attempts to understand individuals by examining their interpersonal and social competence, physical health, and psychological and emotional well-being. It is a health promotion model, which focuses on changing behaviours to prevent or alleviate disease. Stressors, harmful behaviours/lifestyles and illnesses can be targeted for change (Krantz et al., 1985). Ridley (1995: 51) asserts that the biopsychosocial model is not 'inherently racist', assuming that it is applied correctly and therefore is suitable for 'treating minority clients'.

Counsellors employing a transtheoretical approach do not stick rigidly to any one therapeutic orientation or theory. Assuming that the counsellors are

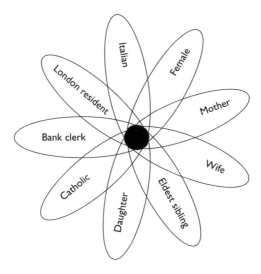

Figure 5.1 *Paola's role map*
Source: Palmer (1999).

adequately skilled, they will select and use whatever approach or technique will help clients deal with their presenting problem(s) or current situation. Sue (1977) suggests that equitable therapy or treatment may be discriminatory whereas the idiographic approach supports the concept of differential but non-discriminatory treatment (Ridley, 1995).

Ridley (1995: 88) suggests twelve actions to help in counselling minority client idiographically:

1 Develop cultural self-awareness.
2 Avoid value imposition.
3 Accept your naivety as a multicultural counsellor.
4 Show cultural empathy.
5 Incorporate cultural considerations into counselling.
6 Do not stereotype.
7 Weigh and determine the relative importance of the client's primary cultural roles.
8 Do not blame the victim.
9 Remain flexible in your selection of interventions.
10 Examine your counselling theories for bias.
11 Build on the client's strengths.
12 Do not protect clients from emotional pain.

Although these actions are self-explanatory, it may be useful to look at a real example where the counsellor is adapting her approach and interventions to the needs of the client. In the following case study, Gita Patel is counselling a young refugee attending the Refugee Project in London:

One young man of 16 had arrived in this country (England) alone after he witnessed his mother's death. He was uncertain whether his father was dead or alive. At the start of the counselling he was very unsettled, could not acknowledge or talk about his mother, almost acting as though she were still alive. His main use of the session was to talk about his school and his home and his social life. The only reason he came to counselling was because of his terrible nightmares which he talked about in a distant way but he said coming to counselling stopped the nightmares, so he would continue to see me. At times it felt like he was avoiding any talk about his real issues and wanted to 'be positive' about everything. After six months the client received his permanent stay in the UK, got into college and found his own place to live. The counselling sessions changed completely. He began to talk about his parents and the pain of losing them, finally able to grieve over his losses. The transient nature of his existence in Britain and his instability had made this young man well defended against any real emotions as he was working hard to survive in an unpredictable situation. Once he knew his life was more stable, he could afford to let himself feel some of his anxieties and worries. An approach that did not see his issues in the context of his seeking asylum may have decided that he was not suitable for counselling or therapy. (Patel, 1997: 30)

It is possible that if Patel had focused on the client's 'real issues' at the beginning of counselling, the client would not have been able to cope with the high levels of anxiety that the issues may have triggered. This could have seriously affected his ability to cope in an already difficult situation as a refugee; perhaps a sensible avoidance by the client at that time. In fact, I suspect that untimely discussion of the 'real issues' would have increased the likelihood of attrition occurring (i.e. premature termination of therapy) and therefore one of the client's major emotional supports would have been lost.

Multimodal therapy: an idiographic approach

Ridley (1984, 1995) and Ponterotto (1987) recommend multimodal therapy as a flexible approach suitable for treating minority clients. The multimodal approach (Lazarus, 1989) rests on the assumption that unless seven discrete but interactive modalities are assessed, treatment will probably overlook significant concerns. The modalities are: Behaviour, Affective responses, Sensory reactions, Images, Cognitions, Interpersonal relationships and the need for Drugs and other biological interventions (Lazarus, 1995). Lazarus believes that the entire range of personality is comprised within these seven modalities. The first letters of each modality produce an easy to recall acronym, BASIC ID.

Ponterotto (1987) added another modality for investigation, which he called 'Interaction with Oppressive Environment'. Assessment of this modality can be useful when counselling ethnic minority clients for a number of reasons:

1 The counsellor acknowledges the oppressive environment.
2 It helps counsellor to understand the difficulties the client may be encountering on a regular basis.
3 Depending upon the circumstances, the counsellor and client can develop a plan of action to deal with the oppressive environment.

The approach is technically eclectic as it uses techniques taken from many different psychological theories and systems, without necessarily being concerned with the validity of the theoretical principles that underpin the different approaches from which it takes its techniques. The techniques are applied systematically, based on data from client qualities, specific techniques and the counsellor's clinical skills (Palmer and Dryden, 1995). Multimodal counsellors are not confined to interventions that may be inappropriate or unhelpful. Instead, they can negotiate with the client interventions addressing each modality (adapted Ridley, 1995: 97). These interventions could include traditional healing practices or at least referral to another therapist who is prepared to undertake this type of work.

Multimodal counsellors are expected to adapt their interpersonal style and approach to the counselling relationship of choice, maximizing therapeutic outcome. This is commonly known by the term 'authentic chameleon' Lazarus (1995) and involves developing differing styles of interaction with different clients. Thus the counsellor needs to decide when and how to be directive, non-directive, warm, cold, supportive, reflective, tough, gentle, informal, formal or humorous (see Milner and Palmer, 1998). In addition, the counsellor will have to decide whether the client prefers a professional who is warm and empathic or would prefer a provider of information, coach or trainer. When being the authentic chameleon, counsellors exhibit different aspects of themselves, which will meet client expectancies thereby helping the therapeutic relationship. Interpersonal mismatches in therapy are less likely to benefit the client. An example of this occurs when a therapist who exhibits type A behaviour (i.e. fast talking, finishes others' sentences, competitive, hostile) has a client who exhibits type B behaviour (i.e. slow talking, thoughtful, 'laid back'). If the therapist does not rapidly adapt to the slower pace of the client, it is very likely that resentment and/or attrition will occur. Interestingly, in supervision the counsellor may state that the client is being 'resistant' when, in fact, it may well be that the counsellor is the 'resistant' one. Likewise, in cross-racial counselling partnerships (see Lago and Thompson, 1997), the counsellor also needs to be sensitive to these issues and not rigidly stick to one interpersonal style or approach. For many counsellors the flexibility required to be an authentic chameleon may be difficult to attain as counselling training often neglects the development of how to relate to clients from different backgrounds or cultures yet still remaining genuine. However, I have observed that many counsellors do actually exhibit the ability to relate to others in a variety of ways such as towards their employers, supervisors, trainers, colleagues, friends,

Table 5.1 *Commonly used techniques and strategies in multimodal counselling and therapy*

Modality	Techniques/interventions
Behaviour	Behaviour rehearsal
	Empty chair
	Exposure programme
	Fixed role therapy
	Modelling
	Paradoxical intention
	Psychodrama
	Reinforcement programmes
	Response prevention/cost
	Risk-taking exercises
	Self-monitoring and recording
	Stimulus control
	Shame-attacking
Affect	Anger expression
	Anxiety/anger management
	Feeling-identification
Sensation	Biofeedback
	Hypnosis
	Meditation
	Relaxation training
	Sensate focus training
	Threshold training
	Yoga
Imagery	Anti-future shock imagery
	Associated imagery
	Aversive imagery
	Coping and motivation imagery
	Implosion and imaginal exposure
	Positive imagery
	Rational emotive imagery
	Time projection imagery
Cognition	Bibliotherapy
	Challenging faulty inferences
	Cognitive rehearsal
	Coping statements
	Correcting misconceptions
	Disputing self-defeating beliefs/schema
	Focusing
	Positive self-statements
	Problem solving training
	Rational proselytizing
	Self-acceptance training
	Thought stopping
Interpersonal	Assertion training
	Communication training
	Contracting
	Fixed role therapy
	Friendship/intimacy training

Continued

Table 5.1   *Continued*

Modality	Techniques/interventions
	Graded sexual approaches
	Paradoxical intentions
	Role play
	Social skills training
Drugs/biology	Alcohol reduction programme
	Life style changes, e.g. exercise, nutrition etc.
	Referral to physicians or other specialists
	Stop smoking programme
	Weight reduction and maintenance programme

Source: Adapted from Palmer (1996).

family, in-laws, shop assistants etc. Therefore, they may have the skills yet are loath to apply them in the counselling setting.

Table 5.1 (adapted Palmer, 1996) includes a list of the most commonly used techniques and strategies in multimodal counselling and therapy. Although many of them are taken from the cognitive-behavioural schools of counselling, this does not preclude other techniques such as meditation, yoga or empty chair, which are from other approaches.

Table 5.2 (Palmer, 1999a) illustrates a counselling programme negotiated with Paola during the first and second counselling session. Once the modality profile has been developed, the client and counsellor mutually agree which intervention to use first. Notice that in Paola's modality profile, relaxation training occurs three times. This could be a useful place to start the counselling programme, as Paola would be able to listen to a relaxation tape daily. Another initial between-session assignment could be to read a handout or book on thinking errors (cognitive distortions) in a self-help book such as *Conquer Your Stress* (Cooper and Palmer, 2000). She could keep a note in a diary of the thinking errors she makes in the course of a day, with a special focus on her interactions with her work colleagues and family. In the following counselling session the counsellor could demonstrate how to use thinking skills to examine and question her thinking errors.

It is usually a good idea to review therapeutic progress every five or six sessions. The modality profile aids this review and is updated as problems are overcome and added to as new information is obtained. Near the end of the counselling programme, the counselling sessions are spaced out to encourage clients to deal with problems as they arise on their own with the goal of reaching total independence of the counsellor. Clients may return for 'booster sessions' after a longer period of time such as six to twelve months. This helps to reduce the idea that they have been abandoned, which can occur in some cases.

Table 5.2　*Paola's modality profile*

Modality	Problem	Counselling programme
Behaviour	Binge eats	Stimulus control; find triggers
	Procrastinates	Dispute self-defeating thinking
	Poor time management	Time management and assertion skills bibliotherapy
Affect (Emotion)	Anxiety about not meeting important deadlines	Anxiety management; dispute beliefs; rational coping statements
	Shame after binge eating	Self-acceptance training
	Depressed about missing her parents and family	Counsellor support and rational discussion
	Feels guilty after speaking to mother	Self-acceptance training and coping statements
Sensations	Palpitations and shaky when anxious	Relaxation training; positive imagery
	Empty feeling before binge eating	Focus on self-defeating beliefs; assess for low frustration tolerance
Imagery	Images of making a fool of herself at work	Coping imagery; time projection imagery
	Images of losing control	Coping imagery
Cognition (Thoughts/beliefs)	I must perform well	Dispute self-defeating beliefs
	I must not let my parents down otherwise I'm worthless	Develop forceful coping statements; self-acceptance training
	We should be together as a family	Examine belief; bibliotherapy
	I can't stand difficulties	Increase tolerance levels to difficulties
Interpersonal	Rows with husband and children	Time-limited communication; dispute unhelpful beliefs; coping imagery
	Passive with work colleagues and boss	Assertiveness training
	Allows mother to manipulate her	Assertiveness and communications skills; focus on underlying beliefs which trigger her guilt and depression
Drugs/ biology	High blood pressure	Liaise with physician; possible medication; relaxation training; bibliotherapy
	Migraines when under pressure	Dispute self-defeating beliefs; relaxation training; biofeedback

Source: Palmer (1999a).

Conclusion

Counsellors wishing to take an idiographic approach will be placing high demands upon themselves as they will need a broad repertoire of therapeutic responses and have to pay close attention to the cultural cues sent and received by the client (see Ridley et al., 1997). However, they may be in a better position to help minority clients (see Palmer, 1999a, b) especially if they become aware of the possible traditional healing practices of their clients and have a knowledge of where to refer clients for these particular interventions.

Note

Article adapted from Palmer, S. (1999a) 'Developing an individual counselling programme: a multimodal perspective', in S. Palmer and P. Laungani (eds), *Counselling in a Multicultural Society*. London: Sage. And Palmer, S. (1999b) 'In search of effective counselling across cultures', in S. Palmer and P. Laungani (eds), *Counselling in a Multicultural Society*. London: Sage.

References

Cooper, C. and Palmer, S. (2000) *Conquer Your Stress*. London: Institute of Personnel and Development.

Krantz, D.S., Grunberg, N.E. and Baum, A. (1985) 'Health psychology', *Annual Review of Psychology*, 36: 346–83.

Lago, C. and Thompson, J. (1997) 'Counselling and race', in S. Palmer (ed.) and G. McMahon (assoc. ed.), *Handbook of Counselling*. London: Routledge.

Lazarus, A.A. (1989) *The Practice of Multimodal Therapy*. Baltimore, MD: Johns Hopkins University Press.

Lazarus, A.A. (1995) 'Foreword', in S. Palmer and W. Dryden, *Counselling for Stress Problems*. London: Sage.

Milner, P. and Palmer, S. (1998) *Integrative Stress Counselling: A Humanistic Problem-Focused Approach*. London: Cassell.

Moodley, R. (1999) 'Challenges and transformations: counselling in a multicultural context', *International Journal for the Advancement of Counselling*, 21: 139–52.

Palmer, S. (1996) 'The multimodal approach: theory, assessment, techniques and interventions', in S. Palmer and W. Dryden (eds), *Stress Management and Counselling: Theory, Practice, Research and Methodology*. London: Cassell.

Palmer, S. (1999a) 'Developing an individual counselling programme: a multimodal perspective', in S. Palmer and P. Laungani (eds), *Counselling in a Multicultural Society*. London: Sage.

Palmer, S. (1999b) 'In search of effective counselling across cultures', in S. Palmer and P. Laungani (eds), *Counselling in a Multicultural Society*. London: Sage.

Palmer, S. and Dryden, W. (1995) *Counselling for Stress Problems*. London: Sage.

Patel, G. (1997) 'Nafsiyat Intercultural Therapy Centre: developing counselling and therapy for young refugees', *RACE Journal*, 14: 30–31.

Ponterotto, J.G. (1987) 'Counseling Mexican Americans: a multimodal approach', *Journal of Counseling and Development*, 65 (6): 308–12.

Raskin, N.J. and Rogers, C.R. (1995) 'Person-centered therapy', in R.J. Corsini and D. Wedding (eds), *Current Psychotherapies*, 5th edn. Itasca, IL: F.E. Peacock.

Ridley, C.R. (1984) 'Clinical treatment of the nondisclosing black client: a therapeutic paradox', *American Psychologist*, 39 (11): 1234–44.

Ridley, C.R. (1995) *Overcoming Unintentional Racism in Counselling and Therapy: A Practitioner's Guide to Intentional Intervention*. Thousand Oaks, CA: Sage.

Ridley, C.R., Mendoza, D. and Kanitz, B. (1994) 'Multicultural training: reexamination, operationalization, and integration', *The Counseling Psychologist*, 22 (2): 227–89.

Ridley, C.R. and Lingle, D.W. (1996) 'Cultural empathy in multicultural counselling: a multidimensional process model', in P.B. Pedersen, J.G. Draguns, W.J. Lonner and J.E. Trimble (eds), *Counselling Across Cultures*, 4th edn. Thousand Oaks, CA: Sage.

Ridley, C.R., Espelage, D.L. and Rubinstein, K.J. (1997) 'Course development in multicultural counselling', in D.B. Pope-Davis and H.L.K. Coleman (eds), *Multicultural*

Counseling Competencies: Assessment, Education and Training, and Supervision. Thousand Oaks, CA: Sage.

Sue, D.W. (1977) 'Counseling the culturally different: a conceptual analysis', *Personnel and Guidance Journal*, 55 (7): 422–25.

Discussion issues

1 Why is it important to consider a client's idiographic experience? Does multimodal therapy take an idiographic stance?
2 What is 'cultural empathy'?
3 What are the benefits of focusing on a client's 'Interaction with her or his Oppressive Environment'?
4 Is being an 'authentic chameleon' authentic from a person-centred perspective?

6

Transcultural Family Therapy

Zoubida Guernina

This chapter addresses the cross-cultural approaches to family therapy in dealing with cultural problems with 'ethnic minority families'. It also identifies some key issues of working psychotherapeutically across cultures. Insufficient training in cultural family therapy could lead to dangerous and misleading assessment. Inadequate diagnosis might be confounded with misunderstanding of norms, beliefs and values of traditional families from non-western countries. This chapter offers a cross-cultural lens or perspective to reconstruct the general understanding of family therapy. Illustrations are given from the author's experience as a psychotherapist in the Intercultural Therapy Centre in London (NAFSIYAT).

Family therapy has been marginalized as a discipline over the years and this might be due to its constant neglect of the distinctive patterns of values, behaviour, beliefs and family ideologies that affect 'cultural minority families'. Ho (1987) argues that family therapy in general has had little contribution to other disciplines because of its inability to deal with the issues in society. This could be compared to someone looking at many countries to get to know them all through one single keyhole.

The term minority, especially in relation to ethnic minority, relates in most western countries to those people seen as in need of help. Rack (1982) suggests that words such as ethnic minority and multicultural could be updated by the word 'cosmopolitan' to stress the importance of contrast and diversity instead of alienation. The mystification of some of these definitions used for ethnic minorities might ignore the real experience of oppression and subordination of ethnic minorities; most of them are descriptive and do not raise the questions of a conceptual framework by which family and cultural problems could be tackled.

There is a host of research in the USA that only elicits the cultural diversity of US ethnic groups (Foley, 1982; Herz, 1982; Kaslow, 1982; McGoldrick et al., 1982). These studies have provided an interesting but broad approach to family therapy and the role of the notion of culture but fail to present the intrinsic cultural factors in family therapy. The aims of this chapter are to:

- understand the individual interactions within a family system that is constantly required to make changes that might be sparked by constant demands from relatives or from the predominant 'host' culture;

- clarify the assessment (diagnosis) or intervention procedures used for families from other cultures in UK. The techniques used in the Intercultural Therapy Centre are explained through the illustration of case studies from cultural minority families; and
- provide a conceptual framework which indicates the skills and strategies used in a cultural specific intervention with ethnic minority families in the UK.

The socio-cultural factors: their influence on ethnic minority families

Research indicates that families from ethnic minorities are deprived of their legitimate rights in psychotherapy (Cross, 1978; Scarman, 1981; Smith, 1977). These studies show that racism and poverty are the main forces in the lives of many ethnic minorities, who have in addition to adjust to societal constraints created by the value systems of the majority. One of the most pervasive problems is ineffective communication: lack of dialogue from the majority group to the minority group. This creates further conflicts for the ethnic minority families to reconcile the norms and values system inside and outside the family. Littlewood and Lipsedge (1982) stress that the dominant culture actively eliminates people who do not belong to it and produces its own aliens. These have adequate frames of reference for judging the standards of individuals from other cultures. Because of this, they describe behaviour that they do not understand as abnormal or ill.

Children are especially affected by the stigma of social membership in a devalued ethnic group so they learn to look at their family as the important source of identity. For this particular reason it is important for the cultural family psychotherapist 'to look at the dual culture perspective' in the assessment of ethnic minority families.

The dual cultural perspective has been proposed by Norton (1978) who explains that a minority child is torn between two cultural systems: the nurturing environment (family) and the sustaining environment (society). This intercultural dual perspective has been a tool of assessment used by the author in NAFSIYAT for looking at the problem of the family within two subcultures. The intercultural approach focuses on clients having the freedom to choose the appropriate language in therapy to express themselves fully (Kareem and Littlewood, 2000). d'Ardenne and Mahtani (1989) add: 'If clients are counselled in their first language they gain access to important cultural and familiar experiences. The therapist needs to be bilingual or multilingual so that s/he is able to deal with cultural resources and subtleties'. These could be shown in the two cases studied at the Intercultural Therapy Centre in NAFSIYAT (London).

Case studies

Two case studies will hopefully illustrate the usefulness of the dual cultural approach used by Norton (1978). The issues discussed are relevant to family therapy practice by discussing two case studies relevant to multicultural counselling. All the names used in the case studies are ficti-tious in order to protect privacy and confidentiality.

Case study 1

A Moroccan family composed of the mother, father and their children was referred by their GP. Initially the mother, Fadhuma, a 35-year-old, attractive woman of Mediterranean build, was seen by the social services who openly decided that they found it difficult to converse with her because she spoke very little English. She asked permission to speak in her native language; she said she could express exactly her feelings, her emotions and thoughts and felt more at ease speaking Arabic. Her sons were of 16 years, Ahmed; 13 years, Nasser and 10 years, Aicha. Her husband, Ali, was 40 years old.

During the interview, Ali, her husband, who seemed to be the breadwinner, spoke about his wife's problems and described the suffering Fadhuma and her family went through. I indicated to him that he could speak directly to his wife and children and about how he felt about her depression.

Fadhuma self-disclosed: talking about her isolation, low self-esteem and explained her lack of appetite for life, (food, sex, friends, life, etc.), and the inability to stand on her own two feet.

Her husband had emigrated a while ago from Morocco to Britain to work as a translator in Arabic/French with an international company. After five years, Ali asked Fadhuma and the children to come and live with him in London. Fadhuma was apprehensive about leaving her home country, her friends, job and family. Ali's extended family, his mother, brothers and cousins were very much against Fadhuma and the children moving to London and thought that Ali was listening too much to his wife, and should rather get on with his job by himself.

In Ali's mother's view, Fadhuma would cease to exist for the family if she left the extended family home. Also that would present a severe threat to the honour of the family. In spite of the family's disagreement, Fadhuma and the children joined her husband in London. She found a job as a language teacher but it proved difficult because members of staff could not interact with her. She was very depressed and reported that most of her colleagues misused her potential, spelt her name wrongly and did not make an effort to get to know her. While struggling with work permit, immigration questioning and adjust-ing to British culture, her mother-in-law arrived from Morocco.

The mother-in-law was continuously imposing her ideas on the family and interfering in the way things should be at home. The generation gap and the level of acculturation threatened the family functioning. Fadhuma was on the verge of a breakdown and her depression affected her children, who both suf-fered from asthma. Since they have been in London they have developed eczema. During the subsequent sessions it became clear that the husband and children felt caught between Fadhuma and Ali's mother. Also they were not sure whether they would live as Moroccan or British.

Many factors were taken were consideration in the therapy sessions: the impact of immigration, discrimination at both individual and institutional levels. It was also important to focus on the degree of acculturation and its effects on the traditional hierarchical role structure.

I asked each member of the family to redefine their views to show that they are all equal in clarifying the contradictions of the family map, within the complexities of dual cultural perspectives. The ability to speak the same language is very helpful in solving the dilemma between the families. A common language in therapy is important in reducing ambiguities. Rack (1982) argues that speaking the same language goes beyond comprehending the non-verbal, verbal or content aspects of communications. It is very beneficial for communicating, exchanging ideas with the client. The dual cultural perspective outlined by Norton (1978) helped in defining with each member of the family their goals, cultural practices, life styles and social identity.

Case study 2

Amina, a 19-year-old Pakistani girl, came to see me with her mother and two sisters. They told me that Amina had withdrawn from school, from all social contacts and become very unhappy. The family had emigrated from Pakistan. The father worked very hard and spent hardly any time with the family. He was not informed about Amina seeking therapy because it might have been difficult for him to discuss 'women's concerns' as they put it. It is clear during the session that the problem is not just in the structure of the family but in the cultural compositions too. We started together exploring the content rules of the family map. I used the cultural dual approach (Norton, 1978) in relation to the family. Throughout the sessions a clarification was made by which 'ethnic minority families' perceive, understand and compare their ethnic values, beliefs, attitude, behaviour with those of the majority. Amina revealed that she was in love with an English boy in her class. Her guilt increases after she sees her father coming back exhausted from work. She felt she was betraying the family and her cultural beliefs. She decided to stay at home to preserve the family's honour. She felt torn between her desire to be free and have a good time and her self-control and responsibility towards the family. She has been feeling confused and anxious about her inability to keep up with the family religious norms. In her boyfriend's presence, she was unable to do the fasting during Ramadhan.

Both her mother and sister were very worried about her involvement with someone who is not of the same religion. The father was described by the mother as being honest and very rigid and would find his daughter's involvement with a non-Muslim intolerable. If he finds out about her he would take action to send her back to Pakistan or dismiss her from the family.

The paradoxical command between autonomy of the self and respect of the culture was discussed without violating the ultimate principle of therapy: respect of the person—Amina.

The crucial aspect of the therapeutic process is to understand the cultural family functioning system in its minority and majority context. Amina's feelings and behaviour were addressed with her mother and sisters and the therapy explicitly focused on changing the dynamic between members of the family.

Implications for practice

Working cross-culturally in therapy is challenging and demanding. It enhances self-growth and development to understand the various concepts used in a multicultural or cosmopolitan society. Psychotherapists need to develop self-awareness of one's attitude and feelings towards minorities. It helps in acquiring knowledge about other cultures: to develop skills for cultural sensitivity in relating and engaging with various backgrounds; to help families whom you have to adjust to their own social and sexual roles within their families and community (Blair et al., 1981); to have an objective insight, a genuine understanding of the family's cultural beliefs, values, perceptions, expectations and attitude; to consider the family's perspectives, environmental and social conditions, current and future goals.

A deeper analysis is needed in family therapy in a multicultural society. The family in an ethnic minority group responds to complex factors in mainstream society and within the family.

A revision of family therapy in a multicultural society is needed to resolve some of the above problems in the field. This could be a universal enrichment in order to bridge cultural and family differences.

References

Blair, W., Khera, A., Khoot, S. and Patel, R. (1981) 'Level crossing?', in J. Cheetham, W. James, M. Loney, B. Mayor and W. Prescott (eds) *Social and Community Work in Multiracial Society.* London: Harper and Row.

Cross, C. (1978) *Ethnic Minorities in the Innercity: The Ethnic Dimensions in Urban Deprivation in England.* London: Commission for Racial Equality.

d'Ardenne, P. and Mahtani, A. (1989) *Transcultural Counselling in Action.* London: Sage.

Falicou, C. and Carter, E.A. (1980) 'Cultural investigation in the family life cycle', in E.A. Carter and M. McGoldrick (eds), *The Family Life Cycle: A Framework for Family Therapy.* New York: Gardner Press.

Foley, V.D. (1982) 'Family therapy with black, disadvantaged family', in A.S. Gurman (ed.), *Questions and Answers in the Practice of Family Therapy.* New York: Brunner/Mazel.

Herz, F. (1982) 'Ethnic differences and family therapy', in A.S. Gurman (ed.), *Questions and Answers in the Practice of Family Therapy.* New York: Brunner/Mazel.

Ho, M. (1987) *Family Therapy with Ethnic Minorities.* Newbury Park, CA: Sage.

Kareem, J. and Littlewood, R. (2000) *Intercultural Therapy*, 2nd revised edition. Oxford: Blackwell.

Kaslow, F.D. (1982) 'Working with families cross-culturally', in A.S. Gurman (ed.), *Questions and Answers in the Practice of Family Therapy.* New York: Brunner/Mazel.

Littlewood, R. and Lipsedge H. (1982) *Aliens and Aliemists: Ethnic Minority and Psychiatry.* Harmondsworth: Penguin.

McGoldrick, M., Pearce, T. and Giardino, J. (eds) (1982) *Ethnicity and Family Therapy.* New York: Guilford Press.

Norton, D. (1978) 'Black family life patterns: the development of self and cognitive development of black children', in G. Powell, J. Yamamoto, A. Romero and A. Morales (eds), *The Psychosocial Development of Minority Group Children.* New York: Brunner/Mazel.

Rack, P. (1982) *Race, Culture and Mental Disorder.* London: Tavistock.
Scarman, R. (1981) *The Brixton Disorders 10–12 April.* London: HMSO, Cmnd 8427.
Smith, D. (1977) *Racial Disadvantage in Britain. The PEP Report.* Harmondsworth: Penguin.

Discussion issues

1 In what ways have western therapies failed to address important major issues in relation to ethnic minority families?
2 Family therapy has been marginalized.
3 'Cosmopolitan' should replace the words 'ethnic minority' and 'multicultural'.
4 Do counsellors working in a multicultural setting need to be bilingual?

7

Therapy with Intercultural Couples

A Postmodern Approach

Joan L. Biever, Monte Bobele
and Mary-Wales North

Historically, interreligious and interracial dating and marriage have been socially proscribed. For example, in the USA, it was not until 1967 that legal prohibitions against interracial marriage were eliminated nationwide. Further, negative attitudes towards interracial dating and marriage have been slow to change. A 1993 survey by the National Opinion Research Center revealed that 20 per cent of those surveyed believed that interracial marriage should be illegal; however, this was down from 33 per cent in 1973. In spite of social disapproval, the number of persons who marry outside of their racial/ethnic groups has been expanding rapidly over the last two decades. US Census statistics reveal that interracial marriages have increased from 366,000 couples in 1970 to 1,478,000 couples in 1992.

Overcoming social disapproval and negotiating cultural differences may exacerbate the stresses and difficulties in marriages. Given the growing number of intercultural couples and the difficulties they may face, the professional literature has paid surprisingly little attention to this population. There is a growing literature that focuses on multicultural counselling issues (e.g. Pedersen, 1991; Sue et al., 1992; Szapocznik and Kurtines, 1993), which primarily addresses clients who are culturally different from the therapist. Writers who have discussed intercultural couples frequently focus on one dimension of intermarriage, such as religion or race (e.g. Davidson, 1992; Gleckman and Streicher, 1990; Pope, 1986; Sung, 1990). Thus, the focus has been on specific differences between two cultural groups rather than on developing an approach to working with cultural differences in general.

Definitions of couples and culture

The literature in this area usually refers to marital partners, using the term 'intermarriage' to describe this population. For the purposes of this article, the term 'couple' will refer more broadly to two people involved in a committed romantic relationship who share a household, a history and a planned future. Following Morris (1970), culture is understood as 'the totality of socially transmitted behavior patterns, arts, beliefs, institutions, and all other products of human work and thought characteristic of a community or population' (p. 321). The term 'intercultural', rather than the more common terms bi-racial or intermarried, was chosen to represent the broader range of cultural variables on which couples may differ. While any number of differences (e.g. SES, age, cohort, immigration status) between couples could be considered cultural differences, we will address differences in race, ethnicity or religion. The reader is invited to consider the application of these principles to other couples as well.

Effects of cultural differences

Cultural differences may affect couples in various ways over the course of a relationship. Initially, couples may face disapproval or social awkwardness with friends and families. In more extreme cases, financial and/or emotional estrangements may occur. Couples often encounter negative reactions in their communities. White members of interracial couples may encounter discrimination and racial hostility (ranging from stares and rude comments to housing discrimination and threats of or actual violence) that was previously unknown to them. Friends and family may infer motives for choosing a partner who is culturally different, such as rebellion, inferiority complex, or denial of one's own cultural group.

Stresses involved in setting up a household may bring cultural differences to the forefront. Potential conflict areas such as sex-role expectations, attitudes towards work and leisure, holiday traditions, expression of affection and problem-solving strategies are frequently culturally based. Disagreement about these issues may take the form of the partners' blaming each other for not understanding or being unreasonable rather than attributing the difficulties to differing cultural traditions. Similarly, parenting styles may reveal cultural differences between partners and affect interactions with extended family members and other social systems.

These problems may present a pessimistic picture of intercultural relationships. However, there are frequently overlooked advantages to such relationships. Couples may learn and grow from the reactions of family and friends. This may lead to deeper involvement between the partners and more thorough preparation as they reflect and discuss the implications of the relationship before making a commitment. The process of negotiating cultural differences may result in each partner becoming more aware, and accepting, of differences. Likewise, the children of intercultural couples may be more accepting of differences in others (Ho, 1990).

Therapy with intercultural couples presents challenges. Like others, intercultural couples may be polarized and expect a therapist to determine which partner is right. As mentioned above, difficulties in the relationship may be mistakenly attributed to personality or emotional problems of one or both partners rather than stemming from cultural differences. Difficulties in understanding may be exacerbated when the therapist is culturally similar to one of the partners. There are few theoretical or practice guidelines available for the practitioner, but González et al. (1994) argued that some postmodern therapies may be particularly suitable for multicultural counselling. One such approach will be discussed below and the ideas will be applied to work with intercultural couples.

Social constructionism

Postmodern ideas are becoming increasingly influential in academic disciplines such as art, literature and the social sciences. Postmodernism refers to an intellectual movement away from the belief in, and search for, foundational truths. Some have described this movement as a result of the evolving complexity of our understanding: 'the postmodern Mind is one which ... has come to question whether it [reality] is ordered in a way in which man's reason can lay bare' (Smith, 1989: 7). Postmodernism has also been described as 'a linguistic theory that proposes that the social world cannot be treated as an objective system' (Pardeck et al., 1994: 343).

One postmodern theory that has some influence in psychotherapy is social constructionism. Social constructionism suggests that what we know as reality is constructed through interactions with others (Gergen, 1985). Understandings or meanings that individuals attach to any given behaviour, interaction, or event will be determined by the social and cultural contexts in which they occur. Relevant social contexts could include: family, racial/ethnic group, religious identification, work setting, place of residence, and others. From this position, psychological theories are merely agreed upon understandings which have proven to be useful in one or more contexts (Howard, 1991). As no account or interpretation of reality can be considered more accurate than any other, the focus is on how or when ideas are useful.

Application to intercultural couples

Social constructionism offers unique invitations to providing therapy to intercultural couples. The following principles, drawn from social constructionism, are illustrated with examples of our work with intercultural couples.

Collaborative, curious stance

Therapy from a social constructionistic perspective is a collaborative effort between clients and therapists. Therapy begins by exploring clients' unique understandings and theories about the problems that brought them to therapy instead of assessing how the client fits into the therapist's theories about psychological problems, diagnostic categories and change. Therapists ask questions that are based on a need to know more about what has been said or what is not known. Thus, clients might be asked how cultural differences have benefited and hindered their relationship. The understandings that are created about the clients' situations and the culture arise out of a mutual, collaborative construction of meaning. Therapists are always aware that the meanings constructed are not the only ones that could be constructed.

Openness and the generation of alternative understandings

A common goal in social constructionist therapy is expanding descriptions and understandings about the presenting concerns. Andersen (1991), in discussing reflecting teams, suggests that observing therapists keep two questions in mind: 'How else can this situation/behavior/pattern be described?' and 'How else can it be explained?' These questions are useful, as well, for therapists who work alone. By asking such questions, therapists may remain open to, and help generate, new possibilities. This contrasts with many conventional therapies, which encourage the therapeutic process to 'uncover' the correct understanding and explanation for clients' situations. By asking themselves and clients 'How else?' therapists create opportunities for new and different understandings. These new ideas may lead to new problem solving strategies.

Anderson and Goolishian (1992) caution therapists not to understand clients 'too quickly'. When therapists 'understand' clients, the possibilities for expanding and creating meanings become limited. Social constructionistic therapists present ideas tentatively, acknowledging that there are many possible helpful ideas. Offering ideas in a tentative manner invites clients to offer their own thoughts and ideas more freely. Tentativeness also promotes a spirit of mutual collaboration in the therapeutic conversation. Anderson (1995) suggests that tentativeness may be conveyed by the use of unfinished sentences or hanging words and phrases such as 'wondering', 'kind of', or 'maybe'.

With intercultural couples, therapists may ask each partner how persons from their cultural background would typically approach or understand a particular situation. For example, the therapist might say, 'I'm wondering if there are differences in how each of your families would view this situation?' Or the therapist might ask if other ideas or explanations had occurred to them.

Exploration of clients' ideas about cause of problem

Client understandings and explanations are valued because of their potential usefulness; not because of their theoretical (or political) 'correctness'. Furman and Ahola (1988) describe interviewing techniques that explore clients' causal explanations or their impressions of others causal explanations. They note that clients often infer therapists' explanations from the type of questions that are asked. Thus, if therapists spend much of the first session asking about childhood experiences, clients are likely to infer that these early experiences led to the current symptoms. It is important for therapists to understand clients' own causal explanations and clients' impressions of the therapists' explanations. Furman and Ahola highlight the need for therapists to display curiosity and to avoid expressing agreement or disagreement with the clients' explanations. Using the client's explanations may lead to more efficient therapy.

View cultural differences as one explanation of conflicts
Therapists may use knowledge of cultural differences to recognize patterns when present, but should not assume the presence of a pattern until it is evident. The dangers involved when therapists have limited knowledge of clients' cultures have been discussed extensively (e.g. Rogler et al., 1987; Solomon, 1992; Szapocznik and Kurtines, 1993). However, making assumptions based on stereotypical cultural patterns can cause problems as well. There are frequent intragroup differences that can easily be overlooked if therapists assume that they are familiar with clients' cultural groups (Sue et al., 1992; Szapocznik and Kurtines, 1993). For example, a Mexican-American couple seen at our university training clinic did not identify cultural differences as contributing to their marital difficulties. However, the interview revealed that the husband was a fourth generation, middle-class, Catholic, Mexican-American. He strongly identified with the Mexican-American community. The wife was a second generation, wealthy, Jewish, Mexican-American. Her religious beliefs were far more influential than the nationality of her parents. Religious and social class differences permeated this couple's difficulties, yet could have been overlooked in therapy had the therapists assumed that similarity on one cultural dimension meant similarities on all dimensions.

A danger in defining behaviours as originating in culture is that the behaviours may be seen as unchangeable. Thus, problems that are attributed to the cultural characteristics of the partner rather than to interactions between the partners may easily escalate into a standoff as to who is 'right' and perhaps, even arguments about which cultural group is 'better'.

Therapists must balance the usefulness and disadvantages of cultural explanations. For example, a white woman became increasingly depressed over several years after discovering her Cuban-American husband had been involved with another woman. In her mind, her husband's affair meant that he did not love her. However, viewing his behaviour in the context of his family's culture (his brothers and father all had numerous affairs) allowed her to understand that, for her husband, having an affair had little to do with love for his wife. She was also encouraged to see how her husband was different from his family, because as soon as her husband realized his behaviour was causing her pain, he ended the affair and promised to be faithful in the future.

Encouraging a both/and stance
Anderson (1986) suggests that therapists adopt a both/and stance. The both/and stance flows from the postmodern idea of multiple, socially constructed realities and the valuing of diversity. Both sides of a

dichotomy are prized. For example, one distinction frequently made by therapists is that of intercultural differences and intracultural similarities. From a postmodern perspective, it may be more useful to assume that all cultures are *both* similar *and* different. This both/and perspective helps the therapist focus on two useful ideas. One is that there are both similarities and differences *between* cultural groups. Second, and invariably, there are both similarities and differences *within* a particular culture.

The both/and stance extracts therapists from the position of judging who is right in family disagreements. The therapist can focus on how both positions are 'right' by exploring how each position came into being and when each is useful or not useful. For instance, one parent may want to use punishment to discipline the children, while the other prefers praise. The challenge for the therapist is to adapt a position where *both* punishment *and* praise are viable alternatives for the couple. Therapists can explore in which contexts punishment or praise have been most useful and why. Exploring intents or underlying meanings provides a way out of either/or standoffs. When therapists take this stance, even logically inconsistent ideas can co-exist. In the situation mentioned above, the therapist may encourage the couple to explore what behaviours they are hoping to teach their children. If the couple agree on the end goal, then they may be willing to negotiate the means or at least experiment with various parenting strategies and observe the results. Therapists may also ask questions that elicit examples of past parenting successes and the parenting strategies that led to these successes.

Search for liberating traditions within each culture
Waldegrave (1990) suggests that therapists search for 'liberating traditions' within each culture. This idea is based on the belief that some less desirable behaviours may reside within larger cultural traditions, which have value and can be used positively. Searching for larger cultural meanings expands the possibilities that may be available for clients. In the extreme, therapists can look for the 'less bad' of cultural traditions within a given area. For example, when working with clients from cultures that have rigid gender roles, therapists may focus on valuing the skills involved in the traditional roles or developing a new meaning for a given behaviour. For example, an Anglo woman married to a Mexican-American man became angry when she was expected to serve her husband's dinner when they dined at his parents' house. However, when she began to think of this as a sign of respecting her in-laws rather than subservience to her husband, she began to use serving her husband as a way of connecting with the women in his family.

Another strategy is focusing on those aspects of a culture that present the most possibilities for change. What does each partner admire in the extended family of the other? If there are aspects of one partner's culture that are particularly bothersome for the other, therapists may focus on discovering positive intents or effects of those traditions over history.

View impasse as an attempt to impose beliefs/values on other

Harlene Anderson (1986) suggests that therapeutic impasses occur in conversations where each of the participants believes that their own description, or explanation, of a situation is correct and tries unsuccessfully to persuade others to adopt their position. This competition of ideas results in participants becoming increasingly committed to their initial positions. Thus, the conversation becomes 'stuck' with little opportunity for the development of new ideas or behaviours. Such impasses may occur among the various members of the client system or between therapists and one or more members of the client system. This view of impasse reminds therapists to look for the attempted imposition of one or more ideas when therapy seems 'stuck'. Therapists may want to ask themselves questions such as 'Who is trying to convince who of what?', 'What is feared?', 'What is hoped for?', 'Are there beliefs which constrain acceptance of differences?' One way to overcome impasses that involve only one member of the couple is for a therapist to focus on learning more about that person. Of course, impasses may also occur between the therapist and one or both members of the couple. When this occurs, it is useful for therapists to ask themselves what understandings are they imposing on the clients.

Working with stories

A focus on stories or narratives is common in postmodern therapies. For instance, Lynn Hoffman (1990) has described problems as stories people tell themselves. Generally, viewing the presenting problem as a 'story' presupposes that it is possible – perhaps inevitable – that the story will change with each telling. Changing the story changes the meanings that are attached to events, behaviours and interactions. The manner in which stories are used in therapy differs among therapists. White (White, 1993; White and Epston, 1990) focuses on the ways in which clients' stories are constrained by dominant narratives such as patriarchal or oppressive stories.

Sluzki (1992) focuses on transforming the structure of clients' stories to change narratives by attending to the dimensions of time, space, causality, interactions, values and the telling of the story. Each of these dimensions is viewed as a continuum. It does not matter where on the continuum a story falls; the therapist's job is to shift the story to another position. For example, if a couple attributes their problem to cultural differences, the therapist may attribute the differences to personal characteristics. Finally, in the collaborative languaging approach developed by Anderson and Goolishian (1988, 1992), the focus is on developing new stories rather than on providing frameworks for changing stories. Therapy is seen as an opportunity for clients to explore a variety of stories while discouraging, commitment to any one story as the truth (Gergen and Kaye, 1992).

Conclusions

Working with intercultural couples presents challenges for therapists as cultural differences may exacerbate the stresses inherent in relationships. Postmodern therapies such as those based on social constructionism provide a framework for approaching the complexities of intercultural relationships, which is culturally sensitive, collaborative, and strength-based. However, the efficacy of this approach with intercultural couples has yet to be examined.

Acknowledgement

The authors would like to thank Shery French, MS, for editorial assistance.

Note

Portions of this paper were presented at the 102nd Annual Convention of the American Psychological Association, Los Angeles, August, 1994.

References

Andersen, T. (1991) *The Reflecting Team: Dialogues and Dialogues about the Dialogues.* New York: Norton.

Anderson, H. (1986) 'Therapeutic impasses: a breakdown in conversation'. Unpublished manuscript, Houston Galveston Institute.

Anderson, H. (1995) 'Collaborative language systems: toward a postmodern therapy', in R. Mikesell, D.D. Lusterman and S. McDaniel (eds), *Integrating Family Therapy: Handbook of Family Psychology and Systems Theory*, pp. 27–43. Washington, DC: American Psychological Association Press.

Anderson, H. and Goolishian, H. (1988) 'Human systems as linguistic systems: preliminary and evolving ideas about the implications for clinical theory', *Family Process*, 27: 3–12.

Anderson, H. and Goolishian, H. (1992) 'The client is the expert: a not-knowing approach to therapy', in S. McNamee and K.J. Gergen (eds), *Therapy, as Social Construction*, pp. 25–39. Newbury Park, CA: Sage.

Davidson, J.R. (1992) 'Theories about black–white interracial marriage: a clinical perspective', *Journal of Multicultural Counseling and Development*, 20: 150–57.

Furman, B. and Ahola, T. (1988) 'Return to the question "why": advantages of exploring pre-existing explanations', *Family Process*, 27: 395–409.

Gergen, K.J. (1985) 'The social constructionist movement in modern psychology', *American Psychologist*, 40: 266–75.

Gergen, K.J. and Kaye, J. (1992) 'Beyond narrative in the negotiation of meaning', in S. McNamee and K.J. Gergen (eds), *Therapy as Social Construction*, pp. 25–39. Newbury Park, CA: Sage.

Gleckman, A.D. and Streicher, P.J. (1990) 'The potential for difficulties with Jewish intermarriage: interventions and implications for the mental health counselor', *Journal of Mental Health Counseling*, 12: 480–94.

González, R.C., Biever, J.L. and Gardner, G.T. (1994) 'The multicultural perspective in therapy: a social constructionist approach', *Psychotherapy*, 31: 515–24.

Ho, M.K. (1990) *Intermarried Couples in Therapy.* Springfield, IL: Charles Thomas.

Hoffman, L. (1990) 'Constructing realities: an art of lenses', *Family Process*, 29: 1–12.

Howard, G.S. (1991) 'Cultural tales: a narrative approach to thinking, cross-cultural psychology, and psychotherapy', *American Psychologist*, 46: 187–97.

Morris, W. (ed.) (1970) *The American Heritage Dictionary of the English Language.* Boston: Houghton Mifflin.

Pardeck, J.T., Murphy, J.W. and Jung, M.C. (1994) 'Some implications of postmodernism for social work practice', *Social Work*, 39: 343–5.

Pedersen, P.B. (1991) 'Multiculturalism as a generic approach to counseling', *Journal of Counseling & Development*, 70: 6–12.

Pope, B.R. (1986) 'Black men in interracial relationships: psychological and therapeutic issues', *Journal of Multicultural Counseling and Development*, 1: 10–16.

Rogler, L.H., Constantino, G. and Blumenthal, R. (1987) 'What do culturally sensitive mental health services mean?', *American Psychologist*, 42: 565–70.

Sluzki, C.E. (1992) 'Transformations: a blueprint for narrative changes in therapy', *Family Process*, 31: 217–30.

Smith, H. (1989) *Beyond the Postmodern Mind.* New York: Quest Books.

Solomon, A. (1992) 'Clinical diagnosis among diverse populations: a multicultural perspective', *Families in Society: The Journal of Contemporary Human Service*, 73: 371–7.

Sue, D.W., Arredondo, P. and McDavis, R. (1992) 'Multicultural counseling competencies and standards: a call to the profession', *Journal of Counseling & Development*, 70: 477–86.

Sung, B.L. (1990) 'Chinese American intermarriage', *Journal of Comparative Family Studies*, 21: 337–52.

Szapocznik, J. and Kurtines, W.M. (1993) 'Family psychology and cultural diversity: opportunities for theory, research, and application', *American Psychologist*, 48: 400–407.

Waldegrave, C. (1990) 'Just therapy', *Dulwich Centre Newsletter*, 1: 6–46.

White, M. (1993) 'Deconstruction and therapy', in S. Gilligan and R. Price (eds), *Therapeutic Conversations*, pp. 22–61. New York: Norton.

White, M. and Epston, D. (1990) *Narrative Means to Therapeutic Ends.* York: Horton.

Discussion issues

1 How did you react to learning that in 1993, 20 per cent of people in the USA still believed that interracial marriage should be illegal, according to a survey?

2 How might cultural differences affect couples?

3 What has social constructionism got to offer intercultural couples in counselling and psychotherapy?

4 If therapists spend much time in the first session asking about childhood experiences, clients are likely to infer that these early experiences led to their current symptoms.

8

Counselling Black Employees Facing Racism and Discrimination

Nick Banks

This chapter seeks to raise the awareness of counsellors who may be offering stress counselling to black (both African-Caribbean and South Asian) client groups in an occupational setting where the stress is a result of discrimination or racism through organizational or white individual employee's practice. In this context, raising awareness means enabling the counselling psychologist with less understanding of the discussed issues to be able to identify difficulties related to discrimination and racism that may otherwise be inaccurately located within 'dysfunctioning' of the oppressed individual.

A working definition of 'institutionalized racism' would include the result of organizational policy, procedure and practice, based on overt or covert notions of the inferiority or inability of black people, blocking the entry or advancement of black people within an institution. For example, refusing promotion to a black bank clerk to become a cashier with direct contact with customers if this is not considered in the bank's best interest due to perceived potential adverse reactions from white customers. This would be an example of illegal direct discrimination (under the terms of the 1976 Race Relations Act) and an example of institutionalized racism, even if couched in terms of 'protecting' the black employee. Personal or individual racism, on the other hand, would be related to an individual's beliefs or actions regarding the perceived inferiority of black people even if not consciously acknowledged.

Social psychologists have identified that many people may prefer not to believe relations between people of different cultures and races are largely determined by the groups to which they belong and that this membership influences the nature and quality of the relationships existing between the groups in question (Bochner, 1983). However, the available evidence confirms that perceptions of race and gender affect people's patterns of communication and interaction (Banks, 1997; Davis and Proctor, 1989; Henley, 1977).

Studies looking at the relationship between white employers, black employees and black job applicants have consistently shown that discrimination and disadvantage are high at the point of recruitment, selection, training and promotion. For example, as long ago as 1971 the census showed that the unemployment rate of young African-Caribbean people in Britain was at least twice that of their white counterparts. Little et al. (1978) found that the number of young black interviewees who were unsuccessful at interview was four times that of white teenagers with equivalent qualifications. Smith (1977) found that, as total unemployment increased, black and other minority ethnic groups formed an increasing proportion of the unemployment figures. A PEP (1977) study of nearly 300 companies showed more than half practised some form of discrimination, and a Labour Research survey (1989) noted that 'discrimination and racial harassment are unfortunately all too often part of the experience of working life for black people' (p. 14).

These studies indicate that decisions on whether to hire, offer development opportunities or promote may be taken on the grounds of race alone. It would seem that discrimination, personal and institutionalized racism may be rife in the work-based experience of black employees.

A North American study by Grant et al. (1983) researched the effect that nonsupportive social relations in the workplace may have on black employees. They used the concept of social undermining as defined by 'a negative form of social interaction characterised by active dislike and devaluing of an individual'. Grant et al. (1983) surveyed 1000 African-American social workers, achieving a 52 per cent response rate. The results suggested that social undermining was a factor in black worker stress, with social undermining playing a significant role in both worker–supervisor and worker–co-worker relationships. Respondents reported increased feelings of irritability, anxiety, depersonalization and depression. Undermining in the black worker–supervisor (mainly white) relationship was associated with more somatic symptoms and emotional exhaustion. The researchers argued that although negative interactions occurred less frequently than positive interactions, the negative interactions, when they did occur, appeared to have a greater impact on the employee's job satisfaction and personal well-being.

Black people's awareness and, often, direct experience of undermining and discrimination can enter into and affect the employee–counsellor relationship at both a conscious and unconscious level. Counsellors, too, may bring 'baggage' into the counselling relationship. It is worth exploring the mechanisms by which this may happen.

The impact of ethnic difference

It is the present author's research finding (Banks, 1999) that many counsellors tend to expect that, once rapport and empathy have been established, differences of gender, age and 'race' should pale into insignificance as a meaningful dialogue initiates a supportive relationship. In making a related point, Chaplin (1989), a feminist writer, has claimed that 'it is easier for men to argue that gender is not an issue, whereas for me, as a woman, it is extremely important'. She makes the point that gender differences, whether physical or social, are not equally valued differences. With 'racial' and cultural differences, power and inequality can also enter into and hamper the establishment of the counselling relationship.

Unless unequally valued cultural and 'racial' differences are acknowledged by the counsellor, both as a means of recognizing the possibility of the counsellor's cultural encapsulation and the limitations and possible bias of ethnocentric counselling theory (Banks, 1991), counselling may fail the black client as it will not engage with the client's existing social reality and historical experience. For the black client, the nature of self, and sometimes identity, may be inappropriately considered the essential focus in counselling (Helms, 1990), particularly when experiences of discrimination and racism have the effect of destroying previous levels of positive self-esteem. Counsellors who have an over-individualistic focus in their method of work may miss or ignore the important affects of institutional or social forces impinging on the social reality and working environment of the black employee and thus avoid, perhaps through their own personal difficulty, coming to grips with the issues that represent an essential area of exploration.

Given the prolific amount of evidence (Banks, 1997; Hamilton and Zanna, 1972; Katz et al., 1975; Miller and Dolan, 1971; Pinderhughes, 1989) in which racial differences related to perceived group status and sense of self play an influential role in everyday interaction, it is reasonable to speculate that these same perceptions will influence the counselling relationship. These perceptions can be significant in their impact. For example, differences in status exist in the relative power and authority held by the client and counsellor. When these differences extend beyond those of role, training and expertise and into those of race, considerable impediments to the counselling process, related to the therapeutic or working alliance, will develop.

Rogers (1962) saw the client's relationship with the counsellor as the most important part of the counselling process. He saw the factors of empathy and rapport as significant indicators that a relationship had been successfully entered into for the process of counselling to begin. Empathy means that the counsellor identifies with and experiences someone else's feelings as though they were his or her own. If black clients produce material that is outside the white counsellor's experience, and thus understanding, the likelihood of empathic meeting will be diminished. For counselling to be facilitative, the counsellor must be in an empathic state. In Rogers's view, the counsellor should not challenge the client; it was the client who was the legitimate negotiator of reality, not the counsellor. Allegations or suspicions of discrimination and prejudice should never be dismissed or negated. If they are real for the client, this reality must be valued and explored. Challenges from the counsellor may feel distancing or even persecutory if they are perceived by a client as being a barrier between the counsellor and the client's experience.

It could be argued that, to some degree, empathy is a process of strongly identifying oneself with another. It is reasonable to expect that the counsellor's own sense of self and concept of what constitutes a healthy sense of self will shape his or her presence with the client and determine the essential direction of their work. Empathy will not be possible for the counsellor who brings a personal bias against other 'racial' groups to the counselling relationship. The counsellor's prejudices and negative stereotypes will directly prevent him or her from entering into a meaningful relationship and using professional skills to support black clients.

The overcoming of prejudices is not easy. At a conscious level they can be recognized, and attempts can be made to guard against them, but at an unconscious level little recognition is possible. Counsellors may act in a defensive manner, imposing their own reality on the client's communication to protect themselves at the expense of exploring their own feelings about personal vulnerability.

Psychodynamic theory uses the concept of countertransference to describe the process whereby the counsellor reacts to the clients as if he or she represented someone other than the client (Jacobs, 1989):

- *negative countertransference* may exist where that 'someone else' holds a negative or threatening image for the counsellor; e.g. the black male client being viewed as stubborn, inferior or a 'super stud', or the black female client as aggressive and over-emotional.
- *positive countertransference* may exist where feelings to do with liking and positive regard may emerge. In either case Rogers's view was clear: they distort and block the development of the necessary counselling relationship as neither positive nor negative countertransference is related to the reality of being for the individual client.

Jacobs (1989) has written that transference was a term which Freud gave to a phenomenon that was universal. It was seen as being present in all human relationships and encounters. In the counselling relationship it had the effect of fuelling strong feelings by the influence of past experiences. Thus, the counsellor can enter into and engage in the counselling relationship with a fixed perceptual set, based on racial prejudice and stereotypes that undermine and devalue the client as an individual. If the counsellor has more in common with others in the client's life than the client, the likelihood of this happening may increase.

The risk to white counsellors is that, as part of the majority culture, they will respond in a defensive, invalidating way to those whose experiences are different from their own, reducing the support or 'therapeutic alliance' in a counselling relationship. When this happens the counsellor becomes allied to the persecutor or oppressor and is as far removed from what counselling is generally held to be as could be possible.

North American literature (Sue, 1981) has shown a tendency for black groups to terminate counselling in a mental health context, often after only one contact, at a rate of 50 per cent. This was in marked contrast to a 30 per cent drop-out rate for white clients. In general the researchers have come to the conclusion that it was the cultural inappropriateness of interpersonal interactions between white counsellor and black client which accounted for the differences between white and black client groups. Countertransference may be seen as an issue that needs to be addressed here.

Conversely, the counsellor may experience transference from the client. Transference is the corollary of countertransference: the client acts or behaves towards the counsellor as if he or she were someone else. This may or may not be facilitative depending on the counsellor's skills in identifying and working with this process in a transcultural context. Vontress (1971), in the North American literature, talks about the 'old slave–master hatred relationship' being a regular theme, often unrecognized between white counsellor and black client. A key issue is the dominant–subordinate relationship between two different cultures or ethnic groups (Sue, 1981), which translates itself into self-fulfilling expectancy and behaviour. Sue argued that:

> It is reasonable to believe that members of one cultural group tend to adjust themselves to the group possessing the greater prestige and power to avoid inferiority and feelings [of low self-esteem] yet it is exactly this act that creates ambivalence in the minority individual. (Sue, 1981: 83)

The skilled counsellor who is confident in his or her ability to work with client transference related to workplace discrimination will allow the client to 'act out' what troubles him or her, while interpreting this for the client within an organizational or environmental context to lessen feelings of self-blame and individual inadequacy. For the unskilled counsellor this form, as indeed any form, of transference may be particularly threatening.

The personal impact

Discrimination and racism have the effect of negating people as individuals, their past and present achievements and, ultimately, their self-worth. The effect of this on the employee in the workplace setting is predictable. Anger and hostility may be inappropriately expressed to those colleagues who are undeserving and normally supportive, and over-expressed to those workers who are persecutory without recourse to the appropriate use of work-related complaint procedures (where appropriate procedures exist). This may make the black employee even more vulnerable in the workplace. It has been recognized for some time that a common reaction to stressful situations is anger (Dollard et al., 1939), which ultimately may lead to aggression either expressed overtly or internalized. The Frustration–Aggression Hypothesis accounts for this, although externalized aggressive behaviour is not always inevitable. It is worth noting that displaced aggression by white employees towards black employees may be related to organizational frustration, e.g., scapegoating.

The anger felt by the black client may be internalized and become disabling, drastically impeding the carrying out of the black worker's employment duties and having the undesirable effect of confirming negative images and opinions both to others and, in a more destructive sense, working to lower the clients own self-esteem. The effect of having one's self-esteem reduced can be devastating and its work-related effect can be demonstrated through Maslow's (1984) 'theory of sequential needs'.

Maslow's view was that there existed what he termed a 'hierarchy of needs'. For individuals to reach their full potential, or 'self-actualization' as Maslow termed it, our primary or lower order needs must be met first. There is some cross-cultural evidence to support the use of Maslow's framework in the analysis of employment satisfaction and thus level of occupational stress. Slocum and Strawser (1972) found that both black and non-black accountants rated self-actualization needs and autonomy needs as more important than esteem needs and this was consistent with Maslow's theory.

An attack on the individual's self-esteem in the workplace could have the effect of increasing the individual's need for 'freedom from threat or danger' in Maslow's hierarchy (level 2). The 'belonginess needs' level (level 3) of Maslow's hierarchy, which includes the needs of 'affiliation', 'identification with others' and 'acceptance', is the level of need that both employer and employee may see as a minimum to meet basic job requirements although, for some work-related tasks in certain occupations, it is possible that the level of 'self-actualization' (level 5) is necessary. If oppressive practices cannot be suspended in the workplace, then it is unlikely that the black client can be supported to return to his or her previously effective status. As Rogers suggested, in the atmosphere of an accepting environment an individual, and hence his or her capacity to contribute to work, will flourish. In an unaccepting environment the capacity for work will severely diminish. The tendency to fall into impoverished performance levels can happen when the positive regard needed by us all is lacking. This may cause the black client to feel depersonalization and out of control. As Basch (1989: 513) states: 'the feeling of controlling one's destiny to some reasonable extent is the essential psychological component of all aspects of life'. It is worth noting that studies conducted in the USA (Hamilton and Zanna, 1972; Katz et al., 1975) have shown that, for black people, positive relationships with co-workers tend to rate more highly in the degree of job satisfaction than for white people. Therefore, in a managerial position where positive peer relationships may determine occupational outcomes and future promotion opportunities, the need for supportive co-worker relationships may be even greater for black people.

Dickens and Dickens (1991) have discussed how newly recruited black managers inevitably experience a moderate to high degree of stress. Many white managers tend to see this onset of stress as typical of any new person, black or white, in a new job. However, Dickens and Dickens (1991) argued that the level and nature of stress was different for black people than for white people. The different concerns that arise are related to:

- how, as a black individual, they will fit into the organizational culture;
- how they will socially mix with white people;
- the amount and quality of informal and formal support that will be forthcoming;
- The degree of acceptance their qualifications and experience will achieve among their white peers and subordinates;
- The experience, felt or actual, of the stereotypical white boss/black subordinate role and its effect on interactions with white subordinates.

From this one can see the importance of having an appropriate, formalized organizational induction approach to black employees. This could take the form of mentoring arrangements, training opportunities as allowed under sections 35 and 37 of the 1976 Race Relations Act – and culturally sensitive induction or support programmes. These sections of the Act do not allow 'positive discrimination', which is illegal under the Act, but do allow training bodies or employing organizations to make provisions for special access to training opportunities under 'positive action arrangements'. The distinction between positive discrimination and positive action is technical, and those seeking information on this are advised to contact the Commission for Racial Equality.

Personal or institutional factors?

Existing counselling theory and training tend not to address adequately significance of cultural and 'racial difference', if they address it at all (Banks, 1999). How a counsellor responds to cultural and 'racial' difference is an issue that needs to be considered and planned for at conceptual and emotional levels and, where appropriate, at an organizational policy and procedure level. Brislin (1990) has documented that extensive intercultural contact can lead to stresses that affect people's physical and mental health. Berry (1990) has argued that one of the most obvious and frequently reported consequences of acculturation is that of social disintegration and personal crisis. He noted that 'at the individual level, hostility, uncertainty, identity confusion and depression may set in' (p. 246). Berry and Annis (1974) have identified what they referred to as 'acculturative stress', in which the stresses are identified as having their source in the process of acculturation and that feelings of confusion, anxiety, depression, marginality and alienation come to the fore. A heightened psychosomatic symptom level may also exist.

The term 'acculturation' has been mainly used in anthropological literature to refer to 'those phenomena which result when groups of individuals have different cultures and come into first hand contact with subsequent changes in the original pattern of either or both groups' (Redfield et al., 1936: 149). To be defined as acculturative stress, the changes which the individual experiences should be related in a systematic way to identified features of the acculturation process. Whereas some individuals may see changes as stresses, others may see the changes as benign or as opportunities to be pursued. Whether this concept alone is helpful in understanding the stresses black employees may face within an organization is contentious, and it certainly has limitations. This definition sees acculturation as a group phenomenon and to some extent may explain the difficulties that black employees experience at both the personal and occupational level in Britain working in white organizations with white organizational cultures, although not all black employees are likely to respond in the same way to occupational stress caused by acculturation. This stress response differs immensely from those occupational stresses caused by oppressive racist practice, where the end product is likely to be similar for all black employees. Fernando (1984) offers some helpful insight to stress counsellors for the latter:

> Treatment...is to encourage strategies for self-assertion and control over events – not a 'coming to terms' or changing cognitive sets: identifying racism as the restrictive yoke which prevents patients [clients] from controlling their environment lead to ways of encouraging resistance and self-assertion. (Fernando, 1984: 46)

The message is clear. There is a need to acknowledge the personal, political and institutional structural factors that black employees experience in stress related to racism. For the difficulty is not the stress but the racism. The strategies for counsellor involvement in institutional or racist discriminatory organizational practice are beyond the scope of this chapter. However, the available evidence confirms that perceptions of race and gender affect people's patterns of communication and interaction (Davis and Proctor, 1989; Henley, 1977), and employers may need to address organizational change issues (Dickens and Dickens, 1991) and initiate specific cultural awareness or anti-racist/equal opportunity training programmes.

For the stress counsellor, who may be expected to feed observations and outcomes into a forum that facilitates organizational change, knowledge of the positive, enabling aspects of the Race Relations Act 1976, as previously discussed, is useful, as is an awareness of the organization's equal opportunity policy (where this exists) and how black people may gain access to support networks or enhanced training opportunities. Reviewing personal experiences related to race and considering the black employee's reality are a must if counsellors are effectively to deliver a service and succeed in transcultural counselling, The challenge presented to white counsellors is great, but the potential gains in personal and professional growth are even greater.

References

Banks, N. (1991) 'Counselling black client groups: does existing Eurocentric theory apply?', *Counselling Psychology Review*, 2–7.

Banks, N. (1997) 'Social workers' perceptions of racial difference', *Social Services Research*, 1997, 1. University of Birmingham.

Banks, N. (1999) *White Counsellors Black Client Groups: Theory Research and Practice*. London: Ashgate.

Basch, M. (1989) Quoted in E. Pinderhughes, *Understanding Race Ethnicity and Power. The Key to Efficacy in Clinical Practice*. New York: Free Press.

Berry, J.W. (1990) 'Psychology of acculturation: understanding individuals moving between cultures', in R.W. Brislin (ed.) *Applied Cross-Cultural Psychology*. Cross Cultural Research and Methodology Series, Volume 14. London: Sage. pp. 232–253.

Berry, J.W. and Annis, R.C. (1974) 'Ecology, culture and psychological differentiation', *International Journal of Psychology*. 9: 173–193.

Bochner, S. (1983) 'The social psychology of cross-cultural relations', in S. Bochner (ed.), *Cultures in Contact: Studies in Cross-cultural Interaction*, vol. 1. Oxford: Pergamon.

Brislin, R.W. (1990) 'Applied cross-cultural psychology: an introduction', in R.W. Brislin (ed.), *Applied Cross-Cultural Psychology*. London: Sage.

Chaplin, J. (1989) 'Counselling and gender', in W. Dryden, D. Charles-Edwards and R. Wolfe (eds), *Handbook of Counselling in Britain*. London: Tavistock/Routledge.

Davis, L.E. and Proctor, E.K. (1989) *Race, Gender and Class Guidelines for Practice with Individuals, Families and Groups*. Englewood Cliffs, NJ: Prentice Hall.

Department of Employment (1991) 'Ethnic origins and the labour market', *Employment Gazette*, 99 (2): 52–9.

Dickens, F. and Dickens, J.B. (1991) *The Black Manager: Making it in the Corporate World*. New York: American Management Association.

Dollard, J., Doob, L.W., Miller, N.I., Mowrer, O.H. and Sears, R.R. (1939) *Frustration and Aggression*. New Haven, CT: Yale University Press.

Fernando, S. (1984) 'Racism as a cause of depression: transcultural psychiatry, racism and mental illness', *International Journal of Social Psychiatry*, 4IA9.

Grant, L.M., Biren, A.N., Nagda, B.A., Brabson, H.V., Chess, A.W. and Singh, A. (1983) 'Effects of social support and undermining on African American workers' perceptions of co-worker and supervisor relationships and psychological well being', *Social Work*, 38 (2): 158–64.

Hamilton, D. and Zanna, M. (1972) 'Different weighting of favourable and unfavourable attributes in impression of personality', *Journal of Experimental Research in Personality*, 6: 204–12.

Helms, J. (1990) *Black and White Racial Identity*. Westport: Greenwood Press.

Henley, N. (1977) *Body Politics: Power, Sex and Non-verbal Communication*. Englewood Cliffs, NJ: Prentice Hall.

Labour Research (1989) 'Racial equality at work: top firms fail the test', *Labour Research Survey*, November: 13–15.

Jacobs, M. (1989) *Psychodynamic Counselling in Action*. Beverly Hills, CA: Sage.

Katz, D., Gutek, B.A., Katz, R.L. and Barton, E. (1975) *Bureaucratic Encounters*. Ann Arbor: University of Michigan Press.

Little, A., Day, M. and Marshland, D. (1978) *Black Kids, White Kids. What Hope?* Leicester: National Youth Bureau.

Maslow, A. (1984) *Towards a Psychology of Being*. New York: Van Nostrand Reinhold.

Miller, R. and Dolan, P. (1971) *Race Awareness*. Oxford: Oxford University Press.

O'Reily, C. and Roberts, K. (1973) 'Job satisfaction among whites and non-whites: a cross-cultural approach', *Journal of Applied Psychology*, 57: 295–9.

PEP Study (1977) Quoted in D.J. Smith, *Racial Disadvantage in Britain*. Harmondsworth: Penguin.

Pinderhughes, E. (1989) *Understanding Race Ethnicity and Power. The Key to Efficacy in Clinical Practice.* New York: Free Press.

Redfield, R., Linton, R. and Herskovits, M. (1936) 'Outline for the study of acculturation', *American Anthropologist*, 38: 149–52.

Reik, T. (1948) *Listening with the Third Ear. The Inner Experience of the Psychoanalyst.* New York: Grove.

Rogers, C.R. (1962) 'The interpersonal relationship: the core of guidance', *Harvard Educational Review*, 132: 416–29.

Slocum, J. and Strawser, R. (1972) 'Racial differences in job attitudes', *Journal of Applied Psychology*, 56: 28–32.

Smith, D.J. (1977) *Radical Disadvantage in Britain.* London: Harmondsworth Penguin.

Sue, D.W. (1981) Counselling the Culturally Different: Theory and Practice. New York: Wiley.

Vontress, C.E. (1971) 'Racial differences: impediments to rapport', *Journal of Counselling Psychology*, 18: 1–13.

Discussion issues

1 What is 'institutionalized racism'?
2 How might counsellors and therapists miss or ignore the important effects of institutional or social forces that may impinge on the social reality and working environment of the black employee?
3 Prejudices can be overcome.
4 Why is the drop-out rate so high for black groups?

9

Crisis Counselling

Romeria Tidwell

Crises occur as part of everyday life. Every individual experiences periods when problems and changes are beyond his or her capacity to cope. For a sizeable proportion of low socio-economic status (SES) individuals, minority group members, or those considered 'out of the mainstream', stress is virtually a constant (Chandler et al., 1985). Because impoverishment, personal and institutional racism, migration and lack of acculturation cause many to have to face a host of stressful life events, crises are highly prevalent in the lives of those considered the underclass (Krieger and Sidney, 1996; Lazarus, 1991; Williams et al., 1997). Consequently, those of economically deprived groups, members of minority groups, and members from foreign countries have a great need for psychological counselling and it is being asserted that crisis counselling is a therapeutic 'fit' for such individuals (Chiu, 1996; Dovidio and Gaertner, 1998; Fishbach and Tidwell, 1993–4). *Crisis counselling*, directive, action-oriented, short-term intervention, is not only the most feasible form of treatment when money is an issue, but is perhaps the ideal medium for introducing groups and individuals to psychotherapy (Ponterotto, 1987; Ruiz and Ruiz, 1983; Vontress, 1988).

The two conditions that normally produce an emotional crisis, extremely difficult problems and lack of an appropriate support system, frequently characterize the lives of economically, socially disadvantaged and out-of-the-mainstream individuals. Hafen and Petersen's (1982) four-stage description of the development of a crisis captures well the vicious cycle in which many impoverished, minority group members and out-of-the-mainstream persons find themselves:

1 The person becomes anxious and stressed when a problem occurs.
2 The person's best methods of coping fail, so the problem continues.
3 As the person attempts other solutions, the stress and anxiety become worse.
4 The person gives up in the belief that nothing will have any effect.

By definition, crisis counselling is a process of short duration, an action-oriented approach designed to help the person martial available personal, spiritual, economic, and social resources in order to meet an immediate problem, which may or may not stem from long-standing conditions. It is assumed that crisis counselling comprises both the prevention of negative outcomes and the enhancement of personal growth. The goal of crisis counselling, 'psychological first aid', is to help the individual in crisis return to a higher level of functioning and achieve some positive change (Hendricks, 1985; Talmon, 1990; Walter and Peller, 1992).

The two types of observation that have strongly influenced the development of crisis counselling techniques point directly to the appropriateness of crisis counselling for members of the underclass and individuals considered out of the mainstream of society. Traditional forms of psychotherapy have been found to be inappropriate in some contexts, because most of them are designed to promote major changes in personality and behaviour. Crisis counselling, on the other hand, is an attempt to address the client's experience of being overwhelmed by events and situations. Extended forms of treatment, however appropriate for members of other SES groups and those clearly in the mainstream, may not provide the most powerful, practical means of quickly reducing the underclass patient's tendency to panic, withdraw and become psychologically and/or physically dysfunctional.

Certain situations and circumstances, some internal (e.g. severe illness) and others external (e.g. loss of employment), tend to precipitate a crisis and people experiencing a crisis generally behave in fairly predictable ways (Getz et al., 1974). A crisis is, first and foremost, a particular type of *reaction* to life events; one person might take in stride an event or circumstance that precipitates a crisis for another (Pliner and Brown, 1985). Nevertheless, once the crisis reactions begins, it follows a similar course from person to person. Largely avoiding questions about the ultimate causes of the client's difficulties, crisis counselling takes advantage of the predictability of the crisis reaction to offer a form of direct relief in a specific problem situation.

Crisis counselling provides the immediate help that a person in crisis needs in order to re-establish equilibrium. The goal of crisis counselling is not complete reorganization of the client's personality, but restoration of the client's problem-solving capacity (Sandoval, 1988). The primary aim is to effect change by increasing the client's awareness of his or her behaviour and thinking. Rather than leading to changes in the structure of the personality or the family, crisis counselling leads, when it is successful, to changes in the current pattern of functioning (Talmon, 1990).

In crisis counselling, the therapist almost always assumes a directive stance, the role of active participant (Fishbach and Tidwell, 1993–4). The general intervention strategy recognizes the primacy of taking action (Sandoval, 1985). It is best if the therapist can intervene immediately, soon after the person begins experiencing him- or herself as in crisis. In listening to the facts of the situation, the therapist engaging in crisis counselling usually attempts to reflect the client's feelings and help the client accept the events that have precipitated the crisis. Encouragement is given to the client to have short discussions about the problem situation and to minimize dwelling on the problem in a way that would prolong this state of counselling. The therapist neither supports blaming not gives false reassurance. Instead, the counsellor acknowledges the client's desire for action by quickly clarifying and defining goals that will lead to actions. The goals tend to be short term rather than long term. Emphasis is placed on breaking out of stuck patterns. Both goals and ways to achieve goals are concrete and specific. The therapist generally tries to enlist the client in focused problem solving directed at re-establishing the client's social support network, strengthening his or her self-concept and encouraging self-reliance. By helping the client re-establish equilibrium, a successful intervention triggers action on the part of the client to resolve or substantially reduce the problems that brought him or her into therapy (Cruz and Littrell, 1998; Sandoval, 1985).

Crisis counselling meets the needs of many impoverished individuals, minority group individuals and individuals considered out of the mainstream because it is concise, action oriented and incorporates a solution-focused approach with a limited time frame (Talmon, 1990; Walter and Peller, 1992). A short, specified time span for therapy appears to be appropriate for many underclass and minority group members (Mays, 1985). Crisis counselling is both briefer and more limited in scope than traditional types of counselling and psychotherapy; a duration of from one to eight sessions is the norm.

Traditionally, one of the psychotherapist's major goals is to prevent the client from becoming too dependent on him or her. In crisis counselling, on the other hand, there are times when the counsellor or therapist will encourage the client's dependency, because such dependency is the best way to help the client survive an extreme short-term disequilibrium. The crisis counsellor listens less and talks more. The greater amount of talk by the therapist is consistent with his or her active role in providing information and devising problem-solving strategies (Sandoval, 1985).

Crisis counselling and traditional methods are driven by different sets of ethical and practical considerations. Crisis counselling rarely involves techniques that are chiefly relevant to personality change, including confrontation, self-disclosure and modelling (Egan, 1986; Sandoval, 1988). Because time is usually at a premium, crisis counselling is more goal directed than other types of therapy (Aguilera and Messick, 1978).

Crisis counselling and the underclass

The differences between crisis counselling and more traditional forms of psychotherapy point directly to the needs of the underclass. There are a number of reasons why non-directive, long-term techniques are likely to be ineffective for low SES individuals, minority group members and those out-of-the-mainstream individuals, who do not identify well with the sometimes ethnocentric goals of traditional psychotherapy (Tyler et al., 1985).

Moreover, crisis counselling would appear to be especially appropriate for members of groups subject to a high frequency of stressful events (Krieger and Sidney, 1996; Lazarus, 1991; Williams et al., 1997).

Persistence in psychotherapy presupposes a kind of faith in the face of seemingly overwhelming immediate problems. A person who is 'stressed out' is not likely to have such patience with techniques that can only promise an eventual lessening of stressful reactions. The relation between actual life events and the feelings of anxiety that characterize the crisis experience are often not clear. An emotional crisis is a natural response to truly unpleasant events. In some instances a crisis reflects deep-seated emotional problems; in others, racial harassment, for example, it is not clear that the crisis experience results from hidden emotional problems.

Crisis counselling is an accessible type of psychotherapy, a form of help and self-help relatively new to some communities and individuals. Crisis counselling does not demand self-identification as 'sick' or 'troubled' – a distinct advantage when potential clients are predisposed to see a visit to a psychotherapist as an admission of craziness. Many individuals and cultures are willing to accept help with a problem, but do not consider themselves in need of psychotherapeutic treatment.

Crisis counselling presents an accessible form of psychotherapy that does not depend heavily on traditional Western concepts of self-analysis. The techniques for treating crisis depend little on theoretical assumptions that, although they appear to be adequate to many of those steeped in western cultural traditions, are probably inadequate for use in describing the universal conditions of emotional distress. From the beginning, for example, proponents of psychodynamic theory have had limited success, at best, when they have attempted to apply its terms to other cultures. Crisis counselling, oriented to the present problem rather than to a set of culturally contaminated values about the structure of psychopathology, is highly suitable for many individuals who, by definition, fall out of the cultural mainstream.

To exist outside the mainstream of society implies nothing negative in itself, and undoubtedly there is much to be said for separation from society's norms. Such separation, whether it is by choice or by deliberate exclusion, does imply a higher risk of poverty. Poverty, in turn, vastly increases the probability of life events that actually threaten the social and even the physical integrity of the individual. Job insecurity, family dislocations and the high probability of being the victim of violent crime are all parts of the underclass experience.

Crisis counselling has the potential to bring help to individuals and groups who need counselling but are either unwilling or unable to get traditional psychotherapy. Crisis counselling is inexpensive and brief. Because it is symptom oriented, crisis counselling may appeal to impoverished individuals, who often have neither the time or the patience for other forms of therapy. Beyond these considerations, the universality of the crisis experience provides a common meeting ground for counsellor and counsellee (Aguilera and Messick, 1978).

Conclusion

An emotional crisis is a turning point, a moment of 'psychological equilibrium in a person who confronts a hazardous circumstance that for him constitutes an important problem which he can ... neither escape nor solve with his customary problem solving resources' (Caplan, 1964: p. 53). Tension and anxiety increase along with the individual's feelings of helplessness. Being thrown off balance in this way can be very painful, but it can also lead the person to new ways of coping and new ways of being. At its best, crisis counselling can be part of important personal change. If an emotional crisis is, as has been suggested, a point of transition, the successful resolution of the crisis is more than 'a return to normalcy'. It is a change to more effective ways of addressing the challenges of living.

Crisis counselling for the underclass, minority group members, and those out-of-the-mainstream individuals and groups can, therefore, involve helping such persons take a new form of control over their lives. While there are some situations in which crisis counselling is not suitable – for problems such as potential suicide, sexual abuse, eating disorders and other severe situations – the individual who resolves a problem that seemingly felt overwhelming is likely to come away from the counselling experience feeling stronger than he or she did before the crisis began (Talmon, 1990). A change in the basic pattern of functioning for the low SES patient, the minority group person, or the out-of-the-mainstream individual may lead the client in the direction of overcoming other situations that keep him or her at a disadvantage and from experiencing the stressors associated with physical and psychological distress (Krieger and Sidney, 1996; Lazarus, 1991; Williams et al., 1997).

References

Aguilera, D. and Messick, J. (1978) *Crisis Intervention*. Saint Louis, MO: C.V. Mosby Company.

Caplan, G. (1964) *Principles of Preventive Psychiatry*. New York: Basic Books.

Chandler, L.A., Million, M.D. and Shermis, M.D. (1985) 'The incidence of stressful life events of elementary school-aged children', *American Journal of Community Psychology*, 13: 743–44.

Chiu, T.L. (1996) 'Problems caused by mental health professionals worldwide by increasing multicultural populations and proposed solutions', *Journal of Multicultural Counseling and Development*, 24: 129–40.

Cruz, J. and Littrell, J.M. (1998) 'Brief counseling with Hispanic American college students', *Journal of Multicultural Counseling and Development*, 26: 227–39.

Dovidio, J.E. and Gaertner, S.L. (1998) 'On the nature of contemporary prejudice: The causes, consequences, and challenges of aversive racism', in J. Eberhardt and S.T. Fiske (eds), *Confronting Racism: The Problem and the Response*, pp. 3–32. Newbury Park, CA: Sage.

Egan, G. (1986) *The Skilled Helper*, 3rd edn. Monterey, CA: Brooks/Cole.

Fishbach, S.M. and Tidwell, R. (1993–4) 'Burnout among crisis-intervention counselors and its relationship to social supports', *California Journal for Counseling and Development*, 14: 11–19.

Getz, W., Wiesen, A., Sue, S. and Ayers, A. (1974) *Fundamentals of Crisis Counseling.* Lexington, MA: Lexington Books.

Hafen, Q.B. and Petersen, B. (1982) *The Crisis Intervention Handbook.* Englewood Cliffs, NJ: Prentice Hall.

Hendricks, E.J. (1985) *Crisis Intervention: Contemporary Issues for Onsite Interveners.* Springfield, IL: Charles C. Thomas.

Krieger, N. and Sidney, S. (1996) 'Racial discrimination and blood pressure: the CARDIA study of young black and white women and men', *American Journal of Public Health,* 86: 1370–78.

Lazarus, R.S. (1991) *Emotion and Adaptation.* New York: Oxford University Press.

Mays, V.M. (1985) 'The black American and psychotherapy: the dilemma', *Psychotherapy,* 22: 379–88.

Pliner, J.W. and Brown, D. (1985) 'Projections of reactions to stress and preference for helpers among students from four ethnic groups', *Journal of College Student Personnel,* 26: 147–51.

Ponterotto, J. (1987) 'Counselling Mexican Americans: a multimodal approach', *Journal of Counseling and Development,* 66: 20–23.

Ruiz, P. and Ruiz, P.P. (1983) 'Treatment compliance among Hispanics', *Journal of Operational Psychiatry,* 14: 112–14.

Sandoval, J. (1985) 'Crisis counseling: conceptualization and general principles', *School Psychology Review,* 14: 257–65.

Sandoval, J. (1988) *Crisis Counseling, Intervention, and Prevention in the Schools,* pp. 3–19. New Jersey: Lawrence Earlbaum.

Talmon, M. (1990) *Single-session Therapy: Maximizing the Effect of the First (and often only) Therapeutic Encounter.* San Francisco, CA: Jossey-Bass.

Tyler, F.B., Sussewell, D.R. and Williams-McCoy, J. (1985) 'Ethnic validity in psychotherapy', *Psychotherapy,* 22: 311–20.

Vontress, C. (1988) 'An existential approach to cross-cultural counseling', *Journal of Multicultural Counseling and Development,* 16: 73–83.

Walter, J.L. and Peller, J.E. (1992) *Becoming Solution-focused in Brief Therapy.* New York: Brunner/Mazel.

Williams, D.R., Yu, Y., Jackson, J.S. and Anderson, N. (1997) 'Racial differences in physical and mental health', *Journal of Health Psychology,* 2: 335–51.

Discussion issues

1 What are your thoughts about the term 'the underclass'? Is the term applicable to Britain?
2 What is a crisis?
3 Why might crisis counselling benefit minority groups?
4 The crisis counsellor listens less and talks more.

10

Counselling Foreign Students

A Review of Strategies

P.L.S. Khoo, M.H. Abu-Rasain and G. Hornby

This chapter focuses on the unique counselling needs of foreign students as reflected from a review of the literature. As more and more students from developing countries opt to further their education in the west, knowledge about counselling foreign students is of increasing interest. Distinctive aspects of foreign student clients and the typical problems faced by them are described. The issues which need to be addressed and the competencies which need to be developed in order to effectively counsel foreign students are discussed. Finally, specific strategies for counselling foreign students are suggested in the context of general guidelines for cross-cultural counselling.

> When international students arrive at overseas universities, the circumstances suddenly and simultaneously impose a variety of competing and sometimes contradictory roles that must be learned. When the requirements of those roles are realistically perceived and effectively learned, the student's experience is likely to be successful, but when the roles are not accommodated, the resulting identity diffusion and role conflict may affect the student's emotional well-being, and present serious obstacles to the achievement of educational objectives. (Pedersen, 1991: 10)

Even though international students are from a whole variety of countries and cultures, they are expected to conform to the culture of their host country. This is not much of a problem for students from western countries, but it can prove difficult for students from developing countries whose customs are often so different from their host country's. This chapter considers counselling for foreign students, especially those from developing countries. That there is a need for such counselling is suggested by reports such as that by Banham on the high proportion of mental breakdowns among Nigerian students at British universities (as cited in Sen, 1970). Getting the most out of their time in the host country depends on the foreign students' ability to adapt to their new socio-cultural setting and their ability to get along with others (Sen, 1970). The faster they adjust, the faster they can get down to studying.

Distinctive aspects of foreign student clients

Foreign students are people in transition

Foreign students will only be in the host country temporarily. They are in a state of transition having left the security of their home country to come to a foreign land to achieve their academic goal. Although this phase of their lives will only last for a few years, it can be both trying and traumatic. Once in the host country, foreign students tend to question their purpose and identity. In addition to dealing with changes in personal growth, they also have to contend with an alien environment (d'Ardenne and Mahtani, 1989).

> Foreign students must decide where they want to be on a continuum between functional adjustment to the host culture – just learning to do what they must do in order to get by – and assimilation – taking as much of the host culture as possible and making it their own. (Thomas & Althen, 1989: 206)

Foreign students have different basic assumptions and values

Foreign students in western countries often have trouble adjusting to the informal nature of the locals. Another complaint is that domestic students are always so busy that they find it difficult to make friends with them. Foreign students are mostly from cultures which are quite different. They come from societies where people are integrally related with others and everyone is expected to conform. Fernandez (1988) says that Asian children are brought up in a society where filial piety and deference to elders are stressed. Nigerians too are brought up to respect their elders and those in authority (Idowu, 1985). Often in their countries, there is a hierarchy in which males are seen as superior. According to Sue and Sue (1990), relationships in traditional Asian cultures tend to be more authoritarian and hierarchical and the father is effectively the ruler of the family. Theirs is a culture where only close friends and relatives can be trusted and it would be inappropriate and even dangerous to reveal oneself to others.

According to Pedersen (1991), foreign students rely more on fellow nationals for help with personal problems since counselling would result in a loss of status. Many foreign students feel that their problems cannot be solved by talking to a counsellor, attending workshops, reading self-help books or by practising new behaviours. They may believe that their problems are fated to occur and it is beyond the control of others to solve them. According to Sue and Sue (1990), Third World groups tend to have an external locus of control which means that they believe that actions and their reinforcing events occur independently of each other and the future is decided more by chance and luck. They believe that their problems must be borne. Therefore, counsellors who deal with foreign students may first need to convince them that something can be done about their problems.

Foreign students are living in an unfamiliar setting

Although all students are under pressure to excel in their studies, foreign students may have other problems to contend with as well. They face difficulties with the language and the different education system. On top of that, they may also have trouble with immigration authorities and financial problems. In a study conducted by Xia (1991) on the adjustment process of Asian students at the University of Wisconsin, it was found that Indonesian and Chinese students experienced more problems with the English language, finances and religious issues while Malaysian students faced problems with language, studies, finances and religion as well as with immigration authorities. Moon (1991) found that Korean students, on the other hand, found the most difficulty with English and finances.

Foreign students have a distinctive social support system

Foreign students typically have a different social support system from domestic students. Not only are their family and friends far away, they may also not understand the experiences that the student is going through. So, the student may turn to their fellow nationals in the same university for help. Foreign students tend to create a subculture of fellow nationals as their primary support system (Pedersen, 1991). Furnham and Alibhai (1985) found that foreign students preferred their co-national friends to help them with emotional difficulties, because of language and cultural similarities. Pedersen (1975, as cited in Pedersen, 1991) found that most of the 781 foreign students at the University of Minnesota went to a fellow national for help with personal problems. This was reported to be because fellow nationals were accessible and acceptable to them as helpers.

Foreign students have different communication styles

Even the way foreign students communicate is often different and this style should be taken into consideration during counselling sessions as it does play a part in developing a good relationship. Their communicative styles may differ in terms of vocal volume, eye contact, turn taking in conversation and degree of directness as well as differing types of persuasive argument. Even the choice of room, the furniture, decor, the arrangement of the chairs and lighting can affect the counselling process (d'Ardenne and Mahtani, 1989).

Foreign students may not share the counsellor's conception of the counsellor's role

Counsellors are trained to listen and help clients explore their concerns and feelings. In this way, the counsellor and client will seek a solution together. The typical foreign student client on the other hand expects counsellors to express their opinions and do most of the talking. For example, it is reported that Nigerian students' upbringing conflicts with the method of counselling that emphasizes self-help. They expect to be given a 'cure' by the counsellor (Idowu, 1985). When Pedersen (1991) reviewed the literature on counselling expectations of foreign students, he found that Chinese and Iranian students had higher expectations of counsellor empathy while African and Iranian students had higher expectations of directiveness, expertise and concreteness. Foreign students, on the whole, had higher expectations of counsellor nurturance. Pedersen (1991) also mentioned that their sample of Chinese students were less motivated and felt less responsible for their improvement. Mau and Jepsen (1988) found that Chinese and American students had different attitudes toward counsellors and counselling processes, in that Chinese students saw the counsellors as directive and as the decision-maker when compared to American students.

According to d'Ardenne and Mahtani (1989) therapists generally prefer clients who are young, attractive, verbal, intelligent and successful (the YAVIS syndrome). Clients from minority groups are often seen as less attractive, less verbal, unintelligent and less successful. This is also stressed by Sundberg (1981, as cited in Sue and Sue, 1990) who commented that therapy is perceived as not for the quiet, ugly, old, indigent and dissimilar culturally (the QUOID syndrome). Sue and Sue (1972, as cited in Sue and Sue, 1990) identified three possible causes of conflict for Third World groups:

1 Counsellors expect clients to be open to a certain degree.
2 Counsellors expect clients to talk about their personal problems.
3 Counselling is seen as ambiguous.

Asian cultures associate maturity and wisdom with the ability to control emotions and feelings, which gives the counsellor a negative impression of the client. Therapy is often referred to as 'talking therapies' which prefer clients to be verbal, articulate and able to express emotions and feelings clearly. This potentially places the minority client at a disadvantage. According to d'Ardenne and Mahtani (1989), the counsellor and client need to discuss the counselling process and the counsellor's role, as well as the client's responsibility and interaction in the counselling relationship to avoid misunderstandings about their respective roles.

According to Sue and Sue (1990) the reason minority group individuals underutilize and prematurely terminate counselling is because the services offered are usually inappropriate for culturally different clients. They suggest that it is important to provide counsellors with educational experiences that encourage sensitivity and the appreciation of the history and needs of the culturally different. Sue and Sue (1990) state that mental health professionals are responsible for:

(a) facing up to biases, stereotypes, values and assumptions about human behaviour;
(b) being aware of the world view of the culturally different client;
(c) developing appropriate help-giving practices that take into consideration the culture and background of the culturally different client.

Problems faced by foreign students

The problems faced by foreign students are numerous and varied. They have been addressed by several authors including Elsey and Kinnell (1990), Livingstone (1960), Sen (1970) and Thomas and Althen (1989). The major problems are discussed below.

Adjustment to new culture

A typical problem faced by foreign students is adjusting to a new culture. According to Thomas and Althen (1989) cultural adjustment is a 'psychological process that focuses on the attitudinal and emotional adjustment of the individual to the new environment' (p. 220). The authors go on to say that most writers generally agree on three distinct stages of adjustment. The first stage or the *honeymoon stage* is when individuals are excited by the novel experience. Then comes the second stage or the *crisis stage* which is when culture shock is most intense. At this stage, individuals are confused as they encounter new values, behaviours, beliefs and lifestyles. The third stage is the *recovery stage*. This is when individuals begin to appreciate and understand the new culture. Oberg (1960, cited in Thomas and Althen, 1989) added a fourth stage which is the *adjustment stage*. This is when individuals begin to function effectively in the new culture.

Livingstone (1960) also suggested dividing the experiences of foreign students into four stages or phases. The first three phases are similar to the stages mentioned above. The first phase, which is the *spectator phase*, is filled with curiosity, expectation and enjoyment. The second phase is the *involvement phase*, where students are confronted with the demands of the environment on them. The third or the *coming-to-terms phase* is marked by achievements which restore their confidence. The final phase which is the *pre-departure phase* is filled with anxiety as foreign students prepare to return to their home countries.

Thomas and Althen (1989) use a conceptualization of cultural adjustment which is based on the understanding that different personalities will respond differently to new cultures, a view which is also taken by Sen (1970) in her study of overseas students and nurses. This becomes clear when the way different students deal with the same situation is considered. While some may meet it as a challenge to be overcome, there are others who become hostile or shrink into their shells.

Culture shock refers to the negative aspect of cultural adjustment. It is the normal process of adaptation to cultural stress. Its symptoms include psychological strain, a sense of loss, rejection, confusion, surprise, anxiety and feelings of impotence (d'Ardenne and Mahtani, 1989). Adler (1975, as cited in Thomas and Althen, 1989) suggested that there are five stages in the development of culture shock. They are the *contact stage*, the *disintegration stage*, the *reintegration stage*, the *autonomy stage* and the *independence stage*. In the contact stage differences seem intriguing. During the disintegration stage, cultural differences are obvious and start to intrude on the individual's well-being. The reintegration stage finds differences rejected and the individual preoccupied with likes and dislikes. In the autonomy stage, the individual is able to negotiate most new situations. The independence stage is when differences and similarities are valued positively and are accepted.

Academic differences

Foreign students encounter a different education system which requires different study skills. On top of having to adjust to a new academic system, they have to live up to the expectations of family and friends back home. As Sen (1970) noted, foreign students are under immense internal and external pressure to succeed. Livingstone (1960) said that it would be disastrous for a foreign student to return to his or her home with a poor degree, but to fail to get a degree altogether would be a shame almost too much to bear. For example, according to Fernandez (1988), within Asian societies achievement and education are status symbols, which is why Asians tend to be perfectionists when it comes to studies and are burdened with shame when they fail.

Conflicts among fellow nationals

Political, religious and social conflicts may arise among fellow nationals in the university community. It can be serious enough to divide the community. When this happens, the students' studies will be affected. The counsellor should never assume that all fellow nationals get along just because they are away from home (Thomas and Althen, 1989).

Impact of developments in home countries

Changes in the foreign students' home country which occur while they are away studying, whether political, economic or social, will affect them (Thomas and Althen, 1989). For example, the Gulf War created many difficulties for students from the Middle Eastern countries involved.

Cross-cultural male–female relationships

Students from male-dominated societies may find difficulties adjusting to a society where male and female roles are largely regarded as interchangeable. Misunderstandings could arise in daily interactions whether socially or romantically. This is because of the different ideas about 'proper' male–female relationships in host countries (Pedersen, 1991).

Mental disturbances

Social isolation, depression and paranoia are common mental disturbances faced by some foreign students. These are considered to be due to culture shock as well as the adjustment stress faced by such students. This is illustrated by foreign students who face a complicated series of crises connected to entering university and adjusting to a foreign culture as well as keeping in touch with their own identity (Pedersen, 1991).

Financial difficulty

When foreign students face monetary problems, they have limited avenues to turn to. They are neither allowed to work nor eligible for state financial aid programmes. This can be very stressful for the students. Idowu (1985) and PEP (1965) found that the most severe problems experienced by African students were financial.

Anxiety from fear of immigration authorities

Students who live in the host country for a specific purpose have to deal with various authorities such as the police, the Home Office or immigration authorities, because they need to register their address and to obtain or extend a visa. Therefore, some students live in fear of being deported if they violate immigration regulations.

Stressful relationships with locals

Another potential source of anxiety for foreign students occurs when they have less harmonious relationships with academic advisers, roommates and landlords. These difficulties can arise from misunderstandings of the appropriate behaviour in particular situations (Pedersen, 1991).

Racial discrimination

This is another problem faced by some foreign students. According to Sen (1970), African, Asian and West Indian students may experience more prejudice and discrimination because of their colour. Racial discrimination mostly occurs in public places like shops, buses and dance halls.

Dealing with newfound freedom

Students from a sheltered and structured society sometimes find themselves overwhelmed with a sense of freedom which they may or may not want. From a society where they have to conform, they are at a loss when they are suddenly faced with this newfound freedom (Thomas and Althen, 1989).

Dealing with death of family or friends back home

It is traumatic to lose a relative or friend, but it is even more so when one is unable to return home and take part in the ceremonial rites and grieve in the customary way (Thomas and Althen, 1989).

Deciding where to live after graduation

It can be quite stressful for foreign students to decide whether to stay in the host country or to go back to their home countries at the conclusion of their studies. They have to weigh the pros and cons carefully before making a final decision (Thomas and Althen, 1989).

Anxieties about returning home

Problems of re-entry are mentioned by Pedersen (1991). For those who have decided to go home, they may face particular problems about readjusting to their own cultures. This is because they have probably changed in their time abroad, whereas their families and friends typically expect them to be the same as when they left.

Problems foreign students bring to counselling

The problems foreign students typically face can be discerned from the problems they bring to counselling. Littlewood (1992) suggests that non-Europeans prefer to express their distress as either physical or religious rather than psychological problems. According to Fernandez (1988), South East Asians are reserved and shy about personal problems because they do not want to be looked down upon. Idowu (1985) says that disclosing personal problems to a counsellor is seen by Africans not only as a sign of weakness, but also as divulging family secrets. Studies conducted by Tanaka-Matsumi and Marsella (1976) and Kleinman (1977) suggest that when students suffer from somatic complaints without an organic basis, they may in fact be experiencing depression.

According to Church (1982) the most prevalent problems reported by foreign students have to do with language, finances, their studies, homesickness and adjusting to social customs. Foreign students usually seek assistance with problems that they feel are acceptable to discuss with someone outside their circle of family and close friends. These problems include those that concern work, finances or immigration laws. They seldom begin discussions with a personal problem. For Nigerians, personal matters can only be discussed with family and friends (Idowu, 1985). So, in many cases, counsellors may have to spend more time developing trust and a closer relationship before they can delve deeper to get to the root of the problem.

Issues in counselling foreign students

According to Thomas and Althen (1989), there are four issues that arise when counselling foreign student clients.

Cultural stereotyping

It is human nature to generalize about other groups of people with whom one has limited or superficial contact. This applies to counsellors who deal with foreign students as well. Their training provides little exposure to muticultural counselling and as a result, the problem of counsellor stereotyping arises. Some negative stereotypes of foreign students are their poor command of English, their clannish nature, and their tendency to be manipulative. Some positive stereotypes are that foreign students are intelligent, motivated, courteous, polite and conscientious. The problem of counsellor stereotyping can be decreased with counsellors becoming more aware of their own stereotypes of foreign students and by finding ways to overcome them.

Factors affecting foreign students' situation

Every foreign student is different. A foreign student's situation is a function of a number of factors. They include cultural background, personality, the country of origin, the number of fellow nationals in the university community, the local community's reception of foreign students, social status at home, age, English language proficiency, amount of time in host country, availability of suitable food and the opportunity to perform religious practices.

Difficulty in identifying the source of problems

In cross-cultural counselling, it is more difficult to diagnose the problem. This is because cultural factors have to be taken into consideration as well. A foreign student's problem could be due to a combination of intercultural problems, interpersonal problems as well as pathological disorders.

Although counsellors should be sensitive to cultural differences, there is such a thing being too culturally sensitive. This is when counsellors attribute everything to cultural differences. Counsellors must therefore be balanced in their approach and achieve 'cultural competence' (see later in this chapter).

Doubts about appropriateness of conventional western approaches to counselling

Counsellors may have doubts about the suitability of western approaches in counselling foreign students. For example, Carl Rogers's person-centred approach is generally considered to be less effective with foreign clients. This is because the approach sees clients as being in control whereas foreign students tend to have an external locus of control (Fernandez, 1988). Foreign clients typically want firm guidance and to be told what to do.

Developing competencies for counselling foreign students

> Counsellors cannot be experts on all the world's cultures, but they can develop a sound understanding of their own cultural values and the way their own culture affects people from elsewhere. (Thomas and Althen, 1989: 209)

Parker (1988) learned three concepts that helped him become an effective cross-cultural counsellor. First, counsellors should be aware of their own attitudes towards minorities and change the negative ones. Second, counsellors should have knowledge about the cultures of minority groups. Third, counsellors must develop counselling skills which are consistent with the goals of minority clients. In addition to that, Parker (1988) suggested ways to develop sensitivity, knowledge and skill. They include becoming personally involved with minority groups, reading ethnic literature, practising counselling ethnic minorities and exploring personal feeling and beliefs about minorities.

Sabnani et al. (1991) suggested that there are five stages in the development of the white counsellors' competencies in cross-cultural counselling. In the first stage, there is a lack of awareness of one's own culture as well as other ethnic cultures. In the second stage, there is awareness of one's stereotypes and racist feelings of superiority and its influence on members of ethnic groups. In the third stage, there is an inclination to over-identify with minority groups. The fourth stage sees a withdrawal into one's own culture. The fifth stage is the redefinition and integration stage where one develops an identity which incorporates 'whiteness'.

Paul and Anne Pedersen (1989) suggest the cultural grid as a dynamic approach to cross-cultural counselling. According to them, it 'provides a means of understanding and describing a person's intended and culturally learned expectations and values' (p. 133). Its advantage is that it increases the accurate assessment of a person's behaviour in the context of that person's culture. The cultural gird identifies an individual's 'personal cultural orientation' by combining personal cognitive categories with social system variables within the individual's intrapersonal perspective. The grid also analyses the interpersonal perspective between two individuals by separating cultural and personal elements of the relationship.

According to Barker (1990), the basic skills needed to satisfactorily handle problems faced by foreign students are the ability to listen, the ability to observe, the use of body language and the ability to ask effective questions. According to Sue and Sue (1990), a culturally skilled counsellor is one who views cultural differences as something positive to be addressed.

The most comprehensive consideration of this issue has been provided by Sue et al. (1992) who have proposed 31 competencies which specify attitudes, skills and knowledge needed for effective cross-cultural counselling. These concentrate on three aspects of counsellor functioning: counsellors being aware of their own values and biases; counsellors being aware of the culture and background of their clients; and counsellors needing to acquire appropriate cross-cultural interventions strategies. These are outlined below.

1 *Counsellors have to be aware of their own values and biases.* They need to explore their own values and respect differences that exist between them and their foreign student clients. This is important because counsellors who are insensitive to their values may impose them on their minority clients.

   They need to be conscious of their own race and culture. Being knowledgeable of how discrimination, stereotyping and race may affect them personally, counsellors will recognize how these can affect their clients and the counselling process. They need also to be comfortable with the differences between themselves and their clients regarding culture, race and beliefs.

   They need to check their communication style when they are dealing with their clients, because breakdowns in communication may be attributed to the dynamic between them and their clients (Thomas and Lago, 1989).

2 *Counsellors need to be aware of the culture and background of their clients.* Obviously, counsellors cannot be experts in every culture, but they should acquire minimum knowledge of their clients' cultures. Klineberg (1985: 34) pointed out that:

> Cultural factors are important to counsellors, and they have the responsibility of learning all they can about the cultural background of their clients. It is too much to ask that they become specialists on all the cultures of the world; it should not be impossible for them, however, to become aware of

the range of values and patterns of behaviour of which human societies and individuals are capable and to learn as much as they can about the particular ethnic groups that constitute their clientele.

3 *Counsellors need to acquire appropriate cross-cultural intervention strategies and adapt a range of helping responses to the needs of their clients.* They should respect indigenous help that can be given to the clients from their own community, because such help may take place in religious contexts (Egan, 1990).

Counsellors need to be aware that psychological tests which are used in the counselling process have biases, because many of them are standardized for specific cultures. They should be aware of the support system outside the counselling process, because many studies have found that foreign students preferred a fellow national to help them with personal problems (Furnham and Alibhai, 1985; Pedersen, 1991).

Counsellors need to be able to send and receive both verbal and non-verbal messages as accurately and appropriately as possible. Ivey et al. (1987) suggested a model to enable counsellors to be effective in multicultural counselling. This model emphasizes careful listening and attending skills.

Effective multicultural counsellors need to seek possible resources that can help them in their job, for example, referral to traditional helpers or professionals from the same culture as their clients. In addition, Pedersen (1991) emphasized the importance of informal counselling as a helpful resource to be used with culturally different clients.

Strategies for effective counselling with foreign students

The following are modifications in style and approach that western-trained counsellors can incorporate to be more effective in counselling foreign students (Thomas and Althen, 1989).

Modifying communicative style

Counsellors can modify their communicative styles to adapt to those of their clients in order to make them feel more comfortable. Some of the things to consider are vocal volume, form of interaction, length of acceptable silence, length of conversational turn, eye contact and degree of explicitness and openness. This is mentioned by d'Ardenne and Mahtani, (1989). According to them, the counsellor needs to determine the client's basic interpersonal skills and communication skills as well as particular abilities that are characteristic of collectivist cultures. They also emphasize the importance of non-verbal signals in communication.

Modifying counselling strategies

In order to decide on the best treatment strategy to use, the counsellor should know the client's cultural values. A study by Thomas (1985, cited in Thomas and Althen, 1989), found that counsellors who paid attention to the wants, wishes and desires of family and community as they related to a student client were considered more effective and culturally aware. According to Sue and Sue (1990) many cultures view the psychosocial unit of operation as the family, group or collective society. When dealing with foreign students, counsellors should be conscious of the foreign students' need to be identified with their family and community. This would go a long way in helping their clients.

Modifying counselling styles and client expectations

A more directive approach tends to work better with foreign students. This is because foreign students typically like to go to an expert to be told what to do. According to d'Ardenne and Mahtani (1989), Asians may not respond well to a reflective approach that focuses on feelings. Therefore, in order to deal more competently with foreign student clients, counsellors should not only be prepared to modify their styles, but also to examine their clients' expectations of counselling.

Explaining the adjustment process

Explaining to foreign student clients that it is normal to experience unhappiness, loneliness and frustration when adjusting to a new environment may help them deal more positively with the experience.

Dealing with adjustment-related depression

Therapeutic techniques based on cognitive and behavioural models of depression can be used with foreign students undergoing adjustment stress. The objective of cognitive therapy is to change negative, self-defeating cognitions. This will enable the individual to 'recognize the association between dysfunctional thinking and his or her own feelings and behaviours' (Coleman and Beck, 1981, as quoted in Thomas and Althen, 1989: 234). One of the goals of behavioural therapy, on the other hand, is to increase the client's activity level. This is based on the assumption that more activity will increase the probability of positive reinforcement from the surroundings. Other aims are controlling behavioural excesses, like excessive negative thoughts as well as helping to enhance the students' social skills.

Addressing presenting concerns first

Foreign students usually seek counselling with problems that concern their studies, although their underlying personal problems are often their major concern. Counsellors should address the presenting problem first before moving on to more personal issues.

Acknowledging cultural differences

Acknowledging the cultural difference of both counsellor and client from the very beginning can go a long way in helping the working relationship. The counsellor should acknowledge the cultural values of the foreign student client.

General guidelines for cross-cultural counselling

These suggestions are selected from those recommended by the American Psychological Association (1993) in the counselling of ethnic, linguistic, and culturally diverse populations. Those listed are particularly relevant to the counselling of foreign students.

1 Counsellors should educate their clients on the goals, expectations and scope of counselling as well as the counsellor's own orientation.
2 Counsellors should be aware of research and issues related to their clients, which in this case are foreign students.
3 Counsellors should acknowledge ethnicity and culture as important parameters in understanding psychological processes.
4 Counsellors should respect the roles of family and community values and beliefs in the client's culture.
5 Counsellors should respect clients' religious beliefs.
6 Counsellors should try to communicate in the language requested by the client. If this is not possible, the client can be referred to another counsellor.
7 Counsellors should think about the impact of adverse social, environmental and political factors when dealing with clients.
8 Counsellors should try to eliminate biases and prejudices.

Pedersen (1980, as cited in Pedersen 1991) states the following implications for counselling foreign students.

1 Counsellors should not over-emphasize or under-emphasize the cultural differences between them and the student.
2 Counsellors should identify specific skills to help foreign students adapt to specific situations and roles.
3 Counsellors should specify the alternatives and reduce the ambiguity of conflicting roles.

4   Foreign students should be allowed to bring a fellow national to the counselling session for support.
5   Counsellors should encourage the bonds between foreign students and their fellow nationals as a form of support.
6   Counsellors should strive to facilitate students' orientation to the host culture which is a continuous process and requires contact with students before they arrive, during their studies and after they have returned home.
7   Counsellors should help students deal with re-entry problems for when they return home.
8   Counsellors should help foreign students consider how their values and perceptions are changing due to their stay in a foreign country.

Conclusion

Counsellors should realize that foreign students have to deal with adapting socially and emotionally as well as academically to a culture that can be alien and frightening. Although counselling is the last resort for foreign students when they are faced with problems, counsellors can play a very important part in helping them cope with life in a foreign land. Foreign students will rarely seek help with personal problems, even though they are troubled by them. Therefore, it is up to counsellors to reach out to foreign students to explain the kind of help they can give. For example, counsellors should make it clear that they are available as necessary to discuss academic and financial worries, English language problems and immigration concerns as well as the personal and social difficulties foreign students may experience.

References

American Psychological Association (1993) 'Guidelines for providers of psychological services to ethnic, linguistic, and culturally diverse populations', *American Psychologist*, 48: 45–8.
Barker, J. (1990) 'Staff development and training', in M. Kinnell (ed.), *The Learning Experiences of Overseas Students*. Buckingham: SRHE and Open University Press.
Church, A. (1982) 'Sojourner adjustment', *Psychological Bulletin*, 91: 540–72.
d'Ardenne, P. and Mahtani, A. (1989) *Transcultural Counselling in Action*. London: Sage.
Egan, G. (1990) *The Skilled Helper: A Systematic Approach to Effective Helping*. Pacific Grove: Brooks/Cole.
Elsey, B. and Kinnell, M. (1990) 'Introduction', in M. Kinnell (ed.), *The Learning Experiences of Overseas Students*. Buckingham: SRHE and Open University Press.
Fernandez, M. (1988) 'Issues in counselling Southeast Asian students', *Journal of Multicultural Counselling and Development*, 16: 157–66.
Furnham, A. and Alibhai, N. (1985) 'The friendship networks of foreign students: a replication and extension of the functional model', *International Journal of Psychology*, 20: 709–22.
Idowu, A. (1985) 'Counselling Nigerian students in United States colleges and universities, *Journal of Counselling and Development*, 63: 506–9.

Ivey, A.E., Ivey, M.B. and Simek-Downing, L. (1987) *Counseling and Psychotherapy: Integration Skills, Theory and Practice.* London: Prentice Hall.

Kleinman, A. (1997) 'Depression, somatization and the "new cross-cultural psychiatry"', *Social Science and Medicine*, 11: 3–9.

Klineberg, O. (1985) 'The social psychological of cross-cultural counselling', in P.B. Pedersen (ed.), *Handbook of Cross-Cultural Counseling and Therapy*. Westport: Greenwood Press.

Littlewood, R. (1992) 'Toward an intercultural therapy', in J. Kareem and R. Littlewood (eds), *Intercultural Therapy: Themes, Interpretations and Practice*, pp. 3–13. Oxford: Blackwell.

Livingstone, A. (1960) *The Overseas Student in Britain*. Manchester: Manchester University Press.

Mau, W. and Jepsen, D.A. (1988) 'Attitudes toward counsellors and counselling process: a comparison of Chinese and American graduate students', *Journal of Counselling and Development*, 70: 136–41.

Moon, D. (1991) 'Problems affecting the education of Korean students in United States Universities', *Dissertation Abstracts International*, A52/12: 4238.

PEP (Political and Economic Planning) (1965) *New Commonwealth Students in Britain. With Special Reference to Students from East Africa*. London: George Allen and Unwin.

Parker, W. (1988) 'Becoming an effective multicultural counselor', *Journal of Counselling and Development*, 67: 93.

Pedersen, P. (1991) 'Counseling international students', *The Counseling Psychologist*, 19: 10–58.

Pedersen, P. and Pedersen, A. (1989) 'The cultural grid: a complicated and dynamic approach to multicultural counselling', *Counselling Psychology Quarterly*, 2: 133–41.

Sabnani, H.B., Ponterotto, J.G. and Borodovsky, L.G. (1991) 'White racial identity development and cross-cultural counselor training: a stage model', *The Counseling Psychologist*, 19: 76–102.

Sen, A. (1970) *Problems of Overseas Students and Nurses*. London: National Foundation for Educational Research.

Sue, D.W. and Sue, D. (1990) *Counseling the Culturally Different – Theory & Practice*. New York: Wiley.

Sue, D.W., Arredondo, P. and McDavis, R.J. (1992) 'Multicultural counselling competencies and standards: a call to the profession', *Journal of Counselling and Development*, 70: 477–86.

Tanaka-Matsumi, J. and Marsella, A.J. (1976) 'Cross-cultural variations in the phenomenological experience of depression: Part 1, Word Association Studies', *Journal of Cross-Cultural Psychology*, 7: 379–96.

Thomas, K. and Althen, G. (1989) 'Counseling foreign students', in P.B. Pedersen, J. Draguns, W. Lonner, and J. Trimble (eds), *Counseling Across Cultures*. Honolulu: University of Hawaii Press.

Thomas , J. and Lago, C. (1989) 'Counselling and race', in W. Dryden, D. Charles-Edwards and R. Woolfe (eds), *Handbook of Counselling in Britain*. London: Tavistock.

Xia, Z. (1991) 'Asian students' adjustment problems at the University of Wisconsin—Madison', *Dissertation Abstracts International*, A52/11: 3832.

Discussion issues

1 What are the unique counselling needs of foreign students?

2 Foreign students are people in transition.

3 What are the competencies for effective cross-cultural counselling?

4 Foreign students rarely seek help with personal problems.

11

Buddhism and Counselling

Padmal de Silva

The value and utility of techniques and approaches found in religious and spiritual traditions in the context of therapy and counselling are recognized by many present-day writers and practitioners (Mikulas, 1983). Many see the arena of counselling as a broad field, into which ideas and practices from different sources can and should be incorporated as necessary. Given the diversity of clients that one is called upon to help, and the wide variety of problems and predicaments that they bring, it is natural that practitioners turn to a diversity of sources in search of the right concepts and techniques in a given situation.

Buddhism has been used particularly widely in this way. Several present-day therapy settings have used Buddhist techniques and ideas, and the reports available suggest a positive and fruitful outcome. For example, Kishimoto (1985) has reported on the use of Zen Buddhist techniques for neurotic patients in Japan, and there are reports on the use of Early Buddhist techniques with groups of alcoholics and drug addicts in Kandy, Sri Lanka (e.g. de Silva and Samarasinghe, 1985).

The relevance of Buddhism to counselling

There are several ways in which Buddhism can be relevant to the practice of counselling. The most obvious is the need to find suitable techniques in counselling Buddhist clients, to whom many of the Western techniques may seem alien and therefore be less acceptable. The problems inherent in using techniques developed in the industrialized West with client populations from a different cultural background are now well recognized (e.g. d'Ardenne and Mahtani, 1989; Ward, 1983). The attitude of optimism that prevailed among therapists and counsellors some decades ago – that good techniques will always work, irrespective of whom they are applied to – is no longer widely held. An approach or a technique has to be seen by the client as making sense, and has to fit into his/her overall life view, in order that he/she may comply fully with therapeutic instructions. Such compliance is a necessary condition for the success of the intervention. The literature has numerous examples of client–technique mismatch and its negative consequences and – conversely – of the benefits of matching client and technique. Singh and Oberhummer (1980), for example, describe the successful use of the Hindu concept of Karma yoga in therapy with a female Hindu client.

The value of Buddhist concepts and techniques in treating and counselling Buddhist clients, then, should be obvious. The examples provided earlier, of the uses of Buddhism in therapeutic settings in Japan and Sri Lanka, provide empirical support for this.

Second, Buddhism has always had a counselling and therapeutic role, in the wide sense, in Buddhist communities. Even in the present day, Buddhist monks are turned to for advice, support and counselling by lay Buddhists. This happens in Thailand, Burma, Sri Lanka and elsewhere (see Gombrich, 1988). The Buddhist monk is seen as someone who can take a detached and objective view of a problem, and provide sensible solutions, or at least support and consolation. This tradition is historically well grounded, as the Buddha himself (563–483 BC) was, in his life, very much a counsellor in this way. The life of this Buddha is replete with examples of the Master providing emotional support and comfort, and often advice and counselling, to those who needed help (Kalupahana and Kalupahana, 1982; Saddhatissa, 1970).

Some of these instances are striking for their dramatic quality, as in the case of Patacara. This young woman's infant son died, and she carried the body of the child asking anyone and everyone to restore him to life. Eventually she came to the Buddha. The Buddha said to her that he would indeed restore her son to life, but in order to do so he needed some mustard seeds from a household where no one had ever died. The young mother then went from house to house, asking at each if there had ever been any deaths there. During this exercise, the truth dawned on her, as the inevitability of death became clear to her disconsolate mind. This facilitated not only her acceptance that her child was no more, but also her insight into the human predicament.

This story, not untypical of the Buddha's dealings with lay persons, is fully recounted in several sources (e.g. de Silva, 1984). The Buddha also often offered advice to husbands, wives, parents, masters, servants, the royalty, and those in various professions, who had problems. This is the tradition that is still found in Buddhist communities, with monks functioning in a counselling role for their lay brethren (Saddhatissa, 1970).

Third, Buddhism has a strong and pragmatic lay ethic which provides a framework for counselling those in need of help. Buddhism is not a religion with the ultimate and/or the hereafter as its sole concern. Much attention is paid to the day-to-day life of lay persons. Buddhism accepts that only a small minority will renounce lay life and devote themselves entirely to a life of personal and spiritual development. The majority do not do this, and remain as lay persons. For them, the Buddha's advice was that they should lead a life which was conducive to the well-being of themselves and others (Saddhatissa, 1970; Tachibana, 1926). This meant that people were reminded of their duties, rights and social and personal obligations. The criteria of what was ethically correct was whether it was conducive to the individual's or his/her fellow-beings' happiness and satisfactory living. For example, people were advised against the abuse of alcoholic substances, not because it went against some religious dogma or principle, but because the behaviour had demonstrable ill effects. These included: loss of wealth; proneness to ill health; proneness to socially embarrassing behaviour; disrepute; and ultimate mental derangement (see de Silva, 1983). This clearly pragmatic social ethic of Buddhism makes it particularly well placed to offer help to those who are afflicted by the day-to-day problems of living, such as grief, disappointment, anger, fear and jealousy.

Finally, Buddhist literature contains references to a large number of specific strategies for behavioural change. These are clearly behavioural and cognitive strategies, as they operate directly on the behaviour or cognition in question. As has been shown in detail elsewhere (e.g. de Silva, 1984; Mikulas, 1981), these Buddhist techniques foreshadowed many of the cognitive and behavioural techniques that have been developed in recent decades in Western psychology and psychiatry. The fact that many of these techniques are more or less the same as their modern counterparts also means that they already have empirical validation, as the latter have been tested in numerous clinical trials and controlled case-studies. The repertoire of specific techniques that Buddhism has for counselling is impressive indeed. These include: systematic use of rewards and punishment; fear reduction by graded exposure; modelling; self-monitoring; stimulus control; overt and covert aversion; use of family members for implementing a behaviour-change programme; and specific techniques, including distraction and over-exposure, for unwanted intrusive cognitions.

Preventive work

There is a further aspect of Buddhism which is relevant to counselling in the wider sense of the term. Buddhism offers much that can help in the prophylaxis, or prevention, of psychological disorder and distress. That is a fundamental aspect of Buddhism, as its main goal is to deal with the human predicament. Alongside success, joy and happiness, life contains failure, sadness, gloom and despair. Friendships and other relationships are fraught with problems. Those we are attached to move away, or die. One may lose one's career, wealth, and offspring. Buddhism recognizes, as a fundamental truth, this distressing state of affairs, which co-exists with the seemingly happy and successful aspects of life. This is the conundrum to which the Buddha devoted his life. In the present day, where competitiveness, material success, strong attachments and power are the order of the day, there are numerous inevitable problems that bring distress to one. The overall Buddhist attitude geared towards reducing attachments, and the specific techniques aimed at managing the vulnerability of the individual to the effects of the vast and powerful array of stimuli around him or her, both have something to offer in reducing the chances of distress and disorder. If one learns not to be attached too strongly to others, not to be overdependent, not to be incessantly acquisitive, not to equate happiness with material wealth, power or fame, then the probability of a breakdown in such a person must be reduced. This preventive aspect is possibly one of the most valuable potential contributions of Buddhism to the practice of counselling. Both the overall philosophy and the specific behaviour-change techniques, including meditative practices, have a role to play in this context.

Discussion

It is not suggested that all counselling should take a Buddhist stance. Counselling needs to draw upon a wide range of sources, and Buddhism happens to be one among these sources, and a particularly rich one at that. The use of its concepts and techniques for appropriate clients and appropriate problems can only enhance the practice of counselling. The ultimate test of any technique or idea is whether it produces the desired results. The implication of this is that Buddhist ideas and techniques, used in the context of counselling, need to satisfy this test: they should have efficacy. As noted earlier, some of the specific Buddhist strategies for behavioural change already have the backing of empirical evidence. This is because their modern counterparts have been subjected to rigorous trials with various client populations. As for those Buddhist techniques and concepts that do not have modern counterparts, there is a need to evaluate them empirically. Such evaluation is entirely in keeping with the overall spirit of enquiry found in the Buddha's approach to problems. If such evaluation demonstrates that they can produce the desired results, then they can be incorporated into the repertoire of techniques in counselling practice today.

References

d'Ardenne, P., and Mahtani, A. (1989) *Transcultural Counselling in Action.* London: Sage.

de Silva, P. (1983) 'The Buddhist attitude to alcoholism', in G. Edwards, A. Arif, and J. Jaffe (eds), *Drug Use and Misuse: Cultural Perspectives.* London: Croom Helm.

de Silva, P. (1984) 'Buddhism and behaviour modification', *Behaviour Research and Therapy,* 22.

de Silva, P. and Samarasinghe, D. (1985) 'Behaviour therapy in Sri Lanka', *Journal of Behaviour Therapy and Experimental Psychiatry,* 16.

Gombrich, R. (1988) *Theravada Buddhism.* London: Routledge.

Kalupahana, D.J. and Kalupahana, I. (1982) *The Way of Siddhartha.* Boulder, CO: Shambhala.

Kishimoto, K. (1985) 'Self-awakening psychotherapy for neurosis: attaching importance to oriental thought, especially Buddhist thought', *Psychologia,* 28.

Mikulas, W.L. (1981) 'Buddhism and behaviour modification', *The Psychological Record*, 31.
Mikulas, W.L. (1983) *Skills of Living*. Lanham, MD: University Press of America.
Saddhatissa, H. (1970) *Buddhist Ethics*. London: Allen and Unwin.
Singh, R. and Oberhummer, I. (1980) 'Behaviour therapy within a setting of karwa yoga', *Journal of Behaviour Therapy and Experimental Psychiatry*, 11.
Tachibana, S. (1926) *The Ethics of Buddhism*, London: Curzon.
Ward, C. (1983) 'The role and status of psychology in developing nations', *Bulletin of the British Psychological Society*, 36.

Discussion issues

1   How can Buddhism be relevant to the practice of counselling?
2   Good techniques will always work.
3   Buddhist techniques foreshadowed many cognitive and behavioural techniques.
4   There is a need to evaluate Buddhist techniques and concepts.

Good Practice in Transcultural Counselling

An Asian Perspective

Amanda Webb Johnson
and Zenobia Nadirshaw

> European models of counselling are not devised to take account of
> ethnic minority experiences and culturally different life experiences. The
> models need to be changed when dealing with ethnic minorities.
>
> (African Caribbean mental health worker)

Among a wide range of mental health professionals, there is growing
concern about the way in which services are provided in Britain's multiracial and pluralistic society. Psychiatric services have failed to respond
to the needs and secure the confidence of Britain's ethnic communities
(Fernando, 1990; Littlewood and Lipsedge, 1982). What is more disturbing is that services are often discriminatory, culturally insensitive and
inappropriate. Counselling and therapeutic practice have not escaped
this. For example, it is widely acknowledged that members of the ethnic
communities are more likely to receive medication and have less access
to 'talking therapies' such as psychotherapy or counselling than their
white counterparts. The evidence indicates that people from South Asian
communities in particular are rarely referred to psychotherapy services
(Campling, 1989; Ilahi, 1988).

There is a common perception among those providing counselling and
therapy services that members of South Asian communities do not really
suffer from mental health problems, and that any problems which they
may have are contained within their families and communities. This has
been substantiated in the research literature and explained in terms of
Asians manifesting greater 'psychological robustness' than the indigenous
population (Cochrane and Stopes-Roe, 1977). Elsewhere the low rate of
reported mental illness has been attributed to fear of stigmatization and
a 'somatization' of mental distress (Rack, 1982). Such perceptions have
also informed a widespread belief that South Asians do not need or want
to use services. Consequently, the level of service provision for these communities has remained unsatisfactory. This is not helped by the fact that
consultation with members of such communities about the planning and
delivery of services has been sadly lacking.

Yet the experience of many mental health professionals and the evidence from a number of studies now question and challenge this view. One community survey revealed an alarmingly high rate of emotional distress within South Asian communities and little outlet for expressing this distress (Beliappa, 1991). It was found that the low uptake of services was due to factors such as lack of awareness of services, lack of confidence in their effectiveness and appropriateness, perception of cultural and language barriers, and fear that confidentiality would not be preserved, rather than a reluctance to use services per se. Another study in Tower Hamlets showed that the Bangladeshi respondents were experiencing more serious life events and reporting more symptoms of psychological disturbance than their indigenous neighbours (MacCarthy and Craissati, 1989).

We would like, therefore, to set the record straight and voice the concerns of a growing number of professionals: that South Asians do have mental health problems; that their mental health needs are not being met and that we all have a professional duty to develop counselling and therapy services that are appropriate and meaningful to this section of our population. In order to set about doing this, however, we need to look at why the existing services, and the concepts of mental health/illness and models of therapy on which they are based, may not be appropriate or sensitive to South Asian clients. We also need to address some of the common assumptions and stereotypes that are held about South Asian communities.

Eurocentrism in western psychiatry

It is evident that western 'knowledge' – facts, logic, science, reason – holds sway in multiracial Britain. We need to remind ourselves that because of the range of ethnic backgrounds, fundamental differences exist between British (western) systems and other systems – for example, in the field of psychiatry and mental health. Concepts of mental health, illness and mental disorder within a white, westernized frame of reference need to be challenged. In the historical context of psychiatry it has been implicitly assumed that this western way of thinking and analysing people's minds is superior to other ways that are not derived from the west, i.e. from black (African) and/or Third World countries (including Asia).

The current medical model of psychiatric illness/mental health implies a mind–body dichotomy, a strong adherence to a classification system, and clear-cut distinctions between psychology, religion, medicine and spiritualism. In contrast, these different disciplines or sciences are integrated together to form a holistic approach within the Asian 'culture'. In the British (western) way of thinking, distress is seen as arising from a pathology in either mind or body. In the east (Asia), it is seen as a lack of harmony at some level or other. The goals of therapy are different in the two cultures. The quest for 'understanding' in western thought is for facts; in the east, for feeling. Gaining self-knowledge through meditation in the east is different from gaining insight in western psychotherapy and counselling through accumulating information about childhood experiences. The goals of many western therapies are to get rid of or control symptoms, or to control emotions by suppressing them. The goal of eastern religions and psychology is enlightenment through individual striving and seeking, with its emphasis on personal, subjective experience and meditation, rather than through taking action (Fernando, 1991).

Challenging stereotypes

One of the prevailing assumptions about the 'Asian community' (and the reason we choose the term 'South Asian communities') is that it represents a homogeneous group of people who share a common culture and heritage. Since there are as many diversities as similarities between people of South Asian origin in terms of culture, language, religion and historical legacy, the existence of a monolithic 'Asian culture' becomes an untenable concept. Moreover, there is often little appreciation of the extent to which cultures have developed and changed, and that members of the South Asian communities have adopted into their own value systems, to varying degrees, the values and cultural patterns prevalent in Britain.

The increased political sensitivity in the area of race relations has meant that it is no longer deemed appropriate or sensitive to talk openly about racial stereotypes. People fear that they will be branded racist or prejudiced if they express any views on this subject. An unfortunate result of tabooing this area of debate is that implicit prejudices are often left implicit and are therefore perpetuated. We feel that it is time to bring these underlying assumptions and stereotypes into the open and thus challenge the foundations for them. The most common stereotypes about the South Asian communities are:

(a) 'Asian culture' is stifling and denies freedom to the individual.
(b) 'Asian culture' is dominated exclusively by men; women play a dependent, submissive role.
(c) Asians are obsessed with religion.
(d) Asians have arranged marriages, and arranged marriages are not happy.
(e) Asians are psychologically more robust than the indigenous population.
(f) Asians do not want to use the available therapeutic services.
(g) Asians are not 'psychologically minded'.
(h) Asians want directive treatment rather than non-directive therapy: they want to be told what do to.
(i) Asian culture attaches a deep-seated stigma to mental illness.

(j)   Asians somatize mental distress and present only physical symptoms.
(k)   Asians 'look after their own' within their extended family networks.

'Asians look after their own'

Although it is often claimed that South Asians 'look after their own' within their extended families and do not need services, in reality this type of extended family is far from representative of South Asian households today, either in the Indian subcontinent or in Britain. One survey (Brown, 1984) revealed that only 16 per cent of South Asian households in Britain are extended families. Furthermore, although the extended family may offer care and support to its members, it is also a source of tension and conflict – for example, from intergenerational differences in attitude and behaviour.

Many counsellors and therapists would agree that marital and family relationships are frequently the most common cause of mental health problems for South Asian communities. Beliappa (1991) found that the most severe concerns for women were related to marital relationships. Yet none of these women felt that the family was an appropriate source of help for their difficulties. In fact, only 13 per cent of her sample saw the family as a viable means of support for any problems they were experiencing. As one woman explained: 'It is not actually appropriate to talk about one's situation within the family – so mental distress remains hidden, bottled up.'

In short, the myth of the extended family lending support to its members is misguided, and prevents service providers from developing meaningful and sensitive services for South Asian communities.

Stigmatization

There is a widely held belief that mental health problems are not acknowledged within South Asian communities because of the perceived effect that the stigma will have on an individual's family and wider community. For example, the stigma attached to mental illness may affect dowry and marriage prospects for other members of the family, or lower the family's status in the community.

It is well recognized, however, that the stigma of mental ill-health is not restricted to South Asian communities but is prevalent in all communities, including the indigenous population. Although statistical evidence is lacking, Beliappa's small-scale study (1991) did reveal findings which question the extent to which stigmatization of mental illness exists within South Asian communities. Of more relevance to counsellors and therapists is that by over-emphasizing the impact of stigma on these communities. they absolve themselves from the responsibility of making the therapeutic process sensitive and meaningful to South Asian clients.

Somatization

It is often asserted that people from non-western cultures, and particularly those from the Indian subcontinent, communicate their emotional distress in somatic or physical terms, in contrast to those from western cultures who express their distress in psychological terms. This has led to a common stereotype amongst mental health professionals that South Asians are not psychologically minded and lack the capacity for insight necessary for certain 'talking therapies'. They are seen as more likely to describe physical symptoms such as aches and pains, sleeplessness, and so on.

There is, however, no conclusive evidence that Asians 'somatize' more than any other ethnic group. One study in Manchester revealed no significant difference in the reporting of somatic symptoms between Asian and white British groups of patients (Bhatt et al., 1989). Beliappa (1991) found that her Asian respondents did not somatize their distress and were able to recognise the psychosomatic nature of their problems. For example, one woman described her health in this way:

> It doesn't hurt me anymore. But I am severely affected. I have had many miscarriages. I smoke when I am tense. I don't rebel anymore. I've withdrawn. I tend to cry a lot. I'm always ill with stomach problems, I cannot eat. I'm very depressed. I recognise that it is my present state of mind that is affecting my health.

It is now more widely recognized that all ethnic groups including the white population have a tendency present emotional difficulties with somatic symptoms, and that somatization may be a reflection of social class and educational background rather than ethnic origin.

It has also been suggested that the individual's perception of the professional may affect the reporting of symptoms (Krause, 1989). For example, if a person expects the professional to give physical treatment, then he/she may seek physical treatment by presenting physical symptoms accordingly. Krause proposes that illness communications occur in a particular context of shared understandings about health and illness which professional and client hold in common. In situations where such concepts and the subsequent behaviour are not shared by therapist and client, i.e. where they belong to different cultures, communication difficulties may occur.

To conclude, somatization is not limited to non-western cultures, nor does it apply to all members of South Asian communities. In situations where physical symptoms only are presented, we would encourage therapists and counsellors to look beyond the presenting symptoms when making their assessment, and to take account of the influence of the different values and belief systems that the individual brings into the therapeutic situation.

The transcultural perspective

For too long, western models of therapy have been based on white, middle-class assumptions which fail to address the experiences and values of the ethnic communities. If this chapter has any effect, we hope that it will be to emphasize to its audience that there is another perspective: one which has to be acknowledged and incorporated into any theoretical debate or service planning for people from South Asian communities. This perspective has been termed 'transcultural' or 'transracial'.

d'Ardenne and Mahtani (1989) have suggested that transcultural therapy is based on the following requirements:

(a) The therapist's sensitivity to the cultural variations and the cultural bias of his/her approach.
(b) The therapist's increasing understanding of the cultural background of his/her clients.
(c) The therapist's ability and commitment to developing an approach to counselling which meets the cultural needs of his/her clients.
(d) The therapist's ability to respond to the greater complexity of working across cultures.

Transcultural therapy recognizes that the individuals' experiences are inextricably linked with their wider social and political context. Therapists are encouraged to develop some appreciation and understanding of the social, economic, historical and cultural factors affecting the client and their impact on the therapeutic process and relationship (Fatimilehin, 1989; Skodra, 1989).

Since the number of professionals belonging to the ethnic communities is limited, many white professionals will be working with clients whose ethnic background differs from their own. In these situations, they will encounter different expectations and values, and unfamiliar symbolic systems, such as language, concepts, attitudes to 'illness' and 'cure', attitudes towards seeking help, and culturally determined variations in the expression of distress (MacCarthy, 1988).

In transcultural therapy, professionals have a duty to increase their understanding of the culture, life history and social circumstances of the people with whom they are working. This does not mean, however, that the professional is expected to become a 'cultural expert'. 'Knowledge' of culture alone will not progress the therapeutic relationship as effectively as the attitudes and skills of the therapist which are brought to the therapeutic situation (Nadirshaw, 1992).

In transcultural therapy, the therapist is faced with the challenge of judging the extent to which the client's cultural background is relevant to the presenting difficulty. Where the client and therapist share a similar cultural background, these socio-cultural factors may be taken for granted, and their significance to the client's problem may be overlooked.

Conversely, where the client and therapist belong to different cultures, these cultural factors can be over-emphasized and exaggerated in interpreting the client's experiences and behaviour (Callias, 1988).

Therapists need to acknowledge the relevance of their client's background without relying too heavily on cultural explanations to understand their clients' problems. Therapists need to be aware of their own assumptions about cultural variations and maintain an open-minded, non-judgemental approach to their clients' difficulties.

Transcultural therapy also takes into account the experience of discrimination and oppression faced by members of the ethnic communities, and views 'illness' as a result of an individual's interactions with a sometimes hostile environment rather than as something intrinsically rooted in the individual. It acknowledges the dislocation and alienation experienced by members of migrant communities and the particular difficulties which may be faced by younger people who have been born and brought up in Britain.

Many professionals believe that a shared cultural background does not guarantee a successful therapeutic relationship and that therapists with the appropriate skills can work across cultures. However, in order to provide a meaningful and valuable service for South Asian communities, the client's preferences must be respected and he/she must have the opportunity to exercise some choice over the identity of his/her therapist.

The therapist's variables

At present, there are no well-established theoretical models of transcultural therapy to substitute for traditional approaches. Innovative projects in America and Britain, however, have achieved considerable success with clients from the ethnic communities (Jackson, 1983; Marsella and Pedersen, 1981: also Nafsiyat Intercultural Therapy Centre, White City Mental Health Project). We believe that for successful therapy with clients of South Asian origin, the different models and schools of therapy in which therapists and counsellors have been trained are perhaps not as significant as the role and influence of the therapist's variables in the process and outcome of the therapy. These variables include:

(a) the therapist's credibility in the client's mind;
(b) the therapist's ability to let the client dictate the goals and purpose of the therapy;
(c) the therapist's ability to convince the client that he/she is understood;
(d) the therapist's ability to communicate effectively with the client – for example, by listening actively and showing empathy and unconditional positive regard;

(e)   the therapist's ability to show genuine respect for his/her client's cultural values and to refrain from imposing his/her own frame of reference on the client's experiences and behaviour;

(f)   the therapist's assumptions and values concerning the experiences of people from the ethnic communities;

(g)   the therapist's ability to address and confront his/her own stereo-typical/prejudiced views and racist assumptions;

(h)   the therapist's awareness of how his/her own cultural values can be imposed, perhaps unconsciously, on the client and can affect the interpretation of the client's experiences: for example, a white female therapist's prejudice towards an Asian female client's problems relating to her arranged marriage;

(i)   the therapist's ability to increase his/her awareness of the cultural, religious, social and political factors which impact upon the lives of members of the ethnic communities;

(j)   the therapist's ability to become acquainted with the strengths of the client and to treat the client as an individual.

Some recommendations

Although we cannot provide any tried and tested formulae for successful therapy with South Asian clients, we can offer the following guidelines for counsellors and therapists which will go some way towards meeting their needs:

1   Avoid generalized assumptions based on Eurocentric and racist atti-tudes. They are inappropriate and insensitive to South Asian com-munities. Treat each client as an individual.

2   Acknowledge the reality of racism and discrimination in the lives of Asian people and how this impacts upon the therapeutic process. Power relationships between therapist and client may reflect the imbalance of power between the indigenous population and the ethnic communities, or between the different genders in society.

3   Take account of the structures within South Asian communities which serve to strengthen and support their members. By recogniz-ing the potential for empowerment and self-help in these communi-ties, we can draw upon these strengths when working with an individual.

4   Adopt a more flexible approach to other therapeutic values, beliefs and traditions, and respect them as offering a different and equally valid perspective. For example, the services of traditional healers, such as matajis and hakims, and alternative medicines can be used in con-junction with western techniques.

5   Listen to and accept the client's own way of viewing his/her difficul-ties and the meaning he/she attaches to them. We may also need to

reevaluate the aims of the therapeutic process with Asian clients in terms of personal and social intervention.

6   Be aware that within South Asian communities the client may not just be the individual in the therapy room: his/her family and significant others may have an important role to play in the therapeutic process.

7   Maintain an open, flexible approach so that it is the client and not the therapist who dictates the goals of the therapy and how the therapy proceeds. Factors such as the identification of the 'problem', and time-keeping, need to be mutually negotiated between therapist and client.

8   Redefine current concepts of mental health and illness by incorporating religious, ethical and spiritual dimensions. The true worth of the Asian 'model' of mental health needs to be honestly examined.

These recommendations for good practice are not exclusive to South Asian communities but can be applied to the whole population. However, it is only by responding to the needs of those most poorly served, including the ethnic communities, that we can move closer to providing an equitable therapeutic service to all.

References

Beliappa, J. (1991) *Illness or Distress?: Alternative Models of Mental Health.* London: Confederation of Indian Organisations.

Bhatt, A., Tomenson, B. and Benjamin, S. (1989) 'Transcultural patterns of somatisation in primary care: a preliminary report', *Journal of Psychosomatic Research,* 33.

Brown, C. (1984) *Black and White Britain: the Third PSI Survey.* London: Gower.

Callias, M. (1988) 'Clinical work with children and families', in N. Bouras and R. Littlewood (eds), *Stress and Coping in the Greek Communities in Britain.* London: Division of Psychiatry, Guy's Hospital.

Campling, P. (1989) 'Race, culture and psychotherapy', *Psychiatric Bulletin,* 13.

Cochrane, R. and Stopes-Roe, M. (1977) 'Psychological and social adjustment of Asian immigrants to Britain: a community survey', *Journal of Social Psychiatry,* 12.

d'Ardenne, P. and Mahtani, A. (1989) *Transcultural Counselling in Action.* London: Sage.

Fatimilehin, I. (1989) 'Psychotherapy for blacks', *Changes,* 1 (2).

Fernando, S. (1990) *Race and Culture in Psychiatry.* London: Croom Helm.

Fernando, S. (1991) *Mental Health, Race and Culture.* London: Macmillan/MIND.

Ilahi, N. (1988) 'Psychotherapy services to the ethnic communities', report of a study Ealing Hospital, London. Unpublished paper.

Jackson, A.M. (1983) 'Treatment issues for black patients', *Psychotherapy: Theory, Research and Practice,* 20.

Krause, B. (1989) 'The sinking heart: a Punjabi communication of distress', *Social Science and Medicine,* 29.

Littlewood, R. and Lipsedge, M. (1982) *Aliens and Alienists: Ethnic Minorities and Psychiatry.* London: Penguin.

MacCarthy, B. (1988) 'Clinical work with ethnic minorities', in F. Watts (ed.), *New Developments in Clinical Psychology,* vol. 2. Chichester: Wiley.

MacCarthy, B. and Craissati, J. (1989) 'Ethnic differences in response to adversity: a community sample of Bangladeshis and their indigenous neighbours', *Journal of Social Psychiatry and Psychiatric Epidemiology,* 24.

Marsella, A. and Pedersen, P. (1981) *Cross-Cultural Counselling and Psychotherapy*. New York: Plenum.

Nadirshaw, Z. (1992) 'Therapeutic practice in multiracial Britain', *Counselling Psychology Quarterly*, 5 (3).

Rack, P. (1982) *Race, Culture and Mental Disorder*. London: Tavistock.

Skodra, E. (1989) 'Counselling immigrant women: a feminist critique of traditional therapeutic approaches and re-evaluation of the role of the therapist', *Counselling Psychology Quarterly*, 2 (2).

Discussion issues

1 The goals of western and eastern therapies are different.

2 How does the myth of the South Asian extended family lending support to its members prevent service providers from developing meaningful and scientific services?

3 What skills are needed to convince the client that she or he is understood?

4 The services of traditional healers and alternative medicine can be used in conjunction with western techniques.

13

Understanding Mental Illness Across Cultures

Pittu Laungani

Mental illness is an ubiquitous concept. Its pervasive influence extends into areas of medicine, biology, genetics, psychiatry, psychoanalysis, psychology, anthropology, sociology and a variety of other related disciplines. Given its multi-disciplinary interests, the arguments surrounding the nature, the etilogy and the treatment of mental illness have never been satisfactorily resolved. Whether mental illness is best conceptualized as a biological disease pattern, a genetic abnormality, a learning disorder, a form of family pathology, a crippling existential condition, a mystical experience, a social construction rooted in its historical and cultural reality etc. remains unclear. Conflicts remain.

Even within a single culture, opinions vary as to what constitutes mental illness, and how the term itself shall be defined and conceptualized. In the west, the term mental illness has been the subject of considerable controversy, which has often been quite bitter. Over the years, several theoretical and empirical models of mental illness have been formulated, ranging from the medical (or organic) model, the classical psychoanalytical model, to the family pathology model, the existential model, the psychedelic model, the behavioural and the cognitive models. For a variety of historical reasons, the medical model – notwithstanding its serious shortcomings – has gained ascendancy over others (Laungani, 2000). The proliferation of models, instead of aiding our understanding of mental illness, has, in fact, made the understanding of the problem even more difficult. The difficulties get compounded and seem almost insuperable when one attempts to understand mental illness across cultures – particularly in non-western cultures.

The major obstacle that stands in the way of a clearer understanding of mental illness across cultures is the one which revolves round the issue of Universalism-Relativism. Let us briefly visit the realm of Universalism and Relativism for a clearer understanding of the issues involved.

Universalism-Relativism

Is mental illness culture specific? Or is mental illness universal? Or is it both, universalistic and culture specific? The well-known anthropologists of the past era, such as Boaz (1911), Benedict (1946), Malinowski (1927),

Mead (1930, 1935) and others, often asserted that all mental illness was culture specific, in the sense that it was relative to a given culture. By relativism they meant that each culture developed its own conceptual system of rules to which people of that culture subscribed. Deviations from certain types of rules were construed as forms of mental aberrations and were dealt with in culturally appropriate ways, e.g. exorcism, prayer, removal of spells, to indigenous forms of medication. To understand mental illness in another culture it was therefore necessary to understand the system of rules and the assumptions which guided the private and social behaviours of people in that culture.

The notion of relativism became very popular for another reason too. It was assumed that the adoption of a relativistic position would put an end to any form of pejorative, racist, genetic judgements of other cultures, and there would be no need to 'order' cultures on a measurable scale of superiority or inferiority, civilized or primitive etc. The adoption of such an approach would also, it was believed, help to reduce, if not eliminate altogether, the oft-voiced accusations of scientific, educational, cognitive, and economic imperialism of which western countries, *not without justification*, have been charged (Jahoda and Krewer, 1998).

However, the acceptance of relativistic doctrines creates its own peculiar problems. The question is, how is one to make sense of the rules of another culture? By what means does one attempt to understand the internal rules of another culture? Opinions on this are divided. One might learn the language, one might learn the rules of the cultural system, but that alone is not enough to guarantee a clear understanding of the principles underlying the rules of the culture. But as Doyal and Harris (1986) point out, learning the rules of the culture in itself is not enough. In certain instances, one would have to suspend judgements concerning whether a given rule was true or false, rational or irrational. If, for instance, one were to be told that the reason why a woman who had just delivered a baby was depressed (assuming one was able to understand the nuances of meanings associated with the word depression and find parallels to one's own understanding of depression in general and post-natal depression in particular) was because of the angry fluttering of birds in her stomach during her pregnancy, one would be totally bewildered by such information. The critics of relativism argue that if the rules of the language of another culture do not have built into them canons of formal logic and conceptions of rationality, it becomes difficult, if not impossible, to interpret behaviours in any meaningful manner. Under those circumstances, no judgements of mental illness or health can be made.

This line of reasoning, however, is in itself contentious because the above argument acquires substance only when one accepts what might be referred to as 'western notions of rationality' and 'Aristotelean canons of logic' as the universal standard against which other conceptions of rationality and logic are to be judged. It is clear from the manner in which Doyal and Harris have expounded their views that they are unfamiliar with other systems of logic, in particular the Nyaya and the Vaisesika systems of analytic philosophy, which were expounded in India around 450 BC (Dasgupta, 1961–2; Kane, 1932–1960; Radhakrishnan, 1923/1956; Radhakrishnan and Moore, 1957). On the other hand, they may have deliberately chosen to regard the Nyaya and Vaisesika systems of logic and philosophy as being irrelevant to their main argument concerning relativism.

Although the adoption of a relativistic position is seemingly quite attractive, there are other reasons why relativism does not lend itself to a ready acceptance. First, as Popper (1972) points out, the uncritical acceptance of relativism leads to an epistemological cul-de-sac. Above all, it does not permit one to transcend one's cultural boundaries; one is forever doomed to languish within the narrowly defined boundaries of one's culture. In other words, the adoption of a relativistic position prevents one from undertaking any form of comparative analysis (Laungani, 1998).

Second, relativism in recent years has come to acquire a variety of ideological connotations, and is often used as a gag to stifle any recognition of genuine differences in opinions, beliefs, values and behaviours. It is in that sense potentially dangerous, for its acceptance creates no room in it for any genuine understanding of cross-cultural differences in a variety of fields, including mental illness. It is hardly surprising that the value of relativism as a valid explanatory concept has come to be seriously questioned by several writers, including Bloom (1987), Feyerabend (1987), Gellner (1985), Musgrove (1982), Stace (1958) and Williams (1985).

But to question relativism does not necessarily mean that there are no mental disorders which are not culture specific. Many obviously are, and have been specifically recognized as such. Clear catalogues of culture-specific disorders have been examined by Al-Issa (1982), Draguns (1994), Kleinman (1980), Marsella (1982), Rao (1986) and several others working in the area.

Just as there are culture-specific disorders, it is reasonable to hypothesize that mental illness is a universal existential experience. An analogy might help to establish this point. Until the 1960s there was a prevalent belief within mainstream academic psychology that the expression of emotions was culture specific (Matsumoto, 1996). Surprisingly, the belief ran counter to the astonishing revelations of Charles Darwin in his remarkable book *The Expression of Emotions in Man and Animals* (1872). It was believed that the Japanese in particular did not express emotions in the manner in which they were expressed by people in America and other western countries. The myth of the culture-specificity of the expression of emotions was destroyed by the remarkable experiments of Ekman and several others working in the field (Ekman, 1972, 1973, 1985, 1994; Ekman and Freisen, 1975; Ekman and Heider, 1988; Matsumoto, 1989, 1992, 1996). The above research studies clearly established the universality of the expression of emotions.

That people lose control over their lives, that people become depressed, unhappy and withdraw into a world of their own, unbounded by constraints of time, space and reality; that people abandon their will to live, seek oblivion in alcohol, resort to uncontrollable and meaningless acts of cruelty and violence; that people are haunted by feelings of guilt, remorse, fear and shame are all common universal human experiences. They exist around us. They may even affect us directly or indirectly. The problem is not that these problems do not exist. They exist everywhere. They problem is how one construes them logically and rationally. For it is the construction of an experience, its interpretation, and the meaning one assigns to the experience which involves making all sorts of assumptions. It is those assumptions which are often culture specific and not the experience itself – as has been mistakenly assumed by some cultural relativists.

Let us now consider the problems related to mental illness in India and Britain. To undertake a meaningful comparative analysis, it is necessary to devise a comprehensive conceptual model which would explain the nature of mental illness, its diagnosis and its treatment in the two cultural groups. Although India and Britain have been singled out for a detailed analysis, it should be emphasized that the overarching conceptual model explains differences and similarities not just between the two cultural groups but also between western and eastern cultures.

Conceptual model of cultural differences

It is suggested that there are four interrelated *core values* or *factors* which distinguish western cultures from eastern cultures, or more specifically, Indian approaches from British approaches to the understanding, diagnosis and the treatment of mental illness. The four core values or factors are:

> Individualism – Communalism (Collectivism)
> Materialism – Spiritualism
> Free Will – Determinism
> Cognitivism – Emotionalism

It should be noted that the two concepts underlying each factor are not dichotomous; they are to be understood as extending along a continuum, starting at, say, Individualism at one end, and extending into Communalism at the other. A dichotomous approach tends to classify people in 'either-or' terms. Such an approach is limited in its usefulness. Categorical approaches, particularly in relation to personality research, were popular four or five decades ago, but were abandoned and replaced by more complex, multi-factorial models. People seldom fit into neat theoretically formulated and/or empirically derived categories. The sheer complexity and variability of human behaviours and responses within and between groups even within a single culture precludes serious attempts at such categorical classifications. Categorical taxonomies may offer neat quantifiable numerical values, but their usefulness in understanding differences and similarities in core beliefs, attitudes and values between cultures is limited, if not dubious.

A dimensional approach, on the other hand, takes account of human variability. It has the advantage of allowing us to measure salient attitudes and behaviours at any given point in time and over time. It also enables us to hypothesize expected theoretical and empirical shifts in positions along the continuum both within and between cultural groups. Each of the hypothesized dimensions subsumes within it a variety of attitudes and behaviours which to a large extent are influenced by the norms and values operative within that culture. The theoretical and empirical bases of these factors have been described at length elsewhere (see Laungani, 1990, 1991, 1991a, 1991b, 1992, 1995, 1996, 1997; Sachdev, 1992).

Values are best defined as the currently held normative expectations that underlie individual and social conduct (Laungani, 1995a). They form the bases of social, political and religious order. They are often the result of past legacies, religious and philosophical. Since these beliefs are passed on over centuries, their roots get deeper and deeper. They cannot be easily severed. Values become an integral part of our psychological and existential being. Although subject to change, values to a large extent remain stable. However, over time, values may change. Several factors, e.g. migration from one culture to another, political, scientific and technological upheavals, war, pestilence, natural disasters, may result in rapid changes in the individual's personal behaviour and value systems.

It is suggested that the salient attitudes, values and behaviours of groups of people may be more Individualism oriented and less Communalism oriented, and vice versa. In fact, the salient values and behaviours can be represented at any point along the continuum, and may, over time, change in either direction. Such a formulation enables us to measure the influence of culture change upon individuals.

Before discussing each factor, it needs to be pointed out that the concepts to the *left* of each factor are applicable more to the British (and to western cultures in general) and those on the *right* to the Indians (and to eastern cultures in general).

Individualism – Communalism (Collectivism)

Individualism

Individualism has come to acquire several different meanings: an ability to exercise a degree of control over one's life, the ability to cope with one's problems, an ability to change for the better, reliance upon oneself, being responsible for one's actions, self-fulfilment and self-realization of one's internal resources, and the pursuit of one's own chosen goals in a culture which respects and cherishes pluralistic (and even conflicting) values. Triandis (1994) points out that individualism, in essence, is concerned with giving priority to one's personal goals over the goals of one's ingroup. While Triandis (1995) distinguishes between vertical and horizontal individualism, Kim (1997) characterizes individualism in terms of three features, which he refers to as (a) emphasis on distinct and autonomous individuals; (b) separation from ascribed relationships such as family, community and religion; (c) emphasis on abstract principles, rules and norms that guide the individual's thoughts, feelings and actions. Individualism, according to Kim (1997), asserts the position of rationalism, universalism, detachability and freedom of choice, and rejects a traditional, ascribed, communal and medieval social order.

Individualism has also been the subject of considerable debate among western thinkers (Bellah, 1985; Berry, 1994; Hofstede, 1980, 1991; Kagitcibasi, 1997; Lukes, 1973; Riesman, 1954; Sinha and Tripathi, 1994; Spence, 1985; Triandis, 1995; Waterman, 1981). Some writers have argued that the notions of individualism are incompatible, even antithetical with communal and collective interests. The 'dog-eat-dog' philosophy is seen as being divisive, inimical in terms of the promotion of communal goals, and in the long run it alienates fellow beings from one another. However, there are others – among them Sampson (1977) being the more outspoken of the defenders of individualism – who extol its virtues. Individualism, it is argued, is in keeping with the philosophy of humanism, which emphasizes, among other things, the notion of the 'dignity of man', its disentanglement from theology and religion, and its espousal of scientific enterprise as the fundamental bases for understanding the universe (Cooper, 1996). In recent years, the increasing popularity of individualism can also be attributed to the Weberian spirit of capitalism and free enterprise. Sampson (1977) sees no reason why the philosophy of individualism should not also nurture a spirit of co-operation and co-existence.

1 How does the notion of individualism affect our understanding of mental illness? Individualism tends to create conditions which do not permit an easy sharing of one's problems and worries with others. Individualism, as Albert Camus pointed out in his famous book *The Myth of Sisyphus* (1955), creates an existential loneliness in people which is compounded by a sense of the absurd, which is an integral part of the human condition. Camus warned that there is no easy escape from this human condition. The emphasis upon self-reliance – the expectation of being responsible for one's success or failure – imposes severe stress upon the individual and can lead to severe psychiatric disorders. Consequently, any failures with attendant feelings of guilt are explained in individualistic terms.

2 The philosophy of individualism has a strong bearing on the notion of *identity*. Identity, in western society, is construed by psychologists and psychiatrists of virtually all theoretical persuasions, in *developmental terms*, which starts from infancy. In the process of development,

one's identity – according to received wisdom – passes through several critical stages from childhood to adolescence, into adulthood (Paranjpe, 1998). To acquire an appropriate identity which asserts one's strengths, which is located in reality, which reflects one's true inner being and which leads to the fulfilment or realization of one's potential is by no means easy. It often results in conflict, which if unresolved leads to severe stress, and in extreme cases to an identity crisis (Erikson, 1963; Maslow, 1970, 1971; Paranjpe, 1998; Rogers, 1961, 1980). The ideology of individualism, in that sense, is inimical to the acquisition of a stable identity.

3   Another dominant feature of individualism is its recognition of and respect for an individual's physical and psychological 'space'. People do not normally touch one another for that is seen as an encroachment of one's physically defined boundaries. Second, the taboos related to physical touch are so strong that, even in times of grief, they are not easily violated (Laungani, 1997). Even eye-to-eye contact between two people is normally avoided. Several studies have shown that the effects of violating another person's physical space lead to severe stress and in extreme cases to neurosis (Greenberg and Firestone, 1977; Rohner, 1974).

4   Closely related to the concept of physical space is that of 'psychological space'. This is concerned with defining boundaries which separate the psychological self from others. It is an idea of immense value in the west, respected in all social situations. It comes into play in all social encounters, from the most casual to the most intimate. One hears of people feeling 'threatened', 'upset', 'angry', 'awkward', 'confused' etc. when they feel that their subjectively defined space is invaded. Thus anxiety or depression or grief is seen primarily as the sole problem of the afflicted individual. One does not intrude, one does not volunteer support for fear of invading the other person's 'psychological' space. Vine (1982) reviewed the major studies in the area related to crowding – the invasion of psychological space – and found that violating another person's psychological space gives rise to stress and other forms of mental disorders. A separate study (Webb, 1978) has shown that, in extreme cases, it leads to neuroses and other psychosomatic disturbances.

5   The importance of physical and psychological space in maintaining social relationships can best be understood in relation to the concept of privacy. Privacy implies a recognition of and respect for another person's individuality. It is concerned with defining boundaries which separate the self from others – both physically and psychologically. It is an idea of immense value in the west, respected and adhered to in all social relationships. The need for defining one's psychological and physical boundaries starts virtually from infancy. Several studies have demonstrated that the invasion of privacy also leads to severe stress (Greenberg and Firestone, 1977; Rohner, 1974).

6   Individualism has also had an effect on the size of the British family structure which from the postwar period onward has undergone a

dramatic change (Eversley and Bonnerjea, 1982). Although the nuclear family is still seen as the norm, it is by no means clear how a 'typical' British family shall be defined. With the gradual increase in one-parent families – at present around 20 per cent – combined with the fact that just under 25 per cent of the population live alone, the present nuclear family structure is likely to change even more dramatically. The changes in the size and structure of families, combined with high levels of social and occupational mobility, may have 'destabilized' society, creating a sense of loss of community life, particularly in the urban metropolitan cities. As a result, mental illness may often go unnoticed and the afflicted person may be denied appropriate care and treatment.

Communalism (Collectivism)

Insofar as the concept 'collectivism' is concerned, I prefer the word 'communalism' instead. A culture is not just a motley crowd or collection of people; it is much more than that. In selecting a word which is seemingly neutral in its sociological and particularly political connotations, there is the implicit danger of reintroducing the old notions of 'group mind', which were abandoned several decades ago. The fact that people in eastern cultures live in communities which are joined by kinship, linguistic, religious and caste relationships would merit the use of the term communalism instead of the sterile, implicitily racist, but politically correct term collectivism.

Indian society, not unlike other eastern societies, is a family-based and community-oriented society (Kakar, 1981; Koller, 1982; Lannoy, 1976; Laungani, 1997, 1998; Mandelbaum, 1972; Sinari, 1984; Sinha and Kao, 1997). A community in the sense in which it is understood in India and other eastern countries has several common features. People within a group are united by a common caste-rank, religious grouping, and linguistic and geographical boundaries. There are similarities in dietary customs, religious beliefs and practices, and leisure pursuits. All the members within a community generally operate on a ranking or a hierarchical system. Elders are accorded special status within the community and are generally deferred to. In Indian family life, one's individuality is subordinated to collective solidarity, and one's ego is absorbed into the collective ego of the family and one's community. The prescriptive norms of the community serve as markers which help define behaviours, including those considered aberrant, deviant, insane and traumatic. Consequently when an emotional problem – whether it is financial, medical, psychiatric, sexual or religious in nature – affects a given individual in a family, it tends to get perceived as a 'communal' event, affecting the entire family, and in certain instances, the sub-community. The family concerned makes a concerted attempt to find a satisfactory solution to the problem.

Other communalist (collectivist) cultures including China, Taiwan, Korea, Hong Kong, Philippines, Thailand, Nepal, Pakistan, Iran, Turkey, Portugal, Mexico, Peru, Venezuela and Colombia also share most of the features described above (Cheng, 1996; Gulerce, 1996; Hofstede, 1980; Jing and Wan, 1997; Kim, 1997; Matsumoto, 1996; Sinha et al., 1996; Ward and Kennedy, 1996; Yang, 1997). For instance, Kuo-Shu Yang (1997) in his excellent analyses of the traditional Chinese personality refers to the tight, close-knit bond between the individual and his/her family:

> Chinese familism disposes the Chinese to subordinate their personal interests, goals, glory, and welfare to their family's interests, goals, glory, and welfare to the extent that the family is primary and its members secondary. (Yang, 1997: 245)

Again, Kuo-Shu Yang (1997) points out that in order to attain harmony within the family it is essential for the individual to 'surrender or merge into his or her family, and as a result, lose his or her individuality and idiosyncrasies as an independent actor' (p. 245).

What influence does communal life have on mental illness?

1   It is expected that for an individual to stay part of the family and of the community, the individual will submit to communal norms, and will not deviate to an extent where it becomes necessary for the deviant to be ostracized. The pressure to conform to family norms and expectations can cause acute stress and anxiety in individual members in the family, leading, in some instances, to psychotic disorders and hysteria (Channabasavanna and Bhatti, 1982; Sethi and Manchanda, 1978). On the whole, it would appear that extended family networks provide inbuilt safety measures against mental disturbances. The emotional and physical intimacy shared by all members within a family group acts as a buffer against the stressors from which the European counterpart is not protected.

2   It should also be pointed out that while personal choice is central to an individualistic society, it is virtually non-existent in a communalistic society. Occupations are largely caste-dependent, and caste of course is determined by birth. One is born into a given caste and destined to remain in it until death. One's friends too are an integral part of one's extended family network; pressures from the elders and threats of ostracism ensure that one stays within the confines of one's caste and community. One has little choice even in terms of one's marriage partner, for although the 'style' of arranged marriages in recent years has undergone a change within Indian society – particularly among the affluent middle classes in the urban sectors of the country – they are still the norm. One's life, to a large extent, centres round the extended family. The pressures which prevent a person from choosing his/her own future often lead to severe stress and psychiatric disturbances.

Table 13.1   *Major features of Individualism and Communalism*

Individualism	Communalism
Emphasis on high degree of self-control may often lead to anxiety, depression and other psychiatric disturbances	Collective pressures at conformity may lead to anxiety, depression, and other psychiatric disturbances
Pressures related to emphasis on personal responsibility	Pressures related to emphasis on collective responsibility
Achievement of a stable identity potentially traumatic and stressful	Identity ascribed at birth (caste system) may impose restrictions on individual development of identity
Emphasis on self-achievement	Emphasis on collective achievement
Individual needs may often override the needs of the family	Individual needs are often subordinated to the collective needs of the family
Emphasis on nuclear and one-parent families	Emphasis on extended families

Table 13.1 shows the major features of Individualism and Communalism.

Materialism – Spiritualism

Materialism

This refers to a belief in the existence of a material world, or a world composed of matter. What constitutes matter is itself debatable; the question has never been satisfactorily answered (Trefil, 1980). If matter consists of atoms, it appears that atoms are made of nuclei and electrons. Nuclei in turn are made up of protons and neutrons. What are protons and neutrons made of? Gell-Mann (see Davies, 1990) coined the word quarks. But quarks, it appears, have their own quirks. In other words, the assumed solidity of matter may indeed turn out to be a myth (Davies, 1990).

The notion of the solidity of matter was robustly debated by Heisenberg in his now famous research paper on indeterminacy in quantum theory in 1927 (Heisenberg, 1930). Such debates, however, are confined to journals of philosophy and science. At a practical, day-to-day level, aided by empiricism, one accepts the assumed solidity of the world which one inhabits – but not without paying a heavy price. For such an acceptance gives rise to the popular myth that all explanations of phenomena, ranging from lunar cycles to lunacy, need to be sought within the (assumed) materialist framework. This is evidenced by the profound reluctance among psychiatrists, medical practitioners and psychologists in general to entertain explanations which are of a non-material or supernatural in nature. In fact, the structure of psychiatry with its espousal of the organic (or the disease) model rests on a materialistic epistemology. The medical model has been the ruling paradigm with regard to research and clinical work in psychiatric disorders, including schizophrenia. For almost a century, the medical model has continued to exercise an undisputed hegemony over other models and has continued to dominate this area of work.

In recent years the hegemony of the medical model has come to be seriously disputed (Laungani, 2000). The attack has come from several disparate groups. These include clinical psychologists, counsellors, psychotherapists, health professionals, feminists, blacks, members of other ethnic minority groups, and those who are seen as the disaffected members of society. Some question the validity of the medical model of schizophrenia. Others attack it on socio-political grounds, arguing that the medical model is socially inequitous. It can be (and is) used to incarcerate different members of society who do not subscribe to the broader social norms and mores or society. But despite the attacks, the medical model continues to exert an extremely powerful influence in psychiatry (Laungani, 1996).

The few psychiatrists who have steered away from non-materialistic explanations, or have shown the willingness to consider alternative, non-material explanations, comprise a very small minority within traditional psychiatry. Most of them are only too aware that anyone offering such explanations of mental illness is in danger of incurring the wrath of the scientific community. For such explanations fall within the purview of the *pre-scientific* communities, or in other words, *superstitious* and *backward* societies to be found mainly in the underdeveloped (or developing) Third World countries.

With the decline in the belief in the demonological model in western societies – certainly among the medical and psychiatric profession – there is reluctance among those members of the public who might wish to attribute the cause of their inexplicable mental disturbances to the malevolent powers of supernatural forces. To offer such explanations might in itself be seen as an indication of serious mental disturbances! For the acceptance of a materialistic framework is incompatible with a non-material explanation and leads to a logical contradiction: a spirit by definition is non-material.

Spiritualism

The espousal of *materialist* and *positivist* epistemologies, so vital in the west, meets with lukewarm approval in Indian thinking. The external world to Indians is not composed of matter. It is seen as being illusory. It is *maya*. The concept of *maya*, as Zimmer (1951/1989) points out, 'holds a key position in Vedantic thought and teaching' (p. 19). Since the external world is illusory and subject to continuous change, external reality cannot but be illusory. If reality is not external to the individual, wherein lies reality? Zimmer (1951/1989) argues that reality or its perception lies within the individual, and not, as westerners believe, outside the individual. According to Zimmer (1951/1989) this tends to make Indians more inward looking and westerners more outward looking. Also, given the illusory nature of the external world, the Indian mind remains unfettered by materialistic and positivistic boundaries, which are often seen as constraints to our perception of reality. The Indian mind may therefore resort to formulations where material and spiritual, physical and metaphysical,

Table 13.2   *Major features of Materialism and Spiritualism*

Materialism	Spiritualism
The world is 'real', solid and physical	The world is illusory; it is *maya*
Rejection of contradictory explanations of mental illness	Co-existence of contradictory explanations of mental illness
Mental illness explained by means of 'natural' phenomena	Mental illness explained by means of natural and supernatural phenomena
Reality external to the individual	Reality internal to the individual
Reality perceived through scientific enterprise	Reality perceived through contemplation and inner reflection, through spiritual transcendence
Mental illness may be explained in genetic and organic terms in psychiatric literature	Mental illness may be explained in terms of the influence of inauspicious cosmic events affecting the individual

natural and supernatural explanations of phenomena coexist with one another. To a westerner if A is A, A cannot then be not-A. If dysentery is caused by certain forms of bacteria, it cannot then be due to the influence of the 'evil eye'. The two are logically and empirically incompatible. But in certain forms of Indian thinking, A is not only A, but under certain conditions A may be not-A.

Indian beliefs and values revolve round the notion of *spiritualism*. The ultimate purpose of human existence is to transcend one's illusory physical existence, renounce the world of material aspirations and attain a heightened state of spiritual awareness. Any activity which is likely to promote such a state is to be encouraged. For it is through transcendence – inward-seeking consciousness – that one is able to attain salvation, or *moksha*.

In keeping with the notion of spiritualism, mental illness in India may also be explained in terms of sorcery, bewitchment, and by the possession of one's soul by evil and malevolent spirits (Kakar, 1982). The belief in magical explanations is widespread, and there are persons specially qualified to understand the workings of evil spirits. In times of serious and sudden illnesses within the family, such 'experts' are summoned by the family members to exorcise spells, cast out the effect of 'evil eyes', undo the malevolence of magic, undertake religious ceremonies to counteract the negative influences of inauspicious events, etc. in order to help the afflicted person to recover (Kakar, 1982).

Table 13.2 summarizes the major features of Materialism and Spiritualism.

Free Will – Determinism

Free Will

There does not appear to be a satisfactory end in sight to the philosophical and scientific wrangles concerning the nature of free will, predestination, determinism and indeterminism. The Aristotelian legacy, although it has undergone several transformations, has remained with us for over two thousand years (Flew, 1989). Prior to Newton's spectacular achievements, determinism was enmeshed in its theistic and metaphysical connotations. After the publication of Newton's *Principia* in 1687, the concept of determinism was partially freed from its theistic connotations and a non-theistic and mechanistic view of determinism in science, and indeed in the universe, gained prominence. A scientific notion of determinism, with its emphasis on causality, or conversely, its denial of non-causal events, found favour among the rationalist philosophers who embraced it with great fervour (Popper, 1972). However, it was not until the emergence of quantum mechanics in the early twentieth century that determinism in science, if not in human affairs, once again came to be seriously questioned. In keeping with his own views on the subject, Popper (1988) avoids the terms determinism and free will altogether. He proposes instead the term indeterminism, which he argues is not the opposite of determinism nor is it the same as free will.

Notwithstanding the unresolved debates in philosophy on the subject, there is a peculiar dualism in western thinking concerning free will and determinism. Research in the natural and physical sciences, in medicine, psychiatry, biology and other related disciplines, including psychology, is still based on the acceptance of a deterministic framework – hence the concern with seeking causal explanations, and with predictability in accordance with rational scientific procedures of prediction. Yet at a social, psychological and commonsense level, there is a strong belief in the notion of free will.

Free will might be defined as a *non-causal, voluntary action*. However, at a commonsense level it suggests responsibility for one's actions, or control over one's actions. Moral actions of any kind would be impossible without a belief in the notion of free will. Thus free will allows an individual to do what he/she wills, permits the individual to choose between a set of alternatives, and in so doing take 'credit' for his/her successes, and accept blame for his/her failures and mishaps. This feature of western society entraps a person into his or her own existential predicament. There does not appear to be an easy way out.

Determinism

Indians, by virtue of subscribing to a deterministic view of life, in a teleological sense at least, are prevented from taking final responsibility for their own actions. The notion of determinism plays an extremely crucial role in Indian thinking. *The law of karma*, which involves determinism and fatalism, has shaped the Indian view of life over centuries (O'Flaherty, 1976, 1980; Sinari, 1984; Reichenbach, 1990; Weber, 1963). In its simplest form, the law of karma states that happiness or sorrow is the predetermined effect of actions committed by an individual, sometimes either in his/her present life or in one of his/her numerous past lives. Reichenbach (1990) points out that the law of karma is not concerned with the general relation between actions and their consequences. It is usually held to apply to the moral sphere and is concerned with the moral quality of actions and their consequences. Thus according to the law of karma we receive the results of our own actions and not another's. The sins of the father are not visited upon the children. And given the deterministic nature of the law of karma, things do not happen because we make them happen. Things happen because they were destined to happen.

The belief in the law of karma does not, as is mistakenly assumed by many, negate the notion of free will. As von-Furer-Haimendorf (1974) pointed out, karma, in an important sense, is based on the assumption of free will. The theory of karma rests on the idea that the individual has the moral responsibility for each of his or her actions, and hence the freedom of moral choice.

One can see how the law of karma is invoked to explain not only the onset of mental illness but all sorts of misfortunes which may befall upon an individual. If one's present life is determined by one's actions in one's previous life, it follows that any illness – mental or physical – that strikes an individual in a family was destined to happen. This idea is not as strange as it might appear at first sight. For in the west too it is not uncommon to attribute the causes of psychiatric disorders to the patient's past experiences (viz. infantile traumatic episodes, faulty or maladaptive learning, hereditary predispositions, genetic abnormalities, chemical imbalances, etc.) However, in India the notion of past is carried into one's previous life or lives. Pandey et al. (1980) in a study of informants of psychiatric patients in India found that the most commonly stated causes of psychotic disorders was attributed to physical causes and sins and wrong deeds in their previous and present life. These findings have been corroborated by Srinivasa and Trivedi (1982) who, in their study of 266 respondents selected from three villages in South India, attributed, among other factors, 'God's curse' as one of the most common causes of mental disorders.

The attribution of one's actions in one's previous life to psychotic disorders takes away the sting and the stigma from suffering. No blame is apportioned to the afflicted individual; it was his or her karma. It was destined to happen. Determinism thus engenders in the Indian psyche a spirit of passive, if not resigned, acceptance. This prevents a person from plunging into an abyss of despair – a state from which westerners, because of their fundamental belief in the doctrine of free will, cannot be protected. The main disadvantage of determinism – and there are many – lies in the fact that it may lead initially at least to a state of existential, and in certain instances, moral resignation, compounded by a profound sense of *inertia*. One takes no proactive measures; one merely accepts the vicissitudes of life without qualm. While this may prevent a person from experiencing anxiety it also prevents the person from overcoming the distressing condition.

Table 13.3   *Major features of Free Will and Determinism*

Free Will	Determinism
Emphasis on freedom of choice	Freedom of choice tends to be limited
Behaviour is often planned and proactive. Steps may be taken to deal individually with a serious problem	Behaviour often tends to be reactive. Attempts are made to find collective solutions to problems
Success or failure is due largely to individual effort	Although effort is important, success or failure is related to one's karma
Self-blame or guilt is a residual consequence of mental illness	No guilt is attached to the person suffering from mental illness
The notion of free will contains its own sets of contradictions: a person may will him/herself to die, but a person cannot will him/herself *not* to die	The notion of determinism contains its own sets of contradictions: no person can take credit or accept blame for his/her success or failure; all that is due to the influence of one's karma
Mental illness may often lead to victim-blaming	No blame is attached to victim

The major features of Free Will and Determinism are summarized in Table 13.3.

Cognitivism – Emotionalism

Cognitivism

This is concerned with the way in which the British and the Indians construe their private and social worlds. In broad terms, it has been suggested by Pande (1968) that British society is *work and activity centred* whereas Indian society is *relationship centred*. These different constructions of their private and social worlds are not accidental cultural developments. They stem from their inheritance of their different philosophical legacies.

In a work and activity centred society, people are more likely to operate on a cognitive mode, where the emphasis is on rationality, logic and control. Public expression of feelings and emotions – particularly among the middle classes in Britain – is often frowned upon. The expression of negative feelings causes mutual embarrassment and is often construed as being vulgar. Even in situations where it would seem legitimate to express feelings openly, without inhibition – at funerals, for instance – the British are guided by control, which suggests that one must not cry in public, one must at all times put on a 'brave face'; one must, above all, never lose one's dignity. Dignity is preserved or even socially enhanced through restraint. If one has to cry, one must do so in the silence of one's heart, in the privacy of one's home. The unwillingness or the inability to express emotions openly – even in those situations where it might seem legitimate and even desirable, such as at funerals – is a theme that has caused considerable concern to other writers in the field (Gorer, 1965; Hockey, 1993; Sarbin 1986).

An inability to express affective feelings related to death and bereavement may also lead to severe neuroses because of unresolved grief, which in turn may prevent the person concerned from 'letting go' and thus coming to terms with the death of a loved one.

It is not surprising therefore that in a work and activity centred society, a need arises for the creation of professional and semi-professional settings which permit the legitimate expression of specific feelings and emotions, and their handling by experts trained in the specific area. Thus one sees in western society the growth of specialist counsellors, including bereavement counsellors, cancer counsellors, AIDS counsellors, palliative care counsellors, marriage guidance counsellors, family therapists, rational-emotive therapists, and last but not least, psychotherapists and psychoanalysts of different theoretical persuasions.

In such a society, relationships are formed on the basis of *shared commonalities*. One is expected to 'work at a relationship' – in a marriage, in a family situation, with friends, with colleagues at work, and even with one's children. In a work and activity oriented society, one's identity, one's self-image and self-esteem grow out of one's work and one's attitude to work. Work defines one's sense of worth.

However, work and its relation to self-esteem acquire meaning only when seen against the background of time. Our conception of time is both objective and subjective. At an objective level time is seen in terms of an Einsteinian dimension, where each hour is divided into fixed moments of minutes, seconds and milliseconds. Each moment (at least on earth) expires at the same speed – an hour passes not a moment sooner, not a moment later. At a subjective level, however, there are variations in our perceptions of time. In a work and activity centred society, one's working life, including one's private life, is organized around time. To ensure the judicious use of time, one resorts to keeping appointment books, calendars, computer-assisted diaries; one tries to keep within one's time limits. One is constantly aware of the swift passage of time, and to fritter it away is often construed as an act of criminality. Time therefore comes to acquire a significant meaning in a work and activity centred society. McClelland (1961) has shown that people in general, and high achievers in particular, use metaphors such as a dashing waterfall, a speeding train, etc. to describe time. The fear of running out of time, the fear of not being able to accomplish one's short-term and long-term goals on time, is seen as one of the greatest stressors in western society. Even casual encounters between friends, between colleagues at work, operate on covert agendas. Meeting people is seldom construed as an end in itself. It is a means to an end, with time playing a significant role.

Emotionalism

Non-western societies, to a large extent, are *relationship centred* and operate on an *emotional* mode. The fact that people live in close physical proximity and share their lives with one another forces them into operating on an emotional mode. In such a society, feelings and emotions are not easily repressed, and their expression in general is not frowned upon. Crying, dependence on others, excessive emotionality, volatility and verbal hostility, both in males and females, are not in any way considered as signs of weakness or ill-breeding. Since feelings and emotions – both positive and negative – are expressed easily, there is little danger of treading incautiously on others' sensibilities and vulnerabilities, such as might be the case in work and activity centred societies.

In an extended family structure, emotional outbursts are, as it were, 'taken on board' by the family members. Quite often the emotional outbursts are of a symbolic nature – even highly stylized and ritualistic. To appreciate fully the ritualistic component of emotional outbursts among Indians, be they Hindus or Muslims, one must visualize it against the backdrop of the living conditions in India. In the urban areas – for those who are fortunate enough to live in a pukka house (houses built with bricks, cement and mortar), it is not at all uncommon for a family of eight to ten persons to be living together in one small room. Given the extreme closeness of life, the paucity of amenities, the absence of privacy, the inertia evoked by the overpowering heat and dust, the awesome feeling of claustrophobia, it is not at all surprising that families do often quarrel, fight and swear at one another (and from time to time assault one another too). But their quarrels and outbursts are often of a symbolic nature – for otherwise such quarrels would lead to a permanent rift, the consequences of which would be far more traumatic than those of living together. There is in such outbursts a surrealistic quality: at one level they are frighteningly real – the words and abuses hurled at one another, callous and hurtful – yet at another, bewilderingly unreal. They serve no function other than the relief which such 'cathartic' outbursts bring.

However, it should be recognized that in a hierarchical family structure each member within the family soon becomes aware of his or her own position within the hierarchy, and in the process of familial adjustment, learns the normative expressions of emotionality permissible to the person concerned.

One of the major disadvantages of being in a relationship-centred society is that one is forced into relationships from which one cannot or is unable to opt out without severe sanctions being imposed upon the individual. Several studies have shown that one's inability to sever enforced relationships based on birth and caste often leads to severe stress and neurosis (Channabasavanna and Bhatti, 1982).

The factor of time which, as we saw, is of such great importance in western societies, does not have the same meaning in a relationship-centred society. At an objective level, time is construed in virtually the same way as it is in the west. But at a subjective level time in India is seen in more flexible and even relaxed terms. Time, in Indian metaphysics, is not conceptualized in linear terms. A linear model of time signifies a beginning, a middle and an end, or, in other words, a past, a present and a future. Time, in Indian philosophy, is conceptualized in circular terms, which means that time has no beginning, no middle and no end, or, if there is a beginning, it remains unknown. These differential conceptualizations have serious implications for our understanding of mental disorders in both cultures.

For instance, at a day-to-day observational level, one does not notice among Indians the same sense of urgency which appears to have become the hallmark of western society. Time in India is often viewed as 'a quiet, motionless ocean', 'a vast expanse of sky'. It is interesting to note that in Hindi there is only one word – *kal* – which stands for both yesterday and tomorrow. It also stands for time. One gauges the meaning of the word from its context. Their flexible attitude to time is often reflected in their social engagements: they tend to be quite casual about keeping appointments; being late for an appointment, keeping another person waiting, does not appear to cause them any undue stress.

There are, however, exceptions to this flexible construction of time. They occur in those situations which are considered auspicious: undertaking an important journey, fixing the time of christenings, betrothals, weddings and funerals in particular. In such auspicious situations one is expected to consult the family Brahmin priest, who then consults an almanac from which he (most Brahmin priests are male) calculates the most auspicious time for the commencement of that particular activity. Such events because of their religious significance are seldom left to chance. One seeks divine guidance and planning in their execution. Inability to start such auspicious activities at the exact time can lead to severe stress, accompanied by feelings of guilt.

The major features of Cognitivism and Emotionalism are summarised in Table 13.4.

It is time to take stock. A close examination of the four factors shows quite clearly that there are fundamental differences between eastern and western cultures (and in our specific case, India and Britain) with regard to the genesis of mental illness. In India the familial, social, emotional and religious conditions unique to India (and to other eastern cultures in general) play an exceedingly important role in understanding the nature and the causes of mental illness. In Britain and in other western countries these factors have a lesser role to play. Mental illness is related to the social conditions which promote a philosophy of individualism with its emphasis on self-reliance, complemented by a belief in free will which asserts that one must trust one's own ability to solve one's problems by logical, rational and scientific means.

Having discussed the genesis of mental illness, what are the therapeutic alternatives available to the two cultural groups? Since the therapeutic practices in western societies are well known, we shall concentrate on the diverse therapeutic practices available in India.

Table 13.4 *Major features of Cognitivism and Emotionalism*

Cognitivism	Emotionalism
Emphasis on rationality and logic	Emphasis on feelings and intuition
Feelings and emotions tend to be kept in check	Feelings and emotions tend to be expressed freely
Emphasis on *achievement* of identity	Identity is *ascribed* at birth due to being born into a given caste
Anxiety is related to the *acquisition* of identity	Anxiety may be related to the 'imposition' of a familial and caste-related identity
Emphasis on work and activity	Emphasis on relationships
Relationships are often a by-product of work	Work is often a by-product of relationships
Relations based on shared interests	Relations based on caste and family

Therapies in India

Psychiatric treatment

Wig and Saxena (1982) point out that psychiatrists in India continue to use the classificatory systems of ICD-9 and the DSM-IV in their clinical work. Psychiatric treatments include confinement into a psychiatric institution, use of drugs, ECT, custodial care, etc. Several psychiatrists, however, have expressed dissatisfaction with the classificatory systems highlighted in the DCM-IV and have suggested changes and revisions which would take into account important social and cultural factors in classification. In any event, the uses of the above classificatory systems are limited for at least two reasons.

First, the ratio of psychiatrists to the general population in India is a little over one psychiatrist to every million people (Rao, 1986). There are only about 45 mental hospitals in the entire country. There is hardly any undergraduate training in psychiatry in the medical schools. Mental illness in India is estimated to affect some two to seven persons per thousand population in India (Rao, 1986). Given the present population of over 950 million people in India, it would seem therefore that between two and four million are affected by mental illness of one form or another. This, however, is a conservative estimate, for according to Wig and Saxena (1982) schizophrenia affects over 1 per cent of the adult population. Given the size of the population, the regional and linguistic variations, and the great 'rural–urban divide' in terms of social, educational and economic differentials, it is impossible for the present psychiatric services to meet the needs of the afflicted persons in India. It is evident therefore that the various forms of psychiatric treatment, including the use of psychotropic drugs, ECT and other forms of therapies are limited in their uses. They are confined to psychiatric institutions, which are located to a large extent in the urban areas of the country. Moreover, psychiatric institutions in India tend to be overcrowded and understaffed. In addition to the above problems, there are limited economic resources, lack of trained personnel, limited availability of drugs, high dropout rate of patients from treatment, lack of awareness among general medical practitioners, lack of integration of indigenous and modern systems of medicine, all of which collectively impose severe constraints on the work done by health professionals, including psychiatrists.

Second, psychiatric institutions arouse pejorative, stigmatizing and even hostile images in the minds of people. For a person to be admitted into a psychiatric institution is the ultimate admission of a family member's insanity. It is a label which families, for social reasons, are anxious to avoid. The label often transfers to the entire family, making it difficult in many cases for parents to find suitable spouses for their children, particularly for their daughters. Parents of eligible daughters are loath to consider forming marital liaisons with families where there is known insanity. Thus people in general are profoundly reluctant to have their near and dear ones admitted into psychiatric institutions – unless of course they have no choice in the matter. Admission into a psychiatric institution may often be seen as the last resort – after all the other alternatives have been tried and exhausted.

Yoga therapy

In India there is a greater reliance on indigenous therapeutic treatments. The WHO Report (1978) points out that there are over 108 colleges of indigenous medicine in India, with over 500,000 practitioners of one of the following indigenous forms of healing: Ayurveds, Unani and Yoga. Yoga appears to be the most popular form of treatment used is psychological disorders all over the country. Evidence of the efficacy of yoga therapy is quite convincing (Satyavathi, 1988). Encouraged by the results of yoga therapy, Vahia (1982) even suggested that yoga represents a new conceptual model of health and disease. Although several studies have pointed to the effectiveness of yoga therapy (Bhole, 1981; Dharmakeerti, 1982; Neki, 1979; Nespor, 1982), it is not seen as a panacea for all types of disorder.

Religious therapies

Since in many instances mental illness is perceived as a visitation from malevolent gods, it is an accepted practice to take the afflicted person to a well-known shrine, a temple, or to a Muslim *darga*. It might be of interest to note that in this instance there is a powerful pragmatic mixture of religious beliefs: Hindus often visit Muslim *dargas*, and Muslim families undertake to visit a temple or a well-known guru, attributed with divine healing powers. Sudhir Kakar in his excellent book *Shamans, Mystics and Doctors* (1982) cites remarkable case studies to that effect. The visitations to shrines, temples, mosques may take several forms. The afflicted person 'surrenders' his/her will to the guru by sitting near the guru, 'feasting' his/her eyes on the guru; the *darshan* (blessed vision) of the guru is attributed with immense spiritual and healing powers. In other instances, the guru may encourage the person to recite prayers, meditate, read from the scriptures, perform religious rites – all of which are attributed with healing properties. Special emphasis is paid to the intense, and in some instances symbiotic relationship between the guru and the follower. The guru – follower therapeutic procedure, on the whole, tends to adopt a *directive approach* rather than a *non-directive* one. The guru attempts to guide the afflicted person through all his/her afflictions, offers hope and prayer. In return it is beholden upon the follower to abide by all the teachings and prescriptions of the guru. For the therapeutic enterprise to progress smoothly, it is essential that the guru is perceived as being a person of immense sagacity and wisdom. The guru must have no obvious pecuniary interests in the outcome of the treatment. The guru must also be seen to be living on the 'margins' of society. In other words, the guru, in keeping with Indian cultural traditions, must be seen as being truly and totally detached from material comforts and aspirations.

The well-to-do often undertake long, arduous and expensive pilgrimages to the holy cities, such as Varanasi, Hardwar and Prayag in Uttar Pradesh, where the holy rivers, Ganga, Jamuna and Saraswati, meet in confluence. There they perform elaborate religious ceremonies, feed hundreds of mendicants, bathe the victim (and themselves) in the River Ganges, which is attributed with divine cleansing powers.

At home, the women pray, undertake regular fasts, refrain from eating meat, and practise extremely severe austerities to ensure the restoring of the victim's mental and physical health.

Demonological therapies

Mental illness (with its accompanying somatic symptoms) in India is also explained in terms of sorcery, bewitchment and evil spirits (Kakar 1982). The patient afflicted by these disorders is considered blameless because the illness is seen as the work of demons and other malevolent spirits, or *shaitans*, who take possession of the patient. Why a demonic spirit should take possession of one individual and not another is attributed to the belief that spirit possession is due to the envy of neighbours at the visible affluence and success and good health and good fortune of the afflicted person. Belief in the evil eye – commonly refered to as *najar* or *dishti* – is quite strong and widespread among Indians. A child who meets with an accident or falls seriously ill and contracts an infections disease might be the victim of an evil eye (Fuller, 1992; Laungani, 1988). Social acceptance of such attributions has served to legitimize the belief in the evil eye and its malevolent variants. In addition to wearing charms, amulets and sacred threads (the symbol of the 'twice-born' high caste Hindu), parents might symbolically blacken the child's face with ash or coal dust or even kohl to ward off the dangers of the evil eye. A plain and 'ugly' child is less likely to become a victim of the evil eye than a pretty child.

But when such prophylactic measures fail, persons specially qualified to remove spells and counter-spells, exorcize demons and other spirits such as *bhoots, balas* and *shaitans,* are summoned by the family members of the afflicted persons.

All over India one finds an army of faith healers, mystics, shamans, *pirs* (holy men), *bhagats* (religious persons) and gurus. They are accorded the same (if not greater) respect and veneration as the medically trained psychiatrists in India. It is not uncommon to find the relatives of a distressed person consulting many such specialists for effective treatment.

Astrological therapies

Beliefs in astrology and the malevolent influences of planets on one's life are strongly ingrained in the Indian psyche. The belief that one's life is influenced by the nine planets, referred to as *grahas,* headed by the sun, is widely prevalent in India (Madan, 1987). Madan points out: 'These planetary movements affect the lives of people variously, depending primarily upon the time (*kala*) and place (*sthana*) of their birth' (p. 54). It is quite customary to have a child's horoscope cast upon its birth. The heavenly configuration of planets at the moment of birth is seen as a determinant of life chances. A carefully cast horoscope reveals a person's fate, which is written on a person's forehead (Fuller, 1992). The horoscopes are also consulted prior to finalizing betrothals. In the event of a serious planetary mismatch in the horoscopes of the couple, the parents may decide not to proceed with the betrothal of their respective children, or may decide to undertake arduous religious ceremonies which would propitiate the evil influences of the planets on the future of the couple. Mental illness too is often attributed to the malevolent influence of the planets, particularly Saturn, *shani.* Shrines containing images of Saturn and other planets are found in all parts of India. On the day when Saturn moves from one house to another, people all over India offer prayers – some expressing relief at having survived the last 30 months, and others fearful and anxious at having to get through the next 30 months without calamitous misfortunes (Fuller, 1992).

Indigenous Ayurvedic therapies

Ayurveda is a traditional Indian system of medicine. Its fundamental goal is to bring about and maintain a harmonious balance between the person, the person's body and the person's psyche. In modern western terminology it might be construed as a form of holistic medicine. However, its roots run deeper. There is a shared belief among Indians and people from South Asia that Ayurvedic medicine has no beginning since it reflects 'the laws of nature inherent in life and living beings and thus mirrors their unchanging essence' (Kakar, 1982: 221). Ayurvedic medicine is focused more on treating the person rather than the disease. Illness occurs when there is a humoral imbalance between the psyche-soma identity, leading to different types of insanities to the specific imbalances.

For effective treatment it is as important to understand the person as the disease which is to be treated. The emphasis of treatment is on purification. Purification treatment may often consist of purges, emetics, enemas and bleeding. However, these practices, to large extent, appear to have fallen into disuse. They are still practised in certain parts of South India. They have been replaced by other traditional herbal remedies. Since the Ayurvedic goal is to restore a harmonious balance, the treatment procedures tend to be diverse. There is a strong emphasis on rigid dietary practices. This is in keeping with the belief that certain types of foods produce certain mental states (both desirable and undesirable) and therefore can only be eaten at certain times of the day. The patient is also encouraged to undertake regular physical exercises, including breathing exercises, or *pranayamas*. The final emphasis is on the acquisition of desirable personal and social habits, which include ways of relating to oneself and to others, and the imbibing of those thoughts, attitudes, beliefs and values which promote a harmonious balance between the person, the soma and the psyche.

Conclusion

Clearly no culture or society has all the answers concerning the nature and treatment of mental illness. It is only when cultures meet – on equal terms and as equal partners both as research scientists and as clinicians – and express a genuine willingness to share and learn from each other that one might find tentative answers to the questions which concern us all. But for some cultures to assume that there is little or nothing of value which they might profitably learn from another culture is inimical to the creation of a genuine multicultural society.

References

Al-Issa, I. (ed.) (1982) *Culture and Psychopathology*. Baltimore: University Park Press.
Bellah, R.N. (1985) *Habits of the Heart. Individuation and Commitment in American life*. Berkeley, CA: University of California Press.
Benedict, R. (1946) *The Chrysanthemum and the Sword*. Boston: Houghton Mifflin.
Berry, J.W. (1994) 'Ecology of individualism and collectivism', in U. Kim, H.C. Triandis, C. Kagitcibasi, S.-C. Choi and G. Yoon (eds), *Individualism and Collectivism: Theory, Method and Applications*, pp. 123–136. Thousand Oaks, CA: Sage.
Bhole, M.V. (1981) 'Concept of relaxation in shavasana', *Yoga Mimamsa*, 20: 50–56.
Bloom, A. (1987) *The Closing of the American Mind*. London: Penguin.
Boaz, F. (1911) *The Mind of Primitive Man*. New York: Macmillan.
Camus, A. (1955) *The Myth of Sisyphus*. London: Hamish Hamilton.

Channabasavanna, S.M. and Bhatti, R.S. (1982) 'A study on international patterns and family typologies in families of mental patients', in A. Kiev and V. Rao (eds), *Readings in Transcultural Psychiatry*, pp. 149–61. Madras: Higginbothams.

Cheng, C.H.K. (1996) 'Towards a culturally relevant model of self-concept for the Hong Kong Chinese', in J. Pandey, D. Sinha and D.P.S. Bhawuk (eds), *Asian Contributions to Cross-Cultural Psychology*, pp. 235–54. New Delhi: Sage.

Cooper, D.E. (1996) *World Philosophies. An Historical Introduction*. Oxford: Blackwell.

Darwin, C. (1872) *The Expression of Emotions in Man and Animals*. New York: Philosophical Library.

Dasgupta, S.N. (1961–2) *History of Indian Philosophy*, vols 1–5, 3rd edn. Cambridge: Cambridge University Press.

Davies, P. (1990) *God and the New Physics*. London: Penguin.

Dharmakeerti, U.S. (1982) 'Review of "Yoga and cardiovascular management"', *Yoga*, 20 (6): 15–16.

Doyal, L. and Harris, R. (1986) *Empiricism, Explanation and Rationality: An Introduction to the Philosophy of the Social Sciences*. London: Routledge.

Draguns, J.G. (1981) 'Psychological disorders of clinical severity', in H.C. Triandis and R.W. Brislin (eds), *Handbook of Cross-Cultural Psychology*, vol. 5. Boston, MA: Allyn and Bacon.

Draguns, J.G. (1994) 'Pathological and clinical aspects', In L.L. Adler and U.P. Gielen (eds), *Cross-Cultural Topics in Psychology*, pp. 165–78. Westport, CT: Greenwood Press.

Ekman, P. (1972) 'Universals and cultural differences in facial expressions of emotion', in J. Cole (ed.), *Nebraska Symposium of Motivation*, 1971, vol. 19. Lincoln: University of Nebraska Press.

Ekman, P. (1973) *Darwin and Facial Expression*. New York: Academic Press.

Ekman, P. (1985) *Telling Lies*. New York: Norton.

Ekman, P. (1994) 'Strong evidence for universals in facial expressions: a reply to Russell's mistaken critique', *Psychological Bulletin*, 115: 268–87.

Ekman, P. and Freisen, W.V. (1975) *Unmasking the Face*. Englewood Cliffs, NJ: Prentice Hall.

Ekman, P. and Heider, K. (1988) 'The universality of a contempt expression: a replication', *Motivation and Emotion*, 12: 303–8.

Erikson, E. (1963) *Childhood and Society*. London: Penguin.

Eversley, D. and Bonnerjea, L. (1982) 'Social change and indicators of diversity', in R.N. Rapaport, M.P. Fogarty and R. Rapaport (eds), *Families in Britain*, pp. 75–94. London: Routledge & Kegan Paul.

Feyerabend, P. (1987) *Farewell to Reason*, London: Verso.

Flew, A. (1989) *An Introduction to Western Philosophy*. German Democratic Republic: Thames and Hudson.

Fuller, C.J. (1992) *The Camphor Flame: Popular Hinduism and Society in India*. Princeton, NJ: Princeton University Press.

Gellner, E. (1985) *Relativism and the Social Sciences*. Cambridge: Cambridge University Press.

Gorer, G. (1965) *Death, Grief, and Mourning in Contemporary Britain*. London: Cresset Press.

Greenberg, C.I. and Firestone, J.J. (1977) 'Compensatory response to crowding: effects of personal space and privacy reduction', *Journal of Personality and Social Psychology*, 35: 637–44.

Gulerce, A. (1996) 'A family structure assessment device for Turkey', in J. Pandey, D. Sinh and D.P.S. Bhawuk (eds), *Asian Contributions to Cross-Cultural Psychology*, pp. 108–118. New Delhi: Sage.

Heisenberg, W. (1930) *The Physical Principles of the Quantum Theory*. Berkeley, CA: University of California Press.

Hockey, J. (1993) 'The acceptable face of human grieving? The clergy's role in managing emotional expression during funerals', in D. Clark (ed.), *The Sociology of Death*, pp. 129–48. Oxford: Blackwell.

Hofstede, G. (1980) *Culture's Consequencs: International Differences in Work-related Values*. Beverly Hills, CA: Sage.

Hofstede, G. (1991) *Cultures and Organizations: Software of the Mind*. Maidenhead: McGraw-Hill.

Hui, C.H. and Triandis, H.C. (1986) 'Individualism–collectivism: a study of cross-cultural researchers', *Journal of Cross-cultural Psychology*, 17: 222–48.

Jahoda, G. and Krewer, B. (1998) 'History of cross-cultural and cultural psychology', in J.W. Berry, Y.H. Poortinga and J. Pandet (eds), *Handbook of Cross-cultural Psychology, vol. 1. Theory and Method*, 2nd edn. pp. 1–42. Boston, MA: Allyn & Bacon.

Jing, Q. and Wan, C. (1997) 'Socialization of Chinese children', in H.S.R. Kao and D. Sinha (eds), *Asian Perspectives on Psychology*, pp. 25–39. New Delhi: Sage.

Kagitcibasi, C. (1997) 'Individualism and collectivism', in J.W. Berry, M.H. Segall and C. Kagitcibasi (eds), *Handbook of Cross-Cultural Psychology, vol. 3. Social Behavior and Applications*, 2nd edn, pp. 1–49. Boston: Allyn and Bacon.

Kakar, S. (1981) *The Inner World – A Psychoanalytic Study of Children and Society in India*. Delhi: Oxford University Press.

Kakar, S. (1982) *Shamans, Mystics and Doctors*. London: Mandala Books.

Kane, P.V. (1932–60) *History of Dharmashastra*, vols 1–5. Poona: Bhandarkar Oriental Research Institute.

Kim, U. (1997) 'Asian collectivism: an indigenous perspective', in H.S.R. Kao and D. Sinha (eds), *Asian Perspectives on Psychology*, pp. 147–63. New Delhi: Sage.

Kleinman, A. (1980) *Patients and Healers in the Context of Culture*. Berkeley: University of California Press.

Koller, J.M. (1982) *The Indian Way: Perspectives*. London: Collier Macmillan.

Lannoy, R. (1976) *The Speaking Tree*. Oxford: Oxford University Press.

Laungani, P. (1988) 'Accidents in children – an Asian perspective', *Public Health*, 103: 171–6.

Laungani, P. (1990) 'Turning eastward – an Asian view on child abuse', *Health and Hygiene*, 11 (1): 26–9.

Laungani, P. (1991) 'Preventing child abuse and promoting child health across cultures', Paper presented at the United Nations Conference on Action for Public Health, in Sundsvall, Sweden, 9–15 June.

Laungani, P. (1991a) 'The nature and experience of learning. Cross-cultural perspectives'. Paper read at a Conference on Experiential Learning. University of Surrey, Guildford, 16–18 July.

Laungani, P. (1991b) 'Stress across cultures: a theoretical analysis'. Paper read at the Conference of the Society of Public Health on Stress and the Health Services at the Royal Society of Medicine, Wimpole Street, London, 25 July.

Laungani, P. (1992) 'Assessing child abuse through interviews of children and parents of children at risk', *Children and Society*, 6 (1): 3–11.

Laungani, P. (1995) 'Stress in eastern and western cultures', in J. Brebner, E. Greenglass, P. Laungani and A. O'Roark (eds) (series eds C.D. Spielberger and I.G. Sarason), *Stress and Emotion*, vol. 15, pp. 265–80. Washington, DC: Taylor and Francis.

Laungani, P. (1995a) 'Patterns of bereavement in Indian and English societies', *Bereavement Care*, 14 (1): 5–7.

Laungani, P. (1996) 'Research in cross-cultural settings: ethical considerations', in E. Miao (ed.), *Cross-Cultural Encounters. Proceedings of the 53rd Annual Convention of International Council of Psychologists*, pp. 107–36. Taipei, Taiwan: General Innovation Service (GIS).

Laungani, P. (1997) 'Death in a Hindu family', in C.M. Parkes, P. Laungani and W. Young (eds), *Death and Bereavement Across Cultures*. London: Routledge.

Laungani, P. (1998) 'Client-centred or culture-centred counselling?', in S. Palmer and P. Laungani (eds), *Counselling Across Cultures*. London: Sage.

Laungani, P. (2000) 'Cultural construction of schizophrenia: a proposed paradigm shift', *Dynamic Psychiatry*. 32 (3–6): 267–92.

Lukes, S. (1973) *Individualism*. Oxford: Blackwell.

Madan, T.N. (1987) *Non-Renunciation: Themes and Interpretations of Hindu Culture*. Delhi: Oxford University Press.

Malinowski, B. (1927) *Sex and Repression in Savage Society.* London: Routledge.

Mandelbaum, D.G. (1972) *Society in India*, vol. 2. Berkeley: University of California Press.

Marsella, A.J. (1982) 'Depressive experience and disorder across cultures', in H.C. Triandis and R.W. Brislin (eds), *Handbook of Cross-Cultural Psychology.* Boston, MA: Allyn and Bacon.

Maslow, A. (1970) *Motivation and Personality*, 2nd edn. New York: Harper and Row.

Maslow, A. (1971) *The Farther Reaches of Human Nature.* New York: McGraw Hill.

Matsumoto, D. (1989) 'Cultural influences on the perception of emotion', *Journal of Cross-Cultural Psychology*, 20: 92–105.

Matsumoto, D. (1992) 'American-Japanese cultural differences in the recognition of universal facial expressions', *Journal of Cross-Cultural Psychology*, 23: 72–84.

Matsumoto, D. (1996) *Unmasking Japan: Myths and Realities about the Emotions of the Japanese.* Stanford, CA: Stanford University Press.

McClelland, D.C. (1961) *The Achieving Society.* Princeton, NJ: Van Nostrand.

Mead, M. (1930) *Growing up in New Guinea.* New York: Morrow.

Mead, M. (1935) *Sex and Temperament in Three Primitive Societies.* New York: Morrow.

Musgrove, F. (1982) *Education and Anthropology: Other Cultures and the Teacher.* Bath: John Wiley.

Neki, J.S. (1979) 'Psychotherapy in India: traditions and trends', in M. Kapur, V.N. Murthy, K. Satyavathi and R.L. Kapur (eds), *Psychotherapeutic Processes*, pp. 113–34. Bangalore: National Institute of Mental Health and Neurosciences.

Nespor, K. (1982) 'Yogic practices in world medical literature', *Yoga*, 20 (1): 29–35.

O'Flaherty, W.D. (1976) *The Origins of Evil in Hindu Mythology.* Berkeley, CA: University of California Press.

O'Flaherty, W.D. (1980) *Karma and Rebirth in Classical Indian Traditions.* Berkeley, CA: University of California Press.

Pande, S. (1968) 'The mystique of "Western" psychotherapy: an Eastern interpretation', *Journal of Nervous and Mental Disease*, 146 (June): 425–32.

Pandey, R.S., Srinivasa, K.N. and Muralidhar, D. (1980) 'Socio-cultural beliefs and treatment acceptance', *Indian Journal of Psychiatry*, 22: 161–66.

Paranjpe, A. (1998) *Self and Identity in Modern Psychology and Indian Thought.* New York: Plenum Press.

Popper, K. (1972) *Objective Knowledge: An Evolutionary Approach.* Oxford: Clarendon Press.

Popper, K. (1988) *The Open Universe: An Argument for Indeterminism.* London: Hutchinson.

Radhakrishnan, S. (1923/1956) *Indian Philosophy*, vol. 2. New Delhi: Oxford University Press.

Radhakrishnan, S. and Moore, C.A. (eds) (1957) *A Sourcebook in Indian Philosophy.* Princeton, NJ: Princeton University Press.

Rao, V. (1986) 'Indian and Western Psychiatry: A Comparison', in J.L. Cox (ed.), *Transcultural Psychiatry*, pp. 291–305. London: Croom Helm.

Reichenbach, B.R. (1990) *The Law of Karma: A Philosophical Study.* Honolulu: University of Hawaii Press.

Riesman, D. (1954) *Individualism Reconsidered.* New York: Doubleday Anchor Books.

Rogers, C. (1961) *On Becoming a Person.* Boston, MA: Houghton Mifflin.

Rogers, C. (1980) *A Way of Being.* Boston, MA: Houghton Mifflin.

Rohner, R.P. (1974) 'Proxemics and stress: an empirical study of the relationship between space and roommate turnover', *Human Relations*, 27: 697–702.

Sachdev, D. (1992) 'Effects of psychocultural factors on the socialisation of British born Indian children and indigenous British children living in England', unpublished doctoral dissertation. London: South Bank University.

Sampson, E.E. (1977) 'Psychology and the American ideal', *Journal of Personality and Social Psychology*, 15: 189–94.

Sarbin, T.R. (1986) 'Emotion and act: roles and rhetoric', in R. Harré (ed.), *The Social Construction of Emotions.* Oxford: Blackwell.

Satyavathi, K. (1988) 'Mental health', in J. Pandey (ed.), *Psychology in India: the State-of-the-Art, vol. III Organizational Behaviour and Mental Health*, pp. 217–88. New Delhi: Sage.

Sethi, B.B. and Manchanda, R. (1978) 'Family structure and psychiatric disorders', *Indian Journal of Psychiatry*, 20: 283–8.

Sinari, R.A. (1984) *The Structure of Indian Thought*. Delhi: Oxford University Press.

Sinha, D. and Tripathi, R.C. (1994) 'Individualism in a collectivist culture: a case of coexistence of opposites', in U. Kim, H.C. Triandis, C. Kagitcibasi, S.-C. Choi and G. Yoon (eds), *Individualism and Collectivism: Theory, Method and Applications*, pp. 123–36. Thousand Oaks, CA: Sage.

Sinha, D., Mishra, R.C. and Berry, J.W. (1996) 'Some eco-cultural and acculturational factors in intermodal perception', in J. Pandey, D. Sinha and D.P.S. Bhawuk (eds), *Asian Contributions to Cross-Cultural Psychology*, pp. 151–64. New Delhi: Sage.

Sinha, D. and Kao, H.S.R. (1997) 'The journey to the East: an introduction', in H.S.R. Kao and D. Sinha (eds), *Asian Perspectives in Psychology*, pp. 9–22. New Delhi: Sage.

Spence, J.T. (1985) 'Achievement American style: the rewards and costs of individualism', *American Psychologist*, 40: 1285–95.

Srinivasa, D.K. and Trivedi, S. (1982) 'Knowledge and attitude of mental diseases in a rural community of South India', *Social Science Medicine*, 16: 1635–9.

Stace, W.T. (1958) 'Ethical relativity', in M.K. Munitz (ed.), *A Modern Introduction to Ethics*. Glencoe, IL: The Free Press.

Trefil, J. (1980) *From Atoms to Quarks: An Introduction to the Strange World of Particle Physics*. London: Athlone.

Triandis, H.C. (1994) *Culture and Social Behaviour*. New York: McGraw-Hill.

Triandis, H.C. (1995) *Individualism and Collectivism*. Boulder, CO: Westview.

Vahia, N.S. (1982) 'Yoga in psychiatry', in A. Kiev and A.V. Rao (eds), *Readings in Transcultural Psychiatry*, pp. 11–19. Madras: Higginbothams.

Vine, I. (1982) 'Crowding and stress: a personal space approach', *Psychological Review*, 2 (1): 1–18.

Von-Furer-Haimendorf, C. (1974) 'The sense of sin in cross-cultural perspective', *Man*, 9: 227–34.

Ward, C.A. and Kennedy, A. (1996) 'Crossing cultures: the relationship between psychological and socio-cultural dimensions of cross-cultural adjustment', in J. Pandey, D. Sinha and D.P.S. Bhawuk (eds), *Asian Contributions to Cross-Cultural Psychology*, pp. 289–306. New Delhi: Sage.

Waterman, A.A. (1981) 'Individualism and interdependence', *American Psychologist*, 36: 762–73.

Webb, S.D. (1978) 'Privacy and psychosomatic stress: an empirical analysis', *Social Behaviour and Personality*, 6: 227–34.

Weber, M. (1963) *The Sociology of Religion*, vol. 4. London: Allen & Unwin.

WHO Report (1978) 'The promotion and development of traditional medicine', *WHO Technical Report Series*, 622. Geneva: WHO

Wig, N.N. and Saxena, S. (1982) 'Recent developments in psychiatric diagnosis and classification', *Continuing Medical Educational Programme*, 1: 53–62.

Williams, B. (1985) *Ethics and the Limits of Philosophy*. London: Fontana Press.

Yang, K.S. (1997) 'Theories and research in Chinese personality: an indigenous approach', in H.S.R. Kao and D. Sinha (eds), *Asian Perspectives on Psychology*, 236–64. New Delhi: Sage.

Zimmer, H. (1951/1989) *Philosophies of India*. Princeton, NJ: Princeton University Press.

Discussion issues

1 Mental illness is a ubiquitous concept.
2 Does the concept of mental illness aid or abet the therapeutic process?
3 What is psychological space?
4 'Materialism versus spiritualism' is an unhelpful construct.

14

'I Say What I Like'

Frank Talk(ing) in Counselling and Psychotherapy

Roy Moodley

It was a summer evening. Five of us had just left an executive meeting of SASO[1] and were strolling on the campus of University College Durban (for Indians), an aged army barracks on Salisbury Island. Suddenly I fell into the swimming pool. This old colonial construction, the leftovers of the British Empire, offered only death—I could not swim. Immediately one of the four jumped in, waded tall through the water and pulled me out. That was Steve Biko. It was 1971. I was 19 then and Steve was 25. Six years later, he was murdered in detention by four white men from the South African Apartheid Police. These men were pardoned in 1997, as a result of confessing to the Truth and Reconciliation Committee chaired by Archbishop Desmond Tutu. The event at the swimming pool began to surface as a significant experience over the 17 years I spent in exile in Britain. The literal rescuing from the water evolved into a metaphor as I engaged with counselling and psychotherapy as an analysand, therapist and trainer.

While I was in South Africa recently, my family and I visited Steve Biko's grave. At the time, as a BPC[2] member, I was prevented from attending the funeral. During our walk in the cemetery I remembered the swimming pool incident and mentioned it to Ntsiki Biko, Steve's wife. We laughed. 'I still can't swim,' I said, 'but I learnt to walk tall.' This statement left me wondering about the kind of empowering strategies in Biko's writings that offer me strength and keep me 'sane' in multicultural Britain. Many of Steve's papers on black consciousness were written for the SASO newsletter as 'I write what I like' and signed 'Frank Talk'. I have attempted to use this title, altering it slightly, in the search for a way of working with black people in counselling and psychotherapy.

Introduction

The philosophical quest that engages all of us is the eternal one that seeks answers to our existence. We are 'driven' to dis-cover, un-cover or re-cover that part of humanity that is always hidden, sublimated and remains out of reach. On this journey we confront love, hate, life and death—sometimes the latter first. Counsellors and psychotherapists are also at the forefront or the borderlines of this process, interpreting the inner reality of the client and facilitating the 'drivers' to acquire a balance with the external environment. In fact, Freud strongly believed that the central reality of the individual was an internal one. Although he later revised his position on the interrogation of the socio-economic and political institutions as merely collective defences of the chaos of the inner world, he nevertheless continued to maintain his position, as does psychotherapy today.

Endowed with this heritage, many counsellors and therapists would be reluctant to contemplate the direct 'interrogation' of social, economic and political factors in the 'interpretation of the inner world of the client. However, this situation is rapidly changing as a result of many factors, including the feminist interrogation of the psychoanalytic literature (see Irigaray, 1985a, 1985b; Kristeva, 1986; Millet, 1971; Mitchell, 1974), postcolonial theory (see Bhabha, 1994; Fanon, 1967; Said, 1978, 1993; Spivak, 1988) and minority groups' questioning of hegemonic masculinities in the practice of counselling and psychotherapy. Fanon (1967), for example, clarifies this challenge, which inevitably involves making the universal individual and the public private, when he says:

> It is not I who make a meaning for myself, but it is the meaning that was already there, pre-existing, waiting for me ... waiting for that turn of history ... black consciousness is immanent in its own eyes. I am not a potentiality of something, I am wholly what I am. I do not have to look for the universal. (Fanon, 1967: 134–5)

Fanon radically questions the formation of both individual and social authority (Bhabha, 1987). Walton (1995) argues that Fanon's attempt in the 1950s was a solitary 'critique of racialised constructions of subjectivity' and that in 'most psychoanalytic literature, which was concerned almost exclusively with white subjects, racial difference was only an intermittent and peripheral force of attention' and that '"race" was blackness and seemed to have nothing to do with the "civilised" white human subject' (p. 780). Carter (1995) points out that 'race has become less salient because mental health clinicians, scholars and researchers are more conformable examining presumed cultural and ethnic issues than addressing racial issues' (p. 4). He also contends that 'race' is misunderstood when culture and ethnicity are assumed to encompass racial issues, as many writers are inclined to do.[3]

In *I Write What I Like*, Biko (1978) proposes a philosophy, or a psychology, or perhaps simply an idea, that provides black people with a tool to examine and re-examine the whole issues of 'race' and racial identity: a concept which interrogates that 'already there, pre-existing, waiting for me, that turn of history, meaning'. It is a process by which the negative socio-economic and political conditions that influence self-concept and personality developments are laid bare, exposed and challenged. This chapter attempts to explore Biko's philosophy of black consciousness and how it can add to an understanding of racial and cultural identity development. Racial and ethnic identity development is at the leading edge of thinking on multicultural counselling in the USA at the present time (Lago and Thompson, 1996; Lee, 1994). A number of racial and identity models have been already been developed (Atkinson et al., 1989; Cross, 1971; Sue and Sue, 1990). The chapter also discusses a particular strategy in the management of the conversations, 'frank talk'(ing), when counsellors and psychotherapists work with cultural diversity.

The philosophy of black consciousness

The writings of 'Frank Talk' are based on the idea of expressing freely what one feels and what one knows to gain and regain one's sense of humanity. In an innovative discourse on the nature of black consciousness and the process of redefining oneself in the light of the experiences of racism and oppression, Biko (1978) contributed a new and relevant theory of personality development for black people:

> The first step therefore is to make the black man come to himself; to pump back life into his empty shell; to infuse him with pride and dignity, to remind him of his complicity in the crime of allowing himself to be misused ... This is what we mean by an inward looking process. This is the definition of black consciousness. (Biko, 1978: 9)

This inward-looking process, although gendered[4] in its text, represents a theory of self-discovery. It constitutes a process whereby the individual can recognize the learned helplessness aspects of her/his personality, explore ways of unlearning them and develop a perspective that defines his/her sense of being. Biko further adds that the black child has tended to hate her/himself and the rich heritage to which he/she belongs and that this situation must be reversed. He lucidly points out that:

> So negative is the image presented to him that he tends to find solace only in the close identification with the white society ... part of the approach envisaged in bringing about 'black consciousness' has to be directed to the past, to seek to rewrite the history of the black man ... a people without a positive history is like a vehicle without an engine. (Biko, 1978: 29)

Black consciousness is also understood as a process which 'seeks to give positivity' (p. 30), encourages 'the oneness of community' (p. 30), and aims 'to infuse the black community with a new-found pride in themselves, their effort, their value systems, their culture, their religion and their outlook to life' (p. 49). The conscientization process demands that people grapple realistically with problems, develop an awareness, analyse the situation and find answers for themselves with the purpose of finding some kind of hope.

Although Biko's analysis was grounded in the context of the South African situation at a particular time, it must be recognized that the experiences of contemporary British black communities are not markedly different when it comes to experiencing the negative aspects of 'race' at a subjective level. Indeed, issues of 'race' and ethnicity in multicultural Britain have been well documented, including a growing critical literature within the field of counselling and psychotherapy (d'Ardenne and Mahtani, 1989; Eleftheriadou, 1994; Kareem and Littlewood, 1992; Lago and Thompson, 1989, 1996). For example, Burke (1986) indicates that 'counsellors and psychotherapists should consider the significance of race-related material in their analysis of human function and behaviour' (p. 139). Lago and Thompson (1989), in reviewing the position of transcultural counselling in Britain, summon up the situation by stating that 'whether covert or overt, very real dilemmas confront counsellors in terms of how subjects related to racism are managed in the process of counselling' (p. 208). Gilroy (1990) reminds us that the emphasis on political racism tends to create the illusion that racism rarely exists outside the political and institutional frame.

The subtleties of social racism, non-verbal racism, symbolic racism or sometimes just plain petty biases are enough to 'pain' the most composed of human personalities. The other forms of racism that can contribute a great deal to the pathological process of individuals in society need to be recognized in any therapeutic intervention with black clients. The initial challenge is to locate the historical racial agenda of the therapeutic project— for example, Freud and Jung's racist notions (see Dalal, 1988). Some of these ideas have continued into the present day. For instance, Kennedy (1952), after treating two black women, observed that their neurosis was a result of conflicts arising from 'a hostile white ego ideal. The self-hatred generated by the fact of not being white started with earliest infancy' (p. 325). Waite (1968) listed at least five types of resistance that were used by black clients with regards to 'race'. These notions are clearly racial stereotypes.

Alienating false images of identity

The formation of the 'ego' and the development of the 'self' are aspects of an individual's identity development. Ontological concerns are also inclusive of the psychosocial, political and cultural experiences of an individual which inform the construct(ion) of his/her consciousness. The development of the 'ego' takes place through a process of identification of 'the image outside itself'. In other words, the individual identifies with an image outside him/herself (Lacan, 1977). The Cartesian *ego cogito* advocates the mutual dependency between 'I' and the 'other' in which the 'other' is basically construed as the 'other I'. Postmodernism, on the other hand, has been anti-Cartesian, in developing the notion that the ego derives from an original encounter with 'other' (Theunissen, 1984). In the light of the above ontological theories, people from ethnic minority communities are engaging in the 'I' and 'other' process in the development of 'race' and cultural identity, but problematized through their experience of colonialism and postcolonialism.

In the process of therapy with some black clients, the therapist may need to consider these issues before undertaking any depth analysis of the client's conversations. It may be necessary to deconstruct the 'race' and cultural identity so that 'false images' are brought to consciousness and understood. For some clients, the identification with the 'false image' becomes an identification with the real of the 'other'—that is, with 'whiteness'.

These ideas confirm the thinking that is reflected in the writings of Biko—the black person becomes the object onto which white people project their 'race thinking' (Husband, 1982). In turn, the black person would seek to identify outside him/herself, with the white 'race'. This dislocation of identity is made more profound as a result of the experiences of racism. Negative 'race thinking' is projected onto black people, who in turn identify with the aggressor. So it seems that a repeated cycle of mutual negativeness takes place. In therapy, this can be replicated with both the client and the counsellor locked into each other's 'otherness'. Such a process invariably 'wounds rather than heals'.

In attempting to alienate the false images of the client's identity, the therapist's clinical skills in communicating ideas, feelings and reflections (interpretations) are paramount. It seems particularly important, irrespective of the theoretical approach the counsellor uses, that the conversations between the two people are 'frank' and free to the extent that 'fear' of each other is 'interrogated' in the sessions and neither relegated to the safety of supervision (for the therapist), nor made to serve as a defence mechanism (for the client). 'Frank talk'(ing) is not a subversive footnote but a method which moves the client from the margins to the centre of 'self' empowerment, as demonstrated in the vignette below.

I say what I like: Jo-Anne

Jo-Anne is a 40-year-old black woman. She has steadily progressed from being a nurse to a schoolteacher and eventually taught at a college of education before taking early retirement. It was at this stage that I met Jo-Anne when she came in for counselling. At the first session, Jo-Anne sought information on the kind of process she was going to engage in and the methods and models of therapy that were going to be used. She indicated that she had a fair knowledge of the counselling process and had attended many courses during her time as a schoolteacher. She asked me about my training, whether I had had any counselling and therapy myself, my experience as a counsellor, and how I felt about working with women, especially black women from the diaspora.

Clearly here was a client who seemed to know what she wanted with these 'up-front' questions and 'frank talk'(ing), before we even started. I said to Jo-Anne that I am usually considered a psychodynamic therapist, but I also draw on my training and experience in cross-cultural coun- selling, humanistic psychology and dramatherapy. In fact, at times I am inclined to think that there is something integrative or eclectic about my work. Or put another way, I work within a multicultural perspective, meaning that I am 'black consciousness' aware and acknowledge cultural healing practices. 'And what about the core theory?' she asked. 'Eurocentric,' I replied, with some reluctance. But (very emphatically) I added that I, as a black practitioner, brought to it my experience, my cri- tique and my cultural ways of thinking and feeling about therapy: that I would be aware and take account of the unconscious in the issues she would be presenting in therapy. Furthermore, I would be attempting to understand some of the presenting problems, using the 'frank talk' philosophy of black consciousness and development which I thought was already her style.

Although the concept of exploring racial and cultural metaphors and symbols was new to her, she agreed to try it out. The process of identify- ing unconscious metaphors and separating them from the 'race' con- structed images to eventually focus on the deep inner conflicts of childhood interested her as a process for her self-development and growth. She indicated that she would be comfortable with such a model and would contract for counselling. In fact, the 'frank talk' method of communication corresponded to her own style of being 'up-front'. 'It's the way black people do it', 'not like the English way where you have to read between the lines, if you want to know what they want', 'a direct way with no hid- den agendas', were some of the descriptions shared by Jo-Anne about this method of communication.

I am always anxious about how much information about the process I need to offer the client. I was once told (perhaps on a training course or at a counselling conference) that too much information can result in the client opting out altogether from the process. Using ideas of practice in this way can raise questions about the power dynamics in the therapeutic relation- ship. Could this be challenged by 'frank talk'(ing)? However, in the case of Jo-Anne this seemed acceptable since she requested it herself and felt a need to explore in depth some of the issues that were confronting her at this stage in her life. The first session, while acting as a 'diagnostic', explanatory and interview session, also offered an opportunity, using this particular method of communication, to 'fast-track' a quality rapport.

The counselling sessions with Jo-Anne were conducted, sometimes on a weekly basis, sometimes fortnightly, and sometimes monthly, for almost a year. She was a meticulous time-keeper and adhered strictly to the therapeutic hour of 50 minutes. Ironic as it seems, this was one of the many values that could be termed western which Jo-Anne held dear. At first it did not seem contradictory to her that she agreed with some aspects of western therapeutic methods and at the same time demanded an exclusively non-Eurocentric approach. She approached the interpretation of racial and cultural symbols and metaphors with the imagination of a creative literary writer. Symbols of ancient Zimbabwe and classical Egypt were images in her 'visions', dreams and daydreaming, suggesting the all too familiar theme, the opposite of the white 'out of Africa' retreat, this 'into or going back to Africa' which for some black people tends to happen at critical moments in 'self' evaluation, usually during states of depression.

With Jo-Anne the images occurred several times. 'This all sounds very romantic,' I said once, 'but what does it all mean to you?' Jo-Anne appeared to be agitated and angry. Her response was, 'How can you understand, you are not African although you were born there.' Indeed, Jo-Anne too was neither African nor born there, nor had been there, nor had any conscious intention to go to Africa. No doubt with the kind of complexities that clients/patients experience in multicultural societies, and the inaccessibility of many of these experiences to the therapist (as a result of the limitations of psychoanalytic/therapeutic theory), the therapy is made more complex, even in a case such as this where there is a racially matched dyad.

I asked her what she meant by considering herself 'black'. This exploration led to the issues of identity, of being a black person, a black woman, a mother and a professional in multicultural Britain. 'The black consciousness of myself for myself ... particularly in private moments ... was most treasured,' she said. She felt that slavery and racism contributed a great deal to the 'image' of black women in society. She talked for a while about the black body being the historical and cultural site of the European 'gaze' of the other. I became concerned midway through the process that this might easily become a defence for Jo-Anne, to avoid the deep exploration of her self. Although this might have developed into an intellectually creative game, it nevertheless led to a crucial stage in the transference. An analysis of the history of black people in the diaspora and the consequences of slavery, migration, de-culturalization and black Europeanization could have become an academic exercise, but through talking about it Jo-Anne explored her genealogy of 'race' at a deep personal level.

I want to conclude the narrative of Jo-Anne with a particular aspect of therapy which pinpointed the need for psychoanalytic theory to take account of the search of the client/patient for lost objects or lost symbols outside the therapeutic ritual. In Jo-Anne's case it seems that another journey was made to retrieve these artefacts through a traditional healer. About two-thirds of the way through the therapy, Jo-Anne cancelled all the other sessions. Many months later, she returned for a final session to tell me that she was seeing a local Obeahman (a practitioner of traditional African Caribbean medicine) and that her situation was all right. Clearly it seems that Jo-Anne was at a stage that necessitated this move from a western-trained therapist to a traditional black healer. Perhaps a temporal shift of the psyche to another world view, one that was much more culturally or psychically significant—a retreat to hibernate from the frost-bitten winters of 'race thinking' and 'race feeling'. Jo-Anne appears to reflect Biko's words regarding the process of black consciousness and therapy: 'has to be directed to the past, to seek to rewrite the history ... a people without a positive history is like a vehicle without an engine'. Her images and 'visions', indeed her narrative, were to place herself in history and then rise above it. Her discovery through 'frank talk'(ing) was her genealogy of 'race'.

Frank talk(ing)

Theorizing black consciousness in the context of Jo-Anne's narrative has been an attempt to add to the debate on racial identity and personality development. The challenge for the therapist is in the communication method used to de-construct the 'text' of the client. In the 'frank talk' method of communication, Jo-Anne and the therapist were in agreement that their conversations would be free, open and 'frank', especially about issues of 'race', culture and ethnicity. The transference and counter-transference processes were confronted, face-to-face as it were: no 'episte-mologies of suspicion' to guide the interpretation, even at the earliest stage of the conceptualization of the transcultural approach. The shroud that covered the neglected issues of 'race' were painfully exposed. Historicizing 'race' then did not consume the discourse of therapy, leaving the patient abandoned on some psychic desert and marooning a very anxious therapist on another island. For Jo-Anne it was a very painful and deeply moving journey but one that remained within the inner-city hamlets: that is to say, she reaffirmed her racial identity through 'frank talk'(ing) her therapy. 'Race' is a social construct that transcends all other experiences because it is the most visible of all cultural differences and needs to be understood as the most significant difference (Carter, 1995).

Another theorizing of Jo-Anne's presentation or representation could easily be (re)textured in clinical manuals such as DMS-IV. These categories are understood to embody illness in western European cultures, but for many people outside this network of meanings the labelling and subsequent 'treatment' remains a problem. The meaning of illness for an individual is grounded in, though not reducible to, the network of meanings an illness has in a particular culture (Good and Good, 1982). The therapist may need to take cognisance of the client's specific culture and healing traditions as well as their socio-political experiences. For example, the racism-related complexes experienced by whites and their internalization by black communities clearly raise questions concerning the relationship between the therapist and the patient. These include the

Chosen People myth (Toynbee, 1948),[5] the Prospero complex (Mannoni, 1956),[6] the white Supremacy complex (Hillman, 1986),[7] the Virgin Mary complex (Moodley, 1991),[8] and the Sepulchre syndrome (Moodley, 1991)[9].

Some of these complexes, whether embodied by hegemonic masculinities or not, are seductive in relation to the 'other'. Therapists can be left vulnerable to such discourses of intersubjectivity. The question of the therapist's appropriateness and readiness to practise is always a delicate one, but made 'invisible' when it comes to black clients/patients. It is through the subtlety of the countertransference process that the projection of such unconscious inheritance is displaced, reinforcing for many clients a sense of their racial and cultural inferiority, which at the same time consciously appearing to espouse equality (Moodley, 1992).

Clearly there is a need for white therapists seriously to consider issues of white racial identity development, particularly when working with minority clients. Said (1978) offers a poignant reminder of our global context when he argues that the Orient was 'Orientalized' to establish 'a relationship of power, of domination, of varying degrees of a complex hegemony' (p. 5). The therapeutic relationship has the potential for such a discourse. Therapy with black clients/patients can become a site for some of the European project(ions), and complexes. These may be internalized as inferiority complexes and phantasies of 'otherness': for example, black masculinity as the all-embracing phallus and other negative identities. Berry and Sipps's (1991) study showed that 'in the counselling environment, if the client devalues characteristics in the counsellor so that a more similar counsellor will be less attractive' (p. 120). On the other hand, Smith (1985) found that black American women had low levels of trust and disclosure in the counselling relationship with whites, and preferred black therapists. She suggests that a lack of awareness of, sensitivity to and knowledge of the black women's history and culture led to the problems that the therapists experienced. 'Frank talk'(ing) in this context may offer a different way of working: therapists and clients/patients have an opportunity to raise concerns about the attractiveness of the therapist and the appropriateness of the therapy. Sometimes, if these issues are not classified early in the process, clients/patients may terminate therapy as a way of avoiding conflicts and confusions which may arise in cross-racial dyads.

It is not only where the client is at, in his/her 'race' and cultural identity development, but an emphasis needs to be placed on the counsellor's and therapist's process as well. Whether we look at Cross's (1971) five-stage theory of negro-to-black conversion,[10] or at developments from it such as the Sue and Sue (1990) racial/cultural identity development model,[11] they in one form or another have the potential to offer a particular point of identity reference in therapy. Sabanani et al. (1991) state that the research on black identity development is much more advanced than white identity development and that more research needs to be done on the latter. They also propose a five-stage developmental model for a white counsellor's identity development[12]. Whichever model one chooses to use, it seems imperative that the issue of white counsellor identity development is taken seriously in the therapeutic practice with black people.

The therapist's awareness of her/his identity in relation to the client supports high-level communication in therapy. This means that the function of interpreting, analysing and extrapolating meaningful relationships of clients' presentations is at a well-developed level. For instance, a highly skilled practitioner using Biko's ideas could easily make appropriate interventions with black clients. Karenga (1982) reminds us that such a method was used by Charles Thomas, founder and chair-person of the Association of Black Psychologists in North America. The 'instructive intervention' method, as it was known, was based on changing negative self-perceptions to positive one, on self-mastery, and on increasing social competence and personal fulfilment. Thomas also rejected simple treatment therapy and urged community engagement in therapy.

In 'frank talk'(ing) with Jo-Anne, resistance was clearly identified and confronted. Some of these forms of resistance involved self-devaluation, intellectualization and the expression of overt hostility. Many of these process are often recognized by counsellors and therapists in white middle-class clients but fail to be recognized in ethnic-minority clients. There are other resistance strategies employed by black clients that may be easily observed by the 'frank talk' method. There is also the possibility that they may not arise because of the 'up-front' and frank way in which the counsellor or therapist would communicate when using the 'frank talk' method. These resistance strategies include:

- Clients can show more lack of understanding of the verbal utterances of the counsellor than they actually experience. Clients may slip into idiomatic expressions, pronunciations, Creole, Patois or other culture-specific colloquialisms that the counsellor or therapist is not aware of or tuned into.
- Clients can appear to be shy and withdrawn, and offer a position of being 'cool', until they 'sus' out the hidden agenda of the counsellor.
- Clients can offer a confusion of the concept of time with the counsellor or therapist. They may be late for appointments or not turn up at all. Clients may also turn up on a different day and insist that that was the arranged day and time.
- Clients can easily get confused in knowing what to disclose and when to disclose it.

'Frank talk' appears to overcome the need that is so often experienced by counsellors of a different 'race' or culture to interrogate the client about his/her own cultural norms and values. It also prevents the need to explore superficial cultural constructs that can sometimes become an obsession on the part of the counsellor. In summary, then, 'frank talk'(ing) is about:

- communicating ideas and thoughts freely and without the inhibition of colonial and postcolonial phobias of cultural inferiority;
- recognizing that the life process has been influenced greatly by the processes of racism and oppression; understanding racism and its consequences;
- interpreting deviance and discomfort as both a personal response to and an influence of the environment; translating projective identification in the light of the oppressor and thereby displacing internalized negative aggression;
- constructing a real sense of 'self' and finding a sense of 'being' as opposed to 'not being'. Concepts such as non-white, non-European and other hyphened negatives reflect this position of non-'being'.

Conclusion

Racial and cultural identity theories are becoming relevant and appropriate in counselling and psychotherapy with ethnic minority clients/patients. Biko's ideas on black consciousness, 'frank talking' and self-concept development are part of the wider challenges that are confronting and transforming counselling and psychotherapy with black clients. The defining moment with Jo-Anne in the above vignette was at the point of entry, when she questioned the appropriateness of the western therapeutic approach. Hall (1992) reminds us that black people 'speak from a particular space, out of a particular history, (and) out of a particular experience' (p. 258), which makes certain forms of therapy limited in their relevance. For example, traditional notions of time and space may need to be (re)considered. Being with a black client may perhaps be a transition from moment to moment, in and out of known spaces and knowledge(s), for the therapist. Where the intervention appears to be patronizing or limited, the client retreats, temporarily concluding the relationship, sometimes to recover their humanity. 'It seems imperative that counselors who want to ease the therapy process for Black clients should achieve some understanding of their clients as racial beings and should acquire a level of sophistication in discussing racial, issues in therapy' (Thompson and Jenal, 1994: 490).

Clearly the 'psychic retreat' which Jo-Anne chose to undertake with a traditional healer could be understood as a recognition that black clients can be aware that the western therapeutic model is inadequate because it is primarily or only a 'talking cure'. It is highly possible that traditional healers relate to their clients outside the boundaries of space and time, as these are usually perceived. It seems that a transcultural model of therapy, to be effective and relevant to the needs of members of the black communities, must seek to integrate those elements of traditional healing which complement and extend the healing process. There is no doubt that the concerns which Jo-Anne felt at that particular point in the therapy, and the suggestion of seeing someone new, would have created anxieties, which she resolved by refusing to attend. However, it needs to be acknowledged that her degree of introspective focusing reached a point where she was able to progress further into the psychic field through the facilitation of an Obeahman. Black consciousness, it seems, would incorporate the convergence of this kind of duality of treatments. It also seems apparent that members of the ethnic minority community tend to consult the traditional healers at some point in their lives (Ineichen, 1990; Rack, 1982), perhaps to (re)construct an identity which also takes them outside the nomenclature of socio-political realities of everyday existence, 'race' being one of them.

Acknowledgement

I am very grateful to the editor and the referees for their detailed comments on earlier drafts of this paper.

Notes

[1] The South African Students' Organization is a Union for black students, founded by Steve Biko in 1968. He became its first President in 1969.

[2] The Black People's Convention was founded by Steve Biko in 1972 to empower black people through a political understanding of themselves.

[3] Social construction theorists claim that 'race' is a product of specific histories and geopolitical experiences. Sometimes it is used as an 'empty signifier', covered in ideological meanings that promote particular interests.

[4] Talahite (1990) cites Cheryl Carolus, an executive member of the United Women's Organization and a former black consciousness militant, who criticized the philosophy by saying that 'asserting your blackness went hand with asserting your maleness' (p. 27).

[5] Toynbee (1948) writes that: 'the Europeans have regarded themselves as the Chosen People—they need feel no shame in admitting that every past civilization has taken this view of itself and its own heritage' (p. 107).

[6] Mannoni (1956) in exploring Defoe's (1903) *Robinson Crusoe* and Shakespeare's *Tempest* suggests that the Island is a reference to Africa, 'the dark continent', a larger metaphor for the 'other' to be projected on to, and the shipwreck a metaphor for the breakdown or failure of white consciousness, allowing for the repressed qualities to surface. He defines this as the 'Prospero complex' (p. 109). He asserts that European 'projected upon ... colonial peoples the obscurities of their own unconscious—obscurities they would rather not penetrate' (p. 19). Fanon's (1967) critique of Mannoni's analysis offers an interesting paradox, making the point that Mannoni 'takes it upon himself to explain colonialism's reasons for existence' (p. 107), and inferring that the analysis fails to see the missing dimension of capitalist exploitation which Fanon feels is a prime reason for arousing in the people 'the feelings of inferiority' (p. 108).

[7] Hillman (1986) explores through Jungian lenses the landscapes which inform the psyche's geography of the white unconscious. He concludes that the ontological fantasy of reality as consisting as paired opposites is a manifestation of the white mind and its narcissistic defence against the wounds of self-awareness. He maintains that to move beyond white supremacy is to give up the opposites.

[8] This complex refers to a desexualized relationship (as in the birth of Jesus) where the sexual experience results in guilt which is then projected on to the 'other'. Davis (1981) expresses how this notion proliferated racist ideologies in America, especially the deep South, justifying the mass lynching of black men for the 'myth of the black rapist' (p. 172).

[9] This term is used here to indicate the symbolic reference of the death, burial and resurrection of Christ: a reintegration of the divided and 'splitted' self; a wish to return to the self before the mirror stage. Benvenuto and Kennedy (1986, p. 172) cite Safouan's concept of the sepulchre as a dwelling where 'all love includes a death wish ... a wish to return to the *inanimate state that the subject was as signifier before he was born*'. It is a drive or as in Freud's 'trieb' (instinct) to go beyond the projection of the repressed negative self and to kill this repressed negative self once it has been projected on to the 'other'. This achieves a single unity of self, translating the symbolic into the real.

[10] The five-stages are: pre-encounter (pre-discovery), encounter (discovery), immersion-emersion, internalization, and commitment.

[11] Sue and Sue's (1990) identity development model for black and white people has the following stages: conformity, dissonance, resistance and immersion, introspection, and integrative awareness. These have a different set of constructs for each of the 'race' groups.

[12] The five stages are:

Stage 1 (Pre-exposure/Precontact): Awareness of one's own culture and cultures of other ethnic groups. Stereotypes brought to the fore and checked with reality. Acquiring specific cultural knowledge of other cultural groups.

Stage 2 (Conflict): Confronting one's own racial stereotypes and racism. Dealing with the feelings of guilt.

Stage 3 (Prominority/Antiracism): Awareness of tendencies towards over-identification or towards paternalistic attitudes and the impact of these on ethnic minorities.

Stage 4 (Retreat into White Culture): Feelings of fear and anger elicited by responses to behaviour and attitudes in stage 3.

Stage 5 (Redefinition and Integration): Developing an identity that claims whiteness as part of the process of society. Making white identity important.

References

Atkinson, D.R., Morten, G. and Sue, D.W. (1989) 'A minority identity development model', in D.R. Atkinson, G. Morgan and D.W. Sue (eds), *Counselling American Minorities*, pp. 35–52. Dubuque, IA: Brown.

Benvenuto, B. and Kennedy, R. (1986) *The Works of Jacques Lacan: An Introduction*. London: Free Association Press.

Berry, G.W. and Sipps, G.J. (1991) 'Interactive effects of counsellor–client similarity and client self-esteem on termination type and number sessions', *Journal of Counseling Psychology*, 38: 120–25.

Bhabha, H.K. (1987) 'What does the black man want?', *New Formations*, 1: 118–24.

Bhabha, H.K. (1994) *The Location of Culture*. London: Routledge.

Biko, S. (1978) *I Write What I Like*. London: Heinemann.

Burke, A.W. (1986) 'Racism, prejudice and mental illness', in J.L. Cox (ed.), *Transcultural Psychiatry*. London: Croom Helm.

Carter, R.T. (1995) *The Influence of Race and Radical Identity in Psychotherapy*. London: Wiley.

Cross, W.E., Jr (1971) 'Towards a psychology of liberation: the negro-to-black conversion experience', *Black World*, 20: 13–27.

Dalal, F. (1988) 'Jung: a racist', *British Journal of Psychotherapy*, 4: 263–79.

d'Ardenne, P. and Mahtani, A. (1989) *Transcultural Counselling in Action*. London: Sage.

Davis, A. (1981) *Women, Race and Class*. London: Women's Press.

Eleftheriadou, Z. (1994) *Transcultural Counselling*. London: Central Books.

Fanon, F. (1967) *Black Skin, White Masks*. New York: Grove Press.

Gilroy, P. (1990) 'The end of anti-racism', *New Community*, 17: 71–83.

Good, B.J. and Good, M.-J.D. (1982) 'Towards a meaning-centred analysis of popular illness categories: "fright-illness" and "heat distress" in Iran', in A.J. Marsella and G.M. White (eds), *Cultural Conceptions of Mental Health and Therapy*. Dordrecht: Reidel.

Hall, S. (1992) 'New ethnicities', in J. Donald and A. Rattansi (eds), *'Race', 'Culture and Difference'*. Buckingham: Open University Press.

Hillman, J. (1986) *Notes on White Supremacy: Essaying on Archetypal Account of Historical Events*. Dallas, TX: Spring.

Husband, C. (1982) 'Introduction: "race", the continuity of a concept', in C. Husband (ed.), *'Race' in Britain: Continuity and Change*, pp. 11–23. London: Hutchinson.

Ineichen, B. (1990) 'The mental health of Asians in Britain: little disease or underreporting?', *British Medical Journal*, 300: 1669–70.

Irigaray, L. (1985a) *Speculum of the Other Woman* (trans. G.C. Gill). Ithaca, NY: Cornell University Press.

Irigaray, L. (1985b) *This Sex Which is Not One* (trans. C. Porter). Ithaca, NY: Cornell University Press.

Kareem, J. and Littlewood, R. (1992) *Intercultural Therapy: Themes, Interpretations and Practice*. London: Blackwell.

Karenga, M. (1982) *Introduction to Black Studies*. Los Angeles, CA: University of Sankore Press.

Kennedy, J. (1952) 'Problems posed in the analysis of black patients', *Psychiatry*, 15: 313–27.

Kristeva, J. (1986) 'Freud and love: treatment and its discontents', in T. Moi (ed.), *The Kristeva Reader*, pp. 240–71. Oxford: Blackwell.

Lacan, J. (1977) *Ecrits: A Selection* (trans. A. Sheridan). London: Routledge.

Lago, C. and Thompson, J. (1989) 'Counselling and race', in W. Dryden, D. Charles-Edwards and R. Woolfe (eds), *Handbook of Counselling in Britain*. London: Tavistock/Routledge.

Lago, C. and Thompson, J. (1996) *Race, Culture and Counselling*, Milton Keynes: Open University Press.

Lee, C. (1994). Introductory lecture. *Conference on Race, Culture and Counselling*, University of Sheffield, July.

Mannoni, O. (1956) *Prospero and Caliban: The Psychology of Colonization* (trans. P. Powesland). London: Praeger.

Millet, K. (1971) *Sexual Politics*. London: Hart-Davis.

Mitchell, J. (1974) *Psychoanalysis and Feminism*. Harmondsworth: Penguin.

Moodley, S.R. (1991) 'A theoretical model for trans-cultural counselling and therapy'. MPhil thesis, University of Nottingham.

Moodley, R. (1992) 'Interpreting the "I" in counselling and guidance: beyond an antiracist approach'. Keynote speech, *Derbyshire FE Counselling and Guidance Conference*, February.

Rack, P. (1982) *Race, Culture and Mental Disorder*. London: Tavistock.

Sabnani, H.B., Ponterotto, J.G. and Borodousky, L.G. (1991) 'White racial identity developments and cross-cultural counselor training: a stage model', *The Counselling Psychologist*, 19: 76–102.

Said, E.W. (1978) *Orientalism*. London: Routledge & Kegan Paul.

Said, E.W. (1993) *Culture and Imperialism*. London: Chatto & Windus.

Smith, E.M.J. (1985) 'Counseling black women', in P. Pedersen (ed.), *Handbook of Cross-Cultural Counseling and Therapy*. New York: Praeger.

Spivak, G.C. (1988) *In Other Worlds*. London: Routledge.

Sue, D.W. and Sue, D. (1990) *Counselling the Culturally Different: Theory and Practice*, 2nd edn. New York: Wiley.

Talahite, A. (1990) *Race and gender in the novels of four contemporary Southern African women writers*. Unpublished PhD thesis, University of Leeds.

Theunissen, M. (1984) *The Other* (trans. C. Macann). Boston, MA: Massachusetts Institute of Technology.

Thompson, C.E. and Jenal, S.T. (1994) 'Interracial and intraracial quasi-counseling interactions when counselors avoid discussing race', *Journal of Counseling Psychology*, 41: 484–91.

Toynbee, A.J. (1948) *Civilization on Trial*. Oxford: Oxford University Press.

Waite, R.R. (1968) 'The negro patient and clinical theory', *Journal of Consulting and Clinical Psychology*, 32: 427–33.

Walton, J. (1995) 'Re-placing in (white) psychoanalytic discourse: founding narratives of feminism', *Critical Inquiry*, 21: 775–804.

Discussion issues

1 In what way did Biko contribute to a new and relevant theory of personality development for black people?

2 Are racial stereotypes still prevalent in therapy?

3 'How can you understand, you are not African although you were born there.'

4 The 'frank talk' method of communication can benefit the therapeutic relationship.

PART THREE
ETHNIC MATCHING IN COUNSELLING

Many papers have been written on the topic of ethnic matching in counselling and psychotheraphy. Some extreme views exist on this subject. Part Three takes forward some of the issues raised in Part One of this book, and also considers gender and race in counselling practice.

In Chapter 15, Alladin suggests that a strict and inflexible insistence on ethnic matching of the client and counsellor risks the danger of segregation. He notes that Pedersen et al. concluded that the research on client counselling preferences for same-race counsellors were mixed and raised more questions than answers. The important of ethnic or racial identity in cross-cultural counselling is considered and the danger of the projection of racism by either party is raised.

In Chapter 16, Ward and Banks analyse the facilitative effects of gender and race in counselling practice. A case study approach is used to illustrate the positive effects to the therapeutic relationship of a different gender and ethnicity between the client and counsellor. The process of transference was seen as crucial to effecting both positive processes and outcome of therapy.

In Chapter 17, Moodley and Dhingra undertook a study to focus on the issues arising from cross-cultural/racial matching with white clients and black counsellors. They interviewed black counsellors and ascertained some of the strategies used to deal with the therapeutic relationship. One concern was the limited supervision that the counsellors were offered, and often with practitioners who were not familiar with the dynamics of 'race' culture and ethnicity.

Although Part Three only consists of three chapters, if provides an interesting insight to some of the many issues raised by ethnic matching in counselling.

15

Ethnic Matching in Counselling

How Important is it to Ethnically Match Clients and Counsellors?

Waseem J. Alladin

The short answer to this complex question is 'It depends'. It may help to consider the rationale behind ethnic matching. When counsellor and client share the same cultural background, empathic understanding and self-disclosure are more easily facilitated. However, most counsellors and counsellor trainers are white, middle-class people whose values and communication styles may differ from those of ethnic minority clients, especially those of lower socio-economic status. Thus, white counsellors may unwittingly engage in cultural oppression by imposing western values on ethnic minority clients. Further, ethnic minority clients, because of a historical exposure to and current experiences of racism, may have a damaged ethnic or racial identity which would hinder the development of a therapeutic alliance with a white counsellor. Thus understanding the client's ethnic or racial identity development is important in cross-cultural counselling.

Ethnicity is a group classification of individuals sharing a unique social and cultural heritage (customs, language, religion) from generation to generation. It therefore follows that ethnicity and race are not necessarily synonymous, though common usage of the term 'race' in the literature really ought to refer specificity to ethnicity or culture. According to Sundberg (1981), culture – a convenient label for knowledge, skills and attitudes that are learned and passed on from one generation to the next – implies a way of life which can become so ingrained that people are not conscious of assumptions they make of themselves and others. In this discussion I will therefore assume that ethnicity and culture are interchangeable terms and focus on black people as one example of an ethnic minority group.

The case for and against ethnic matching

The Eurocentric bias in counselling approaches has been highlighted time and again (see Alladin, 1989). Counselling consciously or unconsciously promotes mainstream (majority) cultural values which leads to a culturally encapsulated counsellor, and if the client does not share the counsellor's values the lack of congruence could lead to premature termination by the client or the failure to agree on the goals of counselling. But what's all the fuss about? Surely counselling is a helping process and considerations of colour, ethnicity, religion, etc. should not come into it? Not surprisingly, there are shades of opinion about the desirability of ethnic matching for successful outcome in counselling.

Let us first consider somewhat extreme views which insist on ethnic matching or reject outright any need for ethnic matching. One extreme view is that the white counsellor cannot possibly counsel the 'black psyche' and would merely perpetuate the 'colonial master–slave' relationship. More accurately, a white counsellor who has not developed awareness of cultural issues, denies the presence of racism and the impact of colonization and is unable to empathize with the oppression that many black clients feel in a dominant white society, is obviously not going to develop a helping relationship. Such a counsellor should not be surprised by 'premature' termination or blame the client for 'lack of motivation' or even a presumed 'inability to benefit from counselling'.

A strict and inflexible insistence on ethnic matching of client and counsellor risks a danger of segregation, with white clients being seen only by white counsellors and black clients being seen only by black counsellors. This not only clashes with the principle that counsellors should offer services to all citizens, but is contrary to the notion of generic counsellor training. Matching black clients with black counsellors assumes that the black counsellor necessarily shares the same values and ignores possible class differences. Further, as Kareem (1992) warns, matching done purely on the basis of race or colour can imprison both the counsellor and the client in their own racial and cultural identity. It also diminishes the human element which must be an integral part of all professional encounters.

To contrast our discussion with another extreme view, consider Patterson (1978) who rejects the principles and practices of cross-culturalism:

The role of counselling and psychotherapy is to facilitate the development of self-actualization in clients. Cultures can be evaluated in terms of their contribution to the self-actualization of their members. The major conditions for the development of self-actualizing persons are known, and must be present in counselling and psychotherapy as practised with any client regardless of culture ... The problems of practising counselling or psychotherapy in others' cultures are viewed as problems of implementing these conditions. Certain characteristics of clients which present obstacles to the implementation of the conditions are associated with certain cultures. Until cultural changes lead to change in these characteristics, counselling or psychotherapy will be difficult and in some cases impossible with certain clients from certain cultures. Structuring and client education and training may change client expectations and make therapy possible. In any case, however, to accede to client expectations, abandoning methods which have been demonstrated to be related to self-actualization as an outcome of counselling or psychotherapy, is to abandon self-actualization as the goal, and to accept goals which are often inconsistent with self-actualization. (Patterson, 1978: 133)

This 'colour- and culture-blind' view is naive and denies the real world in which people live. As Draguns (1989) notes, Patterson's critique rests on several misunderstandings of cross-cultural counselling in theory and in practice. The goal of cross-cultural counselling is not to change the culture but to enable change to take place in the client. Cross-cultural counsellors also reject the notion that whatever does not aim at self-actualization is not counselling. Counselling, Draguns suggests, starts with distress that the client cannot alleviate or with a problem he or she cannot solve.

In counselling the culturally different client, the counsellor may unwittingly engage in cultural oppression, that is, the unconscious imposition of mainstream cultural values on to the client. Any counsellor should be able to counsel effectively irrespective of ethnicity. In other words, all counsellors should acquire cross-cultural competencies so that they can deal effectively with culturally different clients.

Others take the view that the client's preferences for a white or black counsellor should always be respected. In principle this seems commendable. However, a risk is that this preference can sometimes hide avoidance both on the part of the client who requests it and the counsellor who accedes to it, if the reasons for it are not explored honestly.

The benefits of developing cross-cultural competence

The same ethnicity counsellor–client dyad has both advantages and disadvantages which vary according to the theoretical background of the counsellor. For example, Tyler et al. (1985) consider the various pairings of white and ethnic minority counsellors and clients (see also Lago and Thompson, 1989). A black client can have a therapeutically helpful and unique learning experience from working with a white counsellor if his or her racial/ethnic uniqueness can be valued and appreciated without condescension. The white counsellor, in turn, can gain a far deeper and less intellectually contained sense of the pain and destructiveness of discrimination, of the ways in which counsellors may use their theories to rationalize their prejudices, and of the strengths the black client can bring to his or her struggle with racism and with himself on herself.

Research on ethnic matching

Pedersen et al. (1989) conclude that the findings from research on client counselling preferences for same-race counsellors are mixed and raise more questions than answers. Some reasons for this are inadequate research methodologies and measures and the limitations of using a narrowly defined concept of 'race'. To encompass the complexities of cross-cultural relationships, other variables such as the client's racial identity, social class and counselling style preferences need to be considered. Since the research literature on ethnic matching can reduce premature termination rates but does not seem to make a significant difference to therapeutic outcome. Case examples from counselling practice, on the other hand, confirm, at the very least, the need to be aware of racial and cultural issues and to accommodate different world views. As Thomas and Althen (1985) put it (in the context of counselling foreign students, for example), to be effective with foreign clients, counsellors must learn to adapt their counselling styles and their expectations to accommodate the differing world views and cultural value orientations of their foreign clients.

The importance of ethnic or racial identity in cross-cultural counselling

The white counsellor (and the black client) may stereotype each other and be surprised by an oppressive silence or even open hostility. Edwards (1983) stresses that a general disposition shared by some black people is that personal problems should not be discussed outside the family: 'Never tell your business to strangers; black people have to be careful about who they talk to.' Edwards notes that some black clients may have knee-jerk hostility reactions which include statements like: 'That's none of your business … What do you want to know that for? … How would I know? I mind my own business', and cautions against interpreting the client's responses in a literal, concrete way. The counsellor should view such reticence about self-disclosure or hostility as signals of anxieties and as styles of self-protective armour. On the other hand, to react defensively, Edwards (1983) warns, is to give legitimacy to the client's need for self-protection. In these eventualities, it is essential that the counsellor use a model of racial identity to understand the blocks to the relationship.

Helms (1984) outlined a model of racial identity, focusing on the dynamics of cross-racial dyads so that counsellors can acquire a better understanding of how best to treat the culturally different client. Of course, both counsellor and client have their own ethnic identities. According to Helms (1990) white racial identity development refers to the process through which a white person (here the counsellor) first acknowledges racism, abandons racist attitudes and finally develops a non-racist persona. Black racial identity development refers to the process through which a black person (here the client) relinquishes negative racial stereotypes that to be black is 'bad' and inferior to whites, recognizing the oppressive existence of many black people under white dominance and finally developing pride in being black and a more positive self-esteem.

Alladin (1986) has pointed out that in cross-racial dyads there is a danger of the projection of racism by either party. For example, some clients (and counsellors!) may conveniently and wholly blame racism for all their problems but then refuse to accept any personal responsibility for challenging it or taking steps which could help change their situation. On the other hand, some counsellors (and clients!) may collude in denying racism when it exists for fear of arousing strong emotions. A typical dyad in cross-cultural counselling is that of black client and white counsellor. Jones and Seagull (1983) suggest that in cross-racial interactions it is important for white counsellors to examine feelings aroused, such as white racial guilt for colonial oppression of blacks, countertransference and their need to be powerful. If these issues are not adequately resolved then obviously they would inhibit the development of a therapeutic alliance.

Atkinson and Thompson (1992), in their review of the research on racial, ethnic and cultural variables in counselling, conclude that if race/ethnicity is relevant to the client's problem, then a racially/ethnically similar counsellor who is perceived as expert and trustworthy will exercise greater influence on the client's attitudes.

The problem is, how does the practising counsellor ascertain whether race/ethnicity is relevant to a particular client's problem? One hint from the research literature (see Abramowitz and Murray, 1983) is to look at premature termination rates. A counsellor who finds a disproportionate number of his or her culturally different clients dropping out prematurely can infer that race/ethnicity is relevant and has probably been ignored or mismanaged in counselling.

However, the development of awareness about racism and racial identity, and recognition that cultures different from that of the counsellor are not deviant or deficient, coupled with an understanding of different ways of being (for example, communication styles, world views, patterns of self-disclosure) can make counselling a truly helping and challenging relationship, irrespective of ethnicity for both counsellor, and client.

References and further reading

Abramowitz, S.I., and Murray, J. (1983) 'Race effects in psychotherapy', in J. Murray, and P.R. Abramson (eds), *Bias in Psychotherapy*. New York: Praeger.

Alladin, W.J. (1986) 'Clinical psychology and ethnic minorities: an inside view', *Clincial Psychology Forum*, 5: 28–32.

Alladin, W.J. (1989) 'Counselling women and ethnic minorities: problems and prospects', in special issue: Counselling women and ethnic minorities. *Counselling Psychology Quarterly*, 2 (2): 101–4.

Alladin, W.J. (1993) 'Transcultural counselling: theory, research and practice. DCP Reference Library in Clinical Practice', *British Journal of Clinical Psychology*, 32: 2.

Atkinson, D.R. and Thompson, C.E. (1992) 'Racial, ethnic, and cultural variables in counselling', in S.D. Brown, and R.W. Lent (eds), *Handbook of Counseling Psychology*, 2nd edn. New York: Wiley.

Comas-Diaz, L. and Jacobsen, F.M. (1991) 'Ethnocultural transference and countertransference in the therapeutic dyad', *American Journal of Orthopsychiatry*, 61 (3): 392–402.

Draguns, J.D. (1989) 'Dilemmas and choices in cross-cultural counseling: the universal versus the culturally distinctive', in P.B. Pedersen, J.G. Draguns, W.J. Lonner and J.E. Trimble (eds), *Counseling Across Cultures*. Honolulu: University of Hawaii Press.

Edwards, S. (1983) 'Cultural and ethnic perspectives: black cultural attributes and their implications for counseling black clients', in V. D'Andrea and P. Saloavey (eds), *Peer Counselling: Skills and Perspectives*. Palo Alto, CA: Science & Behavior Books.

Helms, J.E. (1984) 'Toward a theoretical explanation of the effects of race on counseling: a black and white model', *The Counselling Psychologist*, 12 (4): 153–65.

Helms, J.E. (1990) *Black and White Racial Identity: Theory, Research and Practice*. Westport, CT: Greenwood Press.

Jones, A. and Seagull, A.A. (1983) 'Dimensions of the relationship between the black client and the white therapist: a theoretical overview', in D.R. Atkinson, G. Morten and D.W. Sue (eds), *Counselling American Minorities: A Cross-Cultural Perspective*, 2nd edn. Dubuque, IA: William C. Brown.

Kareem, J. (1992) 'The Nafsiyat Intercultural Therapy Centre', in J. Kareem and R. Littlewood (eds), *Intercultural Therapy: Themes, Interpretations and Practice*. Oxford: Blackwell.

Lago, C. and Thompson, J. (1989) 'Counselling and race', in W. Dryden, D. Charles-Edwards and R. Woolfe (eds), *Handbook of Counselling in Britain*. London: Routledge.

Patterson, C.H. (1978) 'Cross-cultural or intercultural psychotherapy', *International Journal of the Advancement of Counselling*, 1: 231–48.

Pedersen, P.B., Fukuyama, M. and Heath, A. (1989) 'Client, counselor and contextual variables in multicultural counselling' in P.B. Pedersen, J.G. Draguns, W.J. Lonner and J.E. Trimble (eds), *Counseling Across Cultures*. Honolulu: University of Hawaii Press.

Sundberg, N.D. (1981) 'Cross-cultural counseling and psychotherapy: a research overview', in A.J. Marsella and P.B. Pedersen (eds), *Cross-cultural Counseling and Psychotherapy: Foundations, Evaluation and Cultural Considerations*. New York: Pergamon Press.

Sue, D.W. and Sue, D. (1990) *Counselling the Culturally Different*, 2nd edn. New York: Wiley.

Thomas, K. and Althen, G. (1989) 'Counselling foreign students', in P.B. Pedersen, J.G. Draguns, W.J. Lonner and J.E. Trimble (eds), *Counseling Across Cultures*. Honolulu: University of Hawaii Press.

Tyler, F.B., Sussewell, D.R. and Williams-McCoy, J. (1985) 'Ethnic validity in psychotherapy', in G.R. Dudley and M.L. Rawlins (eds), Special issue: Psychotherapy with ethnic minorities. *Psychotherapy*, 22 (22) Supplement: 311–20.

Discussion issues

1 How important is it to ethnically match clients and counsellors?
2 What is the case for and against ethnic matching?
3 Ethnically matching clients and counsellors can 'imprison both the counsellor and the client in their own racial and cultural identity'.
4 All counsellors should acquire cross-cultural competencies.

16

An Analysis of the Facilitative Effects of Gender and Race in Counselling Practice

Pat Ward and Nick Banks

In the area of transcultural therapy a frequent issue of debate is that of the benefits of matching the ethnic group of client and counsellor. While some writers argue that this is paramount to enable the therapeutic process (Atkinson, 1983; Harrison, 1975; Sattler, 1977), others question its importance and see it as having less influence, for example, to issues of social class (Garfield and Bergin, 1986; Sue and Zane, 1987). Whatever the viewpoint, in considering the need to match the ethnicity of counsellor with the ethnicity of client, little attention has been paid to the positive facilitative transference effects that may ensue from having a therapist of a different ethnicity coupled with being of a different gender. As early as 1965, Bellack and Small argued: 'Because of the emphasis on positive transference the selection of the proper therapist for each patient assumes great importance. The factors that may be involved include the therapist's age, sex, most comfortable role and cultural suitability' (p. 41).

This chapter uses a case study approach to illustrate the positive effects that being of a different gender and ethnicity may bring to the therapeutic relationship. An attempt is made to demonstrate the benefit that a client may obtain through positive use of transference promoting a therapeutic alliance in the transcultural therapy encounter in a white woman counsellor, back male client dyad.

Counsellor and client backgrounds

The counsellor was a white woman, in her early forties, in a mixed 'race' relationship working in a general practitioners surgery in a social work/counselling position, in an inner city area with a large African-Caribbean population.

The client, David, was a man of African-Caribbean origin born in Britain who was in his late twenties. He was unemployed and had previously held semi-skilled manual jobs. He had a white English girlfriend who was also a counselling client of the present counsellor. In addition to his girlfriend, David also had a wife who was a white east European recent immigrant. She had one male child by David. David simultaneously maintained the relationship with his wife and girlfriend without the wife being aware. David initially presented to the counselling services in a drop-in session to discuss housing difficulties. This showed itself to be a 'cover' for his real need. He subsequently came for 26 drop-in sessions, sometimes twice weekly, sometimes once every two weeks. He appeared unable consistently to keep appointments, preferring to come when a crisis in his relationship appeared. It became apparent that David's needs were related to an inability to make and take decisions for himself, difficulties with low self-esteem, relationship issues and anger management. David saw his mother as a warm supportive and caring woman but dominant and overbearing. He was ambivalent in his feelings towards her, seeing her as over-critical and controlling, although he still felt highly dependent on her approval. He had lived with his mother until the age of 25 and then briefly lived with his wife before returning to live with his mother. His mother had always made decisions for him and he had not developed the skills of decision making. His earliest memory was of sleeping in his cot as an infant with his mother's hand comforting him through the bars of the cot as she slept by his side.

Emotional expressiveness and relationship issues

That there was some ambivalence in his relationship with his mother was shown by his reasons for being less attracted to previous black girlfriends. David's view was that black women were 'overpowering, loud and bossy'. He did not feel comfortable with them as partners for fear that they would be over-controlling of him and limit his freedom to develop. Thus, it seemed that black women were perceived as controlling and suffocating 'mother figures' who were limiting of autonomy and growth for David. However, David showed a need to attach this controlling role to other women, white or black. This displayed itself in the counselling relationship where once David came in to counselling agitated and some-what confused saying, 'I need someone to tell me what to do. I need help to make a decision', 'You tell me what to do.' He was fearful of making decisions that would be wrong as he felt that the few decisions he had made in the past had either been faulty, too hasty or made too late to have the desired effect. The counsellor, instead of explaining that it was not her role to make decisions for the client, took the path of exploring what made it important to be given a decision when he had previously stated the difficulty he had with women whom he saw as over-controlling and dominant. This created some frustration in David who saw this behaviour as 'withholding' – another form of control. At one point David became overwhelmed with emotion and filled with tears began to cry and left the room. He came back some four weeks later apologizing for crying and showing what he saw as 'weakness'. It transpired during the counselling session that he was embarrassed by his display of emotion and although he initially felt unable to come back had considered the warm acceptance of the counsellor and had then felt able to return. As he said, 'I thought about it and said to myself no, she [the counsellor] wouldn't get angry at me leaving. You would understand. You'd still see me as a man.'

The value of a man showing emotional expressiveness and being in touch with one's emotions was explored. David tended to spend the first twenty minutes or so of the counselling session trying to formulate his thoughts and find the words for what he wanted to say. Involvement or prompting at this initial stage by the counsellor may have been seen as over-intrusive, having the effect of blocking David's autonomy and development of self-expression and self-control. It transpired that one of his relationship difficulties was the frustration and anger that he felt in his wife's inability to show 'warmth and feeling like a white western woman'. Thus a view of black women as overpowering, loud and bossy was in contrast with white western women as 'warm and feeling' for David.

Cultural conflict or lack of emotional attachment?

David's wife had admitted that he might find her 'emotionally cold'. 'That's how we are in east Europe, we learn not to show how we feel.' He wondered whether this cultural difference made it likely that his 'mixed relationship' could survive. However, what was apparent was that the major difficulty between David and his wife was not one of cultural difference but one of lack of emotional attachment. David had disclosed that he had married Petra due to her becoming pregnant with his child. He felt obligated to the child and his mother and so married Petra to allow her to stay in this country. David had acted out a rescue fantasy with both mother and child and now felt trapped and resentful at creating a matrimonial tie in which he felt little emotional commitment to the woman. He claimed his sole reason for staying with Petra was out of a feeling of responsibility for his 18-month-old son. 'If I left her they'd [the Home Office] send her back. I couldn't bear to think that my son would blame me for the loss of his mother. When he got older, he'd say, "did you do that? What kind of a man are you to let my mother be thrown out of the country?" I couldn't live with him thinking bad about me.' It was clear that David's main reason for staying with Petra was about feeling unable to terminate the relationship due to emotional obligations towards his son. David's assumption was that if his wife left the country she would leave her son with him. He had not explored this with her and it was, in fact, highly unlikely. The thought of a different reality was much too painful for David to consider. In seeking emotional fulfilment, David had sought the company of another (white) woman, Julie, whom he claimed he loved. 'She's all the things I need but I just can't leave Petra.' This longing to leave Petra and inevitably, his son, for Julie was a source of great conflict for David. At one level he realized Petra would resist him having custody, but at another level he acted in denial. He felt he could go to no one to discuss this conflict as he believed his friends might betray his trust to see the 'excitement' which would follow. He felt unable to share his dilemma with a mother he was trying to break free from. This need to reach a decision made him turn to a counsellor. The initial visit was to test how he perceived the counsellor. Could she be trusted or would she tell Petra and indeed could he use her to do his work for him and tell Petra? During the first few sessions it became apparent that much of the difficulty in emotional communication and expression was his own and not Petra's, although she appeared to internalize a view of herself as having the difficulty. The emotion which he had most difficulty in expressing in a positive way was that of anger. He would seemingly contain his anger and then erupt in a shouting rage. This had the effect of closing down any communication about disagreement or expression of feelings by his wife as she had discovered that he could become violent if challenged.

David explored with the counsellor how a woman may perceive and feel about a man crying openly. He wanted advice on how to arrange his relationship to make his wife more responsive while not yet able to recognize that it was he who had the difficulty in accepting responsiveness and spontaneity in others. This was evident in his behaviour in that he claimed to be highly jealous of his girlfriend who worked in a club serving drinks and as part of her role regularly spoke and openly 'flirted' with men. He could not accept this sociable and outgoing behaviour and saw any informal sociable interaction with men by women he cared for as threatening to his manful self-image. Neither could he feel comfortable with his wife who was much more guarded in her relationships and much less expressive. David needed a safe place to explore his contradictions and conflicts and develop the emotional part of himself that he kept hidden. This appeared to be the real reason for seeking counselling. It was clear that one of the mechanisms at play was one of 'splitting'. David invested black women with all those negative attributes he would not recognize in himself and, at times, those he could not recognize in his mother.

The use of transference

Jacobs (1989) has defined transference as a reaction towards the counsellor as if they represented someone other than the counsellor. Kupers (1981) suggests a more elaborated interpretation of the meaning of transference which is useful for considering its particular significance in the cross-cultural encounter. For Kupers, transference can be viewed as an unconscious distortion a client introduces into therapy by displacing onto the therapist the feelings, ideas and memories that derive from or were directed towards important or influential figures in the client's life. These, of course, can be figures who had a positive influence or a damaging misfortunate influence. Consequently, the client can enter the counselling relationship with a fixed set of perceptions and feelings. As has been suggested (Banks, 1992; Lago and Thompson, 1989) for the black client experiencing the attempts of helping by a white counsellor, historical experiences and memories of racism surfacing in the form of present recall or thinking may act at an unconscious or conscious level by intruding and interfering with the facilitative quality in the counselling relationship. This 'interference' may only be the case if the counsellor does not recognize the positive use of transference or is unable to cope with it arising in the counselling encounter.

Rogers's (1965) view was that the phenomenon of transference was relatively unimportant to the process of therapy and may in some cases block or hinder the progress of therapy. In Rogers's view the client-centred therapist's reaction to transference should be the same as with any other attitude of the client, i.e. to understand and accept those feelings in the client while helping them to realize that those feelings exist within them, not within the therapist. Rogers saw this realization by the client coming about through the therapist not attempting to evaluate, make moral judgements or show approval or disapproval of past behaviours. Thus, in Rogers's view, therapist acceptance will eventually lead to insight in the client and self-acceptance.

However, one of the attitudes that may cause difficulties was one which Rogers referred to as 'aggressive dependence'. This was typically displayed by the client who believed that he or she was incapable of making their own decisions, or managing themselves and insists that the counsellor must take over and give more direction. Rogers further described the client with this type of difficulty as someone who may feel annoyed because he or she does not feel they are being understood, or receiving the guidance that they feel they need. Therefore, a feeling of antagonism may arise with the client towards the therapist. It is illuminating to note that this description tends to fit one that is often given as an example of the dynamic of the cross-cultural counselling encounter with white therapist and black client (Alexander et al., 1981; Goldstein, 1981; Pedersen et al., 1989; Sue and Sue, 1991). We can speculate that Rogers may have identified this with black clients more than with white. He fails to address the possibility of this need in black clients and what this may mean for client centredness when applied across cultures. We are left with the possibility that Rogers himself may have had some difficulty with the interracial or cross-cultural encounter but, as a defence, projected these difficulties onto the client as aggressive dependence. Thus, it appears that client-centred therapy may not be client centred when used to address client need across cultures by formulating a 'diagnostic category' that allows counsellors to 'pigeonhole' a specific cultural need.

Rogers (1965) provides us with more information that allows us to speculate further on the particular pressures that a black client may experience when he argues that 'transference attitudes are perhaps more likely to occur when the client is experiencing considerable threat to the organisation of self in the material which he is bringing into awareness' (p. 218). It was the counsellor's view that this was the case with David. The more he spoke and revealed about himself to the counsellor, the more he revealed to himself. It was as though 'discussing' himself caused him to consider his motives and question his motivation.

In further considering transference, Rogers (1965) went on to say 'a true transference relationship is perhaps most likely to occur when the client experiences another as having a more effective understanding of his own self than he himself possesses' (p. 218). This perception of greater understanding seems to have shown itself in David's demand for advice. David appears to have been attracted to an 'internal decision-making resource' he saw women as naturally having. David perceived the therapist as having a greater understanding of himself then he had, as the therapist was 'white wife', 'girlfriend' and, in her gender and age, an all-knowing, powerful 'mother figure' – three transference objects in one. In seeking decisions from a white woman therapist he was both attempting to gain insight into how a white woman may feel and see his predicament and he was able to avoid the over-reliance on black women whom he perceived as controlling. This view of black women was not a process of internalized racism as it was his actual differing experience of black and white women and, in particular, his experience with a significant black female figure – his mother. However, due to early experiences with his mother he had developed a distorted and immature mother fixation which had caused him to 'select' black women who were similar to his mother as a means of exploring and possibly controlling her through controlling them. His resultant inability to do so was confirmation of the power and dominance of black women. As the counsellor had a recognized temporary role, self-exploration carried no long-term commitments as with his mother or Petra, but like his relationship with Petra 'interaction' could be had 'on demand' by use of drop in sessions.

Cultural transferences as an enabling process

For counsellors whose practice is influenced by a psychodynamic orientation, the process of transference is acknowledged and can be of central importance to psychotherapy. However, there may be in the cross-cultural encounter an additional process in play. Cultural transference, as discussed by Ridley (1989), is a specific form of transference which refers to the emotional reactions of a client of one ethnic group transferred to the therapist of a different ethnic group. This is likely to happen where the client has had previous significant experiences with members of the therapist's ethnic group outside of the therapeutic encounter. This was clearly the case with David. In some instances, the client's feelings towards the therapist may have little to do with how the therapist actually treats the client. However, negative feelings, or in some cases positive feelings, can be evoked in the client simply because the therapist is a member of a particular ethnic group. Ridley notes that although not the original source of the client's frustration, the counsellor may show incompetence by not sufficiently handling the transference. The unskilled or uninsightful therapist may fail to recognize the transference or minimize significance if and when it is recognized. A further difficulty may be the therapist's inability to employ constructive interventions to resolve the conflicts underlying the transference. The skilled counsellor should correctly ascertain in transference situations what difficulty interaction with white people is causing. Cultural transference can reveal a client's motivations and ways of behaving in inter-'racial' situations.

Counsellors engaged in cross-cultural situations need to be especially alert to these cultural transference client reactions as they can be of major importance in therapy. As clients re-enact their emotions and experiences of inter-'racial' contact, the skilled counsellor can have a unique opportunity to work with emotional material that might otherwise be inaccessible to the client in therapy. Thus, this presents those in the cross-cultural therapeutic encounter a unique opportunity to truly engage with significant issues the client brings to sessions which may not be successfully explored in the matched ethnic counsellor–client dyad. It is quite likely, as David said, that he could not have explored his relationship with a white woman (women) with a black counsellor. 'No way could I tell a black woman that I was not attracted to black women. I just couldn't.' When challenged by the therapist about his view of black women counsellors, the client said, 'Look, I don't care how good she would be as a counsellor, this is a thing I would never ever discuss with any black woman. No way!' In any case the goal of therapy was not to politically educate the client, but to enable him to explore the dynamic of his own conflict as a means of achieving some insight into his relationship difficulties with all women. With an interpretation that cannot be immediately owned by the client there is little use in pushing it as insight into self may occur between sessions and not always immediately during a session. Some may see this as collusion. However, the responsibility for gaining insight rests with the client and cannot be forced by the therapist. Any attempt to push a point may be interpreted by the insecure client as persecution and dealt with by termination of counselling. Indeed, it is likely that David would have identified any collusive behaviour in the counsellor for himself with the effect of weakening the therapeutic alliance. David was most of all seeking a safe and secure setting to explore his difficulties. In coming to the counsellor David invited personal challenge; not challenge that would lead to conflict of ideology or personal morality, but one that would lead to personal development through supported exploration.

Summary of transference variables

Within this case study example the process of transference was seen as crucial to effecting both positive processes and outcome of therapy. The following issues were of particular significance:

1   The counsellor's personal situation of being in a mixed race relationship with a black man. Pictures of children in the counselling room suggested this. This seemed of central importance to the client who needed to know that his mixed relationship was accepted in a non-judgmental way. The counsellor was told by his girlfriend, Julie (also a client) that he continually asked about the counsellor's relationship and her children's origin. (Note that although a client may discuss their partner with a counsellor, the counsellor may not discuss the partner's, as client, disclosed material with client. This would be a breach of confidentiality.)

2   Another reoccurring theme of importance for the client was one of the influence of being of mixed ethnic origin on the developing child's self and world view. The client simultaneously used the counsellor in this situation as 'girlfriend', 'mother', 'wife' and 'expert' as illustrated by him saying: 'I want you to tell me what I can expect from my child. How will he see himself when he is older? If I leave my marriage will he hate all black men? What can you help me to do so he sees me as a positive role model?' ... 'How would you see me? Would you think I was no good?' 'Will my child see himself as black or will he want to be white? What can *we* do to make certain his mind is settled?'

3   The counsellor's ethnicity and gender were of importance to the client, as these variables coincided with the ethnicity and gender of his girlfriend and wife. The therapeutic encounter was one where the importance and significance of ethnicity, gender and mixed relationships were played out with intense emotion. The client engaged in 'unscripted role plays' as if the counsellor was either girlfriend or wife. Issues of the relationships central to David and David's role with these women found clarification in the therapeutic encounter.

4   The counsellor's gender and age played a central role in allowing the client to examine his relationship with his mother. Issues of decision-making dependency relating to his two partners were 'played out' within therapy with the client continually asking the therapist to take responsibility for the judgements he should make, for example, whether or not he should tell his wife about his girlfriend, abandon his wife for his girlfriend, how to prioritize his budget needs.

There were frequent attempts to transfer the client's dependency on his mother's authority and decision-making role to the therapist. These attempts were resisted to allow the client to take more self-responsibility leading to greater autonomy and independence of decision making.

5   The client's impulsive and spontaneous use of drop-in arrangements was more related to an informal family visiting arrangement than planned use of counselling appointments. For this client the informality helped the process of therapy as he could make decisions as when to come rather than feel obligated to make appointments to please therapist diary needs.

The outcome

David made a decision to leave his wife and live with his girlfriend. He said 'I've spent so much time thinking about this, it's got to be right. I can't stay with a woman I don't love.' His intentions were to continue to contribute to the financial support of his son and visit as regularly as possible with him and Petra. He wished to remain as involved with his son as circumstances would allow to support his son's racial identity needs. He said, 'Just being available to answer his questions will help.' His final words to the counsellor were, 'You've been right not to tell me what to do. I wanted advice from you and you refused. At first I was so mad, but now I see you wanted me to stand on my own feet.'

Conclusion

For the white therapist engaging in the cross-cultural encounter there is an added dimension of responsibility in addition to that one has in the ethnically matched counselling dyad. One aspect of this extra responsibility is to ascertain, through the appropriate use of a supervisor experienced in transcultural issues, whether what is perceived as 'transference' is not in fact 'counter transference' where the therapist is actively playing out her or his own needs in the cross-cultural encounter. The effect of this on the client is bound to be one of further disempowerment. However, there is more to positive process and outcome in counselling than just assessing the existence or strength of transference issues. Wolberg, as early as 1965, indicated: 'unresolved hostilities, needs to maintain too dominant and authoritarian a status in the relationship and detachment ... a therapist will be limited by his (and presumably her) own personality and ways of working' (p. 197). This may be particularly so in the cross-cultural encounter.

References

Alexander, A.A., Klein, M.H., Workneh, F. and Miller, M.H. (1981) 'Psychotherapy and the foreign student', in P.B. Pedersen, J.G. Draguns, W.J. Lonner and J.E. Trimble (eds), *Counselling Across Cultures*, pp. 227–46. Honolulu: University of Hawaii Press.

Atkinson, D.R. (1983) 'Ethnic similarity in counselling: a review of research', *The Counselling Psychologist*, 11: 79–92.

Banks, N.J. (1992) 'Black clients, white counsellors: working with discrimination and prejudice in the workplace', *Employee Counselling Today*, 12–16.

Bellack, L. and Small, L. (1965) *Emergency Psychotherapy and Brief Psychotherapy*. New York: Grune and Stratton.

Garfield, S.L. and Bergin, A. (1986) *Handbook of Psychotherapy and Behaviour Change*, 3rd edn. New York: Wiley.

Goldstein, A.P. (1981) 'Expectancy effects in cross cultural counselling', in A.J. Marsella and P.B. Pedersen (eds), *Cross Cultural Counselling and Psychology: Foundation, Evaluations and Cultural Considerations*, pp. 85–101. Elmsford, NY: Pergamon.

Green, B. (1985) 'Considerations in the treatment of black patients by white therapists', *Psychotherapy*, 22: 389–93.

Harrison, D.K. (1975) 'Race as a counsellor–client variable in counselling and psychotherapy: a review of the research', *The Counselling Psychologist*, 5: 124–33.

Jacobs, M. (1989) *Psychodynamic Counselling in Action*. London: Sage.

Kupers, T. (1981) *Public Therapy: The Practice of Therapy in the Public Mental Health Clinic*. London: Macmillan.

Lago, C. and Thompson, J. (1989) 'Counselling and race', in W. Dryden, D. Charles-Edwards and R. Woolfe (eds), *Handbook of Counselling in Britain*. London: Routledge.

Pedersen, P.B., Fukuyama, M. and Heath, A.E. (1989) 'Client, counsellor and contextual variables in multicultural counselling', in P.B. Pedersen, W.J. Lonner and J.G. Draguns (eds), *Counselling Across Cultures*, 3rd edn. Honolulu: University of Hawaii Press.

Ridley, C.R. (1989) 'Racism in counselling as an aversive behavioural process', in P. Pedersen, J. Draguns, W. Lonner and J. Trimble (eds), *Counselling Across Cultures*, 3rd edn. Honolulu: University of Hawaii Press.

Rogers, C. (1965) *Client-Centred Therapy*. London: Constable.

Sattler, J.M. (1977) 'The effects of therapist–client similarity', in A.S. Gurman and A.M. Razin (eds), *Effective Psychotherapy: A Handbook of Research*, New York: Pergamon.

Sue, D.W. and Sue, D. (1990) *Counselling and Culturally Different*, 2nd edn. New York: Wiley.

Sue, S. and Zane, N. (1987) 'The role of culture and cultural techniques in psychotherapy', *American Psychologist*, 42 (1): 37–45.

Thomas, L. (1992) 'Racism and psychotherapy: working with racism in the counsulting room – an analytical view', in J. Kareem and R. Littlewood (eds), *Intercultural Therapy: Themes, Interpretations and Practice*. Oxford: Blackwell.

Wolberg, L. (1965) *Short Term Psychotherapy*. New York: Grune and Stratton.

Discussion issues

1　Could the issues of social class have more importance to the therapeutic process than matching the ethnic group of client and counsellor?

2　What are the positive and negative effects to the therapeutic relationship of being a different gender and ethnicity?

3　Client-centred therapy may not be client-centred when used to address client need across cultures.

4　Cultural-transference can reveal a client's motivations and ways of behaving in inter-'racial' situations.

Cross-Cultural/Racial Matching in Counselling and Therapy

White Clients and Black Counsellors

Roy Moodley and Shukla Dhingra

Numerous studies in counselling and therapy have explored the issue of cross-racial/cultural matching (Carter, 1995; Heppner and Dixon, 1981; Lago and Thompson, 1989, 1996; Nickerson et al., 1994; Pomales et al., 1986; Sue and Sue, 1990; Wade and Bernstein, 1991). Many have focused particularly on the white counsellor/black client dyad, and the advantages and disadvantages of such matching. The characteristics and effectiveness of the black counsellor/white client dyad has received minimal attention in the counselling literature. In general, the focus has been on white clients' negative reactions towards black counsellors therapeutically (Carter, 1995). The relatively few authors in the field of cross-cultural counselling in Britain, for example, d'Ardenne and Mahtani (1989) and Lago and Thompson (1996), have attempted to explore some of the issues of counselling and therapy in a multicultural context, including the black therapist/white client dyad, but not in any great depth.

The paucity of research in 'race', culture and counselling and the lack of substantive literature on black counsellors/therapists in counselling and therapy have led to misconceptions that reinforce a number of stereotype notions about black people in the mental health field. Of particular consequence is that black people are usually seen as clients, thereby fuelling the argument that black counsellors are more apt to be helpees than helpers. This may also account for the small number of trainees and practitioners in this field. Admission policies on some counselling courses and many institutional employment policies may be subtly contributing to these notions (see Lago and Thompson, 1996). The way intercultural therapy is presently defined may also create the perception that black people are suited for therapy. For example, in cross-cultural counselling the white counsellor and black client norm excludes white people from the process as clients (Sashidharan, 1986). This paradigm reinforces the notion that the black person is 'signified' as 'ill' and can only be helped by the white therapist (see Fernando, 1988; Kareem and Littlewood, 1992; Littlewood and Lipsedge, 1997).

Another perception which problematizes the black counsellor as a professional therapist is the notion that the relatively few ethnic minority counsellors who work in this field are best suited to work chiefly with clients from their own or similar culture background. While in some situations it may be appropriate for same-race therapy to occur (see Mills and Topolski, 1996), it does however place the black counsellor within a very narrow cultural practice, questioning their skills and competence to work beyond the 'race'/culture, gender and disability dynamic in therapy. Our research, although small and not a representative sample of ethnic minority counsellors/therapists in Britain, shows that black counsellors work with just as many white clients as they do with black clients. And, in many cases, black counsellors work with fewer ethnic minority clients than white clients as a result of the demography of the institutions they work in. Some work exclusively with white clients.

In the context of a growing interest in counselling and psychotherapy by ethnic minority groups, both as clients and as practitioners, it seems important that this aspect is researched and evaluated. Using material from a case vignette by one of the authors and from the published literature on cross-cultural counselling, we have attempted to show the strategies that white clients use in accepting black counsellors. We also interviewed a small number of black counsellors/therapists to ascertain their views on working with white clients. This chapter, therefore, is an attempt to consider the black counsellor/white client relationship, examining the particular processes and characteristics that lead to effective outcomes.

Client's choice of a counsellor

A client's preference for a therapist of his or her choice is of particular importance in the relationship and to the eventual outcomes in therapy. Engaging a client at the pre-entry process with the issue of choice of counsellor will support the therapeutic alliance. Clients' awareness and understanding of the process of counselling and therapy will also contribute to positive outcomes. Beutler et al. (1986) suggest that patients who are familiar with psychotherapy may benefit from an informed understanding of what to expect in treatment. The same could be said for counselling. Beutler et al. (1996) suggest that the integrity and strength of the therapeutic alliance may be fortified by assigning therapists to patients with similar demographic backgrounds, sex, age and ethnicity. However, matching done purely on the basis of race or colour can imprison both the professional and the client in their own racial and cultural identity (Kareem, 1992: 24). Making a choice is often closely tied up with a client's actual presenting problem. By addressing the issue of counsellor choice, even before the counselling process begins, clients confront aspects of themselves which contribute to their disturbances and discomforts. In this way, the processes of considering, enquiring and being interviewed for counselling/therapy become paramount in constructing the parameters which may either confine or liberate the client in the relationship with the counsellor.

The opportunity to choose a counsellor is usually available to many white clients but not to the majority of black clients. McLeod (1993) reminds us that counselling remains a predominantly white occupation with relatively few ethnic minority counsellors: 'Black counsellors, by virtue of their training and background, will have been predominantly geared to working with white people, not black people' (Lago and Thompson, 1989: 289). Many white clients who are not offered the opportunity to choose a counsellor may be reluctant to enter into any kind of therapy. Indeed in a postmodern democratic environment, clients may offer resistance to any counsellor irrespective of 'race' or gender if they perceive that their right to choose has been infringed. However, for white clients the appearance of a black counsellor may unconsciously evoke certain prejudices and stereotypes which could lead to the rejection of the counsellor but be interpreted by the client as not having a right to choose. This was reflected by Mary (not her real name), in counselling with one of the authors, who had this to say:

> And I thought maybe she's got different view points, something she's find me really western and really extrovert and lot weird and stuff and I thought maybe there will be some barrier and that you wouldn't be able to help me as much as the other counsellor would, that was white same as me.

At it happens, Mary did not reject her black counsellor but clearly expressed her fear of the 'other'. These issues may not arise in a white counsellor/white client match since it is the norm, and on the surface presents an agreeable and acceptable pairing, even if the client experiences other types of conflict, like differences of gender, personality and so on.

Exploring the question of 'race' in therapy

In our research, the black counsellors we interviewed used a variety of strategies to consider 'race' in therapy with white clients. Some (less than 40 per cent) would take a proactive approach to the subject of 'race' earlier on in the therapy but were clear that the timing and readiness of the client would be key in deciding precisely when the subject was explored. Others (more than 60 per cent) adopted a non-directive approach indicating that they would leave it up to the client and then negotiate the most appropriate way for the 'client to talk about "race" issues'. Almost all the black counsellors we interviewed were sensitive to the complexity and confusions surrounding the issues of 'race', culture and ethnicity. Some black counsellors who used the proactive 'approach were confronted by some of the answers they received. For example, one counsellor asked the question: 'How do you feel about working with me, a black therapist?' She received the following responses from white clients: 'I'm not prejudiced', 'You seem all right', 'You speak good English', 'I didn't realize you were Asian'.

Another counsellor who confronted a client found herself at the receiving end of a barrage of negative perceptions about 'race'. This was difficult for the counsellor to receive initially but good supervision and being clear about her therapeutic approach offered this counsellor strength to understand her client. Six months into counselling, this same client is now emulating the counsellor in dress and other non-verbal manners as a way of identifying with the therapist. Many of the counsellors interviewed felt that the issue of 'race' in the hands of an unskilled counsellor would intimidate and oppress clients. A competent counsellor using positive aspects of themselves offers clients the opportunity to 'risk take', challenge previously held assumptions and transform themselves in counselling. Skilful handling of the therapy will prevent clients from feeling guilty or putting up defences and resistances. This was seen in Mary's therapy, when she said:

> When I first realized that you are a different race to me, I did think she can't be able to help me you know she, eh, especially, I used to live in, eh, a big Asian community around a big Asian community in [...] and they were just so very different to me.

Clearly Mary was able to establish sufficient confidence and trust in the relationship with the black counsellor to share these thoughts knowing that they show her prejudice of the Asian community. In moving from the first person to the third person pronoun – 'I did think she can't be able to help me you know she ...' – Mary was able to reduce her anxiety and also attempted to protect her counsellor from her 'race' based remarks.

Carter (1995) offers a case study in which Tina, a white client, reports that her friend who is 'light skinned' told her that she is lucky to have a black clinician. In the therapy she becomes confused and distressed when 'race' is raised. The excerpt below is a small part of the case study described by Carter (1995):

Tina: Are you very much aware in here that I am White and you are Black? Because I'm not. [Pause]
Therapist: Sometimes. [Silence] I mean, it's hard not to be aware that you're, White.
Tina: Yeah.
Therapist: When I hear you talk about your experiences, then I think some of your experiences can only be understood by seeing you as White. The expectations and perspectives that you hold come about as a result of your racial experiences. So, I'm aware of that. I do have to under-stand you in the context of your race and gender.
Tina: I don't know what that means exactly.
Therapist: Well, it means there're differences between people from various races. I might interact with you differently, talk to you differently: if

you were Asian, for instance, our pattern of communication would be
different. Thus, race affects our work. Do you see what I mean?
Tina: Yeah. I do. (p. 207)

Carter noted that black counsellor/white client dyads like their counterparts are strongly influenced by each participant's racial identity attitude
development and advocated an active introjection of these issues with
clients. In another case study, Tom, a white client, who clearly thought that
his black therapist was 'superior' to him 'by virtue of age, education and
academic experience (i.e. a doctorate) and "down-to-earth"' was 'unable
to share himself and his inner struggles in a consistent and productive
way ... Tom was emotionally closed and defended' (p. 202). Clearly there
are no rules to follow in exploring the issue of 'race' as a variable in therapy: black counsellors must themselves be 'ready' to enter the complex,
confusing, profound and artificial world of 'race'. 'The race of the therapist will inescapably affect the therapy as it does when the therapist is
white and the patient black' (Thomas, 1992: 139). Both black and white
patients use 'race' to express transferences of object relations and
drive derivatives (Holmes, 1992).

White clients' strategies in accepting black counsellors

The negative attitude of white clients to black counsellors must be
acknowledged and understood in the context of a society which reflects
racism in different degrees. In a postmodern, multicultural and multiracial society such as Britain, counselling is always set in a political context. Socio-political variables are now part of the terrain in which black
counsellors and therapists find themselves. Therefore, researchers who
focus on just the negative aspect of the relationship can miss the important strategies which white clients use to develop and maintain the therapeutic relationship with black counsellors. Clients may adopt subtle
strategies to ensure that they are not being 'short-changed'. For example,
the excerpt below shows Mary's way of accepting her counsellor:

Mary: But you have to be professional because you can't be anything else
otherwise you get into a big mess, but I do feel you understand me.
Counsellor: Em.
Mary: I feel understood as a woman.
Counsellor: Em.
Mary: When especially a lot of my issues in patriarchal society in and stuff
like that and I feel you understand me. I can trust you.

Mary's strategy involved a complex and logical reasoning of the counsellor's commitment to the professional role and an assertive request for

good practice. She continues to make sure that she gets her 'money's worth' by recognizing and acknowledging the gender similarity of the relationship. 'Race' then becomes more acceptable because it engages in the discourse of gender and it can also be contextualized professionally. For example, Mary's utterance – 'otherwise you get into a big mess' – is at best a friendly threat or, at worst, litigation. But this is a strong scenario that we are alluding to and clearly from Mary's relationship with her counsellor this was not the case. This last excerpt from Mary's therapy demonstrates that trust and honesty between the white client and the black counsellor is the key ingredient for positive outcomes of the process:

Mary: I think one of the biggest things I got out of counselling was being honest.
Counsellor: I found you very honest. Extremely honest and, and open.
Mary: Yea, it was important for me. I was counselled before again by a woman. And it didn't, didn't help me like it has now. I wasn't being honest with myself, let alone with the counsellor. But this time around I was just so desperate. I was in such a situation with everyone that I knew. I just felt it was time to be honest. I just wanted to take the step and be honest with you.

Honesty in this instance may also be understood as a metaphor, reflecting the various stages of undoing the suspicion and then building the level of trust that the therapeutic process requires for effective outcomes. Lago and Thompson (1996) remind us that 'it is important to respect the enormous risk faced by the client especially when the therapist is so clearly identifiable as a member of the (complained about) racial group' (p. 105). Carter (1995) suggests that:

> In the therapeutic setting, a White client may assume that a Black or visible racial/ethnic therapist should act, think, and feel as he or she does. The White client also believes that the non-White clinician will comply with the client's wishes and conform to the client's stereotypes. This results in a power struggle, because the therapist assumes that he or she is responsible for the direction of the psychotherapeutic process. (Carter, 1995: 205–6)

Not only may the therapist be required to understand the client's projections but he/she has to cope with his/her own fantasies about the client's projections and meanwhile attempt to stay open and receptive to what the client is bringing (Lago and Thompson, 1996: 105). The issue of power in counselling is still not clearly understood and perhaps may need further research in all types of therapeutic relationships. Lago and Thompson (1989) remind us that from the perspective of power, the white counsellor and black client relationship also has a potential danger, namely a perception of the notion of white superiority (p. 27). In our research a number of black counsellors indicated that this may present a problem if the therapist fails to understand 'where the client is coming from' in terms of socio-economic background, poor self-concept, acceptance of their abilities and disabilities, and so on. Sometimes these issues are the very core which underlies the problem clients face in the first place. Many of the counsellors in the research felt that if the therapeutic outcomes were experienced negatively or perceived as unsatisfactory with the black counsellors it may reinforce the 'white supremacy complex' (see Moodley, 1998).

Black counsellors' strategies in managing the relationship

In our study, the black counsellors we interviewed emphasized the complexity of their professional roles as counsellors while at the same time they were aware that their skin colour was part of their practice. This was understood both in terms of their presence in the institution as well as their relationships with colleagues and clients. Many (more than 80 per cent) were overtly anxious to be seen as a professional first but were aware that in the counselling relationship their ethnicity and colour is an important variable. For many counsellors (more than 70 per cent) the problem was not with 'race' and white clients but with 'race' and the institutions they work in. Many indicated that they were often made invisible through staff development policies, subtle employment and promotion policies, and so on. While institutional issues were important to discuss, most counsellors felt that their work with clients overshadowed these institutional policies.

In d'Ardenne's and Mahtani's (1989) example of a black counsellor working with a white client, although the analysis of the therapy is very specific to the one client, Fred, a number of conclusions can be drawn for black counsellors in general. In this case, although the black counsellor has experienced racism and hostility in society, she still has to be aware of how the white client can respond to her. To prepare herself she 'uses her white friends and acquaintances to provide her with insights into the prejudices and fears expressed by the major culture' (p. 35). She is also 'in contact with several discussion and support groups for black counsellors who will help her make sense of all her trans-cultural experiences' (p. 35). Clearly in this way the counsellor has constructed a professional approach to her practice. The client, on the other hand, appears to cope with the 'reversal of power' by literally relating the counsellor to his Asian GP, to whom he has given status. For the client, this kind of coping strategy is vital in forming a favourable relationship with his counsellor and at the same time dealing with the complexity of 'race', culture and ethnicity.

The black counsellor in the above example was able to construct a strategy for maintaining her professional 'health', but many in our research indicated that the limited supervision that they were offered, and often with therapists who were not familiar with the dynamics of 'race', culture and ethnicity, must be a cause for concern by all those who work in this field. We are aware from our interviews that some of the black counsellors were underplaying the 'race' context for a number of reasons. Maintaining an invisibility in the institution may offer rewards and may be a misguided loyalty to the institutional racism which pervades some workplaces. If black counsellors would rather be known as professional counsellors like architects, lawyers and so on), as this may subvert the negative impact of blackness in their practice, the question we need to ask is, Can this stop white clients from seeing them as black?

We are aware from our interviews that many counsellors (more than 60 per cent) believe that not all white clients come into therapy with a conscious awareness of 'race' as a variable to explore in therapy. 'Some white patients who deny any difference between a black therapist and themselves, do so to preserve politeness and to secure against the seepage of unconscious material' (Thomas, 1992: 140). Therefore, it behoves black counsellors to be very sensitive about introducing the concepts of 'race', culture or ethnicity, and to do so only at the request of the client. The interpretations of the transference and the countertransference feeling must be clearly understood within the context of the developing relationship with the client. Counsellors and therapists must work at achieving this position. Dupont-Joshua (1997) suggests that 'counsellors must continually work on their attitudes, on their own racial identity and also work with the aspects of race and culture reflected in the relationship' (p. 284), which she, as a black therapist had to work through: 'very painful issues around my racial identity ... because I know that I cannot work with others on their racial identity unless I work on my own' (p. 282). We talked earlier about counsellors and therapists needing to be aware of 'projecting' on to clients their 'psychological baggages' which are best dealt with in their own therapy.

Conclusion

The process and outcomes of counselling in relation to cross-cultural/racial matching is becoming particularly important as a result of the growth of counselling and the increase in ethnic minority clients and counsellors. In this chapter we have attempted to highlight through some of our findings of a small and limited research project that although black counsellors and white clients enter into a complex relationship vis-à-vis the socio-political variable, they nevertheless can develop a rich environment for effective and creative therapeutic outcomes. This research has convinced us that more research needs to be done using clearly defined and systematic methodologies to investigate the dynamics of the black counsellor with white clients as well as the other growing practice of black counsellors with black clients.

Acknowledgement

We are grateful to the client Mary (not her real name) for giving us permission to use transcribed material in this study, and to all the black counsellors who took part in the interviews.

References

Beutler, L.E., Cargo, M. and Arizmendi, T.G. (1986) 'Therapists variables in psychotherapy process and outcome' in S.L. Garfield and A.E. Bergin (eds), *Handbook of Psychotherapy and Behavior Change* (3rd edn). New York: Wiley.

Beutler, L.E., Zetzer, H.A. and Williams, R.E. (1996) 'Research applications of prescriptive therapy', in W. Dryden (ed.), *Research in Counselling and Psychotherapy*. London: Sage.

Carter, R.T. (1995) *The Influence of RACE and Racial Indentity in Psychotherapy*. New York: John Wiley and Sons.

d'Ardenne, P. and Mahtani, A. (1989) *Transcultural Counselling in Action*. London: Sage.

Dupont-Joshua, A. (1997) 'Working with issues of race in counselling', *Counselling*, 8 (4): 282–4.

Fernando, S. (1988) *Race and Culture in Psychiatry*. London: Croom Helm.

Heppner, P.P. and Dixon, D.N. (1981) 'A review of the interpersonal influence process in counselling', *Personnel and Guidance Journal*, 59: 542–50.

Holmes, D.E. (1992) 'Race and transference in psychoanalysis and psychotherapy', *International Journal of Psycho-analysis*, 73 (1): 1–11.

Kareem, J. (1992) 'The Nafsiyat Inter-Cultural Therapy Centre: ideas and experience in intercultural therapy: in J. Kareem and R. Littlewood, *Intercultural Therapy: Themes, Interpretations and Practice*. London: Blackwell Scientific Publications.

Kareem, J. and Littlewood, R. (eds) (1992) *Intercultural Therapy: Themes, Interpretations and Practice*. London: Blackwell Scientific Publications.

Lago, C. and Thompson, J. (1989) 'Counselling and race' in W. Dryden, D. Charles-Edwards and R. Woolfe (eds), *Handbook of Counselling in Britain*. London: Tavistock/Routledge.

Lago, C. and Thompson, J. (1996) *Race, Culture and Counselling*. Buckingham: Open University Press.

Lago, C. and Thompson, J. (1997) 'The triangle with curved sides: issues of race and culture in counselling supervision' in G. Shipton (ed.), *Supervision of Psychotherapy and Counselling: Making a Place to Think*. Buckingham: Open University Press.

Littlewood, R. and Lipsedge, M. (1997) *Aliens and Alienists* (3rd edn). London: Routledge.

McLeod, J. (1993) *An Introduction to Counselling*. Buckingham: Open University Press.

Mills, M. and Topolski, C. (1996) 'SHANTI: a women's therapy centre', *Counselling*, 7 (2): 108–12.

Moodley, R. (1998) '"I say what I like": frank talk(ing) in counselling and psychotherapy'. *British Journal of Guidance and Counselling*, 26 (4): 495–507.

Nickerson, K.J., Helms, J.E. and Terrell, F. (1994) 'Cultural mistrust, opinions about mental illness, and Black students' attitudes towards seeking psychological help from White counselors', *Journal of Counseling Psychology*, 41 (3): 378–85.

Pomales, J., Claiborn, C.D. and LaFromboise, T.D. (1986) 'Effects of Black students' racial identity on perceptions of white counselors varying in cultural sensitivity', *Journal of Counseling Psychology*, 33 (1): 57–61.

Pope-Davis, D.B. and Coleman, H.L.K. (eds) (1997) *Multicultural Counseling Competencies, Assessment, Education and Training, and Supervision*. Thousand Oaks, CA: Sage.

Sashidharan, S.P. (1986) 'Ideology and politics in transcultural psychiatry' in J.L. Cox (ed.), *Transcultural Psychiatry*. London: Croom Helm.

Sue, D.W. and Sue, D. (1990) *Counseling the Culturally Different: Theory and Practice* (2nd edn). New York: John Wiley and Sons.

Thomas, L. (1992) "Racism and psychotherapy: working with racism in the consulting room – an analytical view" in J. Kareem and R. Littlewood, *Intercultural Therapy: Themes, Interpretations and Practice*. London: Blackwells Scientific Publications.

Wade, P. and Bernstein, B.L. (1991) 'Culture sensitivity training and counselor's race: effects on black clients' perceptions and attrition', *Journal of Counseling Psychology*, 38: 9–15.

Discussion issues

1   Why have the characteristics and effectiveness of the black counsellor/white client dyad received little attention?

2   How much time was spent on the question of 'race' on the counselling training course you attended? Was this sufficient time?

3   For white clients, the appearance of a black counsellor may unconsciously evoke certain prejudices and stereotypes.

4   Both black and white clients use 'race' to express transference of object relationships and drive derivatives.

PART FOUR
RESEARCH

This is the last part of the book. It has three in-depth chapters related to research. It is usual in many books for the research section to come last. Often this is misplaced and misguided, as good practice should prefer-ably be underpinned by research therefore this section needs to come either at or near the beginning of the book. However, I thought it was preferable for the reader to consider some of the complex issues before reaching this section.

Chapter 18 investigates the biases in trainee counsellors' attitudes to clients from different cultures. Pearce found that respondents showed more favourable patterns of attribution for white clients than for clients from three other ethnic groups, Asian, Jewish and West Indian. Knowledge of this bias could be introduced into counselling training to enable discus-sion and cultural understanding to occur. However, it is possible that experienced and qualified counsellors and psychotherapists might also make similar mistakes! This would require relevant continuing profes-sional development to overcome this problem.

In Chapter 19, Clarkson and Nippoda undertake a phenomenological inquiry into the perception of race and cultural issues within one multi-cultural training organization. They distributed questionnaires to 108 co-researchers at the establishment who were either staff or students. Content analysis and frequency measurements were undertaken on the data obtained and a number of categories of statements were identified. They found that the racial and cultural influences were subjectively experienced distinctly as very positive as well as moderately negative. Obviously, this outcome may only reflect this particular training institute but the chapter highlights a useful research methodology that can be applied elsewhere.

The final chapter by Jewel focuses on multicultural counselling research. He reflects on the lack of published British research and that in the last ten years the vast majority of research articles emanated from the USA. He ends the chapter with a number of proposals for future research. If we cut to the chase, the key question that this chapter raises is whether or not more effort will be directed towards research, focusing on the many complex issues of counselling in the multicultural society of Britain during this decade.

Investigating Biases in Trainee Counsellors' Attitudes to Clients from Different Cultures

Anita Pearce

The problems of counselling clients from different cultures have recently been given more attention in Britain (Ahmed, 1986; Cheetham, 1986; Khan, 1991), although most of the established research on this topic has been conducted in the USA (Atkinson et al., 1978; Berman, 1979; Sue, 1978; Sue and Sue, 1990). An issue of particular concern is the counsellors' biasing attitudes towards clients from different cultures.

Khan (1991) points out that the personally held values of the counsellor can and do affect their work, sometimes to the detriment of the client and her/his community. It has been asserted (Ahmed, 1986) that there is a need to focus and understand the dynamics and social forces which create the counsellor's frame of reference. It can be argued that the attitudes and subliminal biases of counsellors are the most important factors in the helping process, because in all kinds of situations counsellors apply their own value systems, usually unconsciously (Banks, 1991).

Rack (1982) notes that the many counselling theories held by western diagnosticians do not always fit into the conceptual models used in other cultures. For example, in western societies counselling is defined as being non-judgemental: the counsellor enables the client to express and explore her/his own feelings, and by being non-directive obliges the client to make her/his own decisions, thus emphasizing individualism, autonomy and self-understanding. But Rack points out that although psychotherapeutic theories of this kind may suit some subjects in individualistic and introspective societies, they cannot be applied everywhere. Counsellors who are trained in Britain have accepted the assumption that the concept of 'self-assertion' is a necessary tool to help the client develop self-esteem. Although this might be applicable to clients from the same white indigenous group as the counsellor, an emphasis on 'self' may cause a client from a different culture to feel frustrated and confused: this applies, for instance, to a culture where there is a greater interdependency within and between family groups. Fontana (1984), examining self-assertion and self-negation in eastern psychologies, argues that whereas in the west many important psychological problems are attributed, in whole or part, to low self-esteem or inadequately developed self-concepts, in non-western cultures the 'self' is often seen as an artificial construct, impeding the way to psychological health, and therapies therefore concentrate on helping the individual recognize this artificiality. The counselling commonly practised in Britain has been formulated on the basis of a western philosophy of life (Fanon, 1967; Sue, 1981) and this often contradicts the traditional beliefs and ideology of those who have come from other cultures and have different religions and value systems. Clearly, in any interpersonal contact, but especially in a therapeutic relationship, it is important to understand and acknowledge the cultural dimensions.

In the present study, the shorthand of 'Asian', 'Jewish', 'White' and 'West Indian' is used. Of course, all these labels are unsatisfactory in some ways. For example, 'Asian' can include people from such differing areas as Pakistan, Sri Lanka and Bangladesh. But it is commonly recognized that regional differences exist in all countries, just as 'British' include people from Scotland and Wales. The convenient shorthand of 'Asian', 'Jewish' and 'West Indian' conveys a specific meaning: it refers to people who have a continuity of history, tradition and culture that has not been part of the indigenous population of the host community and who have different dietary, religious and social needs. As Cheetham (1986) points out, refusal to perceive the different needs of different cultural traditions is treating people unequally, whereas treating people differently according to their real not imagined needs or characteristics is a recognition of the equal worth of different cultures.

The aim of the experiments reported here was to measure the biases of respondents when they were confronted with the case histories of clients from different ethnic groups. It was intended to discover whether the trainee counsellors' perception of the clients' cultural background influenced the respondents' judgement. To keep the variables constant, the respondents were all white female members of the indigenous population. Counselling was a recognized part of their psychology course.

It was hypothesized that the subjects (in-group) would show more favourable patterns of attribution for white clients (in-group) than for clients from the other three ethnic groups (Asian, Jewish and West Indian) (out-groups). It was predicted that different attributions would be made for the four ethnic groups.

The investigations presented to the respondents a vignette of a client case history (the ethnic group to which the client belonged acting as a cue), and the various therapies considered suitable for the client. The dependent measures included a questionnaire to tap readily available psychological processes. An additional paper for personal comments gave respondents the opportunity to make attributions in their own words. It was considered that this would be more natural and less subject to reactivity of instruments than other approaches would have been.

Study I

Subjects

Data were obtained from 12 undergraduate students studying psychology at Manchester Metropolitan University. They were required to prepare a project and to select five options reflecting explorations and applications of psychology. The students, who were white female members of the indigenous population, had all chosen counselling as their main option.

Procedure

The independent variables in this study were incorporated into a vignette of a client case history from Corey (1991) (Figure 18.1). The variation on the case history intake form was the cultural background of the client (i.e. 'Asian' or 'Jewish' or 'White' or 'West Indian'). This single word, which was placed next to the box marked 'Female' on the intake form, stated the ethnicity of the client and was intended to act as a cue. As other independent variables were kept constant, the purpose of the experiment was to discover whether this one cue, the culture of the client, influenced the respondents.

The dependent measures employed were incorporated into a semantic-differential instrument (Osgood et al., 1957) which consisted of bipolar adjectives (i.e. 'strong–weak', 'warm–cold', 'hostile–friendly') relating to the description of the client. A paper for personal comments was also provided.

39 yrs	Female		Married	Middle class

LIVING SITUATION

Lives with husband, two sons, two daughters.

PRESENTING PROBLEM

Client reported general dissatisfaction. She had become aware of some inner conflicts and decided to seek therapy in order to develop a stronger sense of herself. She said her life was rather uneventful and predictable and she experienced panic over reaching the age of 39. She claimed that she was very overweight and has always indulged in eating.

Client was the oldest of six children. Her father was religious, distant and authoritarian. Her mother, though often critical, was totally devoted to her children. During the adolescent period, the client felt frightened of dying and held rigid ideas of morality, which socially isolated her from her peers. At age 19 she married and used her mother as role model.

Figure 18.1   *Client vignette I*

The papers were divided into three sets of four—one for each of the four ethnic groups. The subjects were not aware that the clients' ethnicity differed. The order of the papers on the desks were: first the case history, then a paper for personal comments, and finally the semantic-differential instrument. The experimenter read the standardized instructions to the subjects, who were given an untimed period in which to complete their responses. After the collection of papers, the experimental session ended with an explanation of the purpose of the study.

Semantic-differential results

The data from the semantic differential were computed on a 1–11 scale for analysis of variance (ANOVA). Of the twelve bipolar scales, the analyses of variance indicate significant differences between subjects' responses on three bipolar attributes (Table 18.1). The results showed that for the bipolar attributes 'warm–cold', the subjects who had the case history of the White client found the client to be 'warm', while the subjects with the case history of the Asian and Jewish client rated these clients relatively 'cold'. For the attributes 'hostile–friendly', respondents found the White client to be 'friendly'; conversely, the case history of the Asian, Jewish and West Indian clients more strongly evoked the attribute 'hostile'. For the attributes 'helpful–obstructive', the respondents rated the White client as 'helpful', as opposed to 'obstructive' which was the description elicited to a greater extent by the subjects who had the case history of the Asian, Jewish and West Indian clients.

In general, the results from the semantic differential in this first study showed that the subjects belonging to the White indigenous group gave more favourable responses for the White client than for the Asian, Jewish and West Indian clients. Although the case history of the four clients was identical except for the cue indicating the culture to which the client belonged, the subjects' significant attributions 'warm', 'friendly' and 'helpful' were applied only to the White client. This clearly reflects stereotyping.

The case history of the client stated that the client reported general dissatisfaction with herself and had decided to seek therapy. She claimed that she was very overweight and always indulged in eating. She also experienced panic over growing older. Yet these negative symptoms of the client were discounted when the subjects had the case history of the White client. The descriptions 'warm', 'friendly' and 'helpful' appeared to be the consequence of the respondents' willingness to identify with the White client. The phenomenon of in-group favouritism reflects people's desire to be associated with groups that build their self-esteem (Fiske and Taylor, 1991). It can be suggested that perceiving the other ethnic clients as relatively 'hostile' and 'obstructive' reinforced the subjects' positive social identity.

Table 18.1   *Mean ratings on 1–11 semantic-differential scale for each client (n = 12)*

	Asian	Jewish	White	West Indian	df	F-	p
Strong (1)–Weak (11)	7.66	6.00	6.00	7.66	3	0.538	0.670
Warm (1)–Cold (11)	9.33	8.00	3.33	5.66	3	9.321	0.005
Hostile (1)–Friendly (11)	5.66	5.00	9.33	5.66	3	15.519	0.001
Rigid (1)–Flexible (11)	4.33	4.00	3.00	5.00	3	0.481	0.705
Helpful (1)–Obstructive (11)	6.33	6.00	3.66	5.33	3	4.222	0.046
Anxious (1)–Calm (11)	3.66	4.00	2.33	2.66	3	0.840	0.509
Assertive (1)–Submissive (11)	9.33	7.66	9.00	6.00	3	2.851	0.105
Irritable (1)–Easy Going (11)	4.66	6.66	4.66	5.33	3	1.032	0.428
Insincere (1)–Sincere (11)	6.00	7.33	9.00	7.66	3	1.708	0.242
Unkind (1)–Kind (11)	6.00	6.66	7.66	7.66	3	1.333	0.330
Confident (1)–Unsure (11)	8.66	8.66	9.00	8.33	3	0.063	0.978
Favourable (1)–Unfavourable (11)	5.33	5.66	6.33	6.00	3	0.131	0.939

Personal comments on attribution

The unstructured responses in the personal comments revealed that the subjects given the case history of the Asian client felt that 'although this woman must live in the here and now she must also be aware of her own feelings and how they influence her behaviour'. Here the emphasis seemed to be on enabling the client to explore her own feelings (reflecting a client-centred approach). However, with clients from Asian cultures there are conceptual difficulties arising from different concepts of self. Clients are often taught to hide their feelings (Sue, 1978), and where introspection is not encouraged, a person's identity is more bound up with relationships and roles than with purely subjective experience (Rack, 1982). Awareness of the Asian client's culture was revealed more directly in the comment that the 'cultural situation of this woman may be important. Her situation and feelings are likely to be influenced by her struggles to reconcile two cultures'. This response lends support to Khan (1991) who asserts that, in general, knowledge of the cultural background of the client increases the counsellor's understanding of the client's problems.

The responses from the subjects presented with the case history of the Jewish client revealed a familiar pattern: 'The person-centred therapy, I feel, provides the most appropriate approach for dealing with the client's problems.' For this client, it was quite important for 'the client to express her feelings and attitudes'. Here again, the emphasis on the expression of 'feelings' reflected the subjects' training in client-centred therapy. No mention was made of the cultural background of the client or of cultures where the family and the neighbourhood are important.

A possible reference to cultural conflict could be taken from the comments of the subjects presented with the case history of the West Indian client. The 'source of the conflict' was attributed to 'this lady has lived a life for the wishes of her parents as a sense of duty rather than getting the opportunity to live her own life'. It was noted that for this client there was a sense of duty towards parents; however, the remark 'getting the opportunity to live her own life' was a reflection of western ideals of individual self-assertion.

The subjects' comments concerning the case history of the White client suggested the influence of cultural identity. The statements relating to 'self' seemed to indicate an implicit identification with the client: 'This woman appears to have no positive rewards in her life-style for herself' and 'She has nothing for herself ... she may see herself as too old to make changes'. The subjects stressed that the client's feelings 'has nothing to do with past life experiences'. Therapies dealing with the 'here and now' were advocated to 'give this woman self-awareness and control over her own destiny'. Subjects' responses to 'overeating' were specifically noted for the White client. This was attributed to 'comforting herself due to the conflicts' and 'it is more to do with self-image and her feelings'. It can be suggested that further support for cultural identity was reflected in the comment 'I would want to meet her'. Although generalizations concerning the respondents' positive identification with the White client should be made with caution, nevertheless it appeared from the responses that where the attributions were limited to one's own group (i.e. the emphasis being on 'self'), the subjects perceived different characteristics in the case-history of the White client.

In the personal comments, a number of different causal factors (i.e. expectations about cause–effect relations based on past experience) were mentioned by the respondents. Different attributions were made in relation to the different ethnic groups. The Asian client's behaviour was here seen as being directly or indirectly 'caused' by the cultural situation in which she was placed. In general, the causal factors mentioned by the respondents implied favourable dispositional attributions for the White client. Again, the ethnicity of the client evoked different responses from the subjects.

Study 2

Subjects

Seventy-two students on a registered general nursing course at the South Manchester School of Nursing served as subjects. Part of their training course included interpersonal communication and counselling. They were female, white indigenous members of the 'helping professions' population.

Procedure

The same instruments used in Study 1 were used in Study 2, with the addition of an 'attribution questionnaire'. This was designed to allow subjects to decide whether the client's problem was caused entirely by the client or the situation. The subjects' responses were measured on a 5-point scale ranging from 'not at all', through 'slightly', 'moderately', and 'very', to 'extremely'. The order of presentation and the information introduced to subjects followed the same pattern as in Study 1.

Attribution questionnaire results

The responses from the attribution questionnaire were analysed using analysis of variance (ANOVA) (Table 18.2). The mean scores for 'client' and 'situation' across the four ethnic groups (i.e. Asian, Jewish, White and West Indian) revealed that the mean situational rating for the White client (3.88) was greater than the means for the other ethnic groups. The analysis of variance showed there was a significant difference between the four ethnic groups, when subjects responded to the question 'problem caused entirely by the situation'. In other words, the respondents with the White client's case history rated the client's problem to be caused, to a greater extent, by her situation.

Semantic-differential results

The data from the semantic differential were computed on a 1–11 scale for analysis of variance. The results (Table 18.3) indicated that there were significant differences between subjects' responses on four descriptive attributes, according to the four cultures of the client. The subjects found the White client and the West Indian client to be 'weak', while the attribute 'strong' was elicited to a greater extent for the Jewish client. They found the White client to be more 'flexible' than the Jewish client. 'Sincere' was elicited for the White and West Indian clients, whereas 'insincere' was more strongly attributed to the Jewish client. Again, the rating for the Jewish client was 'unkind', while the subjects found the White client and the West Indian client to be relatively 'kind'.

Discussion

The statistical results from Study 2 corroborated earlier findings (Mann and Taylor, 1974; Stephan, 1977; Taylor and Jaggi, 1974) which indicated that prejudicial and biased attributes would be made to some out-groups. The responses from the attribution questionnaire supported the predictions presented in the hypothesis. The expectations that subjects would show a more favourable pattern of attribution for similar clients (in-group) than for dissimilar (out-group) clients were substantiated by the responses elicited by subjects to the questions which asked whether the client's problem was caused entirely by the client or the situation. This showed that the respondents with the case history of the White client were more likely to find the client's problems to be 'caused entirely by the situation'.

Table 18.2   *Mean ratings for the 'client' and 'situation' attributions across the four cultures*

	Asian	Jewish	White	West Indian	F-	df	p
Client	2.44	2.61	2.38	2.50	0.146	3	0.932
Situation	2.55	3.05	3.88	3.16	3.315	3	0.025

Table 18.3   *Mean ratings on 1–11 semantic-differential scale for each client (n = 72)*

	Asian	Jewish	White	West Indian	df	F-	p
Strong (1)–Weak (11)	4.72	3.66	7.00	6.72	3	4.056	0.010
Warm (1)–Cold (11)	4.83	3.38	4.77	4.83	3	1.034	0.383
Hostile (1)–Friendly (11)	4.16	4.38	6.38	6.38	3	2.487	0.068
Rigid (1)–Flexible (11)	3.44	2.50	5.27	4.50	3	3.022	0.036
Helpful (1)–Obstructive (11)	5.05	3.55	4.55	4.11	3	0.745	0.528
Anxious (1)–Calm (11)	2.11	1.66	3.11	2.27	3	1.600	0.197
Assertive (1)–Submissive (11)	6.27	6.05	7.22	8.88	3	2.220	0.094
Irritable (1)–Easy Going (11)	4.11	3.38	5.72	4.33	3	2.537	0.064
Insincere (1)–Sincere (11)	6.11	4.88	8.16	7.27	3	2.846	0.044
Unkind (1)–Kind (11)	6.50	4.66	8.00	8.00	3	4.189	0.009
Confident (1)–Unsure (11)	8.38	6.66	8.05	8.50	3	0.949	0.422
Favourable (1)–Unfavourable (11)	4.94	4.88	5.55	5.33	3	0.308	0.819

The case history disclosed that the client experienced a negative approach to herself. At adolescence she was socially isolated from her peers and now she claimed she always indulged in eating and reported general dissatisfaction. The respondents found that the White client's negative problems were caused by the situation and these results were significantly different from those for the Asian and Jewish clients.

The results from the semantic-differential scale, given the use of the present methodology, demonstrate that there was a degree of selectivity in how the subjects perceived the different ethnic groups. For example, the subjects found the West Indian client as well as the White client to be 'weak', 'flexible', 'sincere' and 'kind'. These similarities presented conflicting evidence. In attempting to explain this complex phenomenon, reference could be made to the mass media. Although it was not known with any certainty the extent to which the portrayal of ethnic groups in the mass media influenced the content of the stereotype held and accepted by members of the white indigenous group, Dutton (1973) points out that it is possible that the media coverage of black problems in American society makes them a group likely to be recognized as the target of discrimination. In contrast, orientals as a group seldom have any well-publicized protest and therefore it was probable that they would not be perceived as oppressed in the same way. Dutton's study shows that the white person (respondent) must *perceive* the minority group as discriminated against. In the present study, the analyses revealed that the subjects saw the case history of the West Indian client as favourable, contrary to the subjects' responses to the Asian and Jewish clients. It could be argued that Dutton's explanations of perceived discrimination was limited to the media coverage of black problems of American society. But television documentaries in Britain have portrayed discrimination of black groups which may have influenced the respondents' judgements in the present study.

It is of interest, in the context of the present research, to question whether discriminatory behaviour is a generalized norm of hostility towards disliked out-groups. Tajfel (1981) claims that the process is deeper than forming negative value judgements about a specific group and then behaving accordingly. Rather, individuals construct a subjective social order based on the classification of 'we' and 'them', and learn that the appropriate attitude is to favour a member of the in-group and discriminate against a member of the out-group. The mere categorization of a person as a disliked out-group member is sufficient to see that person as less favourable than someone from an in-group (ibid). But in the present study, the findings indicated that sometimes favourable attributions were made to a favoured out-group.

Personal comments on attribution

The subjects' personal comments proposed, for the Asian client, 'giving the lady the opportunity to question her fundamental beliefs which were instilled in childhood'. But as Rack (1982) informs us, in Asian culture introspection is often not encouraged and a person's identity is much more bound up with familial relationships and roles than with purely subjective experiences. Although acknowledging the cultural differences of the Asian client, subjects challenge the concept of cultural diversity by assuming the universality of underlying problems which counsellors encounter. This is revealed in the claim that the client's problems 'could be the problems of any race, colour or creed' and in the comment 'is the fact she is Asian supposed to influence one's thinking?' Pedersen (1981) reminds us that explicit cultural awareness in counselling is a relatively recent development. A major part of cross-cultural counselling has been in the universalistic direction. Cheetham (1986) points out that it is possible to gloss over the cultural aspects of the counselling experience as irrelevant to the tasks in hand. This corresponds to the universalistic fallacy described by Trimble (1983): the belief that human distress is the same regardless of context and site and the conviction that the techniques to counteract it are effective everywhere.

Referring to the 'over-dominating and religious father and on the other extreme a doting mother' in the case history of the Jewish client, the subjects suggested that 'a lot of her (the client's) problems are due to her upbringing as a child' and 'I think this lady has a common problem Jewish women find themselves in, the conflicts of religion, family and expected roles'. Here, as with the Asian client, emphasis was placed on the client's parents, upbringing and childhood. However, in proposing that the client had 'the power to change if she asserted herself', the subjects suggested the method of self-assertion. Although in western societies asserting oneself is normative, and part of the western tradition of psychotherapy, in other cultures it is considered a hindrance to self and well-being (Fontana, 1984). Although the subjects were aware of the Jewish clients 'upbringing and view of life', encouraging the client to be self-assertive ignored the cultural norms of this particular out-group. Proposing the concept of assertiveness, the subjects may be reinforcing the stereotype of this client's culture.

The case history of the White client evoked responses from the subjects that omitted references to 'upbringing', 'culture', 'childhood'. The responses were directed to factors which influenced the client's present life, 'relationship with husband and relationship with children. Would it not be wise to include husband in therapy sessions so that they can sort out their life together?' Noting that 'the client seems a person trying very hard to change the direction of her life and try to take control of it' evoked the added remark from the subjects: 'I admire her very much.' Wintrob and Kim Harvey (1981) point out the problem of the therapist over-identifying with particular aspects of a patient's background, attitudes, values and life experiences. There is a danger of distortion of objectivity and the risk of misinterpretation of clinical data which come from positive over-identification with a group. In the present study the subjects (in-group) showed a favourable identification with the White client (in-group). Further, the subjects advised the client 'that the only person she should be concerned about is herself' and 'have interest in herself as an individual and forget any feelings of guilt'. The client should be 'happy being herself'.

These responses reflect the dominant patterns of counselling in western beliefs. The self which is known by actions and years of dependence develops a core value called self-reliance (Tseng and Hsu, 1979). According to western beliefs, each individual should control her/his own efforts (ibid). It can be assumed that subjects (in-group) trained in the psychotherapies of the west would appropriately emphasise the concept of self with the White client (in-group). Although no specific comments concerning the cultural background of the West Indian client was elicited from the subjects, there were references to childhood experiences and parental influences. The subjects found that 'past experiences in her (the client's) life have rigidly shaped her personality, values and approach to life' and the client was taken back 'to disturbed childhood'. 'Her problems appear to stem from her childhood experiences.' 'She was frightened of her father and modelled herself on her mother.' The subjects recognized that the client's childhood and parental influence constituted the causal structure of behaviour. This was contrary to the responses concerning the White client. The subjects' recommendations for 'much more freedom', 'getting rid of guilt' and indications that the client should show her inner self, her innermost feeling and 'to be herself', revealed the common assumption in counselling that western-oriented therapies are universal and applicable to all cultures.

In the present study, the case history of the clients provided limited information, but this did not prevent the subjects from making implicit value judgements about how the client ought to behave. The subjects were faced with a vignette of a case history of a client and the only indication of the client's ethnicity was the single stimulus item (i.e. Asian or Jewish or White or West Indian) which was placed in a box on the intake form. It is suggested that this cue influenced the subjects' perceptions and that this resulted in biased responses.

General discussion

On balance, it seems reasonable to claim that the present investigation may be seen to contribute to the usefulness of empirical studies to examine the biases of subjects who will be counselling clients from different cultures. The studies supported the contention that subjects who were White Caucasian members of the indigenous population would show a favourable pattern of attribution for the White client, while biased attributions would be made for some out-group clients. Although such a generalized bias cannot easily explain the discrimination against particular out-groups (in this instance, the Asian and Jewish clients), it might be argued that the existence and nature of stereotypes determine our perceptions and judgements and that these stereotypes are shaped by social, economic, political and historical antecedents (Klineberg, 1983). Also, to understand the biases of intergroup evaluations, it is necessary to consider the cultural relations which exist between the ethnic groups concerned (Jaspars and Warnaen, 1982). In the present study, the results seemed to demonstrate that there was a greater cultural gap between the White subjects and the Asian and Jewish clients.

However, the findings from Study 2 also show that biases in trainee counsellors' attitudes may reflect the current influences in society. As mentioned earlier (Dutton, 1973), the media coverage which points out a particular minority group (West Indian) as being discriminated against may be instrumental in evoking attributions which will compensate for deep-seated prejudices. Obviously, therapists experience the same amount of stereotyping and ethnocentrism as the general public (Bloombaum et al., 1968). But the uniqueness of the counselling situation requires those who counsel to become aware of their own biases, values and assumptions about human behaviour. Sue and Sue (1990) are critical of cross-cultural training which often assumes that the mere accumulation of cultural knowledge and the academic teaching of appropriate counselling skills are enough to train an effective cross-cultural counsellor. While the importance of counselling theory, therapy techniques and our traditional understanding of the client's psychological process are not denied, what is missing for the trainee counsellor is self-exploration of one's own biases (Corvin and Wiggins, 1989).

How, then, can trainee counsellors become aware of their own basic cultural biases? Following the findings from the present empirical studies, which revealed biases in the subjects' responses, the present researcher suggests that further studies should indicate to the respondents the implications of their positive and negative attributes towards clients of different cultures. For instance, the subjects could evaluate and discuss the results and comments and consequently become involved in the research. Student involvement could benefit its subjects by helping them to understand their own value systems and to create new cultural understanding through modifications introduced into existing understandings (Miller, 1984).

It is proposed that prior to informing the counsellor trainees that they should be aware of cultural expectations and cultural biases which, it has been claimed (Cheetham, 1986; Sue, 1981; Sue and Sue, 1990), are inherent in the cross-cultural counselling process, an attempt can be made to introduce a similar pattern to the present research. As mentioned earlier, after collecting the respondents' papers, a discussion could take place, dealing with: (a) critical analyses of the investigation and explanations of the counsellors' own biases towards clients from different cultures; (b) awareness of cultural dimensions which can lead to misunderstanding of the causal factors involved; (c) the interpretations that counsellors make can have a variety of emotional and behavioural consequences.

References

Ahmed, S. (l986) 'Cultural racism in work with Asian women and girls', in S. Ahmed, J. Cheetham and J. Small (eds), *Social Work with Black Children and their Families*. London: Bastford.

Atkinson, D.R., Marujama, M. and Matsui, S. (1978) 'Effects of counselor race and counseling approach on Asian Americans: perceptions of counselor creditability and utility', *Journal of Counseling Psychology*, 25: 76–83.

Banks, N. (1991) 'Counseling Black client groups; does existing Eurocentric theory apply?' *Counselling Psychology Review*, 6 (4): 2–6.

Berman, J. (1979) 'Counseling skills used by Black and White male and female counselors', *Journal of Counseling Psychology*, 26: 81–4

Bloombaum, M., Yamamoto, J. and James, Q. (1968) 'Cultural stereotyping amongst psychotherapists', *Journal of Counseling and Clinical Psychology*, 32: 99.

Cheetham, J. (1986) 'Social work with Black children and their families', in S. Ahmed, J. Cheetham and J. Small, *Social Work with Black Children and their Families*. London: Batsford.

Corey, G. (1991) *Case Approach to Counseling and Psychotherapy*. Pacific Grove, CA: Brooks/Cole.

Corvin, S. and Wiggins, F. (1989) 'An antiracism training model for White professionals', *Journal of Multicultural Counseling and Development*, 17: 105–14.

Dutton, D.G. (1973) 'Reverse discrimination: the relationship of amount of perceived discrimination towards a minority group on the behaviour of majority group members', *Canadian Journal of Behavioural Science*, 5: 34–45.

Fanon, F. (1967) *The Wretched of the Earth*. London: Penguin.

Fiske, S.T. and Taylor, S.E. (1991) *Social Cognition*. New York: McGraw-Hill.

Fontana, D. (1984) 'The mind, the senses and the self in Buddhist psychology'. Paper delivered to the *Annual Conference of the British Psychological Society*, University of Warwick.

Jaspars, J.M.F. and Warnaen, S. (1982) ' Intergroup relations, ethnic identity and self-evaluation in Indonesia', in H. Tajfel (ed.), *Social Identity and Intergroup Relations*. Cambridge: Cambridge University Press.

Khan, M. (1991) 'Counselling psychology in a multi-cultural society', *Counselling Psychology Review*, 6 (3): 11–33.

Klineberg, O. (1983) 'Contact between ethnic groups: a historical perspective of some aspects of theory and research', in S. Bochner (ed.), *Cultures in Contact*. Oxford: Pergamon.

Mann, J.F. and Taylor, D.M. (1974) 'Attribution of causality, role of ethnicity and social class', *Journal of Social Psychology*, 94: 3–13.

Miller, J. (1984) 'Culture and the development of everyday social explanation', *Journal of Personality and Social Psychology*, 46: 961–78.

Osgood, C.E., Suci, G. and Tannenbaum, P.H. (1957) *The Measurement of Meaning*. Urbana, IL: University of Illinois Press.

Pedersen, P. (1981) 'The cultural inclusiveness of counselling', in P. Pedersen, J. Draguns, W. Lonner and J. Trimble (eds), *Counseling Across Cultures*. Honolulu: University of Hawaii Press.

Rack, P. (1982) *Race, Culture and Mental Disorder*. London: Tavistock.

Stephan, W. (1977) 'Stereotyping: role of ingroup–outgroup differences in causal attribution of behaviour', *Journal of Social Psychology*, 101: 225–66.

Sue, D.W. (1978) 'Eliminating cultural oppression in counseling: towards a general theory', *Journal of Counseling Psychology*, 25: 419–28.

Sue, D.W. (1981) 'Evaluation process variables in cross-cultural counseling and psychotherapy', in A.J. Marsella and P.B. Pedersen (eds), *Cross-Cultural Counseling and Psychotherapy*. New York: Pergamon.

Sue, D.W. and Sue, D. (1990) *Counseling the Culturally Different*. New York: Wiley.

Tajfel, H. (1981) *Human Groups and Social Categories: Studies in Social Psychology*. Cambridge: Cambridge University Press.

Taylor, D.M. and Jaggi, V. (1974) 'Ethnocentrism and causal attribution in a South Indian context', *Journal of Cross-Cultural Psychology*, 5: 162–71.

Trimble, J.E. (1983) 'Value differentials and their importance in counseling American Indians', in P.B. Pedersen, J.G. Draguns, W.J. Lonner and J.E. Trimble, *Counseling Across Cultures*. Honolulu: University of Hawaii Press.

Tseng, W.S. and Hsu, J. (1979) 'Culture and psychotherapy', in A.J. Marsella, R.G. Tharp and T.J. Cibrowski (eds), *Perspective on Cross-Cultural Psychology*. New York: Academic Press.

Wintrob, R.M. and Kim Harvey, Y. (1981) 'The self-awareness factor in intercultural psychotherapy: some personal reflections', in P. Pedersen, J. Draguns, W. Lonner and J. Trimble (eds), *Counseling Across Cultures*. Honolulu: University of Hawaii Press.

Discussion issues

1 Is counselling non-judgemental from a cross-cultural perspective?
2 Person-centred counselling theory needs to adapt to the challenges of counselling in multicultural settings.
3 What were the main findings of this research paper?
4 Is it surprising that the biases in trainee counsellors' attitudes may reflect the current influences in society?

19

The Experienced Influence or Effect of Cultural/Racism Issues on the Practice of Counselling Psychology

A Qualitative Study of One Multicultural Training Organization

Petrūska Clarkson and Yuko Nippoda

Introduction

We consider it impossible to conduct counselling psychology or any of its related activities out of context. That means that *all* therapeutic activities inevitably and inextricably occur within the idiom and the atmosphere, the climate and the background of the cultures which impinge on it. These 'cultures' or what are called 'structures of feeling' can be related to gender, religion, organization, profession, sexual orientation, class, nationality, country of origin, parts of the country of ancestral origin, language and so on. Any attempt to pay attention to any one of these in particular inevitably highlights the absence of those not studied, not mentioned. Such an effort also risks highlighting some issue from the viewpoint of 'other', at the same time as trying to bridge a gap, and may appear to point out that there are different banks to a river. No wonder complexly motivated silence, professional avoidances and academic neglect characterize these kinds of issues to the extent that indeed we think they do in our professional literature. So, instead of a token mention or a continuing lament about the invisibility of such difficult and sensitive matters in the indexes and the tables of contents of papers and books, as well as in the very texture and structures of our professional disciplines, we bring this tentative attempt at illuminating some integrated research and practice. We look forward to others furthering the work not only in practice and conversation, but also in print.

Britain is increasingly becoming a multiracial society in which professionals are coming into contact with people from a diverse range of cultural and ethnic groups. On many occasions psychologists/counsellors/therapists may find themselves working with people whose culture is substantially different from their own. On this subject, there is very little information and guidance for the counselling psychologist in our professional literature. This is acknowledged by Ray Woolfe in the *Handbook of Counselling Psychology* (Woolfe and Dryden, 1996): 'The fact that there is no chapter in this book on counselling psychology in a cross-cultural context is in itself indicative of the distance that has yet to be travelled' (p. 17). McLeod (1993) also suggests that 'The field of cross-cultural counselling has received relatively little attention in the research literature' (p. 118), while Nadirshaw (1992) argues that:

> There is an increasing concern amongst [ethnic] groups about the lack of available, accessible, adequate, appropriate and relevant services to black people. The concern is ever greater in black and minority ethnic communities as they remain at the receiving end of little or no services. That includes psychotherapy and counselling services.

Nadirshaw's excellent paper includes a list of some 11 assumptions which, in her view, interfere in the attempts of traditionally trained helping professionals to deliver such services appropriately.

Kenney (1994) suggests, based on his research, that European-American students have more commitment to the counselling process than African-American and Asian international students. But, as Nadirshaw and others point out, there may be many good reasons for such a finding. According to Littlewood (1992), ethnic minorities are predominantly working class and their 'relative poverty as well as discrimination [make] access to time-consuming and costly therapy ... less available' (p. 6). Also, some ethnic minorities have a collective society as a cultural background. This may be associated with the notion that it is experienced as a stigma to benefit from therapy services. However, many more people in the world rely on symbolic healing or culturally traditional approaches to personal development than rely on west European models. Eleftheriadou (1994) also mentions that clients who are unsure about the effectiveness of the 'talking cure' may benefit from the work of somebody from their own ethnic/cultural background whose role is equivalent to that of a counsellor, such as a psychiatrist or spiritual healer.

In counselling, psychology, and psychotherapy, too, the theoretical approaches are mainly (if not exclusively) based on white Eurocentric models with little awareness of the influence or inescapable context of ethnicity. This, in itself, as Clarkson (1996) has discussed elsewhere, is oppressive. Helman (1994), too, writes:

> Where patient and therapist come from similar backgrounds, they may share many assumptions about the likely origin, nature and treatment of psychological disorders. However, the proliferation of new 'talk therapies' has meant that, in many cases, the patients may have to *learn* this world view gradually, acquiring with each session a further understanding of the concepts, symbols and vocabulary that comprise it. This can be seen as a form of 'acculturation', whereby they acquire a new mythic world couched, for example, in terms of the Freudian, Jungian, Kleinian or Laingian models. This mythic world, shared eventually by patient and therapist, is often inaccessible to the patient's family or community, who in any case are excluded from the consultation. (Helman, 1994: 280)

Farrell (1979) makes a similar point when he describes how participants are declared 'cured' or 'trained' when they have adopted the WOT (way of talking) of the trainer (or the counselling psychologist).

Anecdotal evidence suggests that most training schools do not pay attention to cultural aspects in ways which satisfy either the trainees on the programmes or the many who apply to come into counselling psychology. (This is irrespective of 'equal opportunities statements' in their literature.) In our experience there are usually only one or two black or Asian people in most professional gatherings (conferences, training courses, etc.); people from a White European background usually predominate.

There are many instances of counselling and psychotherapy sessions which are terminated prematurely because, in the dyad of counselling/ psychotherapist and client from a different culture, the client did not feel understood culturally by the counsellor/psychotherapist. There are probably many that are never even spoken of because the influence of prejudice is out of awareness or because the individuals involved cannot find a way to speak about it. All of us are creatures of one or more cultures— 'structures of feeling'. The notion of culture-free counselling psychology is as implausible as a value-free or neutral counselling (or clinical) psychology (Newnes, 1996).

For the purpose of this research it is important to be in touch with their racial and cultural background, their process and what it means to them. Moreover, d'Ardenne and Mahtani (1989) suggest that it is essential that counselling psychologists and psychotherapists are aware of their own cultural views and biases before dealing with clients' points of view. In his profound chapter, 'Racism and Psychotherapy; Working with Racism in the Consulting Room: An Analytical View', Lennox Thomas (1992) also draws special attention to this kind of awareness when he introduces the therapeutic process of the dyads of the white therapist and the black patient, the black therapist and the white patient, and the black therapist and the black patient.

> It is extremely difficult for any form of racism, accrued from a lifetime of social-isation, to be brought to personal awareness, yet this is indeed what needs to take place, so that our practice is not dominated by what can be termed 'socie-tal racism'. In order to work effectively across cultures and with people of different colour, psychotherapists, I would suggest need first to attend to their own racism, their own prejudices, and their own projections on other racial and cultural groups. Personal attitudes and assumptions need to be re-worked and re-examined. (Thomas, 1992: 133–45)

The basic point of counselling and psychotherapy is 'Who am I?' To know and understand oneself, you have to take into account racial and cultural aspects, since race and culture are essential parts of everybody. 'How does it feel to be *you* with *your* race and cultural background?' would be a very important question to ask yourself. Then you can get to know your own process and experience your subjectivity; and then you can search where you are in terms of other races and cultures.

Psychological counsellors and psychotherapists have many opportunities to see clients from different cultural backgrounds nowadays.

> Cultural factors are important to counsellors, and they have the responsibility of learning all they can about the cultural background of their clients. It is too much to ask that they become specialists in all the cultures of the world; it should not be impossible for them, however, to become aware of the range of values and patterns of behavior of which human societies and individuals are capable and to learn as much as they can about the particular ethnic groups that constitute their clientele. Many counsellors have asked themselves what there is in counseling that is universal and what aspects need tailoring to meet the specific needs of specific groups. I see no alternative to developing awareness of both the universals and the cultural particulars. Finally, counselors should never lose sight of the fact that no two individuals are fully identical in their needs, their problems, and their values and goals. We cannot remind ourselves too often that these three approaches—to human beings in general, to members of particular cultural groups, and to the individual in his or her uniqueness—all require our full attention. (Klineberg, 1987: 34)

In this study, we wanted to get closer to how the people concerned perceive the issues of race and culture affecting counselling, psychology and psychotherapy, particularly focusing on the 'culture' of their training school.

Aims and objectives of this study

Our research population is different from most of the research populations represented in the literature, therefore little can be transferred or generalized. Our intention is more modest: to provide a phenomenological inquiry into the perception of race and cultural issues of a complete group of trainers and staff of a counselling programme. It is a programme dedicated to the valuing of cultural difference, the integration of transpersonal and counselling perspectives. Uncharacteristically, it does not primarily represent 'minority' cultures, but people from all over the world, many who normally live in 'majority cultures' but whom we assume, by virtue of the fact that we inhabit the same planet, have all been touched, in one form or another, by prejudice.

In this project we were not studying the outcome of therapeutic, psychological counselling or the effectiveness of training in a multicultural environment explicitly committed to the values of appreciation of diversity and integration. Phenomenological research as a particular kind of qualitative research methodology attempts to get close to, if not exactly 'capture', the qualities of human experience, as the humans themselves describe their own subjectivity. According to Moustakas (1994), these aspects are not 'approachable through quantitative approaches' (p. 21).

Our work here does not set out to prove or disprove anything in the ways which can be the important goals of quantitative research.

The case for qualitative research as an adjunct, or alternative but valid and valuable approach, to the study of human experience phenomena is further outlined in many other contemporary sources (Denzin and Lincoln, 1994; Polkinghorne, 1992, for example). A issue of *Counselling Psychology Review* (February 1996, 11, 1) deals with this subject in depth and some of the papers from this journal are reproduced in Clarkson (1997).

It is not very easy to find a chapter regarding cross-cultural issues in the books on counselling psychology and psychotherapy, whereas people talk about theories and perspectives on various approaches and other issues. The current situation in these fields is that cross-cultural issues are secondhand. What hinders people from working on this, even though everybody is in touch with culture and our research shows that most people are concerned about cross-cultural issues?

During the process of writing this chapter, we became aware again of the sensitivity and care-fullness experienced in dealing with this delicate area. History and cultural developments bring about changes in what is considered 'politically correct' and sometimes these attempts at formal control of our collective cultural shadows work paradoxically. We wondered whether the inhibiting effect of such fears may be one of the reasons why so few people work, research or publish their opinions and experiences on issues concerning race and culture? We would hope that all sincere work can be welcomed, improved on and encouraged by all who have an interest in this field.

Our personal situatedness in relation to the theme

In accord with this and the philosophy and procedures of qualitative research, it becomes necessary therefore to indicate our personal situatedness to the themes. One of the reasons the group was willing to participate in the research may be, as a participant wrote (unsolicited) on the questionnaire, because the senior counselling psychologist researcher is well known in this community for her work on Bystanding (Clarkson, 1996). Clarkson's interest seeded from personal experience of discrimination, injustice and prejudice from a variety of perspectives as well as growing up in a culture where, for example, the *majority* of the people of the very heterogeneous country were excluded by law from participation in government. Bystanding is more fully contextualized and developed in the book on that particular theme (Clarkson, 1996).

The other co-author is from Japan, which is largely a homogeneous society. Since coming to this multicultural society in the UK, she has been working on crosscultural issues, in particular crosscultural transition (Nippoda, 1993), transcultural collective psychology and issues of the East and West. The more she worked, the more she realized the complexity and the confusing aspects of the issues. Her views have also changed in various ways during the time—and continue to change. She is developing her own theory and perspectives. This research is part of her ongoing learning process from which she hopes her work in the future will develop and grow.

Conceptual realms and literature review

Because of its scope our study implicates all of psychology—'being human'—and we looked specifically at the body of work on the themes of race, racism, ethnicity, cross-cultural, transcultural, and a-cultural practice, identity, language, political science, post-structuralism among many others. A thorough overview is left to others more expert than ourselves, since an insistence on its achievement before attempting a study such as this could paralyse individual researchers from even starting a fraction of the task.

Most of the books and articles on cross-cultural issues focus on how to deal with those issues within a multi-cultural context, rather than within traditional Eurocentric counselling and psychotherapy models. D'Ardenne and Mahtani (1989) explain how the relationship of ethnicity between therapist/counsellor and client could affect the counselling/ therapy process. However, many books which deal with cross-cultural counselling/therapy concentrate on the difference between traditional therapy/counselling and ethnocentric therapy/counselling. They do not tend to pay enormous or detailed attention to how these issues are perceived and experienced by people from all kinds of cultural backgrounds.

Transference can be used in a different way depending on the approaches. d'Ardenne and Mahtani (1989) introduce Smith's (1985) description about transference in a transcultural setting:

> For our purposes [transcultural counselling] 'transference' may be defined as the attitudes and feelings placed by the client on to the counsellor in the thera-peutic relationship. In our own experience, 'transference' has an additional dimension. Clients who have had a lifetime of cultural and racial prejudice will bring the scars of these experiences to the relationship. (d'Ardenne and Mahtani, 1989: 79)

Thomas (1992) also explains that 'It is the therapist's task to recognise and explore pathological fit along racial lines in the transference. This, of course, is not easy when the countertransference is also powerfully bent on enactment' (p. 136).

There is little research in cross-cultural counselling, as noted by Lowenstein (1987): 'There has been virtually no research on the subject of intercultural counseling in Great Britain' (p. 41). Perhaps the best overview is contained in Kareem and Littlewood (1992), to which all readers are referred. It explores themes, interpretations and practice, and includes case examples for teaching and group discussion, inserting quantitative research results in intercultural context. Moorhouse (1992, in Kareem and Littlewood), in her review of past research and the project at Nafsiyat, comes to the conclusion that:

> the view that black and ethnic minority people cannot benefit from formal therapy is wrong. The research also suggests, albeit with small numbers, that people who show severe symptoms as determined by conventional rating scales may benefit from psychotherapy. (p. 98)

At the 1994 conference of the Transcultural Counselling/Psychotherapy Forum held at Goldsmiths College, University of London, it was reported by Nafsiyat that 'Research (a research project funded by the DHSS) left many questions unanswered. Further research is necessary' (Adams, 1996: 40).

Other attempts have been sporadic and are not very well known. Eleftheriadou (1994) mentions that: 'We do need further cross-cultural research in all the social science disciplines and more integration of the information. Because research has been done within different disciplines, there has not yet been synthesis of all the information obtained.' Where there is research which we have not found, this chapter will hopefully act as a call to interested organizations and people to share such research, compare finding, and perhaps collaborate on further projects.

In 1989 Acharyya et al. found that 'the subtle differences of experience and response [of second or third generation immigrants] have yet to be studied' (Moorhouse, 1992: 86). Our interest was not in prescription, but in the *description* of their experience; in fleshing out in words the *experience* of these people (and not primarily in generalization from this population to a wider one by means of 'objective scientism'). However, speculation in order to generate hypotheses for future research is to be welcomed—as is any serious effort to increase our understanding in this most complex and sensitive area, which affects every single one of us—all the time. It is, however, unlikely that a more racially and culturally heterogeneous group on one counselling programme of this size in Britain could be found—and perhaps even elsewhere. The commonality between the participants—if any—was an explicit commitment to multicultural appreciation and the integration of transpersonal concerns with personal growth and development, values which prioritize growth and the richness of diversity and difference.

In our research we have focused on phenomenological experience of race and culture. Everybody is unique and has different experiences. Conventional researchers focus on how therapists/counsellors use diagnoses for ethnic minorities, what kind of interventions would be appropriate or suitable for ethnic minorities, or the outcome of the therapy/counselling. In other words, many research projects focus on the ways in which practitioners deal differently with ethnic minorities compared to white European clients. Of course, it is not appropriate to use the same approaches and interventions with everybody, and practitioners have to pay attention to cultural differences. However, when we were doing this research, somebody said that they are not an ethnic minority; in their culture and society, they are an ethnic majority. We gathered the impression that the phrase 'ethnic minority' and the idea of 'how to deal with ethnic minorities' can perhaps contribute to, as well as ameliorate, the marginalization and isolation of people to whom, for good or ill, or a mixture of intentions, such nominations are applied.

Comparison with Nadirshaw (1992)

Nadirshaw focuses on how traditional Eurocentric therapists/counsellors perceive the issues of ethnic minorities and ways of dealing with such a clientele. Nadirshaw makes several recommendations for good practice, which include examining the relevance of culture in the therapeutic process and the conduct of therapy within the cultural context, although she stresses the acceptance of different value systems and the development of cultural sensitivity. She quotes the findings of Fernando (1991), which showed that expert knowledge about a culture alone does not necessarily lead to successful therapeutic outcomes. Nadirshaw mentions the importance of setting, non-verbal facility, ability to read emotions from other cultures, the necessity of taking into account the transference toward the very therapeutic process itself, contextual familiarity, 'ability to be sympathetic to the oppressed position of the client and create positions of equal power and control', the ideal of having worked through the counsellor's own racist attitudes, beliefs and prejudices and the culturally different influences of gender, the perception of the therapist/counsellor, and the goals and tasks.

> A thorough assessment of how the combined effects of deprivation, disadvantage and racism impinge on the client's personality and identity need to be undertaken ... Imposition of therapist's views about such matters (i.e. labelling, categorizing and classifying) should be avoided and the practice of therapy/counselling in a non-judgemental, non-oppressive manner should be endorsed. (Nadirshaw, 1992: 260)

Finally, Nadirshaw (1992) recommends appropriate and relevant training courses, such as the one run by Nafsiyat, as 'models that mainstream training counselling courses could learn from' (p. 260).

Her research is a call to people who could think about other ways than the current ways. Although our research talks about the current situation of the issues, our focus was different from Nadirshaw's. We have focused on the subjective experience of the counselling trainees and on how the issues of race and culture affect counselling/psychotherapy as a whole, rather than on how to deal with clients from ethnic minority groups. In this research we wanted to assess people's perception of issues of race and culture.

Methodology

Quantitative and qualitative research

This is phenomenological research; it relies on the subjective, phenomenological experience of people, and not their objectification. This research tries to represent these views as assumption-free as possible, although we of course acknowledge that assumptions are always present.

By presenting them to colleagues before and after publication, such explicit and implicit assumptions can at least be brought overtly into discussion and mutual exploration. The report of such responses is intended as another, future phase of the current research project.

However, since we also employed figure and percentage analysis of the descriptions of subjective experience in terms of categorization, it can be said that we also employed quantitative methods to work with and communicate about our data.

Selection of participants

Many organizations were approached when we were seeking institutes who would be willing and able to participate in the research project. We formally contacted some 32 likely organizations for their co-operation in the distribution of the questionnaire. Forty-four completed questionnaires were returned, mostly from people who described themselves as white Europeans.

Only one organization responded favourably within our time frame with a substantial number of replies—108. Forty-five of these were from white European cultural backgrounds and 60 from black or Asian cultural backgrounds. It so happened that it is a counselling training organization where people from 30 nationalities, speaking an even larger number of languages, are in full-time training with trainers, many supervisors and psychotherapists, from a wide range of cultural backgrounds. We think it would be rare in Britain to find a training organization of this size with such a diversity of cultural backgrounds.

All the people in this organization have been exposed to counselling or counselling variants such as growth groups, personal effectiveness facilitation, spiritual direction, psychotherapy from UKCP-registered psychotherapists or psychotherapeutic counselling psychology for short or long periods. Anonymity was respected in this questionnaire in order to facilitate free descriptions of the participants, and some of the participants received a draft of the final paper to which they could freely add comments. This allowed for triangulation (Barker et al., 1994: 81) of our research results.

For the purposes of this study we have not factor-analysed the specifics of these types or periods of experience because our interest at this stage was in (a) how people may describe themselves in terms of race and culture, and (b) how they may think or feel about issues of race and culture affect counselling and psychotherapy. It was enough that 98 per cent had some experience (and the 2 per cent who did not report it, we assume, knowing their general history, would probably have had experiences similar to counselling—for example, in preparation to come on the course). Question 2 was thus a kind of screening device and was not further analysed for the purposes of this research at this stage.

Instrumentation

The short questionnaire used for this enquiry consisted of three sentences to be completed freely by each participant. They were given some 20 minutes to complete it, after which they were all handed in to the senior researcher.

The three questions were as follows:

1   I would describe myself as … (for example, Black, Asian, Afro-Caribbean, White European, etc.)

2(a) My experience of counselling, psychology and psychotherapy is … (for example, I have been in counselling or psychotherapy with an Asian counsellor or Black or White Irish psychotherapist … many years.)

(b) I have been the counsellor, psychologist or psychotherapist of … (for example, Asian, Afro-Jamaican, White European or British clients, etc.) for … months during and/or after training [whatever applies to you].)

3   In my experience/opinion, issues of race and culture affect counselling, psychology and psychotherapy in the following ways …

This research questionnaire was not designed with pre-made boxes or specifically pre-packaged categories within which people had to 'insert' themselves.

The richness of the data obtained in this way supported the open-ended nature of our research questionnaire design—even though from a quantitative view certain 'facts' may be hidden or obscured.

Method of analysis

We collected and typed up the answers from the whole survey. We subdivided the answers to the three questions by scissoring. Each question had its own section. The first question was divided into the categories of ethnicity which the participants used to describe themselves. The result is shown in Table 19.1.

In the second question, we could only pick up the counsellor and client pairings of those who indicated both their own ethnic origin and that of their counsellors. We divided the counsellor and clients into three

Table 19.1   *Self-descriptions of trainee counsellors (obtained from replies to Question 1)*

White European	22	Multicultural, Anglo Irish roots	1
Asian	20	Irish woman	1
Black African	16	White American USA male	1
African	11	North USA Caucasian	1
European	4	Irish Catholic	1
White Irish European	3	Irish	1
Black	3	Human being European	1
White	2	Brown Indian	1
European White Male	2	Asian male	1
Black South African	2	Asian Indian	1
White South African	2	British Context White	1
Black coloured human being	2	Human being with brown skin	1
(As above) with intellect and will	1	A person	1
White European Italian	1	A person who relates to persons	1
Indian Black	1	Child of God	1
White European Female	1		

categories: White, Black and Asian/Indian, and checked the pairing patterns in order to extract the percentage of the pairings. Nonparametric measures of association (Phi coefficient and Cramer's V) were employed to estimate the significance of these relationships.

The answers to the third question were divided into 322 statements. At first we put them into five themed categories: positive statements, negative statements, neutral (the issues do not matter), qualification and unclear. Qualification here means, similar to its definition in the *Shorter Oxford English Dictionary* (1973), 'to modify in some respect'.

We furthermore put positive statements into six categories of themes: Learning and Understanding, Commonality and Individual differences, Overcoming or Awareness of Prejudice, Reparative and Healing, Positive Emotion, and Experience of Enrichment. We also put negative statements into four categories: Experiencing Counselling Errors/Mistakes, Prejudice/Transference, Inferiority or Bad feelings, and De-skilled/Competencies.

In order to attempt some measure of inter-rater reliability, we categorized the statements separately on three separate occasions, by three different raters, from three different ethnic groups: British Afro-Caribbean, White South African and Oriental Japanese. After that, we compared our categorization. On negatives, we had five disagreements, one of which was unclear. On positives, we had no disagreements but two were unclear. Then we counted the number of the statements in each category and found that the percentage inter-rater reliability was 91 per cent.

Results

1   The identities of the trainee counsellors in Question 1 are described by themselves in at least 31 different ways (see Table 19.1).

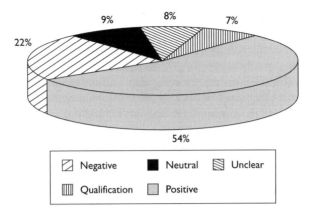

9%   8%   7%

22%

54%

Negative   Neutral   Unclear

Qualification   Positive

Figure 19.1   *Pie diagram to show categories of replies according to percentage*

2   In Question 2, because of the nature of the question, we did not get sufficient data at this stage of our study. The advantage and purpose of the style of the question was to get each participant's own description; the disadvantage was that we lost other kinds of data (this can be rectified and followed up in the future).
3   To Question 3, we received 174 answers of positive statements, 71 of negative statements, 29 neutral comments (the issues of race and culture does not matter), 25 unclear answers and 23 statements of qualification (see Figure 19.1).

The percentages of the five main categories are:

Positive statements	54%
Negative statements	22%
Neutral comments	
(e.g. that the issues race does not matter)	9%
Unclear	8%
Qualification	7%

Discussion of results

In respect to Question 1, there are some distinctive patterns. Half of the categories (16 of 31) and more than half of the statements (61 of 108) referred to skin colour. Eighteen people explained their nationalities: 3 Indians, 9 Europeans, 2 Americans and 4 South Africans. Black people did not enter their nationalities at all, except the South Africans. What does that mean? According to one of the assumptions which Nadirshaw (1992) lists, traditional therapists/counsellors might believe and act as if 'Black communities (Asians, Afro-Caribbeans) represent homogeneous groups, sharing a common culture and heritage, without acknowledging the diversity that exists within each of these groups'. Our findings may indicate that she may be correct about this. However, this obviously does not mean that the Black community lacks consciousness of diversity and a sense of nationality in other contexts.

There were not many people who described themselves as just a human being or person without mentioning race and national identities; it seems to be important for most people to describe race and cultural aspects in order to describe themselves. (People show high awareness of race and cultural identity within themselves.)

In respect to Question 3, as can be seen in Figure 19.1, we divided the responses into five categories of statements. We found many kinds of answers but there were some similarities and we categorized them in accordance with the individual's subjective perception.

Five main categories (see Figure 19.1)

Positive

This pertains to the experience, through the issues of race and culture, brought about by some kind of change for the individual in a positive way. They have learned something new, experienced different things, and broadened their points of view, thus overcoming the past hurt or becoming aware of their own process.

Negative

This indicates that their experience of the effect of race and cultural issues was that of a negative effect on counselling and psychology—feelings of failure, incompetence, anger from prejudice, and so on.

Unclear

The responses in this category showed that the individual acknowledged some kind of effect from the issues of race and culture, but was unable to clearly and precisely articulate what that effect might be. Since we did not personally interview many of the participants (yet), we had to understand what was meant from the sentences; some were ambiguous or did not give the detail to make it clear whether the intended meaning was positive *or* negative—or may have implied both. For example: 'Issues of race have affected me greatly when it comes to other races'; 'Issues of race have affected my experience because we have different racial backgrounds'. Other statements explained how, but they did not give a sense of evaluation—for instance, 'spiritually', 'socially', 'politically', 'psychologically', or 'economically'. However, every statement in this category suggests that the issues of race and culture have *affected* their counselling and psychotherapy.

Qualification

The replies in this category did not give an immediate reaction of effect from the experience but they spoke of a feeling that it had affected them and that, as time goes by, things become better. Also, some mentioned the language barriers and how after some time this might give positive effect. For example: 'It took me some time to trust her because of her colour'; 'An initial fear that I might not be understood in my own context'; 'I would open up gradually and share more as trust builds', and 'I was most affected by a racist client in that I struggled to remain "Rogerian" and yet was empathic to his mugging that reinforced his stereotypical beliefs'. Hence, it is not to say the experiences were positive straight away, and indeed there may some limitation to the degree of positiveness.

Neutral or 'it does not matter'

This category denotes that basically the participants did not think that the issues of race and culture affected them. A few participants commented that 'Race does not matter', 'Not the colour or race' and 'Issues of race did not arise'. However, others stated: 'I am also aware of the commonality of Human experience irrespective of race and culture'; and 'Human experience is the best teacher so I need to accept and respect persons rather than race and culture'. They focused more on the commonality of human beings no matter how different the race and culture. They may be denying, ignoring or minimizing the cultural issues first, maybe in order to stress the commonality. Of course, it should not be assumed that therefore other aspects were not implied or perhaps taken for granted within the context. However, the raters wished to err in the direction of not 'reading into' the statements and refraining from imposing spurious assumptions on the categorization which all three of us (from our very different backgrounds) could not easily agree about. This neutral category is therefore *different* from the sub-category of commonality *and* individual differences in the positive category, and we will explain this difference later.

As a whole, from the research, 91 per cent of the statements showed that there was some effect from the experience of issues of race and culture. Of course the very fact that we asked the question shaped the consciousness of people's responses. Although the difficulties with using either or both of these terms are understood, these are the terms which featured in conversation with participants as well as in the professional literature and the acronyms of groups committed to improvements within such universes of discourse and practice.

Sub-categories of positive statements

We divided the positive statements into six categories: Learning and Understanding; Commonality and Individual Difference; Overcoming Prejudice; Reparative and Healing; Positive Emotion and Experience of Enrichment (see Table 19.2). The percentages are shown in (Figure 19.2).

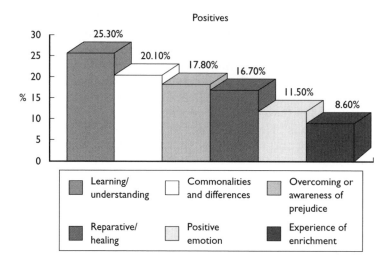

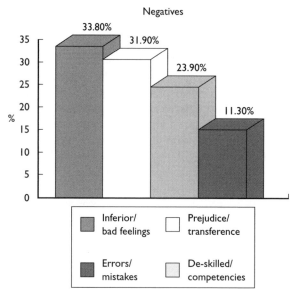

Figure 19.2   *Negatives and positives*

Learning and understanding

In their replies in this category, the participants raised points about learning
something about their own culture as well as other cultures, about their
own limitation, and about acceptance of people from other cultures. For
example: 'I have better understandings of the good and bad things in my
own culture as a result'; 'Issues of race have made me aware how we need
each other in order to survive. Whites had always been paternalistic
towards us blacks but I have discovered little by little how I have to affirm

Table 19.2 *Subdivision of positive and negative responses*

Positives	
• Learning/understanding	44
• Commonality/individual differences	35
• Overcoming prejudice	31
• Reparative/healing	29
• Positive emotion	20
• Experience of enrichment	15
Negatives	
• Inferior/bad feelings	24
• Prejudice/transference	22
• Experiencing counsellors errors/mistakes	17
• Deskilled/competency issues	8

myself in this White-dominated world. I really think the only way is to accept that these racial differences are in themselves a richness that has to be appreciated. Each race has to learn from the other. It has made me aware that we all need self-criticism'; '[Certain cultural beliefs] are not absolutes and can be changed depending on how much a person has allowed themselves to know about and their willingness to change their ideas which they may hold due to lack of true knowledge about it'; 'Only coming into this multicultural setting have I been able to put a more clear and balanced view on my perception of different cultures'.

Commonality and individual differences
We kept these themes together in one category. We judged from the statements that the participants came to respect people from other cultures as human beings with their difference and their uniqueness. For example: 'We all have feelings and emotions'; 'and begin to appreciate their uniqueness'; 'Having been here and experiencing different cultures and races, I found out that all of us (whether black or white or brown or what not) we do have needs, problems, strength, good and bad points'. Also, compared to *Neutral* or *'it does not matter'* in the main categories, the statements here tell us that as a result of experience through race and cultural issues, the participants have realized that human beings have a commonality no matter how great the cultural differences and yet everybody is different and unique. These participants have accepted that these issues affect them – 'I have learned to appreciate the people for who they are', 'I have learned to look at the human being'—and statements in this section on the whole had a different feel to them from those in the *Neutral* or *'it does not matter'* category. Oerter (1996) addresses and acknowledges that individuals across cultures have commonalities in physical and psychological aspects.

Reparation
The replies in this category showed that many people addressed how they have been healed from the experience of race and culture issues. 'Most of

the fear on how to face White people was cleared during these sessions';
'They have helped me to deal with past hurts coming from friction with
people of other races'; 'The issue of race has affected myself in the sense I
overcame the complex of inferiority I had'. Some mentioned a sense of
freedom: 'I was freed', or healing: 'My experience of counselling is that I
have been healed!'; pride: 'to consider myself as good as other different
races and appreciate my racial belonging'. It is the element of reparation,
the experience of a therapeutic healing experience, that separates this
section from the *Learning and Understanding* category which fundamen-
tally seemed to have more to do with knowledge.

Positive emotion

Here, the responses were a description of how positively the participants
felt about the whole process of race and cultural issues in terms of emotion or affect. They used terms and phrases such as: 'openness', 'tolerance', 'free', 'Good and happy because I felt there is nothing wrong with
my culture', and 'live life fully in order to enjoy the here and now'. These
responses focused on feelings like 'I did not feel threatened'; 'Sometimes
it was very touching and very meaningful ... in the way of relationship'.
Though they may contain an element of healing, we felt that because
these statements did not specifically mention the individual's past experience in comparison with the present situation and describe how the individual had changed, they should be in a separate category.

Experience of enrichment

Contrary to much of the writing in this field, which tends to focus on the
problems and the problematique, along with an acknowledgement of
negative experience in this group (see below), there was also a prominent
theme of 'enrichment'. Here are some examples: 'Cross-cultural awareness has greatly broadened and enriched my experience'; 'Issues of race
have sometimes given me the joy of entering a wider world'; 'Helped me
to grow'; 'I really think the only way is to accept that these racial differences are in themselves a richness that has to be appreciated'; 'In general
I was enriched by being with persons of different cultures and race'.

Overcoming or awareness of prejudice

In cultural issues, it is common for people to have prejudices. In an extensive discussion of the theoretical and psychoanalytic components (Clarkson,
1993), I discussed how the root of transference is 'to carry across' and
how in that sense it is usually a necessary component of all learning—
anticipation based on previous learning. It is only when prejudice or anticipation becomes rigid and not capable of changing in the light of updated
information or new experiences that it can be said to be 'neurotic', prejudiced, unhelpful or damaging. On the positive side, the responses of this
inquiry which we categorized as 'overcoming or awareness of prejudice'

described something about becoming aware of and dealing with their own prejudice and coming to deal with their own prejudice such as: 'For the first time I became aware of my prejudice'; 'They have helped me deal with my racial prejudice'; 'As part of the training I had to work through my prejudice'. It sounds as though they have gained realization in order to go forward. How the effects of prejudice and racism were healed or overcome therapeutically through the counselling process in this setting may be the subject of another in-depth study in the future. The very fact that the element of prejudice was addressed in the negative statements, too, opens possibilities for comparison and learning.

Sub-categories of negative statements

We divided the negative statements into four categories: Counselling errors/mistakes; Prejudice and transference; Feeling deskilled and other competency issues; Bad and inferior feelings. The percentages are shown in Figure 19.2.

Counselling errors/mistakes

The responses here showed how difficult people find it to deal with people from different cultures and that notwithstanding the best of intentions negative experiences do occur. Failure to open up because of the cultural difference on both sides makes the relationship artificial and difficult: 'Over-sensitivity to accommodate the cultural differences has led to an artificiality in the sessions' and 'lack of freedom of speech at times'. Some people mentioned 'authentic' Europeans and colluding Black people. Others focused on the power issue: 'Working with a European counsellor I felt I was playing the "Yes father"/Victim role of conformism'; and 'Victim role because the counsellors acted domineering role'. Holloway (1995) explains the power issues in the supervisory relationship. She cites the research of McRoy et al. (1986) on cross-cultural issues in supervision, which found that although supervisees perceive the supervisors as sensitive to cultural issues, they find it difficult to talk about these issues openly. On the whole, these statements indicated that issues of race and culture, as experienced by our respondents, created some difficulties, errors and even failures in counselling on a number of occasions.

Prejudice/transference

These statements contained awareness of the participatnt's own experience of racism and prejudice during counselling sessions, and their feelings of not being understood: 'I experience injustice in putting people in colours, since there is prejudice and stereotype.' Some people mentioned how prejudice and racism affected the therapy relationship. 'Taking for granted that the person comes from a completely different background has caused some embarrassment at times'; and 'Racism has affected my relationship in that she could not understand some patterns of my behaviour'. They mention their own racism and prejudice, too: 'On an occasion or two, my prejudice blocked my [relationship or] understanding of the issue'; and 'I am sure I would have been prejudiced if counselling across the colour'.

Lack of understanding, due to prejudice, could lead to feelings of anger or bitterness: 'The racism has affected me to a certain level, that I have not been able to express myself fully in case the other people did not understand me or made a judgement on me'; 'The feelings of bitterness because of sufferings due to racism'; and 'I feel angry when I hear the prejudices of the Europeans above Africans'. These statements indicate that experiences of blockage in counselling relationships may be due to racism and prejudice. The way in which collective prejudices become sedimented as individual transference is well established. In our research we came upon two statements of transference which, in view of the common usage of the term, we sense as intrinsically negative: 'I still experience transference and countertransference of my past bad experience' and 'I feel countertransference from my counsellor'.

Feeling de-skilled and other competency issues

The statements in which experiences of feeling or being de-skilled and lacking competency arose did not specifically mention mistakes in counselling but, because of the sensitivity of the issues experienced by the participants, their statements seem to reflect that they felt de-skilled and incompetent. For example: 'I feel incompetent even if I have experienced counselling people'; 'I was not in a position to give the correct empathy when counselling the other person'; '[Issues of race and culture] crop up in the nitty-gritty of everyday relationship. I often catch myself being critical/ impatient'; and 'This has led me to develop a lot of defence mechanisms in order to survive in this world'.

The counsellors were also criticized on what sounded like skills and competency issues: 'Black brought dreams which white did not fully understand'; 'My issues could have been better dealt with by an African who wouldn't have difficulties in getting what I was saying'; as well as 'Sometimes I feel like being humiliated and over-inquired'.

Bad and inferior feelings

These are potentially overlapping with the above category, but we separated general bad and inferior feeling statements from those which seem to refer more to the counselling process. This category contains statements of 'feeling inferior', 'feeling oppressed', 'feeling small among other races', and 'exploited'. One participant 'worries about fundamentalism' and for others, the whole experience of race and cultural issues means something bad for them: 'I have been sure white people would not understand my issues as a black person.'

Comparisons

More than half of the people in this survey told us that they have had *positive* experiences through these issues, rather than negative. It is possible that the very exposure in a training setting to so many cultures (some 30 languages, 23 nationalities) develops or helps to develop a more positive mindset in staff ant trainees than is produced in xenophobic or predominantly unicultural organizational or national cultures. Certainly it has been found that one of the primary functions of stereotypes is to preserve the social distance (Taijfel, 1981) and thus to resist the acknowledgement of relationship.

This finding cannot of course be directly compared, but it can be considered in the context of the research of Sutter and McCaul (1993). They found that respondents with more social contact with immigrants, as well as those who had positive experiences with immigrants, tended to score higher on the tolerance measure which they developed and tested. Proximity and acquaintanceship is documented as important in changing attitude (Krech et al., 1962).

The category of statements which is included under both positive and negative headings is *prejudice*. However, the content of the statements was understood to be different. In the positive statements, the participants indicate that the *awareness of prejudice* was a significant experience for them. However, these responses did not give details of any personal change. More information about the individual's feelings and the affects in the counselling process were given in the *negative* category, for example: 'However, even though this happened, I still experience transference and countertransference from my past bad experience.'

Comparing other sub-categories of positives and negatives, the positives mentioned more about what they gained through the experience and thus implied a therapeutic process. However, in the negatives, there were many statements regarding counsellors' qualities or abilities.

On the whole, we found that quite a large number of people feel that the issues of race/racism and culture affect counselling in ways which they experience as positive. This predominance is enhanced when positive statements including qualification are added on. The presence of negative statements with an authentic ring to them could indicate that these statements of positive experiences and value should be taken at least equally seriously in our receipt of this report.

Implications for the practice of psychotherapeutic psychological counselling

There is no study of which we are aware for direct comparison (a) involving this variety of racial and cultural backgrounds; (b) a counselling/

psychotherapy training institution; (c) so explicitly concerned with the integration of counselling and transpersonal dimensions to be utilized in many different countries of the world.

The literature reviewed does not deal in depth with many of the issues raised and space prohibits much further discussion here. However, we would draw attention to the kind of fit between the 're-search' we have engaged in here and our search to resonate to the experiences of our co-researchers in this project as different from the ideals and paradigms of psychological research which espouse 'the heuristics of suspicion', privilege objectivity, accept the possibility of neutrality in the researchers and disqualify responsible involvement (Banister et al., 1994). The kind of phenomenological approach which we have begun to approximate here questions not only traditional quantitative academic psychological research with its factor analyses and null hypotheses, but in particular questions the ideological substructure which supports, sustains and rewards compliance with such northern Eurocentric models. We wanted to know: 'What's it like for you?' rather than 'what is or is not the case to what percentage of probability' in order to reliably and validly generalize from this particular study to the rest of the world.

If we have achieved only a possibility of an awareness of a variety of points of view and multiplicities of experience, and some beginnings of ways to reflect seriously on these, the effort has been worthwhile. Helms (1989) reviewed and compared papers by several authors on racial identity counselling, which implicate various degrees of Eurocentrism. One of the most important Eurocentric values is considered to be dualistic thinking. We have attempted to conduct this research in a way which allows for multiple perspectives—the possibility of doing many different kinds of research—quantitative, qualitative, interview, immersion, phenomenological, observational, action research, etc. We believe the space that needs to be created now for non-binary systems of human experience and that Ani (1994) puts the case best:

> The main cultural force that dictated the creation of the myth [of 'objectivity' and the 'uses of scientism'] and supported its continuance was the fact that it provided pseudoscientific support for the imposition of European ideology ... 'Knowing' and 'understanding' then become more humanly and existentially meaningful than what has been meant by 'scientific knowledge'—defined Eurocentrically. (p. 518)
>
> It leads as well to the questioning of the 'scientific character' of *any* information gathering and its subsequent interpretation. Maquet concludes that subjectivity is encountered *throughout* the 'scientific process'. He attempts to redefine the concept of 'objectivity'. Conventionally, in keeping with Platonic epistemology, it meant 'conformity with the object' and independence from the subject. But, says, Maquet, 'the content of knowledge is never entirely independent; rather it is the result of the meeting of the subject and the object' [Maquet, 1964, p. 54]. This, he says, is true of 'scientific knowledge' generally, for there is always the possibility of different perspectives. Maquet suggests

therefore that the only requisite for 'objectivity' be that one's observations and conclusions are partly determined by the object; elimination of the subject is *not* necessary. (pp. 516–517)

The implications of Maquet's proposed redefinition are radical in the context of the European *utamawazo*. A change that the phenomenologists have been attempting to effect for over a century. It would mean a complete break from the epistemology that is based on the idea and methodology of 'objectification', on which the total separation of 'subject' and 'object'—of the 'knower' from the 'known'—is predicated. Ultimately the implications of a radical change in the definition of knowledge or 'what it means to know' are not only a change in epistemiological methodology, but a change in the European conception of the self, with corresponding changes in the conception of 'other' and behaviour towards others as well. If the traditional mode of European science—'objectification'—loses its position of primacy on their scale of values, the redefinition of the culture itself theoretically becomes possible. (p. 517)

Of course in the space of this chapter we can only discuss a small number of facets, but we attempted to be open to discovery rather than prove or disprove a null hypothesis. Research in the latter paradigm is considered very valuable indeed. However, it needs to be considered along with all the other known and possible paradigms in reflecting on, understanding and being 'touched' by others—epistemiologically, academically and philosophically.

Future research

We could explore these issues further using the results of this research. What we could think of for the future research is to obtain more detailed descriptions of the participants' subjective experiences and the processes involved. In addition, we could compare the differences between and among different self-defined cultural groups. The purpose would be to challenge and inform the current situation where many counselling schools do not pay adequately *experienced* attention to cultural issues although most people are conscious of these issues. (When attention is paid to these issues, it is so in one-sided or simplistic ways which do not always honour the complexity of our multicultural situatedness in the world.) We could not find the significant result regarding pairings this time and, therefore, we would like to progress further on that.

Probably our most important result indicates that people's experience of counselling and psychotherapy could become more positive than negative by experiencing a multicultural environment. Lago (1996) explains that 'The link between research and training is obviously an important relationship, where research can inform trainees and they in their turn may be stimulated towards new research. Research is also required on the efficacy of the training process itself in producing knowledgeable, aware and skilled counsellors' (p. 154).

Recognizing the limits of our present contributions, we would like to refer our readers to the many excellent volumes of work cited in our reference list, particularly the key recommendations for multiculturally skilled counsellors as collated by Sue et al. (1992).

Acknowledgements

We would like to acknowledge with gratitude the input, support and encouragement of our colleagues, especially Melanie Johnson, Kristina Scheuffgen, Tessa Adams, Marie Angelo, Zack Eleftheriadou, Sherna Gayara Chatterjee, Garfield Harmon, Vincent Keter, Len Kofler, Zenobia Nadirshaw, Joan Kendall, Rita Cremona, and all our co-researchers.

References

Acharyya, S., Moorhouse, S., Kareem, J. and Littlewood, R. (1989) 'Nafsiyat: a psychotherapy centre for ethnic minorities', *Psychiatric Bulletin*, 13: 358–60.
Adams, T. (ed.) (1996) *Transcultural Counselling/Psychotherapy Forum: Symposium—Psychotherapy and Black Identity: Addressing the Debate. 22 October 1994.* London: Goldsmiths College, University of London.
Ani, M. (1994) *Yurugu: An African-centred Critique of European Cultural Thought and Behavior.* Trenton: Africa World Press.
Barker, C., Pistrang, N. and Elliott, R. (1994) *Research Methods in Clinical and Counselling Psychology.* Chichester: Wiley.
Banister, P., Burman, E., Parker, I., Taylor, M. and Tindall, C. (1994) *Qualitative Methods in Psychology: A Research Guide.* Buckingham: Open University Press.
Clarkson, P. (1993) *On Psychotherapy.* London: Whurr.
Clarkson, P. (1996) *The Bystander (an end to innocence in human relationship?).* London: Whurr.
Clarkson, P. (ed.) (1997) *Counselling Psychology: Integrating Theory, Research and Supervised Practice.* London: Routledge.
d'Ardenne, P. and Mahtani, A. (1989) *Transcultural Counselling in Action.* London: Sage
Denzin, N. and Lincoln, Y. (eds) (1994) *Handbook of Qualitative Research.* London: Sage.
Eleftheriadou, Z. (1994) *Transcultural Counselling.* London: Central Books.
Farrell, B.A. (1979) 'Work in small groups: some philosophical considerations', in B. Babington Smith and B.A. Farrell (eds), *Training in Small Groups: A Study of Five Groups,* pp. 103–15. Oxford: Pergamon.
Fernando, S. (1991) *Mental Health, Race and Culture.* London: Macmillan/MIND.
Helman, C.G. (1994) *Culture, Health and Illness,* 3rd edn. Oxford: Butterworth-Heinemann.
Helms, J.E. (1989) 'Eurocentrism strikes in strange ways and in unusual places', *Counselling Psychologist*, 17: 643–7.
Holloway, E. (1995) *Clinical Supervision: A Systems Approach.* Thousand Oaks, CA: Sage.
Kareem, J. and Littlewood, R. (1992) *Intercultural Therapy: Themes, Interpretations and Practice.* Oxford: Blackwell.
Kenney, G.E. (1994) 'Multicultural investigation of counselling expectation and preferences', *Journal of College Student Psychotherapy*, 9: 21–39.
Klineberg, O. (1987) 'The social psychology of cross-cultural counselling', in P. Pedersen (ed.), *Handbook of Cross-cultural Counselling and Therapy*, pp. 29–35. New York: Praeger.
Krech, D., Crutchfield, R.S. and Ballachey, W.L. (1962) *Individual in Society: A Textbook of Social Psychology.* San Francisco: McGraw-Hill.

Lago, C. (1996) *Race, Culture and Counselling*. London: Open University Press.

Littlewood, R. (1992) 'Towards an intercultural therapy', in J. Kareem and R. Littlewood (eds), *Intercultural Therapy: Themes, Interpretations and Practice*, pp. 3–13. Oxford: Blackwell.

Lowenstein, L.F. (1987) 'Cross-Cultural research in relation to counseling in Great Britain', in P. Pedersen (ed.), *Handbook of Cross-cultural Counselling and Therapy*, pp. 37–44. New York: Praeger.

McLeod, J. (1993) *An Introduction to Counselling*. Buckingham: Open University Press.

McRoy, R.G., Freeman, E.M., Logan, S.L. and Blackmon, B. (1986) 'Cross-cultural field supervision: implications for social work education', *Journal of Social Work Education*, 22: 50–60.

Moorhouse, S. (1992) 'Qualitative research in intercultural therapy: some methodological considerations', in J. Kareem and R. Littlewood (eds), *Intercultural Therapy: Themes, Interpretations and Practice*, pp. 83–98. Oxford: Blackwell.

Moustakas, C. (1994) *Phenomenological Research Methods*. Thousands Oaks, CA: Sage.

Nadirshaw, Z. (1992) 'Theory and practice: brief report—therapeutic practice in multi-racial Britain', *Counselling Psychology Quarterly*, 5: 257–61.

Newnes, C. (1996) 'BPS Conference: Values in Clinical Psychology'. Unpublished.

Nippoda, Y. (1993) 'Cross-cultural counselling and personal developments in another culture: how the Japanese adapt to Britain'. Unpublished MA dissertation.

Oerter, R. (1996) 'Are there universals and why? A reply to Minoura and Wesiz et al', *Culture & Psychology*, 2: 203–9.

Onions, C.T. (ed.) (1973) *The Shorter Oxford English Dictionary*. Oxford: Oxford University Press.

Polkinghorne, D.E. (1992) 'Postmodern epistemology of practice', in S. Kvale (ed.), *Psychology and postmodernism*, pp. 146–65. London: Sage.

Smith, E.M.J. (1985) 'Ethnic minorities: life stress, social support and mental health issues', *Counselling Psychologist*, 13: 537–79.

Sue, D.W., Arrendondo, P. and McDavis, R.J. (1992) 'Multicultural counseling competencies and standards: a call to the professional', *Journal of Counseling and Development*, 70: 477–86.

Sutter, J.A. and McCaul, E.J. (1993) 'Issues in cross-cultural counseling: an examination of the meaning and dimensions of tolerance', *International Journal for the Advancement of Counselling*, 16: 3–18.

Taijfel, H. (1981) *Human Groups and Social Categories. Studies in Social Psychology*. Cambridge: Cambridge University Press.

Thomas, L. (1992) 'Racism and psychotherapy; working with racism in the consulting room: an analytical view', in J. Kareem and R. Littlewood (eds), *Intercultural Therapy: Themes, Interpretations and Practice*, pp. 133–45. Oxford: Blackwell.

Woolfe, R. and Dryden, W. (eds) (1996) *Handbook of Counselling Psychology*. London: Sage.

Discussion issues

1 Participants are declared 'cured' or 'trained' when they have adopted the WOT (way of talking) of the trainer or counsellor.

2 Equal opportunity statements are a sham.

3 A few participants in this study stated that 'Race does not matter'.

4 How much does research inform your approach to counselling?

20

Multicultural Counselling Research

An Evaluation with Proposals for Future Research

Peter Jewel

Preamble

This chapter, in its original form, appeared as an article in the *Counselling Psychology Review* (May 1994, 9 (2)). I have made only minor changes to that article, because the position which I outlined then still largely applies today, five years on. A trawl through Psychlit, the database for journals and books published in the field of psychology, reveals that almost all the multicultural counselling research of the last five years, and indeed most of the writing too, is still from the USA. A whole journal, *The Journal of Multicultural Counselling and Development*, exists to publish such research, in addition to the large numbers of specialist journals there which also frequently give their pages to such work. Much of this research relates entirely to the North American situation, and almost nothing refers to the very different UK context. So the thrust of my original 1994 article still applies.

Within the US situation, many of the prominent 'experts' have gone on since my original paper to consolidate or extend their position. This is true of Pedersen et al. (1996), Ponterotto et al. (1995) and D.W. Sue (1998). To my knowledge no inherently new approaches have been developed. More and more work has been done with each of the ethnic populations regarded as distinctive that make up the US population, and most of the major theoretical orientations are represented.

In the UK itself, the journal of the BACP, *Counselling*, does publish some indigenous research and articles. Indeed, there is a regular feature, 'Research Matters', designed to 'raise the profile of counselling research and make it more accessible to the majority of BACP members' (*Counselling*, Feb 1996, 7 (1): 18), but there is hardly a coherent body of work. Indeed, since then only one multicultural research paper has been mentioned in 'Research Matters', that of Ann Burrows, given at the BAC Research Conference on 20–21 March 1998 at Birmingham University ('The challenge of increasing access to a counselling service for black, Asian and non-white people, and the links with a research project'). It is still the case that no research of great moment, the kind of groundbreaking research which immediately changes the scent and spawns a number of corroborative studies and also attempts to rebut its strongly argued position, has yet appeared in the UK.

On the other hand, a number of journal articles and several books discussing counselling in today's multicultural UK society have been produced, and they have certainly begun to affect the consciousness of practising counsellors, and also the training courses which are provided for student counsellors. Of these, three particularly important recent texts are, in my view:

Transcultural Counselling, Eleftheriadou, Z. (1994). London: Central Books.
Race, Culture and Counselling, Lago, C. and Thompson, J. (1996). Buckingham: Open University Press.
Counselling in a Multicultural Society, Palmer, S. and Laungani, P. (eds) (1999). London: Sage.

Race, Culture and Counselling has a chapter entitled 'The Challenge of Research' which concludes that research is 'urgently required' (p. 155). This indeed is virtually the same comment on the situation in the UK as I implied in 1994.

On a personal note, my own position has actually altered since then. I have now become convinced, through my development as a person-centred counsellor, that this counselling modality is able to encompass a wide range of multicultural issues as I have experienced them in the current UK counselling context. In my own work with a range of non-European, and non-white clients, and with students of counselling from a range of ethnic backgrounds working in a person-centred way, we have found the person-centred approach to be facilitative and enabling.

This perception too needs to be examined carefully. I would like to see appropriate research assessing the validity of the person-centred approach in the UK multicultural context. Some of Dave Mearns's research questions in *Developing Person-Centred Counselling* (1994: 32–3) could be useful here. Research is of course as vital to person-centred counselling as it is to any other modality. It is often forgotten, especially by critics of Rogerian counselling, that Carl Rogers developed what has since become known as person-centred counselling as a result of his 'initial research orientation' (Kirschenbaum and Henderson, 1990, p. 202). The citation on Rogers's Distinguished Scientific Contribution Award, given in 1956, referred among other things to his use of 'extensive systematic research to exhibit the value of the method and explore and test the implications of the theory' (quoted in Kirschenbaum and Henderson, 1990, p. 201).

Were I writing the chapter now, I would thus add to the suggestions for future research a research design to explore and test the implications of person-centred theory in a multicultural context. That apart, the main 1994 conclusions seem to me as valid today as then.

Introduction

Traditional counselling theories have frequently been criticized for their lack of multicultural relevance, yet even today many UK counsellors assume a prevailing white (and middle-class) culture. This summary of research findings in multicultural counselling has had to rely entirely on evidence from the USA, since to my knowledge very little comparable work has been done in this country.

This section gives a brief overview of the current research, emphasizing its lack of agreed findings and the limitations in methodology. It then focuses on three major questions, asking whether counsellor race/ethnicity, explicit multicultural counsellor education and current research affect the counselling process and outcome.

The final section considers several research proposals that seem to have particular relevance to the issues discussed.

An overview of the current state of multicultural counselling research, with a summary of major research findings

Substantial controversy exists over the notion that ethnic individuals are short-changed in counselling or psychotherapy, and that an ethnically or racially dissimilar therapist–client dyad is undesirable. Much effort has gone into analysing the limitations of the research, which has provided the only real consensus among investigators: 'Not enough research has been conducted, and published research suffers from methodological and conceptual limitations' (Sue, 1988).

Garfield and Bergin (1986), summarizing all the work that has gone before, also note the research limitations. They suggest, for example, that in exploring the role of therapist ethnicity, problems arise with adequate sampling and a failure to control potentially confounding variables. For these reasons firm conclusions are difficult to reach. A clear example of this may be seen in a recent study.

Effectiveness of traditional counselling theories: the Merta, Ponterotto and Brown study

Traditional counselling theories, such as person-centred or psycho-dynamic, have been reportedly perceived by the culturally different as being 'highly ambiguous, possibly threatening, and often irrelevant' (Exum and Lau, 1988; Sue and Sue, 1990). A review of the research in cross-cultural counselling reveals ample support for a directive counselling style for use with the culturally different: this includes Blacks (Berman, 1979); Asian Americans (Exum and Lau, 1988; Sue and Sue, 1990); Hispanic Americans (Pomales and Williams, 1989); Native Americans (Draguns, 1981b); and foreign students (Althen, 1983; Pedersen, 1991).

Such at least are the claims made by Merta et al. (1992) in their article 'Comparing the effectiveness of two directive styles in academic counselling of foreign students'. In this study, the authors compared the effetiveness of two counselling styles, the 'authoritative' and 'collaborative', and asked: Do directive academic counselling styles differentially affect foreign student ratings of peer counselling effectiveness? Does acculturation level affect foreign students rating of peer counselling effectiveness? Do directive academic counselling style and acculturation level interact to affect foreign students ratings of peer counselling effectiveness?

The results according to the authors, 'appear to support the general consensus articulated by Pedersen (1991) that foreign students prefer directive forms of counselling as against non-directive counselling'.

However, there are serious flaws in this study. First, it is an analogue study. The 'as if' design, with its learned role playing, has been frequently criticized, not least by one of the researchers involved in the study (Ponterotto and Casas, 1991). Second, the definition of acculturation level is very crude. (Compare the work of Helms, 1984, 1989, and note the researchers' own comment that the acculturation level 'should be correlated with a scale that allows for comparison of foreign and US students'.) Third, the study utilized just one treatment interview. Fourth, the within-group differences of the foreign students used in the study are huge (all Asian, but from a widely differing range of countries such as the Republic of China, India, South Korea and Singapore, and of an age range from 18 to 44), yet no account is taken of this. Conversely, a group that is entirely Asian, primarily male, primarily graduate students, all at a Midwestern university, is an unrepresentative sample, and cannot justify the conclusion indicated.

The authors do state that 'researchers in cross-cultural counselling need to place greater emphasis on within-group differences among the culturally different'. They also lament the 'absence of reliable and valid measures of adjustment' in the study of foreign student adjustment. They also point out that 'support for directive counselling has been largely anecdotal; research has been minimal and has been limited to studies on individual attributes and general comparisons of directive and non-directive counselling styles'. This article does little to change these perceptions, which are certainly accurate as far as they go. In this way it seems to me representative of much of the work done to date on multicultural counselling, that is to say that very many of the research designs have important limitations, and the conclusions drawn are at times too grandiose for the actual evidence contained within the study.

This particular study has been referred to for two reasons: first because one of the authors, Ponterotto, is a leading researcher and writer in the field, and second because it is relatively recent (Merta et al., 1992). It is perhaps some indication of the fact that the particular methodological difficulties of multicultural counselling research have not yet been overcome.

Race effects in psychotherapy

This has been a second major area of unresolved contention. It has been examined particularly in relation to counsellor/client ethnic match, but because of frequent failure to control client groups on the basis of type or degree of disturbance, amount of therapy received, socio-economic status or gender, such studies are subject to criticism (e.g. Garfield and Bergin, 1986).

Abramowitz and Murray have examined the questions of race effects in relation to American Blacks perhaps more fully than anyone else. In fact, their 1983 article gives the title to this section. In it they asked three questions:

1   whether Blacks and other minorities who seek out traditional mental health services are victims of covert discrimination;
2   whether Blacks are more likely to receive the kind of pejorative psychiatric diagnoses that can label them for life, or to be shunted off to second class or briefer treatments;
3   whether Blacks are unresponsive to conventional therapy as conducted by white professionals.

Having fully examined the evidence, their answer is that there is no simple answer: the reviewers of research in the area run the gamut from negative (i.e. no evidence of discrimination), through inconclusive, to posi-tive (i.e. definite evidence of discrimination). While themselves, with the benefit of hindsight and recent evidence, taking a 'judiciously negative stance' (i.e. accepting 'subtle and circumscribed' racial effects), they throw out a challenge that 'those who would continue to press the charge of pervasive racial bias must explain why racial bias eludes detection when social bias has been found'. To my knowledge this challenge has never been taken up.

Does counsellor race/ethnicity affect the counselling process and outcome?

Client utilization

In the 1970s, what Pedersen (1988) calls 'abundant evidence' began to accumulate suggesting that mental health services were 'being under-utilized' by minority clients (Sattler, 1977; Sue and Zane, 1987; Wade and Bernstein, 1991).

As Sue and Zane (1987) point out, researchers and practitioners exhibit remarkable agreement about the reasons for this state of affairs. They cite several – lack of bilingual therapists, the stereotypes therapists have of ethnic clients, and discrimination. But, according to them, the 'single most important explanation for the problems in service delivery involves the inability of therapists to provide culturally responsive forms of treatment'. The fact that therapists are more likely to be from white middle-class backgrounds (Sue, 1978) 'has given rise to expressed doubts about whether non-minority counsellors can provide an effective therapeutic relationship' for minority clients (Wade and Bernstein, 1991, quoting Vontress, 1971).

Abramovitz and Murray (1983) however sound a cautionary note. Sattler's (1977) widely quoted work was based in fact on only five studies. Their 'closer look' at these reveals 'that only one of them unequivocally indicated an under-representation of black patients in mental health clinics'. And the newer evidence germane to the questions of race differential utilization of psychiatric services they also found 'meagre and ungeneralizable'.

Client preference

The evidence about client preference for counsellor race is also equally mixed. As Pedersen (1988) points out, there is considerable controversy as to whether counsellor and client should ideally be culturally similar. In a much quoted sentence, Harrison (1975) concluded that 'counselees tend to prefer counsellors of the same race'. Sattler (1977) reviewed more than 20 analogue and survey preference studies and reached the same conclusion. Updating these reviews in 1983, Atkinson (1983) reported a 'fairly consistent preference by black subjects for counsellors of their own race', though he found no documentation of a similar effect among other racial/ ethnic groups. Abramowitz and Murray (1983) suggest that 'minority counselees have tended to prefer the same- over opposite-race counsellors', citing Atkinson et al. (1978) and Harrison (1977). Pedersen (1988) also summarizes the client preference literature, indicating that there is a range of conclusions and resultant controversy, and suggesting that this area of research has too often 'addressed distal factors and ignored proximal ones'. In this he is echoing Sue and Zane (1987) who suggest that 'therapists' knowledge of the culture of clients is quite distal to therapeutic outcomes', or that ethnicity of therapist or client, and ethnic match, are 'distal variables' (Sue, S., 1988) and that 'proximal' treatment issues should be more fully addressed.

Process

The effects of a counsellor's race on client perceptions of the counselling process have received increased attention over the past two decades, as Wade and Bernstein (1991) point out. According to Abramowitz and Murray (1983), newer data do suggest that 'the process in cross-racial treatment may differ from the process in treatment involving two persons of the same race'. They cite studies by Jones (1978) and Wright (1975) which suggest the influence of racial matching on the therapeutic process.

Jones (1978) found 'important process shifts between the first and subsequent sessions' in a study of seven white and seven black middle-class neurotic women patients matched with two black and three white therapists.

Wright (1975) randomly assigned black and white college students to several counselling sessions with a black or white counsellor. He found that 'students initially held preconceived notions of the opposite race counsellors, but perceived them as increasingly empathic over the counselling period'. This suggests that the working alliance in the cross-racial dyad is weakest at the outset and supports Griffith and Jones' (1979) observation that the 'race difference appears to have its greatest impact early in the treatment, particularly at the first encounter. If the white therapist can establish effective rapport at the initial contact and build a therapeutic alliance in a relatively rapid fashion, successful outcome can be achieved'. Harrison (1975) indicated that there is 'some evidence that the facilitative functioning of the counsellor is affected by the race of the client, but the studies are few and the findings mixed and inconclusive'.

Abramowitz and Murray (1983), discussing these examples of the lack of any clear effect attributable to the presence of racial differences on the therapeutic process, argue that 'distinctive ingredients should produce distinctive results', and yet there are yet no clear outcome differences. As is so often the case in the field, they recommend more research:

> Solving the problems of identifying the essence of the therapeutic process and measuring change in therapy are two of the most pressing charges to future researchers in this area. (Abramowitz and Murray, 1983: 241)

Outcome

Treatment outcome is perhaps the most important measure of racial effect in counselling and psychotherapy. But there is a 'lack of agreement regarding desirable outcomes for psychology in general, and the inability of present instruments to measure treatment effectiveness makes assessment of cross-cultural counselling outcome almost impossible' (Atkinson, 1985). Sue (1988) asks the question: 'Is there evidence that ethnic minority clients have poorer outcomes from treatment than white clients?' He states that 'most treatment studies have failed to show differential outcomes on the basis of race or ethnicity of clients'. In the absence of hard evidence, Sue, like Atkinson before him, agrees with Abramowitz and Murray's (1983) view that the effects of race-ethnicity on counselling outcome remain unclear. Thus different researches and commentators have been able to take different views as to whether ethnic clients receive positive outcomes when working with white therapists. Sue (1988) lists three alternative viewpoints:

1 The *negative*, as stated by Sattler (1977): 'Therapist's race is for the most part not a significant variable in affecting the subject's performance and reactions'.
2 The *positive* position, presented by, for example, Griffith and Jones (1978): 'The results of analogue studies concerning black–white interactions in interviews simulating counselling situations support the conclusion that white therapist–black patient interactions are frequently ineffective'.
3 The *neutral* position, adopted by a number of researchers: Parloff et al. (1978) stated that 'The review of the research on the race of the therapist does not provide much definitive information about the effects of race per se or of intra and inter-racial matching on the outcomes of therapy'.

The position has not changed since 1983, when Abramowitz and Murray summed it up by concluding that 'no definite conclusions can be drawn at this point. That is, no one really knows how prevalent race effects are in therapy as it is practised today'.

Racial identity development

Sue (1988) points out that ethnicity per se tells us little about the 'attitudes, values, experiences and behaviour of individuals, therapists or clients, who interact in a therapy session'. He suggests that the ethnicity of the therapist or client, and the ethnic match, are 'distal' variables; consequently weak or conflicting results are likely to be found between the ethnic match and the outcome. 'Ethnicity is but one factor, embedded in many others, that may influence therapy outcomes.' He finds three aspects of therapist ethnicity that may have an effect on counselling: first, the physical stimulus of the therapist, which may provoke client expectations, transference reactions and so on based on race; second, an ethnic therapist may be fluent in the client's native language and thus establish a better relationship; third, 'ethnicity may suggest something about one's culture, ways of behaving, values and experiences'. These 'meanings' of ethnicity are more important to a study than ethnicity itself because they are 'less distal and are more likely to influence therapy outcomes'.

Ethnicity is not a fixed, but a developing experience. One of the 'meanings' of ethnicity may be the sense that development in relation to the other ethnic groupings of the society, one's sense of racial identity. In the counselling research literature, most of the work on racial identity development has focused on minority clients, and much less attention has been given to the majority group, or white counsellors' racial identity. This is discussed by Sabnani et al. (1991) who point out that the majority of counsellors and trainee counsellors are from the 'white middle class' (see the survey by Cameron et al., 1989). Sabnani et al. (1991) recognize 'the importance of the counsellors' racial identity development to the cross-cultural counselling process'. They examine the three developmental rather than static models of white racial identity (Hardiman, 1982; Helms, 1984; Ponterotto, 1988a) and propose their own five-stage model. Their thesis is that counsellor's own racial identity development can be an integral component of a training which will help to make him an 'effective' counsellor. Casas (1985) advised researchers to 'stop thinking of race/ethnicity as a single or unitary variable that effects preference and effectiveness'. Sabnani et al. have heeded this is presenting their five-stage model.

But the bulk of the work on white racial identity development has been done by Helms and her associate Carter over the last decade. In 1984 she published a major study, 'Towards a theoretical explanation of the effects of race on counselling: a black and white model', which started from the premise that 'after 30 years of consideration, the question of how the race of the participants influences the counselling process remains unanswered'. The purpose of the paper was to present an interactional model for investigating the cross-race and same-race counselling process. It was based on the premiss that all people, regardless of race, go through a stagewise process of developing racial consciousness, wherein the final stage is an acceptance of race as a positive aspect of themselves and others. Her final conclusion was that individuals at different stages of racial consciousness probably enter counselling with different attitudinal and behavioural predispositions. The 1984 model has led to some valuable research, by herself and others.

The Helms-Carter 1991 study: relationships of white and black racial identity attitudes and demographic similarity to counsellor preferences

In an interesting and complex study, Helms and Carter (1991) have attempted to relate racial identity attitudes to counsellor preference. The research design is particularly complicated in that it introduces another variable, that of demographic similarity. By demographic is meant social class, or more accurately, perceptions of each other's social class by both members of the therapeutic dyad, since neither counsellor nor client would be able to evaluate objectively from each other's appearance or manner. Thus Helms and Carter speak of a 'phenomenological-demographic' perspective, the basic premiss of which is that 'people's preferences are determined by their perceptions of shared demographic membership characteristics'.

Some support for this view is given by Carter's (1991) review of empirical research into cultural values, where he states that: 'the majority of studies in this review seem to support common value systems for poor non-urban people *regardless of race or culture*' (emphasis added). Smith (1989) too, in an article on black racial identity development, suggested that 'ostensible differences and similarities in social class should predict preferences for counsellors regardless of the counsellors' or clients' race'.

Helms and Carter, however, suggest that Smith's (1989) proposition may be in doubt, since in the USA social class is confounded with race to the extent that a larger percentage of blacks than whites is classifiable as 'poor', and vice versa with the 'middle class' or 'wealthy'. Thus an apparent social class preference might in fact be a euphemism for racial prejudice. They also argue that the extent to which clients favour those similar to themselves with respect to membership group characteristics like gender or race is very difficult to assess, and has not been adequately studied (Helms, 1985; 1986).

This article (Helms and Carter, 1991) presents and discusses a complex double study in which assumptions from racial identity and demographic models were used to study white and black participants' strength of preference for counsellors' race and demographic characteristics. Racial identity research has helped to elicit within-group differences on clients' and client-surrogates' differential strength of preference for counsellors who resemble them. Barkham (1990), writing in a different context, and discussing the assumption that clients may seek out therapists with whom they share 'a common belief system', suggests that 'although there is some support to the claim that similarity of academic, intellectual and social values contribute significantly to client outcome (Arizmendi et al., 1985), generally, there is little evidence to support this assumption'. Beutler et al. (1986) have concluded: 'It is unlikely that any single dimension of [therapist] personality or personality similarity is a major factor or inhibitor or therapy benefit'.

The purpose of the Helms and Carter (1991) study was to examine the racial identity and demographic perspectives in two separate studies, one of white, one of black client surrogates. They point out that 'until recently there have been no published theoretical models for anticipating the ways in which white clients will respond to black counsellors', but that Helms' (1984, 1990) white racial identity model can be useful in examining these racial dynamics between white clients and black professionals. Helms (1990) hypothesized that white racial identity evolves through a six-stage process of contact, disintegration, reintegration, pseudo-independence, immersion/emersion, and autonomy. This process is similar in its developmental outline and some of its stages to the earlier widely used Cross (1971, 1978) model of black racial identity development.

Helms and Carter's general hypothesis concerning the racial identity perspective was that 'when counsellor's race was called to participants' attention, racial identity attitudes, but not self-assessed social class or gender, would predict the participants' strength of counsellor preferences'. Similarly with the demographic perspective, 'when counsellor's social class or gender was the dimension being examined, surrogates' self-assessed social class or gender, but not their racial identity attitudes, would predict the strength of counsellor preferences'.

The first of the two studies contained within it plotted white racial identity attitudes against demographic characteristics. It was found that white racial identity attitudes significantly predicted the strength of preference for white counsellors, both female and male. Thus the phenomenological-demographic perspective received little support from white respondents. It was different though in study two, where black identity attitude demographic variables accounted for most of the preference that black participants of lower class backgrounds had for white counsellors.

So the answer to the question 'Which predicts the strength of counsellor preferences best: the racial identity or the demographic perspective?' is certainly, as Helms and Carter indicate, 'rather complex'. Their suggestion is that 'combinations of counsellor characteristics, as well as the race/ethnicity of subject populations, should be varied in future counsellor-preference research'.

It is particularly interesting that this study, statistically very sophisticated and building on some of the best research, using the most flexible and empirically validated model, should nevertheless reach such a tentative conclusion (see Helms, 1995, for an update of Racial Identity Models). Abramowitz and Murray's (1983) tenet is confirmed ten years' later: 'No-one knows how prevalent race effects are in psychotherapy as it is practised today'.

A major finding of Wade and Bernstein's (1991) examination of 'Culture sensitivity training and counsellor's race: effects on black female clients' perceptions and attrition' is that 'black female client perceptions of counsellors and the counselling process were affected more by culture sensitivity training of the counsellors than by counsellor race'.

It is to the effects of training that I now turn.

Explicit multicultural counsellor education: does it affect the counselling process and outcome?

As late as 1977 McFadden and Wilson found in a survey of counsellor educators that fewer than one per cent required their students to study non-white cultures (Casas et al., 1986). By 1986, however, a national survey in the USA found that 33 per cent of the responding programmes (58 out of 95) had required courses or practicums in cross-cultural counselling (Ponterotto and Casas, 1987).

Ponterotto and Casas (1987), listing documentation of the 'widespread ineffectiveness' of traditional counselling approaches and techniques with racial and ethnic minority groups, claim that the counselling profession as a whole 'is failing to effectively meet the mental health needs of racial and ethnic minorities', a point of view echoed by Sue et al. (1992) in their 'Multicultural counselling competencies and standards: a call to the profession', when they argue that 'the major reason for therapeutic ineffectiveness lies in the training of mental health professionals'.

One reason why this may be so is summed up by Ponterotto and Casas (1991): the view of many commentators is that counselling programmes are 'proponents of the status quo' in which counsellors are taught out of traditional western European influenced training models. Thus 'white, middle-class male perceptions of normal and appropriate behaviour are set as the standards to judge, diagnose and treat all clients' (Pedersen, 1987, 1988). As long as training programmes continue to be, for the most, culturally biased, the graduates of these programmes will continue to operate from a biased perspective, what Marsella (1980) called 'ethnocentricity'.

Sue and Sue (1990) referring to the dangers of 'a cultural encapsulation' and its detrimental effect on minorities, note that training recommendations of a number of US Conferences all mentioned the serious lack and inadequacy of psychology training programmes in dealing with 'religious, ethnic, sexual and economic' groups. Selected recommendations included advocating that evaluation of training programmes include not only the content, but also the evaluation of graduates. This point regarding the dual nature of meaningful evaluation of multicultural training programmes, and the importance of assessing the individuals in the programme, is crucial.

Can the usefulness of cross-cultural training be demonstrated empirically? How do we evaluate its relevance to positive outcome in the field?

These are the two crucial questions posed by Harriet Lefley (1985). She goes on to indicate that there have been some attempts to evaluate cross-cultural training effectiveness (e.g. Triandis, 1977), but they are theoretical frameworks or models rather than actual findings on efficacy. Some hard data are available from the Cross-Cultural Training Institute for Mental Health Professional (Lefley and Urutia, 1982) which demonstrated that knowledge acquisition and changes in social distance, attitudes and values were 'accompanied by significant improvements in therapeutic skills with a client of contrasting culture. A major objective indicator was a significant reduction in patient drop-out rates following cross cultural training'.

Ponterotto and Casas (1987) suggest that little is known about the effectiveness of the training provided in various counsellor education programmes. They go on to give brief descriptions of the training pro-grammes of five leading American institutions, noting in spite of some similarities a 'lack of consensus' about objectives, and conclude that 'given the lack of consensus as to the country's leading multicultural-oriented programs … it would be inappropriate to label those programs as cultur-ally competent'. Similar terminology and attitude is seen in an article by D'Andrea et al. (1991) who point out that the field lacks consensus regard-ing 'the type of training considered to be most needed and effective in terms of promoting counsellors' level of multicultural development. This lack of consensus reflects both our current understanding as to what constitutes effective multicultural training as well as the individual counsellor-educator's preference regarding the type of content to be covered by such a course'.

The triad model

One model which has been widely used as a multicultural counselling training device (as well as in other areas of counselling) and has itself been the subject of some attempts at evaluation, is the Triad Model of Multicultural Counselling Training, originally developed by Pedersen in the 1970s and described in full in his *Handbook for Developing Multicultural Awareness* (Pedersen, 1988). It was developed to train mental health practitioners in work with culturally different clients through a micro-counselling laboratory design. A therapist from one culture is matched with a coached client/'anti-counsellor' team from the same other culture for a video-taped simulation of a multicultural therapy session. In the simulation, the therapist tried to build a rapport with the culturally dif-ferent client, offering a counselling solution to the problems presented.

The 'anti-counsellor' seeks to represent the problem element from the client's cultural viewpoint as opposed to the intervention from the culturally different counsellor.

As a result of this role played interaction, the therapist learns to articulate the problem explicitly from the client's cultural viewpoint, diminish his or her defensiveness in working with culturally different clients, anticipate resistance from clients of different culture and practice recovery skills from inappropriate responses made during the simulated interview.

According to McRae and Johnson (1991) this model has been used in several hundred workshops in the USA over the last decade. One person plays the role of counsellor, another the client. The third person plays either a supportive ally to the counsellor (the 'pro-counsellor') or an antagonist force (the 'anti-counsellor') in this dynamic model which is designed to emphasize the relevant cultural values that may have an impact on the counselling relationship. After the role play, the participants observe their taped interactions for evaluation and analysis purposes. Because the role of the pro-counsellor or anti-counsellor is played by someone from the same background as the client, understanding of potential cultural, ethnic or racial conflicts between counsellor and client may be promoted.

Pedersen himself suggests that University of Hawaii prepracticum counselling students trained with the Triad Model 'achieved significantly higher scores on a multiple choice test designed to measure counsellor effectiveness ... than did students who were not trained with the Triad Model' (Pedersen, 1988). Sue's (1979) research indicated that counsellor trainees found the pro-counsellor model to be more effective in the acquisition of knowledge and skills, whereas the anti-counsellor model was more effective in the development of sensitivity and awareness of personal bias and differing cultural values. Neimeyer et al. (1986) indicated that counsellors in the pro-counsellor model found themselves feeling more competent, less confused and more in control than those in the anti-counsellor model.

Types of multicultural counselling training courses

A variety of such courses have emerged over the last twenty years in the USA D'Andrea and Daniels (1991) classify them into four groups, each area focusing on a specific aspect of multicultural counselling:

1 The acquisition of communication skills (Pedersen, 1977).
2 The need to become more aware of one's attitudes towards ethnic minorities (Hulnick, 1971; Parker and McDavis, 1979).
3 The importance of increasing the counsellor's knowledge about ethnic minority populations (Mio, 1989; Parker et al., 1986).
4 Training formats encouraging counsellors to develop their awareness, knowledge and skills (the three Pedersen key words) in this area (D'Andrea, 1990; Pedersen, 1989).

Using this grouping as the basis, D'Andrea and Daniels set up an exploratory investigation. In this qualitative research study they gathered data from a variety of sources using a range of techniques, and 'purposeful sample'. They reviewed appropriate journals, participated in numerous open-ended conversations with counsellor educators, professional counsellors and graduate students, gathered information from conferences, workshops and conventions, and synthesized data one of these authors has as a member of the editorial board of the *Journal for Multicultural Counselling and Development*.

Synthesizing all these findings, they developed a theoretical framework 'thought to be reflective of the different types of multicultural counselling training currently going on in counsellor education'. The model has two levels, each level containing two discrete stages, the Culturally Entrenched stage and the Cultural Awakening stage. Level 2 they call the 'Conscientious Level of Counsellor Education', with its two stages, the Cultural Integrity stage and the Infusion stage. Some of the terminology is borrowed from earlier models of racial identify development, but applied in this case not to individuals but to the programmes of training institutions.

The validity of the model was tested using quantitative research methods, primarily by 'surveying a number of faculty and departmental chairpersons in counsellor education programmes to determine how well the levels and stages of the model fit their training programmes'.

D'Andrea and Daniels suggest that this 'tentative framework', as the 'only known paradigm of its kind', is a model that 'could be used by other researchers interested in testing the validity and reliability of the proposed levels and stages of cross cultural counselling training in a more formal manner'. Thus a potentially useful research tool has been developed and awaits use.

Evaluating the impact of multicultural counselling training

One significant attempt to do this, in the article of the same title, was carried out by the same two investigators as members of a larger team (D'Andrea et al., 1991). The authors note that little research has been done to assess the impact of multicultural counselling courses on student development. There has been little consensus as to the types of training considered most needed or effective in terms of promoting a counsellor's level of multicultural development. Thus the variety of courses now on offer reflect pedagogical diversification in terms of process and content. This in turn suggests substantial differences in approach in designing instructional objectives and learning experiences.

So the authors conducted a series of investigations to examine how various courses affect graduate students. Since there is a lack of empirical studies, they first had to develop an instrument that could be used to measure an individual's level of multicultural counselling competence, the Multicultural Awareness, Knowledge and Skills Survey (MAKSS).

Three investigations took place, into separate counselling courses. They sought to assess the impact of these three multicultural counselling courses in terms of the effect each had on the student's level of multi-cultural counselling awareness, knowledge and skills.

The results suggest that the training format used in the studies to promote student awareness, knowledge and skills in the area of multicultural counselling did significantly affect the project participants. According to the perceptions of the student participants in each of the three counselling programmes assessed, according to the differences between the pre-test and post-test administration of the MAKSS, there is clear evidence that the type of training they received 'may have substantially improved their level of multicultural counselling awareness, knowledge and skills'. Moreover, the apparent effectiveness of the training model to stimulate a noticeable increase in the student's level of multicultural development did not depend on the length of time the training was offered (regular academic semester, summer semester or weekend training format).

Secondly, with respect to within-group gains, the lowest z values were associated not with awareness of knowledge, but with skill, in each group. This may suggest that it is more difficult to promote the acquisition of multicultural counselling skills than to improve students' cross-cultural awareness and knowledge.

McRae and Johnson (1991) report on two studies that have attempted to evaluate the effectiveness of a similar multicultural counselling course at graduate level. Parker et al. (1986) developed a multifaceted approach that nevertheless relied heavily on self-report inventories, with no reliability or validity data provided. Mio (1989) reported that students who participated in a Partners Program that matched them with an immigrant student 'were rated as more culturally sensitive at the end of the semester'.

As McRae and Johnson (1991) point out, although the experiential component of such a course may promote cultural awareness and knowledge, it does not provide much in the way of skills development, nor in 'examining the therapeutic relationship from a cultural perspective'. Lefley's (1985) evaluation model, although it might provide 'a basic foundation for further research in the refinement of models for evaluating multicultural counsellor training', suffers from the same basic limitation:

> Although measures of trainees' attitudes and values provide important data about the pre and post status of trainees, the data provide little information regarding *the actual counselling process that occurs between counsellor and client.* (McRae and Johnson, 1991: 133; emphasis added)

This is the crucial point, and to my knowledge there is as yet no research evidence relating directly to the process or outcome effectiveness of multicultural counselling training. Mark Aveline (1990) stated that 'partial progress has been made towards the subsidiary but important question of what has training added to the therapist's ability', but as far as the main issue of the effectiveness or otherwise of multicultural counselling training, 'the methodology to assess' the question of the therapist competence 'does not yet exist'.

Has multicultural counselling research had an effect on counselling process and outcome?

From a professional perspective, write Ponterotto and Casas (1991), it would be safe to say that racial/ethnic minorities have received minimal benefits from the work of psychologists (Zytowski et al., 1988). Even fewer benefits from the work of researchers, it could be added, for in many ways the available multicultural counselling research has had almost no quantifiable effect.

Over the past decade or two, for example, the arguments over the effectiveness of treatment with ethnic minorities have remained remarkably unchanged, in that strong critics and proponents of psychotherapy with ethnic individuals can still be heard. The available research has failed to systematically reveal outcome differences (Sue, 1988).

Pedersen (1988) has suggested several reasons why a consensus of research methodology has not been developed in the field of multicultural counselling (Draguns, 1981a, 1981b). He suggests this is partly because the emphasis on research across cultures has been on abnormal rather than normal behaviour. He suggest too that the complexity of research on multicultural counselling, by which I presume he means the large number of possible variables, discourages empirical research. Interactions among people, professional institutions and community, are incredibly and notoriously complex.

In most areas of multicultural counselling concerns, the research is limited. D'Andrea et al. (1991), discussing the variety of multicultural courses in counsellor education programmes as a way of improving counsellors' professional training for a diversified, pluralistic society, note that 'little research has been done to assess the impact of this sort of instruction on student development'. The complaint is a familiar one.

Research weaknesses

Many commentators suggests that weaknesses in the available research provide some explanation for its lack of practical impact. Listing what they regard as a variety of such weaknesses, Casas et al. (1986) summarize the view that 'from a research perspective, clients from racial and ethnic minority groups continue to be unknown or misunderstood'. Taking up this issue in 1991, Ponterotto and Casas examined ten major criticisms of multicultural counselling research as referred to in an 80-study database encompassing five major US counselling journals over a recent six-year period. The validity of these frequent criticisms was largely supported by data: of the ten criticisms, two were supported not at all, two partially, and the remaining six entirely. The six valid criticisms of the available research are:

1 Lack of conceptual/theoretical frameworks to guide research.
2 Disregard for within-group or intracultural differences.
3 The use of easily accessible college student populations.
4 Reliance on culturally encapsulated psychometric instrumentation.
5 Failure to adequately describe one's sample in terms of socio-economic status.
6 Over reliance on paper-and-pencil measures as the dependent variable.

The question of relevance

Gelso et al. (1988) note that the relation between research results and practice is complex, far more than a simple matter of applying results to a clinical setting. Discussing Krumholtz's (1968) 'test of relevance', they note its implications that to be worthwhile research must have an effect on what counsellors do in practice. Casas (1984) had equally suggested that 'research should have pragmatic value'.

Gelso et al. (1988) suggest that 'relevance' is to do with the way the results of research raise scientific questions about practice, and also pertains to the contribution to, and modification of, theory. In these senses, 'research may be powerfully related to practice, but the link is highly indirect'. The Gelso article is a report of the summary and conclusions of the research group at the Third National Conference for Counselling Psychology. The discussants suggested:

- that conceptualizations that are a part of research studies are incorporated into the counsellor's concept system about his or her practice;
- that results that are meaningful to the practitioner become a part of his or her conceptual framework.

Examples of this might be the effect of culture sensitivity training (Wade and Bernstein, 1991) or the impact of the Pedersen Triad model as a training approach (Pedersen, 1988).

Sue and Sue (1990) suggest that research can be 'a powerful means of combating stereotypes and correcting biased studies', but they point out that 'unfortunately this self-correcting process of ethnic research has been underdeveloped'. One is left with exactly this sense, having examined the research literature, of underdevelopment.

One small example of its back of impact relates to a recently conducted Delphi poll (Norcross et al., 1992) in which a panel of 75 'experts' forecast future scenarios and a range of major changes. This study employed a sensitive forecasting method – the Delphi methodology – to predict the future of psychotherapy in the USA for the next ten years. There was not a single mention of multicultural counselling.

A set of proposals for future research

In this final section, I consider five research proposals, some using qualitative and some quantitative design, that seem to have particular relevance to some of the issues I have been discussing. They are:

1 An investigation of white counsellor racial identity.
2 A comparison of eastern and western therapeutic modalities for reducing anxiety.
3 An evaluation of the levels of cultural mistrust among blacks receiving counselling.
4 An evaluation of the validity of the Smith (1985) model in working with stressed West Indian women.
5 A single-subject evaluation of multimodal therapy.

The flexibility of multimodal therapy seems to me to have exciting implications for multicultural counselling, as I shall indicate.

White counsellor racial identity

Most commentators agree that more research is needed on white racial identity development (Sabnani et al., 1991). This proposal would examine the attitudes of white counsellors, an area that to my knowledge has not been the subject of much research: in the USA, for example, where virtually all the work has been done, the subjects of white racial identity development have almost all been students (Tokar and Swanson, 1991).

Minority identity models all postulate the possibility of different levels of acculturation and awareness: that is, in this case, there are progressive stages of racial consciousness.

The hypothesis is that successively later stages of white counsellor racial consciousness will be associated with greater ability to work effectively with clients from different racial/ethnic groups.

Instruments

The White Racial Identity Scale (WRIS) consists of 50 items designed to assess attitudes reflective of the six stages of white racial identity development: contact; disintegration; reintegration; pseudo-independence; emersion/immersion; autonomy (Helms and Carter, 1990). Subjects respond to the items using a five-point, Likert-type scale ranging from strongly disagree (1) to strongly agree (5).

The Cross-Cultural Counselling Inventory – Revised (CCCI-R) was constructed by La Framboise et al. (1990). It was developed by converting the cross-cultural competencies outlined in the D.W. Sue (1982) position paper into scale terms. It is a 20-item, six-point, Likert-type scale (1 = strongly agree, 6 = strongly disagree) which assesses the counsellor's ability to work effectively with clients from diverse racial/ethnic groups. It is completed by an evaluator observing the counsellor, and, consistent with the D.W. Sue position paper, the counsellor is evaluated in three areas: cultural awareness and beliefs; cultural knowledge; specific cross-cultural skills.

Regression analysis would be used to measure the correlation between the two sets of variables. There would be control for differences of sex, age, socio-economic status.

Variants

It would be interesting to test the cross-cultural validity of these American instruments by replicating the research in a UK context.

Second, it would be useful to carry out the research in a training context. Counsellor training programmes are considered by many to be proponents of the white status quo (e.g. Atkinson et al., 1989; Katz, 1985). The field of multicultural counselling lacks consensus as to the types of training considered to be most needed (Carey et al., 1990) and effective in terms of promoting counsellors' level of multicultural development (D'Andrea et al., 1991).

Particularly suitable in a training setting would be to make use of another instrument, the Multicultural Awareness, Knowledge and Skills Survey (MAKSS). This is a self-administered written test developed by D'Andrea et al. (1990), consisting of a total of 60 items that are equally divided into three subscales. The questions are presented in multiple choice format, and are designed to obtain a measure of participants' perceptions of their level of multicultural counselling awareness, knowledge and skills. It would be appropriate to use this instrument in place of the Cross-Cultural Counselling Inventory – Revised, in this training context. In that way the correlative experimental design would not need to be changed. The hypothesis in this variant would be that the later stages of white student counsellor racial consciousness will be associated with higher levels of Awareness, Knowledge and Skills.

Comparison of eastern and western approaches for reducing anxiety

Ponterotto (1988b) has suggested that 'research is needed that concentrates on the strengths of minority cultures. Of interest will be an examination of positive coping strategies by minority group members'. Reynolds has reported on his adaptation of Japanese 'Morita' and 'Naikan' therapies into western contexts (Reynolds, 1980; see also Pedersen et al., 1989). Sue and Sue (1990), emphasizing the need to identify the intrinsic helping skill of particular cultures, suggest that 'such a research approach would allow us to eventually develop counselling theories that are different from those we have learned'.

More data is needed on the effectiveness of indigenous counselling approaches (Pedersen, 1988). This simple research design allows a comparative evaluation of effectiveness. Several variants are possible. Let us take as one example a comparison between meditation, cognitive-behavioural therapy and person-centred therapy, and consider their comparative effectiveness in the treatment of generalized anxiety state.

Both cognitive-behavioural and person-centred therapy have been widely assessed. Meditation, both as a term and a mental state, has suffered from considerable abuse, administered mainly by those who make unsubstantiated claims about its therapeutic value in the west. The claims made during the heyday of its popularity by the proponents of one form of meditation, so-called transcendental meditation, 'appear to have been based on studies with insufficient control over confounding variables' (Saeki and Borrow, 1987). Yet, a few 'aspects of the meditational state have been documented: the EEG pattern generally shows alpha waves, oxygen consumption drops, energy expenditure is lowered and subject reports are consistent in describing the experiences as relaxing and salutary' (Reber, 1985).

In the experimental design, a group of subjects presenting with Generalized Anxiety Disorder, half of Indian origin, half white, are randomly assigned to one of four treatment groups: the control group (placed on a waiting list to be offered therapy later), one in which they will receive cognitive-behavioural therapy, one receiving person-centred, the last one in which meditation will be taught. Each group, apart from the control group, will have an experienced therapist who will see each member individually, once a week, in the normal manner. Measurement of anxiety level (on a 1 to 10 self-report scale) will be taken before and after a ten-week period of therapeutic intervention for each individual, or in the case of the control group, a ten-week interval. Hypothesis:

1   There will be significant differences between groups in mean improvement scores.
2   All other groups will do better than the control group.
3.   The improvement scores of whites and those of Indian origin will vary according to which therapy group they are in. This is a two-factor design; the factors are therapy (with four levels) and racial/ethnic background. As a parametric test, analysis of variance (ANOVA) would be used to consider the effects of the two independent variables acting together.

To evaluate the levels of cultural mistrust among black students receiving counselling

This study will entail mixed methodological strategies, using both quantitative and qualitative methods. The former will be similar to the design of research proposal 1. The latter will use qualitative techniques that are becoming more commonly used in research designs.

In the last few years, a number of counselling psychologists have emphasized the value of qualitative methods to counsellors (Ponterotto and Casas, 1991). Gelso et al. (1988) write of a 'clear and strong movement' that wants to take more seriously the experiences, self-perceptions and reports of counselling participants. Alternative research paradigms 'may be characterized by an understanding or the illumination of meanings. For this reason alternative research methods have been referred to as interpretative methods' (Hoshmand, 1989).

Qualitative research is an example of this. It is not descriptive and phenomenological. Since it is inductive, it does not impose any general theory of counselling, but moves only slowly to tentative hypotheses. It has several advantages for this sort of study. It can yield more information than a conventional quantitative study, being very data–rich. Researchers attempt to examine their subjects holistically, to be methodologically flexible, and to ensure a close fit between the data collected and the behavioural reality of the situation (Ponterotto and Casas, 1991). Counsellors should make naturally good qualitative researchers, for the skills needed are exactly those they have trained for as counsellors, i.e. skilled observation and interviewing (Matthews and Paradise, 1988).

This particular study will examine the experience of a non-random, purposive sample of black students receiving counselling. Qualitative methods will include:

1 Participant observation in different settings (home, community, college).
2 Data collection – investigator notes, interviews (taped with the participants' permission) both in a generalized interview approach and standardized open-ended. Peers, family and college lecturers and tutors would also be interviewed, and their perspective be evaluated too.
3 In each case, a case analysis would be built up.
4 Classification of level and types of cultural mistrust would be inferred from participant articulated designations.

Quantitative methods would be similar to the experimental design of proposal 1, using as instruments two scales.

The Racial Identity Attitude Scale-B Short Form RIAS-B (Parham and Helms, 1981) is designed to measure the development of a positive black identity. It is a 30-item, self-report questionnaire, with four subscales, each representing attitudes from one of the first four stages proposed by Cross (1971). Respondents use a five-point, Likert-type scale ranging from strongly disagree (1) to strongly agree (5).

The Cultural Mistrust Inventory (CMI) was developed by Terrell and Terrell (1981) to measure black people's distrust of whites and white-related organizations. It is a 48-point, Likert-type scale scored on a seven-point continuum (1 = strongly disagree, 7 = strongly agree). There are four subscales of the CMI, with each corresponding to one of the domains in which black mistrust of whites might exist: education and training; politics and legal affairs; business and work; social and interpersonal settings.

The hypothesis here would be that successively later stages of black racial identity consciousness (a higher level of positive black identity) is associated with a lower score on the CMI.

Results from the quantitative and qualitative designs will be evaluated together, to build a composite analysis.

An evaluation of the validity of the Smith (1985) Stress Resistant and Delivery Model (SRD) in working with stressed West Indian women

Smith hypothesizes that there are certain culturally patterned ways of responding to stress. She presents a model which asks three secondary questions:

1   What are the life events that might cause stress?
2   What are the personal dispositions and internal mediating factors related to the stress process?
3   What social conditions and external mediating factors are related to the life stress process?

Starting from these questions, her model attempts to go beyond and answer the primary question: How do we go about counselling members of racial minority groups?

This evaluation involves the researchers as a participant observer, who will observe a series of women in counselling sessions, interview them individually, and the counsellor too, to establish and evaluate their individual awareness of stress and their sense of the counselling process, interview peers and family members too, and to evaluate their sense of the presence and force of external stressors, evaluate, systematize, and perhaps even suggest a hypothesis for later investigation. Thus this is a multi-perspective analysis designed to evaluate the validity of Smith's three-stage model, which seeks to identify the sources of stress, analyse mediating factors, both internal and external and decide on the method of delivery to clients.

The investigator will attempt to evaluate the counselling process. Smith's account of her own counselling process shows that she moves from empathy, through an educative role, to a final delivery mode. In doing so she uses a broad range of techniques: How does the counsellor in this investigation follow that pattern? What is the range of deviation from that pattern? What is the counsellor evaluation of process and outcome?

The client's experience will be similarly diagnosed: What is her sense of the counselling process? Has there been a helpful outcome? What is the counsellor evaluation of process and outcome?

Finally will come the investigator evaluation and systematization.

1   What are the themes that run through all the individual cases?
2   What is essential to all these personal cases?
3   Can common external causes be identified?

4 Is there a common psychological organization of the internal sources
   of stress?
5 La Framboise (1985) describes the Smith model as an 'excellent illustration of a culturally sensitive intervention'. How successfully has it
   identified sources of stress, analysed mediating factors and facilitated
   effective methods of service delivery?

A single-subject evaluation of multimodal therapy with an ethnic minority client

In multicultural counselling, it is particularly important to work within a
framework that is flexible in addressing the needs of individual clients,
and at the same time culturally sensitive and relevant. Multimodal therapy attempts to be 'at the cutting edge of clinical effectiveness by continually scanning the field for better assessment of treatment methods'.
Moreover, 'the majority of techniques currently employed within this discipline come from the field of cognitive-behavioural therapy' (Lazarus,
1986). This is a form of therapy 'of which cross-cultural psychology has
made good use' (La Framboise, 1985).

One particularly useful strategy from a multicultural point of view is that
'counsellor and client work together in formulating the modality profile'
(Ponterotto, 1987). 'This team-work approach is culturally important
because it allows the client to express his or her own view on the cultural
relevance of the various planned counselling interventions.' Ponterotto
also, in considering its use with a Mexican/American population with its
'tremendous intracultural diversity', suggests that multimodal therapy may
be valid for all levels of acculturation and a wide range of other variables.

After establishing a therapeutic relationship, the counsellor, working
with the client, will:

1 Draw up a modality profile.
2 Work out a 'firing order' of the seven modalities in relation to the presenting problem.
3 Draw up a structural profile, a cognitive map, to provide direction for
   the counselling process.

Note that under the modality 'Interpersonal Relations' can be considered
environmental factors and conditions, a particularly appropriate heading
with ethnic minority clients (Ponterotto, 1987).

A second important feature of multimodal therapy is that, although
most of the meetings may take place in the therapist's office, 'the flexibility of the multimodal approach leaves open a variety of other settings ...
it may be helpful to shift the locus of therapy outside the office ... the use
of ancillary personnel is also often useful [to] expedite in vivo excursions,
provide reinforcement for adaptive responses, and offer useful modelling
experiences' (Lazarus, 1986). All these possibilities are particularly relevant for ethnic minority clients (Atkinson et al., 1989).

In analysing the data of the counselling sessions, the research questions for consideration are:

1　How genuinely interactive is the process?
2　How and how far do client opinions of the planned counsellor interventions affect the process?
3　How and how far does the counsellor adapt to the client's views of the cultural relevance of the counselling interventions?
4　How far can the client actually plan his or her own therapeutic progress?
5　Is it possible to plot systematically 'client progress over time'? (See Miller, 1985, for a suggestion of three data analysis techniques for use in N = 1 studies, that give graphical presentation of client change during therapy.)
6　What difficulties are there in using multimodal therapy with ethnic minority clients?
7　How far can Ponterotto's claim be accepted that the systematic format of multimodal therapy 'provides maximum opportunity to develop culturally relevant clinical case conceptualizations'?
8　How can the outcome be evaluated?

N = 1 studies, by their very nature, cannot be replicated. Yet it would also be interesting to develop an exploratory series of such studies, each client also being rated on a standard acculturation level scale, to get some sense of the range of possibilities for using multimodal therapy with ethnic minority clients.

Such a multimodal approach is one of the most interesting in the whole field of multicultural counselling, and a fitting note on which to end this account.

References

Abramowitz, S.T. and Murray, J. (1983) 'Race effects in psychotherapy', in J. Murray and Abramson (eds), *Bias in Psychotherapy*. Westport, CT: Greenwood Press.

Althen, G. (1983) *The Handbook of Foreign Student Advising*. Yarmouth, ME: Intercultural Press.

Arizmendi, T.G., Beutler, D.E., Sharfield, S., Crago, M. and Hagaman, R. (1985) 'Client–therapist value similarity and psychotherapy outcome: a microscopic approach', *Psychotherapy*, 17: 161–75.

Atkinson, D.R. (1983) 'Ethnic similarity in counselling: a review of the research', *The Counselling Psychologist*, 11: 79–92.

Atkinson, D.R. (1985) 'A meta-review of research on cross-cultural counselling and psychotherapy', *Journal of Multicultural Counseling and Development*, 13: 138–53.

Atkinson, D.R., Marayuma , M. and Matsui, T. (1978) 'Effects of counselor race and counseling approach on Asian Americans' perceptions of counsellor credibility and utility', *Journal of Counseling Psychology*, 25: 76–85.

Atkinson, D.R., Morten, G. and Sue, D.W. (1986) *Counselling American Minorities*. Dubuque, Iowa: William C. Brown.

Atkinson, D.R., Morten, G. and Wing Sue, D. (eds) (1989) *Counseling American Minorities: A Cross Cultural Perspective, Third Edition*. Dubuque, IA: William C. Brown.

Atkinson, D.R., Morten, G. and Sue, D.W. (eds) (1998) *Counseling American Minorities*. Boston, MA: McGraw-Hill.

Aveline, M. (1990) 'The training and supervision of individual therapists' in W. Dryden (ed.), *Individual Therapy: A Handbook*. Milton Keynes: Open University Press. p. 335.

Barkham, M. (1990) 'Research in individual therapy', in W. Dryden (ed.), *Individual Therapy: A Handbook*. Milton Keynes: Open University Press.

Berman, J. (1979) 'Counseling skills used by black and white male and female counsellors', *Journal of Counseling Psychology*, 26: 81–4.

Beutler, D.E., Crago, M. and Arizmendi, T.G. (1986) 'Therapist variables in psychotherapy process and outcome', in S.L. Garfield and A.E. Bergin (eds), *Handbook of Psychotherapy and Behaviour Change*, 3rd edn. Chichester: Wiley.

Cameron, A.S., Galassi, J.P., Birk, J.M. and Waggener, N. (1989) 'Trends in counseling psychology training programs: the Council of Counseling Psychology training programs survey 1975–1987', *The Counseling Psychologist*, 17: 301–13.

Carey, J.C., Reinat, M. and Fontes, L. (1990) 'School counselor's perceptions of training needs in multicultural counseling', *Counselor Education and Supervision*, 29: 155–69.

Carter, R.J. (1991) 'Cultural values: a review of empirical research and implications for counseling', *Journal of Counseling and Development*. September/October 1991, Volume 70.

Casas, J.M. (1984) 'Policy training and research in counseling psychology: the racial/ethnic minority perspective' in S.D. Bron and S. Lents (eds), *Handbook of Counseling Psychology*. New York: John Wiley. pp. 785–831.

Casas, J.M. (1985) 'The status of racial- and ethnic-minority counseling: a training perspective' in P. Pedersen (ed.), *Handbook of Cross-Cultural Counseling and Therapy*. Westport, CT: Greenwood Press. pp. 267–74.

Casas, J.M., Ponterotto, J.G. and Gutierrez, J.M. (1986) 'An ethical indictment of counseling research and training: the cross cultural perspective', *Journal of Counseling and Development*, 64: 347–9.

Cross, W.E. (1971) 'The negro-to-black conversion experience', *Black World*, 20: 13–27.

Cross, W.E. (1978) 'The Cross and Thomas models of psychological nigrescence', *Journal of Black Psychology*, 5: 13–19.

D'Andrea, M. (1990) *A Syllabus for Multicultural Counselor Training*. Honolulu: University of Hawaii-Manoa.

D'Andrea, M. and Daniels, J. (1991) 'Exploring the different levels of multicultural counselor training in education', *Journal of Counseling and Development*, 70: 78–85.

D'Andrea, M., Daniels, J. and Beck, R. (1991) 'Evaluating the impact of multicultural counselor training', *Journal of Counseling and Development*, 70: 143–50.

Draguns, J.G. (1981a) 'Counseling across cultures: common themes and distinct approaches', in P.B. Pedersen, J. Draguns, W. Lonner and J. Trimble (eds), *Counseling Across Cultures*. Honolulu: University of Hawaii Press.

Draguns, J.G. (1981b) 'Cross cultural counseling and psychotherapy: issues, history, current status', in A.J. Marsella and P.B. Pedersen (eds), *Cross Cultural Counseling and Therapy*. Elmsford, NY: Pergamon Press.

Exum, H.A. and Lau, E.Y. (1988) 'Counseling style preference of Chinese college students', *Journal of Multicultural Counseling and Development*, 16: 84–92.

La Framboise, T. (1985) 'The role of cultural diversity in counseling psychology', *The Counseling Psychologist*, 13 (4): 649–55.

Garfield, S.L. and Bergin, A.E. (1986) *Handbook of Psychotherapy and Behaviour Change*, 3rd edn. New York: Wiley.

Gelso, C.J., Betz, N.E., Friedlander, M.C., Helms, J.E., Hill, C.E., Patton, M.J., Super, D.E. and Wampole, R.E. (1988) 'Research in counseling psychology: prospects and recommendations', *The Counseling Psychologist*, 16: 385–406.

Griffith, M.S. and Jones, E.E. (1979) 'Race and psychology: changing perspectives', in J.H. Masserman (ed.), *Current Psychiatric Therapies*, vol. 8. New York: Grune and Stratton.

Hardiman, R. (1982) 'White identity development: a process oriented model for describing the racial consciousness of white Americans', *Dissertation Abstracts International*, 43: 104A.

Harrison, D.K. (1975) 'Race as a counselor–client variable in counseling and psychotherapy: a review of the research', *The Counseling Psychologist*, 5: 124–33.

Harrison, D.K. (1977) 'The attitudes of black counselees towards white counselors', *Journal of Non-White Concerns in Personnel and Guidance*, 5: 52–9.

Helms, J.E. (1984) 'Towards a theoretical explanation of the effects of race on counseling: a black and white model', *The Counseling Psychologist*, 12 (4): 153–65.

Helms, J.E. (1985) 'Cultural identity in the treatment process' in P. Pedersen (ed.), *Handbook of Cross-Cultural Counseling and Therapy*. Westport, CT: Greenwood Press. pp. 239–47.

Helms, J.E. (1986) 'Expanding racial identity theory to cover the counseling process', *Journal of Counseling Psychology*, 33: 62–64.

Helms, J.E. (1989) 'Considering some methodological issues in racial identity counseling research', *The Counseling Psychologist*, 17: 227–52.

Helms, J.E. (1990) 'Toward a model of white racial identity development' in J.E. Helms (ed.), *Black and White Racial Identity: Theory, Research and Practice*. Westport, CT: Greenwood Press.

Helms, J.E. (1995) 'An update of Helms' white and people of colour racial identity models' in J.G. Ponterotto, J.M. Casas, L.A. Suzuki and C.M. Alexander (eds), *Handbook of Multicultural Counselling*. Thousand Oaks, CA: Sage.

Helms, J.E. and Carter, R.T. (1990) 'Development of the white racial identity inventory', in J.E. Helms (ed.), *Black and White Racial Identity: Theory, Research and Practice*. New York: Greenwood Press.

Helms, J.E. and Carter, R.T. (1991) 'The relationship of white and black racial identity attitudes and demographic similarity to counselor preferences', *Journal of Counseling Psychology*, 38 (4): 446–57.

Hoshmand, L.L.S.T. (1989) 'Alternate research paradigms: a review and teaching proposal', *The Counseling Psychologist*, 17 (1): 3–79.

Hulnick, R. (1971) 'Counselor: know thyself', *Counselor Education and Supervision*, 17: 69–72.

Jones, E.E. (1978) 'Effects of race on psychotherapy process and outcome: an exploratory investigation', *Psychotherapy: Theory, Research and Practice*, 15: 226–36.

Katz, J.H. (1985) 'The sociopolitical nature of counseling', *The Counseling Psychologist*, 13: 615–24.

Kirschenbaum, H. and Henderson, V.L. (eds) (1990) *The Carl Rogers Reader*. London: Constable.

Krumholtz, J.D. (1968) 'Future directions for counseling research', in J.M. Whiteley (ed.), *Research in Counseling: Evaluation and Focus*. Columbus, OH: Merrill.

Lazarus, A.A. (1986) 'Multimodal therapy', in J.C. Norcross (ed.), *Handbook of Cross Cultural Counseling and Therapy*. New York: Praeger.

Lefley, H. (1985) 'Mental health training across cultures' in P. Pedersen (ed.), *Handbook of Cross-Cultural Counseling and Therapy*. Westport, CT: Greenwood Press.

Lefley, H.P. and Urutia, R. (1982) 'Cross cultural training for mental health personnel', *Final Report NIMH Training Grant No.5-T24 – MHI5249*. Miami, FL: University of Miami School of Medicine.

McRae, M.B. and Johnson, J.D., Jr (1991) 'Towards training for competence in multicultural counselor education', *Journal of Counseling and Development*, 70: 131–5.

Marsella, A.J. (1980) 'Depressive experience and disorder across cultures', in H.C. Triandis, and J.G. Draguns (eds), *Handbook of Cross Cultural Psychology*, vol. 6. Boston, MA: Allyn and Bacon.

Matthews, R. and Paradise, L.V. (1988) 'Towards methodological diversity: qualitative research approaches', *Journal of Mental Health Counseling*, 10: 225–34.

Mearns, D. (1994) *Developing Person-Centred Counselling*. London: Sage.

Merta, R.J., Ponterotto, J.G. and Brown, R.D. (1992) 'Comparing the effectiveness of two directive styles in the academic counseling of foreign students', *Journal of Counseling Psychology*, 39 (2): 214–19.

Miller, M.J. (1985) 'Analysing client change geographically', *Journal of Counseling and Development*, 63: 491–94.

Mio, J.S. (1989) 'Experiential involvement as an adjunct to teaching cultural sensitivity', *Journal of Multicultural Counseling and Development*, 17: 38–46.

Neimeyer, G.J., Fukuyama, M.A., Bingham, R.P., Hall, L.E. and Mussenden, M.E. (1986) 'Training cross cultural counselors: a comparison of the pro-counsellor and anti-counsellor triad models', *Journal of Counseling and Development*, 64: 347–439.

Norcross, J.C., Alford, B.A. and Demichelle (1992) 'The future of psychotherapy: delphi data and concluding observations', *Psychotherapy*, 29 (1): 150–58.

Parham, T.A. and Helms, J.E. (1981) 'The influence of black students' racial attitudes or preferences for counselor's race', *Journal of Counseling Psychology*, 28: 250–57.

Parker, W.M. and McDavis, R.J. (1979) 'An awareness: toward counseling minorities', *Counselor Education and Supervision*, 18: 312–17.

Parker, W.M., Valley, M.M. and Geary, C.A. (1986) 'Acquiring cultural knowledge for counsellors in training: A multifaceted approach', *Counselor Education and Supervision*, 26: 61–71.

Parloff, M.B., Waskow, I.E. and Wolfe, B.E. (1978) 'Research on therapist variables in relation to process and outcome', in S.L. Garfield and A.E. Bergin (eds), *Handbook of Psychotherapy and Behaviour Change: An Empirical Analysis*, 2nd edn. New York: Wiley.

Pedersen, P.B. (1977) 'The Triad Model and cross cultural counselor training', *The Personnel and Guidance Journal*, 56: 410–18.

Pedersen, P. (1987) 'Ten frequent assumptions of cultural bias in counseling', *Journal of Multicultural Counseling and Development*, 15: 16–24.

Pedersen, P. (1988) *A Handbook for Developing Multicultural Awareness*. Alexandria, VA: American Association for Counseling and Development.

Pedersen, P. (1989) 'Developing multicultural ethical guidelines for psychology', *International Journal of Psychology*, 24: 643–52.

Pedersen, P. (1991) 'Counseling minority students', *The Counseling Psychologist*, 19 (1).

Pedersen, P.B., Draguns, J.E., Conner, W.J. and Trimble, J.E. (1989) *Counseling Across Cultures*, 3rd edn. Honolulu: University of Hawaii Press.

Pedersen, P.B., Draguns, J.G., Lonner, W.J. and Trimble, J.E. (eds) (1996) *Counseling Across Cultures*. Thousand Oaks, CA: Sage.

Pomales, J. and Williams, V. (1989) 'Effects of the level of acculturation and counseling style on Hispanic student' perceptions of counselor', *Journal of Counseling Psychology*, 36: 79–83.

Ponterotto, J.G. (1987) 'Counseling Mexican Americans: a multimodal approach', *Journal of Counseling and Development*, 65: 308–12.

Ponterotto, J.G. (1988a) 'Racial consciousness development among white counselor trainees: a stage model', *Journal of Multicultural Counseling and Development*, 16: 146–56.

Ponterotto, J.G. (1988b) 'Racial/ethnic research in the Journal of Counseling Psychology: a content analysis and methodological critique', *Journal of Counseling Psychology*, 35: 410–18.

Ponterotto, J.G. and Casas, J.M. (1987) 'In search multicultural competence within counselor education programs', *Journal of Counseling and Development*, 65: 430–34.

Ponterotto, J.G. and Casas, J.M. (1991) *Handbook of Racial/Ethnic Minority Counseling Research*. Springfield, IL: Charles Thomas.

Ponterotto, J.G., Casas, J.M., Suzuki, L.S. and Alexander, C.M. (eds) (1995) *Handbook of Multicultural Counselling*. London: Sage.

Reber, A.S. (1985) *The Penguin Dictionary of Psychology*. London: Penguin.

Reynolds, D.K. (1980) *The Quiet Therapies*. Honolulu: University of Hawaii Press.

Ridley, C.R. (1984) 'Clinical treatment for the non-disclosing black client', *American Psychologist*, 39: 1234–44.

Rowe, W. and Hill, T.L. (1992) 'On carts and horses: the status of white racial identity research', *The Counseling Psychologist*, 20 (1): 189–90.

Sabnani, H.B., Ponterotto, J.G. and Borodovsky, L.G. (1991) 'White racial identity development and cross cultural counselor training', *The Counseling Psychologist*, 19 (1): 76–102.

Saeki, C. and Borrow, H. (1987) 'Counseling and psychotherapy: East and West' in P. Pedersen (ed.), *Handbook of Cross-Cultural Counseling and Therapy.* Westport, CT: Greenwood Press. pp. 223–229.

Sattler, J.M. (1977) 'The effects of therapist–client similarity', in A.S. Gurman and A.M. Razin (eds), *Effective Psychotherapy: A Handbook of Research.* New York: Pergamon.

Sherwood, G. (1980) 'Allied and paraprofessional assistance', in U. Delworth, G.R. Hanson and associates (eds), *Student Services: A Handbook for the Profession.* San Francisco: Jossey-Bass.

Smith, E.M.J. (1985) 'Ethnic minorities: life stress, social support and mental health issues', *The Counseling Psychologist,* 13: 537–9.

Smith, E.M.J. (1989) 'Black identity development', *The Counseling Psychologist,* 17 (2): 277–88.

Sue, D.W. (1978) 'Eliminating cultural oppression in counseling: towards a general therapy', *Journal of Counseling Psychology,* 25: 419–28.

Sue, D.W. (1979) 'Preliminary data from the DISC evaluation report, number 1'. Hayward, CA: California State University.

Sue, D.W. and Sue, D. (1990) *Counseling the Culturally Different,* 2nd edn. New York: Wiley.

Sue, D.W., Arrendondo, P. and McDavis, R.J. (1992) 'Multicultural competencies and standards: a call to the profession', *Journal of Multicultural Counseling and Development,* 20: 64–88.

Sue, D.W., Bernier, J.B., Durran, M., Feinberg, L., Pedersen, P., Smith, E. and Vasquez-Nuttall, E. (1982) 'Position paper: cross cultural counseling competencies', *The Counseling Psychologist,* 10: 45–52.

Sue, S. (1988) 'Psychotherapeutic services for ethnic minorities', *American Psychologist,* 43 (4): 301–8.

Sue, S. and Zane, N. (1987) 'The role of culture and cultural techniques in psychotherapy', *American Psychologist,* 42 (1): 37–45.

Suinn, R. (1985) 'Research and practice in cross cultural counseling', *The Counseling Psychologist,* 13 (4): 673–84.

Terrell, F. and Terrell, S. (1981) 'An inventory to measure cultural mistrust among blacks', *The Western Journal of Black Studies,* 5: 180–85.

Tokar, D.M. and Swanson, J.L. (1991) 'An investigation of the validity of Helms' (1984) model of white racial development', *Journal of Counseling Psychology,* 38 (3): 296–301.

Triandis, H.C. (1977) 'Theoretical framework for the evaluation of cross cultural training effectiveness', *International Journal of Intercultural Relations,* 1: 19–45.

Wade, P. and Bernstein, B.L. (1991) 'Culture sensitivity training and counselor race: effects on black female clients' perceptions and attrition', *Journal of Counseling Psychology,* 38 (1): 9–15.

Wright, W. (1975) 'Relationships of trust and racial perception towards therapist–client conditions during counseling', *Journal of Negro Education,* 44: 161–9.

Zytowski, D.G., Casas, J.M., Gilbert, L.A., Lent, R.W. and Simon, N.P. (1988) 'Counseling psychology's public image', *The Counseling Psychologist,* 16: 332–46.

Discussion issues

1 Good research into cross-cultural or multicultural counselling is non-existent.

2 Does multicultural counsellor education affect the counselling process and outcome?

3 The flexibility of multimodal therapy has exciting implications for counselling in a multicultural society.

4 What possible areas of multicultural research are worth investigating?

Afterword

This edited book contains 20 chapters on a range of topics including counselling and race, approaches, good practice, ethnic matching and multicultural counselling research. These chapters span over a decade and reflect the views of 26 authors. Hopefully their views and findings have increased awareness on the very nature of multicultural counselling. I finish the book with an assertion made by Roy Moodley (1999: 139): 'The challenge for multicultural counselling, in the next decade, would be to include traditional healing practices as part of its discourse, if it is to encourage the active participation of ethnic minorities.' Do you agree?

Reference

Moodley, R. (1999) 'Challenges and transformations: counselling in a multicultural context', *International Journal for the Advancement of Counselling*, 21: 139–52.

Appendix I
Recommended Reading

The recommended list provides a selection of books that may enhance the understanding of multicultural counselling. Publications have also been included that relate to some of the topics covered in this book. For the reader's convenience, I have given the title of the book first.

Against Therapy, J. Masson, 1989. London: Collins.
Aliens and Alienists: Ethnic Minorities and Psychiatry, 3rd edn, R. Littlewood and M. Lipsedge, 1997. London: Routledge.
Applied Cross-cultural Psychology, ed. R.W. Brislin, 1990. Newbury Park, CA: Sage.
Assessing and Treating Culturally Diverse Clients, F.A. Paniagua, 1994. Thousand Oaks, CA: Sage.
Challenges to Counselling and Psychotherapy, A. Howard, 1996. London: Macmillan.
Client Assessment, eds S. Palmer and G. McMahon, 1997. London: Sage.
Clinical Guidelines in Cross-cultural Mental Health, L. Comas-Diaz and E.E.H. Griffith, 1988. New York: Wiley.
Counselling Across Cultures, 4th edn. eds P.B. Pedersen, J.G. Draguns, W.J. Lonner and J.E. Trimble, 1996. Thousand Oaks, CA: Sage.
Counselling the Culturally Different: Theory and Practice, D.W. Sue, 1981. New York: Wiley.
Counselling for Stress Problems, S. Palmer and W. Dryden, 1995. London: Sage.
Counselling in a Multicultural Society, S. Palmer and P. Laungani, 1999. London: Sage.
Culture-centred Counselling and Interviewing Skills, P. Pedersen and A.E. Ivey, 1993. Westpoint, CT: Greenwood/Praeger.
Cultures of Healing, R.T. Fancher, 1995. San Francisco: W.H. Freeman & Co.
Death and Bereavement Across Cultures, eds C.M. Parkes, P. Laungani and B. Young, 1996. London: Routledge.
The Decline and Fall of the Freudian Empire, H.H. Eysenck, 1985. London: Methuen.
Eastern and Western Approaches to Healing: Ancient Wisdom and Modern Knowledge, A. Sheikh and K.S. Sheikh, 1989. New York: Wiley.
Effective Psychotherapy, eds A.S. Gurman and A.M. Razin, 1977. New York: Pergamon.
The Effects of Psychotherapy, H.H. Eysenck, 1966. New York: International Science Press.
A Guide to Treatments that Work, P.E. Nathan and J.M. Gormas, 1997. New York: Oxford University Press.
Handbook of Counselling, eds S. Palmer and G. McMahon, 1997. London: Routledge.
Handbook of Cross-cultural Counselling and Therapy, ed. P. Pedersen, 1987. London: Praeger.
Handbook of Culture and Mental Illness: an International Perspective, ed. I. Alissa, 1995. Madison, CT: International University Press.
Handbook of Multicultural Counselling, eds J.G. Ponterotto, J.M. Casas, L.A. Suzuki and C.M. Alexander, 1995. London: Sage.
In Search of Self in India and Japan: Toward a Cross-cultural Psychology, A. Roland, 1988. Princeton, NJ: Princeton University Press.
Mental Health, Race and Culture, S. Fernando, 1991. London: Macmillan/MIND.
Minority Children and Adolescents in Therapy, M.K. Ho, 1992. London: Sage.

Overcoming Unintentional Racism in Counseling and Therapy, C.R. Ridley, 1995. Thousand Oaks, CA: Sage.

The Practice of Multimodal Therapy, A.A. Lazarus, 1989. Baltimore, MD: Johns Hopkins University Press.

Psychology and Culture, eds W.J. and R.S. Malpass, 1994. Boston, MA: Allyn and Bacon.

Race, Culture and Counselling, C. Lago and J. Thompson, 1996. Buckingham: Open University Press.

Race, Culture and Difference, J. Donald and A. Rattansi, 1992. London: Sage/Open University.

Shamans, Mystics and Doctors, S. Kakar, 1982. New York: Knopf.

Social Foundations of Thought and Action: A Social Cognitive Theory, A. Bandura, 1986. Englewood Cliffs, NJ: Prentice-Hall.

Third World Challenge to Psychiatry, N.H. Higginbotham, 1984. Honolulu: University Press of Hawaii.

Transcultural Counselling in Action, P. d'Ardenne and A. Mahtani, 1989. London: Sage.

Transcultural Counselling, Z. Eleftheriadou, 1994. London: Central Publishing House.

Appendix 2

Professional Bodies and Organizations

African Caribbean Mental Health Association
35 Electric Avenue
London SW9 8JP

Association focusing on African Caribbean mental health.

British Association for Counselling and Psychotherapy
1 Regent Place
Rugby
Warwickshire CV21 2PJ, England
Administration telephone: +44 (0) 1788 550899
Information telephone: +44 (0) 1788 578328
Website: www.bac.co.uk

Provides list of accredited counsellors and relevant organizations. Publishes professional journals and a range of materials.

British Association for Behavioural and Cognitive Psychotherapies
PO Box 9
Accrington BB5 2GD, England
Telephone: +44 (0) 1254 875277
Website: www.babcp.org.uk

Provides a list of accredited cognitive-behavioural and rational emotive therapists.

British Psychological Society
St Andrews House
48 Princess Road East
Leicester LE1 7DR, England
Telephone: +44 (0) 116 254 9568
Website: www.bps.org.uk

Holds a register of chartered psychologists and publishes a range of books.

Centre for Multimodal Therapy
156 Westcombe Hill

London SE3 7DH
Telephone: +44 (0) 20 8853 1122
Website: www.managingstress.com

Provides training in multimodal therapy and offers counselling.

International Stress Management Association (UK)
18 Albury Ride
Cheshunt, Herts EN8 8XF, England
Telephone: +44 (0) 1992 633100
Website: www.isma.org.uk

Provides information about stress management and accredits members.

Chartered Institute of Personnel and Development
IPD House
Camp Road
London SW19 4UX
Telephone: +44 (0) 20 8971 9000
Website: www.ipd.co.uk

Professional body which publishes a range of useful books and materials. Provides information relevant to employees.

Nafsiyat Intercultural Therapy
278 Seven Sisters Road
Finsbury Park
London N4 2HY

Organization which offers intercultural therapy and counselling.

RACE Division
c/o British Association for Counselling and Psychotherapy
1 Regent Place
Rugby
Warwickshire CV 21 2PJ, England
Administration telephone: +44 (0) 1788 550899
Information telephone: +44 (0) 1788 578328
Website: www.bac.co.uk

Division of the BACP that focuses on race, culture and counselling in a multicultural society. Publishes a journal and runs workshops. Membership is recommended for counsellors and psychotherapists practising in the UK with an interest in these areas.

Race and Culture Special Interest Group
c/o British Psychological Society

St Andrews House
48 Princess Road East
Leicester LE1 7DR, England
Telephone: +44 (0) 116 254 9568
Website: www.bps.org.uk

Interest group consisting of BPS members with an interest of race and culture.

United Kingdom Council for Psychotherapy
167–169 Great Portland Street
London W1N 5FB
Telephone: +44 (0) 20 7436 3013
Fax: +44 (0) 20 7436 3013
Website: www.psychotherapy.org.uk

Maintains a register of qualified psychotherapists and publishes a newsletter.

Index

Introduction to Counselling Skills

Text and Activities

Richard Nelson-Jones *Director of the Cognitive Humanistic Institute, Chiang Mai, Thailand*

'As a course book or an aide to individual learning this book contains a wealth of information and guidance based on years of study and practice. It is easy to use because it is clearly sign-posted. I particularly like the way the author addresses the range of issues a student needs to consider before embarking on a counselling course. The structure of building block-by-block, skill-by-skill simplifies assessment' - **Counselling**

1999 • 352 pages

Cloth (0-7619-6185-2) / Paper (0-7619-6186-0)

Counselling in a Multicultural Society

Edited by **Stephen Palmer** *Centre for Stress Management, London and City University* and **Pittu D. Laungani** *South Bank University*

'The chapter authors frequently refer to each other's work – a phenomenon not always commonplace in edited publications. The decision to draw upon the expertise of this team of highly experienced practitioners has certainly paid off. Each chapter is well researched, sensitively written, challenging and thought provoking' - **Counselling**

1998 • 224 pages

Cloth (0-7619-5064-8) / Paper (0-7619-5065-6)

 SAGE Publications
London • Thousand Oaks • New Delhi
www.sagepub.co.uk